Cafe Wisconsin

Cafe Wisconsin

A Guide to Wisconsin's Down-Home Cafes

Second edition

Joanne Raetz Stuttgen

The University of Wisconsin Press

The University of Wisconsin Press
1930 Monroe Street
Madison, Wisconsin 53711

www.wisc.edu/wisconsinpress/

3 Henrietta Street
London WC2E 8LU, England

3   5   4   2

Printed in the United States of America

Library of Congress Cataloging-in-Publication Data
Stuttgen, Joanne Raetz, 1961–
Cafe Wisconsin: a guide to Wisconsin's down-home cafes / Joanne Raetz Stuttgen.—2nd ed.
p.cm.
Includes index.
ISBN 0-299-20114-7 (pbk.:alk. paper)
1. Restaurants—Wisconsin—Guidebooks. 2. City and town life—Wisconsin. I. Title.
TX907.3. W6S78   2004
647.95775—dc22   2004005250

In memory of Joe Kunze
a chief of men

Contents

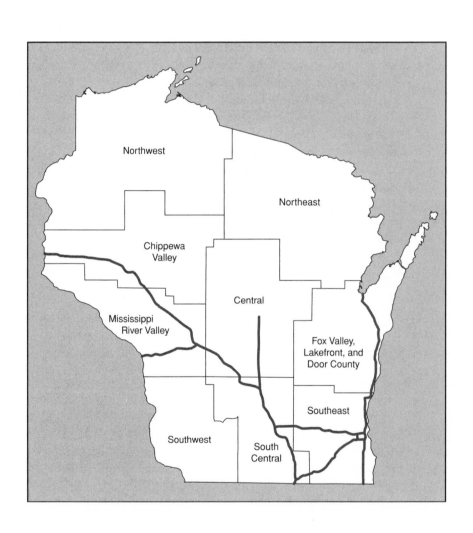

Northwest

Northeast

Chippewa
Valley

Central

Mississippi
River Valley

Fox Valley,
Lakefront, and
Door County

Southeast

Southwest

South
Central

Preface

Getting Started

Welcome to the second edition of *Cafe Wisconsin*. If you are an adventure eater who uses the book as a directory to good home-cooking spots across Wisconsin, you realized long ago that the local cafe scene has changed quite a bit since 1993, the year the first edition debuted. Many cafes have a different cast of characters. Many have a new, updated menu and focus. A few have closed their doors for good.

Over the years, many people have asked for an updated *Cafe Wisconsin*, but for a long time there was room in my life for only one. Then the University of Wisconsin Press came courting, and I said yes. My editor, Raphael Kadushin, and I both thought the second time around would be a cinch. "Just call all the owners on the phone and find out what's new," Raphael suggested.

Five phone calls later I had found five new owners. The notion of a simple revision melted as quickly as real whipped cream on a July day. It was pretty much a new book I was after, and so I hit the road.

Come on. Let's go out to eat.

I did not think up *Cafe Wisconsin* on my own. The inspiration comes from my bicycling friends in Eau Claire, Wisconsin, who joined me for countless Sunday morning rides in search of the ultimate cafe and ultimate piece of pie. We call these excursions pie rides.

As the sun rose above the wooded hills, we'd gather at Eric and Barbara Wheeler's house and roll out of town. Some thirty or forty miles later, we'd lean our bikes against the front of the Downing Cafe in Downing, the Cardinal Cafe in Eleva, the Red Dot Cafe in Augusta, or the Sand Creek Cafe in Sand Creek, where we'd refuel on pie, cinnamon rolls, toast, and coffee for the return trip home.

In this way we came to know the highways running through neighboring counties, the small towns sprinkled in the valleys and cut into the hills. By the lure of good food we came to feel a sense of place and the lingering of the past in the present, and we came to appreciate the power of rootedness and belonging that merges individuals into community.

As a folklorist, I am interested in cultural traditions that maintain a familiar sameness despite change over time and across regions. This is the sort of change that produces the all-American apple pie and its countless variations: mock apple pie, Dutch or French apple pie, apple crisp, apple cobbler, apple pan dowdy. By examining objects that are created by human hands—apple pie—or performances enacted by individuals in social settings—joke telling or card playing—folklorists determine cultural patterns that give form and meaning to human lives, both in the vanished past and in the present.

During my research for both editions of *Cafe Wisconsin*, I sought historical and regional connections between small town, main, and back street eateries by considering food traditions, architecture and ornamentation, ownership and patronage, and social performances, such as dice shaking and coffee klatching. I wanted to discover what roles cafes play in small towns and in the lives of individuals, and why cafes have survived—even thrived—in Wisconsin across time and space.

Other writers have attempted to translate food and eating into a cultural experience. In *Blue Highways* (1982), William Least Heat-Moon deliberately sought out "Ma in her beanery and Pap over his barbecue pit, both still serving slow food from the same place they did thirty years ago." Perhaps best remembered for his "calendar method" of rating cafes, in which a no-calendar cafe is little better than an "interstate pit stop" and a seven-calendar cafe is a golden dream from the past, Heat-Moon whetted the appetites of adventure eaters throughout the country for the deliberately prepared, regionally diverse "slow food" found in obscure eateries along remote byways.

Nearly fifty years before Heat-Moon left his Missouri home for cafes unknown, Duncan Hines's *Adventures in Good Eating*, first published in 1936, was being thumbed by travelers and businessmen the country over. Annually for the next twenty-three years, Hines updated his pocket-sized guide to restaurants serving genuine home-cooked food. His selections leaned more toward glamorous hotel and resort dining rooms in larger cities than unpretentious small town, main street eateries, but in Wisconsin he heartily endorsed the City Cafe in Spooner, the Blue Bowl Cafe in Tomah, and the Rocket Cafe in Ashland. All are long gone.

Until they ceased in 1962, the yearly volumes of *Adventures in Good Eating* were regarded by Hines and his thousands of readers as indispensable companions on any trip, whether across the country or across the city. Although Hines's perspective is genteel, his sentiment is practical and earthy. Hines wrote of his mission in 1942: "How hard it is to find simple dishes finely prepared. Cornbread, fried potatoes, codfish cakes, baked beans, eggs, etc. And when the hungry tourist does find them, how he shouts the glad news to all his friends." Hines didn't have to contend with preprocessed and frozen foods such as instant mashed potato flakes (and now, preservative-laced real mashed potatoes air-sealed in a plastic bag) and frozen "home-baked" (not homemade) pies that frustrate today's adventure eaters.

In "The Great American Pie Expedition" (*New Yorker*, March 27, 1989), Sue Hubbell argues that the use of frozen pie crusts is a sure sign of an inadequate cook, and "probably a mercy, because if left to their own devices they would make worse." Leaving Washington, D.C., with her dog, Tazzie, Hubbell jaunted through the Northeast, the Ozarks, and on into Oklahoma in search of perfect pie. She devised three rules during her travels: 85 percent of cafes located between two businesses will have good pie; good pie is often found near places where meadowlarks sing; never eat pie within one mile of an interstate. I know little about meadowlarks and pie, but I do know about squeeze-in cafes versus off-the-highway truck stops. At the former, you're likely to find from-scratch, fresh-apple pie and at the second, gloppy canned filling "home baked" in a frozen crust.

Jane and Michael Stern's *Roadfood* (first edition 1977, latest edition 2002) is a paperback compendium of humble eateries that serve outstanding regional fare, ranging from catfish and chili dogs to Chicago-style pizza, chitterlings, and corn chowder. For three years, the Sterns traveled with truckers along interstates and major highways, discovering "the essence of America" by sampling its varied roadside tastes.

In Wisconsin, the Sterns tried Cornish pasties in Mineral Point and the hot beef sandwich in Ellsworth. "We find it difficult to be charmed by plain roast beef," they wrote in 1977, "but to Midwesterners it seems to be a never-ending source of eating pleasure." In Trempealeau County, they dropped a mere mile off I-94 into Osseo and discovered the Norske Nook, home of "some of the world's best pies and cakes," a claim that spurred the tiny cafe's climb to phenomenal success. Unfortunately, most of the small town cafes they wrote about in the first edition no longer exist or have changed hands. Two steadfast selections that remain are the Norske Nook, under different ownership, and Borgen's Norwegian Cafe and Bakery in Westby.

As America's pop culture food gurus, the Sterns parlayed their success with *Roadfood* into two other related books, *Eat Your Way Across the U.S.A.* (1997, 1999), which again features the Norske Nook, and *Blue Plate Specials and Blue Ribbon Chefs* (2002). In their latest book about America's "blue-collar culinary scene," the Sterns pay a visit to the Downing Cafe in the basement of the Downing Civic Hall. They are enchanted with the firm-fisted shovel method used by two men wallowing in hot beef and enraptured by the graham cracker cream pie, which you can make yourself from the recipe included in their book.

Unlike the previous authors, in preparing *Cafe Wisconsin* I have concentrated entirely on traditional cafes hiding in small towns off the beaten path. Sorting these out from today's colorful variety of other eateries required a careful definition based on three rather essential requirements: (1) location in the town's original business district and typically on the main street—this pretty much eliminates former drive-ins and fast food franchises turned into family-type restaurants, as well as truck stops and cafes attached to gas stations; (2) an established history in the community; (3) a role as the year-round gathering place for local residents.

Beyond this, traditional cafes are owner operated and have limited seating—usually a few booths and tables with one or more counters and stools. The hours tend to be limited—for example, 5 A.M. to 3 P.M.—and shorter than they were ten years ago. Cafes typically do not serve beer, wine, or liquor. They feature daily, home-cooked specials based on traditional Wisconsin "farm food": meat, mashed potatoes and gravy (affectionately known as MPG), and vegetables. A good general rule is that cafe food is familiar and conservative, rarely trendy, with white bread and devil's food cake taking the place of croissants and schaum torte.

Bear in mind, however, that these are guidelines rather than rules. They must be applied with a certain degree of flexibility. Some cafes are relatively new businesses; some are run by managers instead of owners; some have liquor licenses; and some, like Diane Moulai and Santo Pulvino's Oak Street Cafe in Juneau, even specialize in schaum torte.

This balance between conservatism and change is what lures folklorists to their work. It is also what pulls pie riders out of bed before sunrise and sends them pedaling down county highways in search of good home cooking that is comfortable in its sameness, yet unique in its quality and innovation. Pie riders and other adventure eaters are much like folklorists in their search for things reminiscent of the past and symbolic of a way of life rather than merely a passage through—a way of life shaped by the hand, enriched by the heart, and impressed with community. So we search out cafes that recreate images of home by displaying family photos and offering home-style cooking; that encourage friendships through cribbage games and coffee klatches; that express continuity in their architecture and decoration; that express commitment to community by virtue of their longevity. These cafes comfort us in their sameness; yet, in their uniqueness, they incite us to adventure.

For three main reasons, I have limited my search for traditional cafes to small towns with populations of approximately ten thousand or less. These are the communities not highlighted by bright yellow on the Wisconsin state road map.

First, I wanted to explore Wisconsin backroads and discover humble, small town restaurants that still serve good home cooking.

Second, I wanted to understand how modest cafes—and small communities, too, for that matter—manage to survive in a world that we interpret as being increasingly impersonal, mechanized, and fast paced.

Third—and most important for the adventure eater—in towns smaller than ten thousand, it's almost impossible to get lost. It's always easy to find cafes by their locations on the main business streets, by the soft drink sign hanging over the sidewalk, by the cars and pickups corralled on the street, and by the parade of newspaper vending boxes on the sidewalk out front.

To avoid dead-end meandering down every main street in the state and to make for less work on the road, I began by creating a master list of small town cafes. I first identified all towns on the Wisconsin state road map with populations of ten thousand or less. With the help of various Web sources and the advice of friends throughout the state, I created a master list of potential cafes based on names, addresses, descriptions, and my previous knowledge. Restaurants located on "Main Street" or on low-numbered streets were candidates, as were restaurants with names such as Coffee Cup or Cozy Corner, or any restaurant whose name included a personal name or initials, or the town in which it was located.

Even eliminating such obvious noncafes as Do-Drop Inns, franchises, and resort/supper clubs, I still had a list of potential cafes that was far too lengthy. The magic of cellular allowed me to place calls to each of the eateries on my list at a reasonable expense, and I conducted brief interviews with owners, managers, or employees to determine whether a personal visit was warranted. I asked questions about the history of the restaurant, whether it had a liquor license, the seating capacity, and the type of food being prepared and served. The answers I received determined which restaurants I would visit.

Conducted between June 2002 and March 2003, my visits were spent chatting with owners and customers, taking notes, shaking dice with men's coffee groups, joining in story- and joke-telling sessions, taking tours through kitchens, studying old photographs displayed or dug out of storage by cafe owners, taking photographs of my own, and inspecting building construction, facades, and interior decoration. I conscientiously attempted to visit every cafe on my list (which numbered nearly four hundred), but sometimes I came to a cafe after it was closed for the day or when owners had taken two weeks off for a fishing trip. In cases where a personal visit was not possible, I followed up with a telephone interview or, if I was in the vicinity at a later date, by stopping back for another try.

The 133 cafes featured in the following chapters have distinguished themselves by providing exceptional food and/or atmosphere. My primary qualification for inclusion was good home cooking, which I judged on the basis of favorite "test foods": pie, baked goods, mashed potatoes, soups, hamburgers, and roast beef with gravy—the ubiquitous Wisconsin "hot beef." While all of the featured cafes serve good home cooking, not all of them serve home-cooked everything. Some things have to be forgiven, so exceptional pie sometimes compensates for instant potato buds, and bakery hamburger buns for preformed frozen beef patties.

Next, I considered how open and receptive people were to me as a total stranger, especially whether owners were willing to take time to talk, or whether customers invited me to take part in their pastimes. If conversation came begrudgingly or people were less than articulate, I found myself passing through a cafe particularly quickly as I had miles to go and many cafes to visit.

A cafe's appearance was also important to me. I favored those that were comfortable, pleasant, clean, and homelike. I was thrilled to discover cafes that remain relatively unchanged despite the passage of years, cafes that still sport early-twentieth-century high-back booths, splendid back bars and soda fountains, terrazzo floors and tin ceilings, or mid-twentieth-century polished chrome and Formica.

On the other hand, cafes whose histories had been obliterated in the pursuit of modernization left me empty and uninspired. With their impersonal, computer-printed checks, laminated print-shop menus, and identical, mass-produced waitress uniforms, they feel exactly like franchises, and I have not featured some that otherwise met my classifications.

Lastly, I invited cafe owners to participate in the creation of the book by providing input on the stories I had written. They were able to suggest corrections, clarifications, additions, and sometimes deletions. They also showed me historic photographs, vintage postcards, old menus, advertisements, and other nifty stuff pulled out of drawers and storage cabinets. Some cafe owners chose not to be featured in the book for personal reasons, so if your favorite is missing, this is likely the reason.

The 133 featured cafes are mapped into nine sections of Wisconsin, determined by recognized tourism regions, size, and the total number of small towns and cafes in the area. Within each chapter, featured cafes are listed alphabetically by the name of the town in which they're located. Listings include street addresses or locations, telephone numbers, hours of operation as of January 2004, and names of owners. This information is constantly changing, so I advise you to call ahead to avoid disappointment. Cafes featured in the first edition of *Cafe Wisconsin* and still under the same ownership are designated by 🍽. Because I am repeatedly asked what cafe is the state's "best," I have designated twenty-one cafes, which I consider to be the most outstanding, with ℧. These cafes excel at every aspect of the business, and they are the only cafes I would not hesitate to drive a hundred miles out of my way for.

One hundred and one "Next Best Bet" cafes, which deserve a visit because of notable menu specialties, decor, or people, are listed alphabetically by town at the end of each chapter. All cafes included in the book are listed in the alphabetical index organized by the name of the town in which they're located.

The final chapter is an epilogue, a summary of the many roles that cafes play in small communities and in the lives of individuals. Normally, material of this kind appears as an introduction rather than a conclusion, instructing readers what to expect in the chapters to follow. But that is not how I learned about Wisconsin's small town cafes. I wasn't told what to see. My sight developed. I'd like you to come to understand cafes the way I did: gradually, through the words of owners and customers; through sights and sounds and tastes; through participation in games and gossip; through penetration of the past and perusal of the present.

This book can be used in several ways. It is both a comprehensive directory to Wisconsin's small town cafes and an analysis of the many roles cafes play in small towns. Like *Blue Highways*, it is a journey into the intimate lives of communities and individuals. Like *Adventures in Good Eating*, it is a reliable companion designed to delight and comfort travelers. Like "The Great American Pie Expedition," it is a rejection of the artificial and a celebration of the authentic and homemade. And like *Roadfood*, it is an exploration of regional variations in food traditions that result in Wisconsin food phenomena like the Friday night fish fry and the Door County fish boil, and specialties such as Cornish pasties, Greek gyros, Mexican enchiladas, and Norwegian lutefisk and lefse.

And so, having found small town cafes serving simple dishes finely prepared, this hungry tourist shouts the glad news to all her friends.

Acknowledgments

There are many people to thank. With fondness I thank Eric Wheeler, the indomitable pie rider for whom six o'clock in the morning is never too early, and Barbara Wheeler, who can without hesitation pass up the most perfect of pies for dry wheat toast. Many happy miles were pedaled in the company of Kine Torinus, who talks without breathing; Lance Scott, who orders all-you-can-eat breakfasts and then buys Snickers bars for the trip home; also Liz Tolbert, Mark Blaskey, David and Joan Angell, and my husband, Mark Stuttgen.

Scott Wilson led a small group of us one Sunday in July 1990 to the small Dunn County village of Sand Creek, where we ate sandwiches and malts at the Sand Creek Cafe. It was this pie ride, more than all the others, that inspired this book.

Although I wrote the text that follows, the histories, anecdotes, and many of the words themselves were given to me by cafe owners and their customers. It is their story I tell. I am particularly indebted to owners who generously engaged in hours of conversation, including Sue Brooks of the Arrowhead Restaurant in Winneconne, Jerry Bechard of the Norske Nook in Osseo, Earl Bruinsma of Callen's Restaurant in Union Grove, Cecelia Cruse of the Sand Creek Cafe, Jeff and Rhonda Gulich of the Lake Holcombe Cafe in Holcombe, Louise Halvorson at the Cottage Cafe in Port Wing, Ken Koyen of KK Fiske on Washington Island, Helena Lawinger of the Red Rooster Cafe in Mineral Point, Doyle Lewis of the Unique Cafe in Boscobel, Patricia and Richard Lohmar of the Hixton Cafe in Hixton, Dale and Bertie Mahal of Harry's Restaurant in Port Washington, Kay Nelson of K's Outback Cafe in Orfordville, Donna Perkins of Borgen's Norwegian Cafe and Bakery in Westby, Teri Scott of Teri's Restaurant in Baraboo, Donald Stoik of the Main Street Cafe in Bloomer, and Diane Stroik of the Amherst Cafe in Amherst.

Many of the 170 cafes featured in the first edition of *Cafe Wisconsin* (1993) are now closed or have different owners. I want to recognize the fifty-eight stalwart proprietors I found in the old familiar places: Perry Andropolis, who took over Perry's Cherry Diner in Sturgeon Bay from his parents, Andrew "Jack" and Ann Andropolis; Mark and Tom Badtke, who replace their parents, Russell and the late Edith Badtke, as owners of the

Wilmot Cafe in Wilmot; Kristine Bassett of Kristine's Restaurant in Three Lakes (formerly Alpine Haus Restaurant); Jerry Bechard; Judy Bolier, who took over the Crystal Cafe in Iola from her mother Ann Moerke; Jim and Sue Brooks of the Arrowhead Restaurant in Winneconne; Earl and Charlotte Bruinsma; George F. Callos Sr. of the Island Cafe in Minocqua; Kevin and Rosemary Clarke of Rudy's Diner in Brillion; Cecelia Cruse; Sherri Dessart of the Country Cafe in Babcock; Carolyn Elstad of Carolyn's Coffee Shop in Independence; Jim and Connie Farrell of the Clinton Kitchen in Clinton; Owen and Joan Farrell of OJ's Mid-Town Restaurant in Gillett; Denise J. Fischer of Denise's Cafe in Randolph; Joyce Flanagan and Patty Noble, who bought out Irma Collins, their mother and namesake of Irma's Kitchen in Argyle; Dawn French, daughter-in-law of Donna French, former owner of the Roberts Cafe in Roberts (formerly Donna's Kitchen); Donald and Linda Graff of Graff's Restaurant in Lena; Jim, Joy, and Mark Greenwood of Greenwood's Cafe in Reedsburg; Kendall and Trish Gulseth of the Koffee Kup Restaurant in Stoughton; John and Linda Gustafson of the Country Style Cookin' Restaurant in Hillsboro; Mary Kay Hagen of Mary Kay's Kitchen in Arcadia; Lona Haughian of Lona's Corner Cafe in Haugen; Beverly Igo and Louise Halvorson of the Cottage Cafe in Port Wing; John and Sharon Johnson of the Pier Plaza in Bayfield; Connie Kaplenski of Koni K's in Elcho (formerly named Connie's Elcho Restaurant); Mike and Mary Klug of Mary's Coffee Cup in Montello; Doris Krueger of the Red Dot Cafe in Augusta; Helena Lawinger and Patti McKinley of the Red Rooster Cafe in Mineral Point; Doyle and Nancy Lewis of the Unique Cafe in Boscobel; Evelyn Leystra of Leystra's Venture Restaurant in Cambria; Richard and Patricia Lohmar; James "Mac" and Mary McBrair of the Ideal Cafe in Iron River; Marshall and Janette Maxwell of Daddy Maxwell's Artic Circle Cafe in Williams Bay; Bob and Jeanne Michaelson of the Woods Cafe in Woodruff; Don and Brenda Miller of the Phillips Cafe in Phillips; Steve and Darlene Miller of the Dairyland Cafe in Ridgeland; Lisa O'Brien of O'Brien's Restaurant in Pardeeville; Larry Ourada, who took over the Dixie Lunch in Antigo from his father and mother, Ed and Georgian; Barbara Paar of the Lunch Bucket Cafe in Black Earth; Larry and Susan Palubicki of the Log Cabin Cafe in Crandon; LeRoy and Donna Perkins of Borgen's Norwegian Cafe and Bakery in Westby; Dan Peterson of the Viking Restaurant in Ellison Bay; Bob Prevost of Prevost's Restaurant in Solon Springs; Gloria J. Qualley of the City Cafe in Whitehall; Martha Rommel, who followed her in-laws, Lyle and Margaret "Mardie" Rommel, as owner of the L & M Cafe in Melrose (formerly L & M Chuckwagon Cafe); Dennis and Connie Riebe of the Hungry House Cafe in Prairie du Chien; Connie Roy, who took over the

Main Street Cafe in Siren from her parents, Mike and Susan Roy; Gerry Schubert of Schubert's Old-Fashioned Cafe and Bakery in Mt. Horeb; Teri Scott; Ed and Cindy Starke of Cindy's Country Cafe in Three Lakes; Dennis Starr of the Portage Cafe in Portage; Jim and Lorrie Steffek of Lorrie's Home Town Cafe and Catering in Denmark; Donald Stoik; Diane Stroik; William and Kay Tabbert of Tabbert's Restaurant in Rosendale; and Tom and Denise Thompson of Tom's Country Cafe in Mercer.

Lastly, I owe a heart full of thanks to my son, Peter, who spent the summer I was away blissfully playing on the computer without me constantly yelling at him to get off; to my husband, Mark, who lets me go and welcomes me home; to Joanne Flemming, who read the manuscript and shared a long overdue evening with me in Menasha; to Diana Cook and Adam Mehring at the University of Wisconsin Press, who read the manuscript again (and again); to Mark and Emily Blaskey, who ate roast pork during a Packers game; to Loren West, a fellow adventure eater; to Eleanore Stuttgen, Tom, Kathy, Mallory, and Allie Huber, John and Kine Torinus, Mike and Cathy Weiss, and Eric Wheeler, who always have an open door and an empty bed; and to Raphael Kadushin at the University of Wisconsin Press, who saw the project through from beginning to end.

Northwest

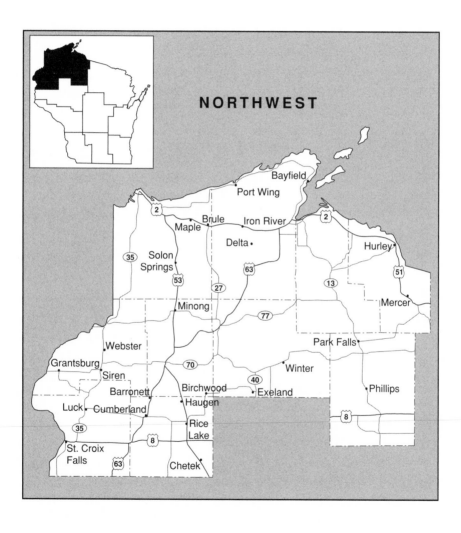

NORTHWEST

Bayfield
Port Wing
Brule Iron River
Maple
Delta
Hurley
Solon
Springs
Minong
Webster
Grantsburg
Siren
Barronett Birchwood
Luck Cumberland Haugen Exeland
St. Croix
Falls Chetek
Rice
Lake
Winter
Park Falls
Mercer
Phillips

BARRONETT
Brickhouse Cafe
2974 Highway 63
(715) 822-3424
April 1–November 30: M closed; Tu–Th 7 A.M.–2 P.M.; F 6 A.M.–8 P.M.;
Sa–Su 6 A.M.–2:30 P.M.
December 1–March 31: M closed; Tu–Su 7 A.M.–2 P.M.
John and Dana Glaubitz

Barronett, on the Barron-Washburn county line, is a tiny speck of a town, a blink-and-you'll-miss-it cluster of turn-of-the-century buildings housing the It's About Time clock shop, a furniture and ironworks shop, a tavern or two, Odden's Norsk Husflid (a Nordic imports shop), Ron and Sue Helstern's woodcarving and sign business, and the Brickhouse Cafe. In 1988 the Helsterns converted a "shell of a building"—formerly a well driller's shop—into Barronett's main street cafe because, Sue explained in 1991, "we really felt that Barronett needed a restaurant."

Today, the Brickhouse Cafe, owned by John and Dana Glaubitz, is an attractive and comfortable mixture of old and new. Natural knotty pine covers the walls and ceiling, complementing the original maple flooring. A handcrafted, laminated golden maple counter is paired with salvaged chrome stools. On a shelf above an old ice-cream freezer sits a 1950s-ish green Hamilton Beach malt machine. The two bay windows overhanging the sidewalk are filled with small pine trees, a black bear, and miscellaneous antiques that speak to the woods and water of Wisconsin's Up North.

On the first blustery day of autumn, a table of travelers wearing wool sweaters and turtlenecks chase away the unwelcome chill by spooning bowls of clam chowder. It is Friday—fish day in Wisconsin—and they have chosen soup over the daily special of fried fish. It is indeed a day for soup, and the Brickhouse Cafe is an altogether pleasant place to be. The natural wood is warm and inviting, and the menu board promises good home cooking to those who have escaped the weather outdoors.

Dana Glaubitz, feeling a bit under the weather with a head cold, explains that from the beginning she and John were committed to making everything from scratch. "We thought we were young enough to take the risk and do it," she says with a small laugh. "We didn't want to look back and say, 'We should've done it.'" Did it they have. As John stands stoop shouldered at the grill in back—he's a tall fellow and has trouble clearing the overhead equipment—Dana tends to the dining room duties while squeezing in a conversation with me.

It was John's dream to have his own little cafe, a dream he developed working in his parents' restaurant in Amboy, Minnesota. Dana grew up in

Spooner, attended UW–River Falls, and then moved to Minnesota, where she met John. Meanwhile, her grandparents were frequent and loyal customers of the Barronett cafe. When they learned it was for sale, they let the young couple know. "We compromised," Dana explains. "He got his cafe, and I got to live near home."

Their compromise is the adventure eater's gain. John and Dana concentrate on authentic, slow-cooked real food prepared by their own hands. Breakfast is served all day—"You'd be surprised how many people eat breakfast for dinner," Dana notes—and competes handily with the favorite Brickhouse burger, made with all of the California accessories plus Swiss cheese, mushrooms, and bacon. On Tuesday and Thursday they shake up the menu with daily specials, and on Friday they honor the Wisconsin tradition by hosting a fish fry. Wednesday is Mexican day and might feature tacos, burritos, or other south-of-the-border offerings, including fried ice cream. The deep-fried dessert is so popular that it is available most other days as well.

BIRCHWOOD
Birchwood Cafe
121 Main Street
(715) 354-3000
M–Su 6 A.M.–2:30 P.M.
Mike and Jan LeBrocq
Back in 1983, there existed a combination laundromat, cafe, and barbershop at the current site of Mike and Jan LeBrocq's Birchwood Cafe, formerly owned by Dave and Jimmie Dimmick. But resorts were populating the Birchwood area, and the seasonal booms rather than year-round stability forced the businesses to close. Meanwhile, Dave Dimmick was teaching school in Menomonee Falls. When the schools were consolidated, the Dimmicks had to make a choice between yearly two-week vacations at their cottage near Birchwood or a life in the lake area. They chose the latter. In 1983 Dave and Jimmie Dimmick expanded the restaurant into the barbershop and updated the laundromat. Ever since, it has been possible to grab a burger while your jeans tumble in the dryer next door.

The Dimmicks built the business "on fresh Rice Lake potatoes and local eggs," Jimmie had told me. When they sold out to the LeBrocqs in 1993, Mike LeBrocq knew better "than to kill the golden goose—only the golden goose isn't a goose, it's potatoes." Not that he had even the slightest chance to do any such thing. "The people definitely let us know they came for the potatoes," he recalls.

Mike graduated from the Culinary Institute of America in 1979 and went to work for a variety of big resorts across the country. He enjoyed preparing the finest and most creative dishes. He met Jan, a Birchwood native, while they were both working at the same Lake Tahoe hotel. The small town, northwoods girl married the Connecticut-born chef. Each was happy in the knowledge that they had escaped the places and lives of their childhood. But life is a funny thing and often calls you back. One day, Jan's brother, a realtor in Birchwood, called up to say hello and mentioned he had a cafe for sale across the street. Mike flew in to take a look and decided it was not only a great opportunity to strike out in business for himself, but also a great way to raise the kids in a close-knit small town. Jan was less sure about the return home. "I had to drag her back here," Mike says. Ten years later, they are both happy with their decision. "You know, it's like living in Mayberry," Mike smiles. "And as long as I have a golf course and ESPN, I'm happy."

The transition from big-time chef to the owner of a "little breakfast place" was eased by a vision of what the LeBrocqs wanted to accomplish. They had enjoyed eating breakfast at the Red Hut Cafe in Tahoe before hitting the slopes, and Mike knew "people like to eat breakfast and like value. They don't want to pay a lot for food." Breakfasts at the Birchwood Cafe consist of all variety of eggs, potatoes, meat, and toast; biscuits and gravy; and more inventive offerings, such as stuffed French toast and specialty hash browns. The bluegill hash browns—Birchwood is the world's bluegill capital—are the favorite and consist of breakfast sausage, Spanish olives, cheddar cheese, taco meat, salsa, and sour cream. Eggs Benedict and bananas Foster French toast are also hits. "I make bananas Foster French toast in the slow season, otherwise there'd be lines out the door. It's crazy," says Mike.

Mike uses his training as a chef to keep things fresh but does express a concern with growing bored with traditional Wisconsin cafe food. Creating new dishes that would sell led to friendly competition among the chefs, something that Mike misses. He bought and operated the Birchwood Inn, a supper club, because "I thought I was getting bored." For several years he enjoyed preparing made-to-order sauces and fine meals, but eventually realized running both restaurants was just too much. He sold the supper club and stayed with the cafe because it allowed time for other interests. He is constantly reassured of his decision by former colleagues who express envy at his work and his life. "They're doing the big, fancy things at five-star restaurants," he notes. "I've done that, and am happy to be here."

Here in Mayberry, that is, where the log-sided cafe is decked out to resemble a northwoods lake cabin. An old fishing boat stands on its square keel end, with the daily specials board fixed to each gunwale. Paddles, oars, fishing nets, creels, poles, minnow buckets, and lanterns are scattered about the restaurant, with an occasional pine tree and black bear tucked in here and there. Black and white photos of fishermen with their catch promise great things in store for those who hit the water after breakfast, or for the men who are able to break away from the coffee table with enough of the morning left to cast a line. "It's the same crew every morning, 365 days a year," Mike says.

CHETEK
Bob's Grill
505 Second Street
(715) 924-4130
M–Sa 5:30 A.M.–7 P.M.; Su 6 A.M.–2 P.M.
Lowell "Buckshot" Trowbridge, owner
Candy Nelson, manager

Candy Nelson is looking forward to a much-needed vacation from Bob's Grill, where she has spent the past twenty-six years as manager. The summer has ended and the vacationers have given back the town of Chetek and the surrounding lakes to the twelve hundred year-round residents, who again enjoy parking on the street in front of the restaurant instead of a block or two away. They're lined up at the counter, sopping up broken egg yolks with toast and downing cups of coffee while sharing the latest news. Among them sits Buckshot Trowbridge, as he does nearly every morning, not really supervising the operations of the restaurant he owns but keeping an eye on it nevertheless. He is content to be just another regular and confidently leaves the work to Candy and her experienced staff.

Six years ago Buckshot bought the landmark corner restaurant from Candy's parents. "He used to drink coffee and eat here," explains Candy, "and my mom and dad asked me to ask him, 'Buckshot, will you buy this place?' and he finally did." He invested in new kitchen equipment, remodeling and redecorating, and wisely persuaded Candy to remain as manager. As a result, Bob's Grill operates just as it has for many years, and Buckshot is guaranteed a reserved space at the counter, the gathering place of choice for the ten o'clock men's coffee group. Especially during the winter. If an off-season stranger happens to take a stool, he'll be asked to step down. "The locals are really used to being spoiled all winter long," Candy says. "We try to make sure the coffee counter is empty."

Named for its first owner, Bob's Grill is known primarily as a breakfast place, especially in the summer when tourists keep the grill sizzling with pancakes, omelettes, and skillets, concoctions of hash browns, eggs, and other ingredients. The locals come early for coffee and talk, and by nine o'clock the summer visitors replace them. "The summer tourists eat huge breakfasts between nine and eleven," notes Candy. "Just when you're sick of making breakfast, they come in."

My sister and her husband have a little cabin on the chain of lakes, and they recommend Bob's fresh buttermilk pancakes, another specialty. The batter is mixed up from real buttermilk. Candy reports, "Our milkman tells us he only delivers buttermilk to us, which means we must be the only ones making fresh pancakes." She is always on the lookout for pancakes on a par with those at Bob's whenever she eats out, "and my ex-husband always said, 'Why? You're going to hate it.' And I never have found pancakes as good as ours."

Other breakfast favorites at Bob's include the real potato hash browns, American fries, and spudniks, huge doughnut balls made from real mashed potatoes. These are the one item that I cannot pass over at Bob's. I love them. Crisp and brown, either plain or coated with granulated sugar, the spudniks are about the size of a golf ball. The recipe comes from Candy's mother, who introduced them at Bob's. They sell for a mere fifteen cents, making complete gluttony affordable. "People order them by the dozens," says Candy.

Tourists eat breakfast all day, but by lunchtime the locals have moved on to hot beef sandwiches, burgers, and the daily specials. "The people in this area like mashed potato meals—potatoes, vegetables, and meat meals," says Candy. They save room—as you should—for the pies made fresh every day.

Tourism has such an impact on Chetek that it is the calendar with which Candy measures out the year. "We start getting busy at fishing opener," she says. "Then there's cabin opener—when people come to open their cabins for the summer. That leads to Memorial Day, the first really big weekend of the year. Summer peaks over the Fourth of July, and we're always glad when that's over. We breathe a big sigh of relief. It winds down to Labor Day when the families disappear because the kids are back in school and people begin closing up the cabins. Hunting opener is another big weekend, and then things settle down to just the locals. Winter is for the locals. It's our time to relax a little."

EXELAND
Village Cafe
11038 Highway 48 West
(715) 943-2321
M 6:30 A.M.–2:30 P.M.; Tu–F 6:30 A.M.–6 P.M.; Sa 6:30 A.M.–2:30 P.M.;
Su 9 A.M.–1 P.M. closed Sundays in winter
Debbie Kisner

At high noon on a winter Thursday, there is scarcely room in the tiny Exeland cafe for another person. The place is filled to capacity with regulars who have come in from the cold to greet friends and neighbors over steaming bowls of chicken and dumplings, the daily special. The short counter is filled with outdoorsmen wearing Carhartt pants and jackets and Sorel boots. It is cold outside, and the front window is covered with a film of steam struggling to convert itself into ice.

I sweep my eyes across the cafe and spy an empty stool at the counter, just under a framed newspaper featuring the Village Cafe and owner Debbie Kisner. The article is by Loren West, who sent me here in search of the same great home cooking and small town magic he found a few years earlier. I seat myself on the chrome and red vinyl stool and turn to assess my neighbors. Looking back at me is a series of bearded faces topped with camouflage caps, each one craned around or over the faces between it and me. "Hi," I say in response to the inquiring looks. The face nearest the front window softens at being addressed, and then offers the typical Wisconsin winter greeting.

"Cold enough for you?"

We have scarcely moved through the perfunctory comments about the weather when the faces rise en masse and turn to brave the cold outside. Within a span of two minutes, the cafe goes from standing room only to nearly empty. "Some days are like this," owner Debbie Kisner tells me as she pauses in the kitchen doorway. "If we could only figure out when it's going to happen, we could be ready."

Joining me at the counter, Art Sampson orders a hamburger and piece of lemon meringue pie. He has just dropped his wife off at the senior center, in the Exeland school that was discontinued a year or two ago. Used to be, the kids from area farms would meet each other at the town school, but since it closed, the kids are sent to the schools in Winter or Bruce. Out where Art lives, the kids on his side of the road go to one school. The kids on the opposite side go to the other. "When the school closed, we lost something. That's for sure," Art says.

Nowadays, it's the seniors who meet at the Exeland school for food and fellowship. Art prefers the cafe because, he says, "I don't want to sit and hear people talk about the pills they're taking." Besides, he has a couple of gift certificates someone gave him for his birthday, which he uses to pay for his burger and pie.

Art was a boy when his parents relocated from Chicago to Sawyer County, where they'd purchased a small farm. Back in the 1930s, most farms were scratched out of the sandy, rocky soil, but Art's parents were fortunate to have found a patch of productive soil. Life centered on the farm and the weekly trips to town.

"Exeland used to be quite a town," Art remembers. "There were five stores and a grocery store. A two-story hotel and a tavern across the street." In the 1940s, the small business district grew with the addition of Ma Carter's Cafe, which Art watched being built. Sixty years later, after World War II service in the Aleutian Islands ("They told me soldiers got a shorter term there because of the severe weather, and I said, 'That's nothing! I'm from Sawyer County!'"), raising a family, selling the family farm, and retiring, Art sits on the same chrome stools at the same counter. On the back wall hangs Ma Carter's sign.

Ma Carter was long gone when Debbie Kisner and her husband moved to Sawyer County from Ohio in the mid-1990s. "He got a farm. I got a cafe," Debbie explains succinctly. With the eyes of the village watching, she set about cleaning and redecorating the old Ma Carter's. Nothing could be prettier than the results. The upper walls are stark white, the lower walls cobalt blue. Behind the gold-flecked, Formica-covered counter, white shelves are filled with a collection of mismatched but complementary blue and white plates—Harker cameoware, Homer Laughlin floral prints, Blue Willow, and more. Cobalt jars and glasses catch the winter sun falling through the front window before splintering it into bright rays.

Eight years into her ownership, Debbie is amazed at how much food gets served in the twenty-seven-seat cafe. Although Sawyer County now has "more tourists than farming," according to Art, most of Debbie's customers are locals. Gesturing to the highway outside, she points out, "Not a lot of traffic goes by here, as you can see." The locals fill the place for breakfast and lunch, when they load up on burgers and the noon special—"We sell out every day," Debbie says—and the latest news.

Debbie promises "homemade everything" and delivers it in the form of fresh, hand-pattied burgers, slow simmered soups, hot beef with mashed potatoes made from peeled and boiled spuds, and pies made daily from scratch. People come for miles for Debbie's peanut butter pie. The lemon meringue pie is worth driving for as well. My piece was tart and puckery, with just enough lumps in the filling to prove it was made on Debbie's stovetop. Lemon meringue pie is one of Art's favorites, and Debbie used to call him whenever she made it. He doesn't come in so often anymore, which is all the more reason I was glad to have him for company at the counter.

Art's son, Carl, is more likely to be found at the cafe on any given day. "He comes in here all the time," Debbie says, as she dials his work number to see if he has a few minutes to talk with me. He does, so I walk across the street to a brick building where fiberglass molding is done.

On weekends and vacations, Carl and his wife enjoy motorcycling with friends. As the state coordinator of the Christian Motorcyclists Association, Carl is often responsible for organizing rides and rallies. This sends him to all corners of the state in search of scenic routes, accommodating campgrounds, and memorable small town cafes.

"My wife and I seek them out," Carl says. "A special treat for ourselves is to go to the small cafes for breakfast. We always have the same thing: eggs, toast, hash brown potatoes, and coffee. We like getting in with the morning crowd, the local talk, what so and so did last night. Wherever we go, it's just like home."

HAUGEN
Lona's Corner Cafe |●|
309 Highway SS North
(715) 234-6110
M–Sa 6 A.M.–3 P.M.; Su 7 A.M.–1 P.M.
Lona Haughian
Having lived several years on a small Barron County farm and being a connoisseur of good home cooking at small town cafes, my friend and fellow pie rider Barbara Wheeler believes there's a direct correlation to feed mills and great cafes. Wherever you find a working feed mill, she theorizes, you'll find a great cafe. Her theory certainly bears witness in Haugen, the Mushroom and Kolache Capital of Wisconsin, where the feed mill is just across the street from Lona's Corner Cafe.

Lona Haughian, a Norwegian who married an Irishman, is the owner of the eatery in this community of Czechoslovakians (don't miss the Bohemian Museum in the old Haugen School during the summer months). She'd been a regular customer, but when the previous owner asked her to buy the place, she turned her down. One night she woke up, sat up in bed, and announced to the Irishman next to her that she was going to buy the cafe. And she did. "That was fifteen years ago already," she tells me, emphasizing *already*.

Fifteen years and one new kitchen. In 2001 a kitchen more than five times the size of the original was built on the other side of the dining room wall. "It's wonderful," Lona exclaims. "I don't know how we ever got along without it." Before moving into the spacious new cookery, Lona prepared all of the food in a tiny space behind the counter, on the kind of stove you'll find in most family kitchens. At the urging of many people, she left a portion of the tiny kitchen behind a screen of lattice "because everyone expects me to be out here," she explains. "Everyone likes me to say hi and goodbye. I want to see my customers, and they like to see the cook."

From the small kitchen or the large, Lona takes pride in offering her customers an expanded menu. She supplements traditional meat, potatoes, and gravy meals with colorful pasta salads; bison sausage, bacon, and burgers from the local bison farm; and a variety of breakfast offerings. "We're basically a breakfast place," says Lona. "My strawberry pancakes and Lona's Omelette are big sellers. I put American fries in the omelettes, so they're a little different." A big breakfast seller is Lona's sausage gravy over baking powder biscuits. Once served as a Sunday special, it was in such great demand that people waited in line on the sidewalk for a chance to sit down in front of a plate of their own. "Then we added Fridays. Now we have it every day. People just love it!" Lona says.

I'm not a fan of biscuits and gravy, but I was tempted to reevaluate my inclination when I spied the man at the next table enjoying a half-order. That was only after I plunged ahead and ordered a cherry kolache, a traditional Czechoslovakian pastry, without consulting either the menu or my waitress. Lona has discontinued offering the pastry as a regular menu item although they can be special ordered ahead of your visit. I was sadly disappointed, having put off my kolache fix until I reached Lona's. My waitress suggested a caramel roll instead, and I took her up on it. It came to the table sweet and heavy with butter and brown sugar goo and chopped walnuts.

But then I realized it was Thursday—taco day at Lona's. I called my waitress back and ordered a taco, instructing her to pack the caramel roll in a Styrofoam box so I could take it with me. Lona's tacos must not be missed.

Taco Thursday started several years ago with Tammy, a former waitress who offered her own recipe for soft tortillas when Lona was looking for something new to make. Filled with taco-seasoned ground beef, shredded lettuce, tomatoes, sour cream, and cheddar cheese, the tacos soon became a huge hit. Reminiscent of eggy crepes or thin Swedish pancakes, the tortillas make the meal.

The Norwegian woman with the Irish last name cooking for Wisconsin Czechoslovakians appreciates the many compliments. But don't expect to get the tortilla recipe. "It's an old Norwegian secret," Lona explains with a smile.

IRON RIVER
Ideal Cafe ◉

Highway 2 and Main Street

(715) 372-8915

M–Sa 6 A.M.–2 P.M.; Su 7 A.M.–1 P.M.

Mary and James "Mac" McBrair

Tucked behind Mac McBrair's tavern in the beige, three-story building left over from the nineteenth century, you'll find Mac's wife, Mary, tending a bar of her own. She serves broasted chicken instead of Schlitz and closes up at two in the afternoon, not two in the morning. The Ideal Cafe, she laughs, "has been around here just about forever. It's the cheapest place in town to eat."

The building was erected in 1892 as a combination hotel-bar-cafe. More than a century later, Mary continues to cater to the locals, tourists, and "snowbirds"—summer residents who leave Wisconsin's iced-over northwoods for warmer climates during the winter months. "We're most popular for our Ideal Breakfast—two eggs, toast, potatoes, choice of ham, bacon, or sausage, and coffee for $3.75," explains Mary. "Breakfast is a really big thing. When we first started, it was lunches. I don't know why it's breakfast now."

In the past ten years, Wisconsinites—including full-time residents, temporary vacationers, and snowbirds—have turned to breakfast as if it's going out of style. Cafe owners throughout the state report that breakfast is their biggest meal of the day. They're serving a lot of breakfasts, and a lot for breakfast. Eggs; omelettes; hash browns and American fries; ham, bacon, sausage, steak, bratwurst patties, corned beef hash, even fish; vegetables and cheese; pancakes, French toast, and waffles; doughnuts, rolls, and other bakery items; toast and jelly—all washed down with gallons of coffee, milk, and juice. Everything is fair game for breakfast, and the more of it the better. Morning, noon, and night, twenty-four hours a day, we eat breakfast. Maybe the explanation lies in what one cafe owner surmised: "It must be that old peasant stock we come from, packing away food for the long days in the fields—or the hard winter."

Mary had exciting plans when she took on running the cafe. She was going to have a "muffin of the day" and experiment with all kinds of fancy cooking. "I never liked to cook ordinary, everyday stuff," she explains. But she soon learned that her customers had other ideas. They liked the ordinary, everyday stuff and wouldn't touch her experiments, such as lentil soup, which they dubbed "lethal soup." Mary quickly learned that she could offer different foods if she "called it what they understand." When the lentil soup was renamed hamburger and bean soup, it became a favorite. Likewise, the chicken cordon bleu sandwich she offered had to be called a chicken breast sandwich with ham and Swiss cheese. "You have to describe the food by the ingredients," she now knows.

As we chat over the counter, Mary busies herself with preclosing cleanup, darting in and out of the kitchen. She knows her local customers by their likes and dislikes, making menus an unnecessary formality. As we talk, a woman enters the cafe and sits at a booth on the far side of the room. Mary pokes her head out of the kitchen, calls out hi, and asks, "Do you want the daily special?" The woman shakes her head and replies, "I'd rather have what I had yesterday." Without having to ask, Mary returns to the kitchen and begins preparing the woman's meal. Now isn't that ideal?

LUCK
Main Dish Family Restaurant
219 South Main Street
(715) 427-2378
M–F 6 A.M.–4 P.M.; Sa 6 A.M.–3 P.M.; Su 7 A.M.–2 P.M.
Jenell and Ralph Britton
Earlier in the day, Jenell Britton received a phone call from people passing through Luck on their way farther north. They had a special request. Could she make them beer cheese soup? They didn't want to miss out on one of their favorite Main Dish dishes, and the vacation just wouldn't be the same without it. Jenell agreed, and though she didn't yet know just who had called—"I guess I'll find out tomorrow"—she was elbow deep into preparations.

Jenell worked for past owners Jo and Norman George before moving on to another job. Shortly thereafter, she was diagnosed with cancer and spent an unhealthy period in which her time, mind, and energy were focused entirely on her ill health. As the cancer came under control, she decided she needed a job to focus on, so she went back to work at the Main Dish. Within a week, the owner offered to sell the business to her. "I wanted to buy it from Jo but things didn't work out. So when I had the chance a second time, I jumped at it," she says.

Only four months into her ownership, Jenell is "back to home cooking again. I'm putting it back the way Norm and Jo had it. I saw Jo and she offered to give me the recipes. I want to go back to all of the homemade dressings, the ranch, everything." She has been trying her hand at replicating Jo's popular pies, soups, and daily specials and reports that it is coming along well. The pies in the glass display case on the counter attest to that, but, she apologizes, "I don't have the banana cream down quite yet. I want to make it with the big meringue and everything."

Jenell's commitment to the Georges' quality home cooking excites Jo, under whose ownership the Main Dish was featured in the first edition of *Cafe Wisconsin*. Jenell has a good model to follow but also is trying to develop menu favorites that are distinctly her own, such as the popular bread pudding served with plain or French vanilla cream. Returning to the high standards that both the locals and tourists have embraced, Jenell knows she has her work cut out for her. But she emphasizes that "everything's going good. It's everything I thought it would be."

With the support and help of her family—"It was a family decision," she says. "We all sat down and talked about it"—including her father, Gary, who has appointed himself the chief handyman, Jenell is sure to succeed. "I plan to be here a while," Jenell promises. She has plans to redecorate the

---

BREAKFAST

HAM & EGGS, TOAST & COFFEE	75¢	BACON & EGGS, TOAST & COFFEE	60¢
1 - EGG, TOAST & COFFEE	30¢	WHEAT CAKES	30¢
FRENCH TOAST	30¢	JUICE	10¢ & 20¢

SANDWICHES

TURKEY	50¢	STEAK	40¢
BACON, LETT & TOMATO	35¢	DENVER OR BEEF	35¢
BAKED HAM	35¢	GRILLED CHEESE	30¢
LETTUCE & TOMATO	30¢	HAMBURGER	20¢
LIVER OR SUMMER SAUSAGE	20¢	EGG, SARDINE OR CHEESE	20¢
CALIF. HAMBURGER	45¢	PEANUT BUTTER & JELLY	25¢

A LITTLE OUT OF THE WAY
BUT - FOR LESS TO PAY

THE OUTFITTERS
MENS & BOYS CLOTHING
SHOES & RUBBER FOOTWEAR
SHOE REPAIRING

ON HIWAY - 35
IN MILLTOWN

WE RECOMMEND
NORTH LUCK MOTEL
& NORTH LUCK CASH STORE
MODERN CABINS & LIGHT GROCERIES
Mr. and Mrs. S. J. Schauls
RT. 1, LUCK, WISC - ON HIWAY 35
PHONE - 38F22 - LUCK

FIDELITY
STATE BANK
YOU'LL FIND CONVENIENT &
PLEASANT DEALINGS WITH THIS BANK
- LOANS - DEPOSITS -
INSURED - INSURANCE
PHONE - 95 LUCK   MEMBER F. D. I. C.

ANDERSON BROS.
TEXACO SERVICE
LUBRICATION WASHING
GREASING - OILS - BATTERIES - TIRES
"Let us service your car while-u-eat"
PH. 151-LUCK-CARS
CALLED FOR & DELIVERED

LUCK
AUTO CO.
McCULLOCH CHAINSAW
ALUMA   JOHNSON
CRAFT   MOTORS
BOATS   sales & service
Phone - 5 - LUCK

WE RECOMMEND
BUTTERNUT
DAIRY CO-OP
GRADE - A - MILK
& DAIRY PRODUCTS
PHONE - 19 LUCK, WISC

L. J. HESSON CO.
Allis-Chalmers Tractors and Machines
FORD CARS & TRUCKS
Sales & Service
COMPLETE TRACTOR
TIRE SERVICE
PHONE - 76 -- LUCK, WISC

dark, paneled interior to look like "an old-fashioned Coca-Cola restaurant," though she is not yet a collector of Coca-Cola items. "I just came up with the idea and will start collecting stuff."

A facelift will invigorate the Main Dish, which reflects the decorating trends of the 1970s. There is timelessness about the place, as if it has stubbornly withstood the many changes that have occurred outside its walls. The decor is the same. The food and its quality are again the same. About the only thing that hasn't been frozen in time are the prices, as evidenced by a menu board resurrected from the basement and hung over the counter. It provides a glimpse into the Main Dish of the mid-1950s, when someone sitting in your very spot at the counter could have ordered a sardine sandwich (that's one menu item that's long gone) for a mere twenty cents. While munching away, that same person could have contemplated a purchase at the Outfitters in nearby Milltown—"A Little Out of the Way But for Less to Pay"—or an overnight stay at the North Luck Motel.

The businesses, like the prices, belong to the 1950s. But you can go back to the future by dropping in to the Main Dish for a bite to eat. If you want beer cheese soup or any other favorite, call a day ahead and ask Jenell to make it. She'll be happy to oblige.

MERCER
Tom's Country Cafe |●|
5233 Highway 51 North
(715) 476-2433
M–Sa 5:30 A.M.–7 P.M.; Su 5:30 A.M.–2 P.M.
Tom and Denise Thompson
One day in 1989 Denise Thompson paused during her work at the local bank, which had recently been bought by a large corporation, and pondered her future. "I thought, 'What else could I be doing with my life?'" she remembers, "and immediately thought about the cafe for sale down the street. That night I told Tom about my idea, and he asked, 'Are you serious?' Yes, I said. We called the real estate agent that very night. . . . So much of this world is so corporate and people are forgetting about other things—the back-to-basics stuff that holds life together."

Denise examined her future as an employee of a faceless corporation and rejected it in favor of the community- and family-centered life she knew as a child growing up in her parents' restaurant, where men's coffee klatches replaced power lunches and family cooperation replaced office networks. About the "spur of the moment" decision to buy Mercer's old cafe, Denise remembers, "I felt really good about this place. I didn't have any nightmares about buying it. I felt positive about this restaurant."

Thirteen years later, Denise credits the success of Tom's Country Cafe ("The family voted on a name, and Tom lost," she laughs) to two "back-to-the-basics" philosophies: "Please the people" and "Family first, job second." The first explains Denise's insistence on "homemade everything," from real potatoes (to the tune of seven hundred to eight hundred pounds a week), scratch pies and soups, "humongous" omelettes "that really bring in the oohs and aahs," and slow-cooked daily specials. Denise says, "Personally, I can't stand instant mashed potatoes. It's whatever you want your standard to be, and mine is the highest, always has been the highest. That's what people like, and you're here to please the people. You do what they want you to do." Denise's commitment to quality is equally reflected in the warm, inviting restaurant, with its golden maple floor, real wood wainscot and oak chairs inside, and rustic, northwoods log siding outside.

The second philosophy keeps the Thompson family central to the life Denise has chosen. She explains, "When we took over this place, we promised ourselves that the kids would always come first. We scheduled everything around the kids, so we didn't end up missing their activities." The Thompson "kids" include Christopher, now graduated from college and raising two daughters of his own; Tammy, a teacher with a little boy; and Shawn, a college graduate who works in computers. "The kids weren't committed to working here," Denise says, "and they all decided they'd rather go into other work. That's fine. None of us wanted to be slaves to this place. But we are a family and this is a family business, and the family holds it together. That's what I mean by back-to-the-basics. I'm really proud of the kids for pitching in and helping out."

The town of Mercer is known as the loon capital of Wisconsin, and you'll find a giant fiberglass loon along the side of the highway welcoming you to town. On the cover of the menu at Tom's Country Cafe you'll find a loon wearing a chef's cap and, on the reverse, this sage bit of advice: "All of our food is prepared with fresh ingredients and cooked daily to order. You can't rush the cooking of a quality meal. Bite your nails . . . be patient . . . it's worth it!"

MINONG
Wendy's Place
749 Business Highway 53
(715) 466-4334
M–F 6 A.M.–7 P.M.; Sa 6 A.M.–5 P.M.; Su 7 A.M.–3 P.M.
Wendy and Terry Holman
A sign hanging over the front porch of Wendy's Place pulls drivers off old Highway 53 with the promise of HOME COOKING. About half are tourists

who fill the worn asphalt parking lot with motor homes and tent trailers. The knotty pine–paneled cafe is a local favorite, too, especially in the summer when seasonal residents return from winter hideaways. Look for them at Table One—"Yesterday morning there were twenty-one of them drinking coffee and shaking dice," reports owner Wendy Holman—between six and nine in the morning and again from three to five in the afternoon, but watch where you sit. The older men and women have their "reserved" chairs and stools. If you happen to sit there, they'll politely inform you that you'll have to move. Around Table One, they know everybody's business and are glad to give it, too.

Just which table is Table One, you ask? You'll know it by the melted portable phone mounted on the wall. This is Buzz's Hot Line, a practical joke ribbing Buzz for the accidental incineration of his cell phone. Seems he had an important call he didn't want to miss, so he took his phone with him when he went out back to burn his trash. Into the can went the crushed cereal boxes, the junk mail, the cell phone. "He was alone when he did it, so no one had to know anything about it. But, of course, he comes in here and tells everyone," chides Wendy. "It didn't take long for Buzz's Hot Line to show up." When he reads about his mishap in this book, Buzz will think twice about telling anyone anything.

Wendy worked seventeen years for the previous owners and bought the place in 1996, making it twenty-five years and counting that she has been associated with the little white cafe on the old highway—the new one bypassing the town of Minong by a few blocks. Wendy has little grudge against the new highway, saying, "It didn't hurt too bad." She notes that the slump in the economy has had a greater effect, except during 2000, the best year ever for the cafe. Perhaps more people were traveling in anticipation of the millennium. In any case, once people find Wendy's Place, they make a point of coming back. "People want real food," Wendy explains, and they get it here. The hot beef sandwich, chicken dumpling soup, and hamburger soup are among the best sellers, but breakfast is always "a big thing." Pies are the frozen home-baked variety, so opt for one of the dessert specials.

Formerly Nelson's Family Restaurant, Wendy's Place has kept the family spirit alive and well. Wendy has her three children, Jenna Latvala, Heather Golembiewski, and son, Mark, working for her, as well as her dad, Bill Visger, who tends the morning grill. Also lending a hand are her cousin, her cousin's son, and her nephew's girlfriend. Keeping the business all in the family requires flexibility, she notes. "Whenever there's a family event, we have to close." The regulars don't mind a bit—as long as they reopen the next day.

PHILLIPS
Bonnie's Diner
126 South Lake Street
(715) 339-3404
M–Su 5:30 A.M.–2 P.M.
Troy Dunbar

Bonnie's Diner is packed at noon, and people who enter and can't find a seat leave with dismay or elect to share tables with people they might not know. I am a bit hurt that no one asks to sit with me, one person at a table for four. I'm hoping for a genuine small town experience, but it doesn't happen.

Bonnie's is clearly the hot lunch spot in Phillips, which is saying a lot because the town has three fine main street cafes. But don't go asking for Bonnie in order to bestow your praises. There is no Bonnie here. Instead, the owner is Bonnie's son, Troy Dunbar, who started his restaurant career washing dishes at age ten. As a mere boy, he never anticipated that someday he'd be spending ten- to eleven-hour days doing everything from making soup to scheduling the help.

I did not feature Bonnie's Diner in the first edition of *Cafe Wisconsin*, and I am at a loss to explain why. I certainly made a mistake, for Bonnie's has wonderful food, right down to the homemade white, wheat, and seeded rye bread. The day I wandered in (after stopping at Fred Smith's don't-miss Wisconsin Concrete Park up the road), I was bored with burgers and meat and potatoes and wanted something a little different to eat. Troy's daily special of stuffed green peppers fit the bill. I ordered it—and had to laugh when a pair of stuffed green peppers came to the table with a scoop of mashed potatoes and beef gravy on the side. The whole plate full of food was far too much for me to eat, so I saved one of the peppers for dinner later in the day. After one bite told me the mashed potatoes were real, I ignored them in favor of two pieces of pie. The lemon meringue had meringue so high, I would have sworn it wasn't homemade. But it was, and it was delicious. So was the chocolate peanut butter pie.

As the lunch hour proved, the locals come to Bonnie's to eat. But they also come to drink coffee and talk, filling two tables every day between eight and ten in the morning. "I find out a lot of different things going on in town," Troy points out. "It gets pretty deep in here some days. You gotta wear hip boots sometimes!" Phillips is still a pretty laid back little town during the summer, explains Troy, and it's not uncommon for the town folk to mix with the travelers who make Bonnie's a regular stop on trips to and from Up North. Once people find Bonnie's, they make a point to come back. And once they taste the good home cooking, "They all ask for Bonnie. They get quite a surprise when they find out I'm Bonnie!"

PHILLIPS
Crystal Cafe
138 South Lake Street
(715) 339-3711
M–Th 6 A.M.–2 P.M.; F 6 A.M.–8 P.M.; Sa–Su 6 A.M.–2 P.M.
Bob and Julie Voda
One of three down-home cafes on the main street through Phillips, the Crystal Cafe is by far the oldest. In 1912 Emma Soeterber expanded the bakery she had opened a few years earlier into the Crystal Cafe, a business she operated while her husband, Herman, worked as a cook in area lumber camps. Each spring he returned to Phillips, and Emma's seasonal widowhood melted away with the snow. When Herman's death two years later left her a widow for good, Emma supported herself for many years as the cafe's sole proprietor. She moved the cafe to its current location in 1917.

With so many years under its belt, the Crystal is alone in bearing witness to the passing years and fads. If its walls could talk, we'd hear stories about the early years: about the rowdy fights and free-for-alls of the woods-roughened lumberjacks, about welcome home celebrations for soldiers returning from World War I, about the semi-professional baseball team that lived in the rooms upstairs and took meals in the dining room. Those were pre-Depression days when area boys with a sizzling fast pitch or bat-cracking swing were hired by local businessmen, who provided them with jobs and a small salary for playing on league teams they sponsored. Fueled by local pride, a love for America's favorite pastime, and Emma's cooking as good as dear old Mom's, these boys were summer sandlot heroes who returned home each fall. Some stayed behind, married local girls and established homes of their own in Phillips.

The Crystal's current owners, Bob and Julie Voda, are Emma's most recent heirs. The Voda family has had a long relationship with the Crystal Cafe, dating back to 1946 when Bob's great-grandmother worked in both the kitchen and the upstairs rooming house. In 2002 Bob and Julie traded in long-distance trucking for the short-distance, day-to-day business of the cafe when they took over for Bob's uncle, Robert Upson, and mother, Dar Kaufman. Dar remains an essential member of the staff, preparing many of the cafe's homemade daily specials and baked goods from recipes that exist not on spatter-stained index cards but as frequently enacted memories in her head. Other family members include Bob's cousin Sharon and Aunt Marie, who help with the kitchen prep work, cooking, and cleaning.

Despite the cafe's age, periodic remodeling has erased much of its vintage flavor. The most noteworthy survivors from the early days are the full front windows and heavy recessed front door, with its beautiful brass latch rubbed smooth and shiny from years of customer grips. Don't preoccupy yourself with history here. Concentrate instead on the Crystal Cafe's "homemade everything," including daily soups, noon specials, baked goods, and what may be the largest selection of pie north of Highway 8. "Lemon meringue, banana cream, coconut cream, and caramel apple with nut are probably the favorites," Julie says. "But people also like the cakes, especially the cream cheese cake and carrot cake."

One cannot live by pie alone (although some days I think I could), so for heartier appetites the Crystal Cafe features "good old-fashioned, traditional food" like roasted meats, real mashed potatoes, and vegetables, all in sizeable portion that would challenge Babe Ruth's appetite. Get your game underway with any of the Crystal's regular breakfast offerings. You'll get around the bases with the homemade buttermilk pancakes and biscuits and gravy. If it's a home run you're hoping for, take a swing at the omelettes and skillets, both in enough varieties to keep the bats ringing. Made with three eggs, the omelettes come in standard varieties and in an assortment of creative concoctions devised by the regulars. The skillets—whole meal combinations of hash browns, scrambled eggs, meat, and veggies—come in Mexican, Western, and other flavorful versions.

If your day is heading into extra innings and you need more than breakfast, the Vodas' customers report that the grilled chicken sandwich and quarter- and half-pound burgers are some of the best they've ever had. Fridays bring the bottom of the ninth, end of the work week fish fry ritual, which continues to grow in popularity. "From what people are telling us, it's one of the best fish fries in Price County," Julie promises.

As long-distance truckers, Bob and Julie often stayed on the road for four or five weeks at a time. This meant countless meals on the road, and they searched for food "as close to home-cooked as you could get. We were always looking for home-prepared, not pre-fab food," Julie recalls. Knowing what they like and what is worth eating—and what is not—make the Vodas eminently qualified to run a home-cooking cafe of their own. "I wouldn't dare serve anything to my customers that I wouldn't eat myself," asserts Julie.

In a town of about sixteen hundred people, the Crystal Cafe must share the appetites and loyalties of the locals with a half-dozen other restaurants. "I sometimes wonder how we all survive," Julie muses, especially during the relatively snowless winters of the past few years. A good winter brings the snowmobilists, ice fishermen, and other cold weather recreationalists and bolsters the economy just enough to get through until the summer tourist season. The regulars, however, remain committed and loyal 365 days a year—though they may have to adjust their daily comings and goings a bit to accommodate the out-of-town visitors. When autumn fades, there is time to relax and celebrate neighborliness.

"For the past three years, we've prepared a full Thanksgiving dinner and offered it free to anyone in the community. Last year we served over 125 meals. It's our way of thanking them for seeing us through another year," Julie says. "After all, we're all in this together."

PHILLIPS
Phillips Cafe 🍽
167 North Lake Avenue
(715) 339-3232
M–Th 5 A.M.–8 P.M.; F 5 A.M.–9 P.M.; Sa–Su 5 A.M.–7 P.M.
Don and Brenda Miller

Don Miller learned the tricks of the restaurant trade while growing up in his parents' restaurants. In 1981 he bought and remodeled the Phillips Cafe, down the road and across the street from Bonnie's Diner and the Crystal Cafe. Today he dishes up good home cooking, including home-made doughnuts and sweet rolls, fresh burgers, thick malts and shakes, and flaky and perfectly fluted pies. Don makes fruit pies once a week and bakes them as needed, but his from-scratch cream pies are made fresh daily. A plastic menu board with snap-in letters lists the pies in Don's repertoire: apple, coconut, blueberry, pumpkin, lemon, rhubarb, chocolate, custard, pecan, raspberry, raisin, banana, cheesecake, butterscotch, oatmeal, peach, and strawberry. Little red arrows guide you to the day's selections, and it's a good thing they do. Having to pick a piece from the master list would be nearly impossible.

The Phillips Cafe is known for its Flavor Crisp broasted chicken, and Don keeps track of just how much of the crispy poultry pieces he sells each year. In 2001 that amounted to fifty-five thousand pieces, or ten tons! I can't imagine what ten tons of broasted chicken would look like laid out piece to piece. It would probably fill the road from Prentice to Phillips.

I'm of the opinion that once you've tasted broasted chicken, you've tasted broasted chicken, so I move on to welcome alternatives, such as today's Mexican tacos, tostadas, and burritos. Other choices might include the inventive daily specials, such as Oriental beef, goulash, Spanish rice, and Mediterranean tomato soup. While waiting for your food to be brought from the kitchen, you can browse through the back issues of magazines kept at the end of the counter. The selection—*Outdoor Life, Field and Stream, Kiplinger's Finance*—represents a small business owner's view of life in the northwoods.

PORT WING
Cottage Cafe 🍽
8805 Highway 13
(715) 774-3565
May 1–October 31: M–Sa 6 A.M.–8 P.M.; Su 6 A.M.–7 P.M.
November 1–April 30: M–Tu 6 A.M.–6:30 P.M.; W 6 A.M.–12 P.M.; Th 6
A.M.–6:30 P.M.; F 6 A.M.–7 P.M.; Sa–Su 6 A.M.–6 P.M.
Beverly Igo, owner
Louise Halvorson, manager

The Cottage Cafe has stood across from the Port Wing village park for the past forty years or so, according to regular customer Irene Nelson. "It was closed for about two years a while back, and were we ever happy when it reopened. We were sure glad to have a place to go for a cup of coffee, because most people don't like to go to a tavern in the middle of the day."

Irene's niece, Beverly Igo, bought the place in 1989 and wisely hired Louise Halvorson as manager and queen of pie makers. Her raspberry pie is the most scrumptious to be found in northern Wisconsin. I asked her how she made it, and she wouldn't tell me. All of the recipes are secret she says, and besides, they're not written down. "They're all locked inside her head," explains Annie, a longtime waitress.

After so many years, both Beverly and Louise are ready to pass the cafe on to new owners and have the business up for sale. The locals and other regular customers, including the swarms of summer motorcyclists and bicyclists ("We put 'Welcome Cyclists' on the sign out front, and that covers both of them"), will expect the new owners, whoever they might be, to continue in the same vein. When real food made from scratch gets under your skin, there's no substitute. That means plenty of real potatoes, hearty breakfasts, casseroles, and no end to the delicious pies.

Carrying on the traditions of the Cottage Cafe includes opening doors and arms to both the "natives" and the "transplants" of the community. The cafe is the community center, the mayor's office, the senior center ("it's better than staring at four walls"), the community switchboard, the gossip center, the heart of the town, say Louise and Annie, and Barb and Jeremiah, mother and son who have come for afternoon coffee and pie. "When Jeremiah was in the air force, he called here for me," Barb says. "If I wasn't here, they knew where I was."

"This is the place to find out all the latest news," Jeremiah explains. "Who hit a deer. Who drove into the ditch. Who's sick, who's died. Whose animals got loose."

"How to get back at the DNR [Wisconsin Department of Natural Resources]—or get rid of them," Barb adds.

It's also the place for the community to rally behind various efforts, including the current fundraiser to finance the volunteer fire department's purchase of Jaws of Life, a device that pries open smashed cars. For a dollar, you can sign your name on a fluorescent green paper shark and help them reach their goal. People from as far away as Prescott, Arizona, and San Dimas, California, are represented on the wall behind the counter. "This is important to all of us," Louise points out, "because it might be the couple from California who get in the accident that requires the Jaws of Life."

It's also the place for the community to thank Beverly, Louise, and the rest of the workers at the cafe for all they contribute. Certificates of appreciation hanging on the walls include one from the South Shore ATV Club and the local school district, which Beverly supports by being a supervised work employer. Although the following poem disappeared from the wall of the Cottage Cafe after remodeling in 1996 (replaced by a sign that reads, "I had to give up jogging because my thighs kept rubbing together and my underpants caught on fire"), its sentiments still perfectly apply:

Small-Town Cafe
The friendly small-town restaurant
Is busy as can be.
It serves as meeting place for all
And town directory.

Its grand aroma fills the air
With coffee, cakes, and pies
And gaily asks all young and old
To stop when passing by.

It stands for pop and ice-cream cones,
For chicken golden brown,
For homespun hospitality
The friendliest around.

Because it knows its clientele,
It's very apt to greet
A guest who has a birthday
With a very special treat.

It stands for warmth and cheerfulness
Where friends are surely found.
The cozy small-town restaurant
Lends pleasure to the town.

SIREN
Main Street Cafe 🍴 ⛌
7719 West Main Street
(715) 349-2536
M–F 6 A.M.–4 P.M.; Sa 6 A.M.–3 P.M.; Su 6 A.M.–11 A.M.
Conny Roy

The sign painted in blue and white on the front window of the Main Street Cafe promises "home-cooked food," and from the back kitchen Conny Roy and her staff deliver. With the taste of lemon meringue pie lingering in my memory, I returned to the Main Street Cafe ten years after my last visit. Even day-old, wrapped in cellophane, and beaded with sugary drops of meringue sweat, the pie brought me back.

"It doesn't feel like anything has changed," reports Conny as she reflects on the years since we last spoke. "We still make the same food—real mashed potatoes, pie—that people around here like."

Other than the beautifully redecorated cafe—it is light and golden with honey-colored pine boards and feather-painted walls—things really haven't changed much at all. Conny is grateful that the tornado that devastated Siren in June 2001 barely brushed the Main Street Cafe, leaving it virtually intact. Antique kitchen items and old black and white photos from Siren's past, brought in by the locals for Conny to copy and frame, still decorate the walls. Men still sit around the round coffee table passing the news and the time, rehashing last night's baseball game play by play. There is still lemon meringue pie, this time fresh and warm from the oven, but I pass it up in favor of a gooey, homemade caramel roll served with real butter in gold foil.

In the sunny kitchen, Conny Roy snaps the ends off fresh garden green beans brought in by a customer. She snaps and talks about the time she spent helping her grandmother with her Minneapolis catering business. Conny has mastered the skills required of traditional Wisconsin cooking: making pies, mashing potatoes, roasting meats, and making gravies. Predictability, she has found, is the key to success. "You can't experiment in this cafe," she says. "They want the same old thing. Oatmeal raisin and chocolate chip cookies. Hot beef. Apple pie. We tried frozen yogurt, oat bran muffins, Egg Beaters. They didn't want any of it."

"The customers more or less dictate to us," she explains. "They get what they want. You do get stuck in a routine and feel like you're making the same thing every day. I don't really like that." She looks at the beans she's cleaning. "So you have meat, potatoes, and vegetables. What else is there to do with beans?"

In 1986 Conny's parents, Mike and Susan, returned to Mike's hometown of Siren and settled on his grandparents' homestead. They had thought about running their own cafe and, despite their lack of experience, they wound up buying the former Ma's Cafe. Susan explained on my visit ten years ago: "Mike had traveled a lot and ate in restaurants. He knew what workingmen liked to eat. His mom ran a catering business, and both of them always had a second sense for food. So this is just like a home kitchen. It's just like cooking at home."

The "home kitchen" on Siren's Main Street attracts mostly senior citizens because, as Conny explains, "the older generation knows this food. Home-cooked food draws this kind of people. The younger crowd goes more for burgers and Mexican food, quicker stuff that's easier to fix."

As Conny readies the beans, Susan mixes batter for homemade dough-nuts and readies tomorrow's batch of sweet rolls. Breakfasts are popular here, especially omelettes and the platter-sized pancakes (kids get special Mickey Mouse pancakes with chocolate chip eyes). Daily specials include roast beef, chicken, lasagna, and meatballs and always an alternative soup and sandwich special. Soups are clever and innovative, like the turkey corn chowder, a favorite of the fish salesman who marks his next visit on the Roys' calendar to indicate when they should plan on fixing it. "He always takes a bucket of it home," laughs Conny.

Conny's elderly customers often come for three meals a day, some so predictably at the same time every day that it's possible to have their food cooked and ready for them when they step through the door. "If they don't come in, we know we'd better check up on them to see if they're okay," Conny tells me. "We'll call them up or ask a friend about them. If we can't find out anything, we'll go over to see if things are all right."

"You do get to know individuals' quirks," she continues. "There's one guy who has a regular routine: one cup of coffee, then food, then when his plate is empty, another cup of coffee. One guy lays his money on the counter to show he's ready to order. They're spoiled here, but sometimes I think we're the only ones who know it."

WEBSTER
Tracks Dining Car Cafe
7457 Main Street
(715) 866-7332
M–Sa 6 A.M.–2 P.M.; Su 7 A.M.–12:30 P.M.
Joel Hakenson and Pam Durkee
At seven thirty in the morning at Tracks Dining Car Cafe, men are drink-ing coffee and divining with dice to see who will pay the bill. It's the start of another day in Webster at the old cafe adjacent to the railroad bed; with its rails and ties pulled, it's now the Gandy-Dancer recreational trail.

Owners Joel Hakenson and Pam Durkee celebrate its association with the railroad with a collection of train-related items, including model trains, a wooden pull toy, framed prints, and a short section of salvaged rail. On the rail sit several flattened pennies and nearby are a few iron spikes, all remnants of Joel's own childhood spent in the nearby town of Barronett. "My dad gave me those," Joel says. "Dad and I did the pennies when I was a kid."

Like the pennies, life's curves have a way of circling around and flattening out, carrying you from place to place, thing to thing—sometimes despite your best intentions. Two and a half years ago, Joel and Pam were thrilled to finally have sold their bar and grill in Herbster. "I vowed I'd never do it again," Joel remembers. Instead, he joined his brother's road contracting business, and while on a job near Spooner he discovered the cafe in Webster was up for sale. Soon thereafter, he and Pam bought the place, trading in, as he says, "the first letters of the old town for those of the new town."

"Cashing in a few favors," the couple rounded up a crew of friends and spent a twenty-four-hour-a-day, seven-day workweek resurrecting the neglected cafe. While the local regulars waited on the sidewalk for the place to reopen, Joel and Pam installed a new furnace and air conditioner, cleaned the place from top to bottom, hung new wallpaper, and readied the kitchen for the first day. They set out a few train items, and then opened the doors. As the locals filled the place and got to know the new owners, they expressed their confidence and approval by bringing in items of their own to display. Little paper cards identify who owns which object.

Within a few short weeks, the regulars had established a predictable daily pattern. At seven thirty, the men's coffee group arrived, followed by married couples breakfasting between ten thirty and eleven thirty, and working people looking for a midday meal between noon and one. The cafe and its new owners quickly became so popular that "it has been standing room only since we took over," Joel says.

Joel and Pam love to cook, but "owning a restaurant has nothing to do with cooking," points out Joel. "You can't cook what you want, but what you sell." His customers tell him what they're hungry for and are quick to let him know when he's made something they aren't interested in trying. That means there are plenty of potatoes, roasted meats, and other familiar favorites. Joel finds soups to be the best outlet for his culinary creativity and is proud of such concoctions as his Guadalajara stew, which he describes as "beef stew with a Latino influence." Once they try his creations, the locals usually are sold. But they've learned not to ask for recipes because Joel doesn't give them out.

In his more reflective moments, Joel considers "the biggest issues in the cafe business, and that is to keep the essence of what a cafe is supposed to be and still make it a profitable business." People want and hope to find the mythical cafe that is clean and bright, old-fashioned in appearance, filled with homemade everything, and frequented by small town characters. The reality is that that image is neither real nor profitable, Joel says. "You can't make money selling a full case of doughnuts for fifteen cents a piece. But that is what people expect. They miss seeing the pie case and doughnuts because that's what a cafe is supposed to be. We all want to walk into a place and see all that homemade—cakes, doughnuts, pies— and smell it, but you've got to be able to sell it."

Joel realizes that the dream is marketable even if the actual product is less so. Instead of dealing with a surplus of unsold or stale baked goods, he limits his production to what can be realistically sold in a given day. Anything that can be held over another day or reused is, and anything that cannot is given away for bear bait. This means that the regulars, as well as the area bears, remain captivated and well fed.

WINTER
Lakewood Cafe
5158 North Main Street
(715) 266-5015
M–Sa 6 A.M.–9 P.M.; Su 6 A.M.–8 P.M.
Jill and Larry Petit

The main street through Winter has been torn up all summer, and even though summer is rapidly coming to a close, there is no haste to pave over the rutted dirt in preparation for winter's snow and ice. The locals have grown accustomed to the inconvenience. It certainly has not stopped their daily and some times multiple daily visits to the Lakewood Cafe. In the face of blowing dust and severely taxed shock absorbers, they make jokes about the road, such as this computer-generated sign hanging on the bulletin board near the front door: "Wisconsin's newest rustic road / MAIN STREET / Winter, Wisconsin."

Last week, when the brother of former owner Virginia Langille died, the road was groomed so the mourners could get through in comfort. That demonstrates the affection the Langille family has earned in this small town. They have been residents for many years, and in 1978, when Les and Virginia Langille returned home and bought the cafe from Virge's sister, Lucille Murphy, there was even more cause to embrace them. Today, their niece, Jill Petit, and her husband, Larry, run what has become a family business.

Once known as Phalen's Hotel, the present brick building was built in 1925, replacing an earlier frame structure that had burnt down. "Back in those days," Virge had told me, "people didn't have a lot of money, and what they did have they kept with them. They didn't use the banks like we do now. So when the first cafe—the wooden one—burned down the owners lost literally everything they had. They went to the bank and had to borrow four thousand dollars. That was in 1925, and they reopened the same year. That tells you how fast they got their business going again. I think that's an interesting story."

When the Langilles became owners, they did a lot of remodeling but didn't erase the historic features of the old cafe. By the time Jill and Larry bought the place in 1997 it was ready for a complete overhaul. Larry's skill as a contractor is evident in the old cafe's new look: fresh, natural pine trim and clean white walls decorated with a simple stenciled leaf design. Larry pushed the dining area into the neighboring building and added a deck for outdoor seating. The building also received new windows and a new door. "The old door never stayed shut," Jill relates. "It got to be the joke around here that when it blew open, people took turns getting up to push it shut."

Jill spent summers living in her parents Minong drive-in and winters attending elementary school in Winter. As a high school student, she waitressed for Les and Virginia and thought it would be an interesting place to own someday. She was working as the town clerk when the opportunity came up, and she knew if she hoped to stay in Winter, she'd need a job to keep her there. She and Larry bought the cafe on October 1, 1997, and opened on Halloween wearing costumes.

For people who have been coming to the Lakewood for years, the changes in its appearance are readily noted. I rather miss the old-time look of the place, including the wood-fronted Coca-Cola cooler and the antique cash register, but I'm thrilled that the old-time quality of the food has not changed a morsel. Jill follows in Aunt Virge's footsteps, making homemade specialties including "gravy off the roast," real mashed potatoes, and tasty pies. "Everything here is homemade, do-it-yourself," Jill says proudly.

Although Jill grew up in a family of women who are good cooks, she never really had the opportunity to test her legacy until she began running the Lakewood. "I think I made two pies in my life before this," she explains, "but I learned real quick by teaching myself. I didn't have any choice but to learn!" She has learned exceptionally well, and with the help of her mom and her mom's sister—both pinch-hitter pie makers—she satisfies the cravings and demands of her customers.

As she stood behind the counter reading what I had written ten years earlier about Les and Virge and the Lakewood, she looked up and said,

"You know, I made rhubarb custard pie just today. Let me buy you a piece."
Ten years after I sat at Les and Virge's counter eating rhubarb custard pie,
I again was sitting there—this time eating Jill's. It is still warm from the
oven and just as delicious. With my first forkful, I am transported to childhood and summer Sunday dinners at my grandma's house. After a meal of
pot roast, mashed potatoes, and gravy, the pie made with rhubarb from the
plants in the backyard is cut into triangle wedges and levered onto plates.
Grandma's pie—like Jill's—was perfect: not-too-sweet, eggy custard filled
with chunks of tender pink rhubarb, baked in a perfectly flaky crust dusted
with granulated white sugar.

"How's the pie?" asks my waiter.

"Perfect. Divine," I say, relishing every bite, every memory.

Next Best Bets

Bayfield
Pier Plaza ⦿

1 Rittenhouse Avenue

The original A & W-turned-dockside-cafe has been torn down and replaced
with a new and improved full menu restaurant that borders on "upscale tour-
isty." But still the local hangout.

Brule
Twin Gables

Highways 2 and 27

Featured in the first edition, the Twin Gables has recently undergone new
ownership. Stop in and try the hot beef—and pick up a Finnish-American
calendar for the coming year.

Cumberland
Our Place Cafe

1233 Second Avenue

Cumberland may be the only town in Wisconsin to have an ordinance against
dice shaking, but that doesn't keep the coffee klatchers from gathering every
morning at this cafe that boasts everything is made from scratch.

Delta
Delta Diner

14385 County Highway H

Wow! An authentic 1940s Silk City Diner dropped into the northwoods, with
inspired real food to match. Opened in December 2003, the Delta's destined to
be a hit. Delta is not on the state road map, so you may want to call for directions (715-372-6666).

GRANTSBURG
Country Cafe
125 West Madison Street
A fine cafe recently under new ownership. Stop in and give them a try.

HURLEY
Cardo's Cafe
410 Silver Street
A local runner training for Ashland's Whistlestop Marathon ran twelve miles in cold and rain just to eat breakfast at Cardo's, an old-time cafe reopened in 2002. That's darned good testimony for Cardo's darned good food.

IRON RIVER
Orchard's Cafe
Highway 2
Known for homemade pasties in six varieties and pie. The interior, however, is only fair to middlin'. The building is a former service station.

MAPLE
Sundown Cafe
Highway 2
Originally Buster's Coffee Pot, a little roadside cafe with a few stools, the Sundown serves up genuine food along with gas for your car.

PARK FALLS
Frontier Inn
177 Division Street (in the Park Mall downtown)
Home cooking all around, but the setting in a mostly vacant downtown mall is less than appetizing.

RICE LAKE
Sherry's Happy Hour Cafe
6 East Freeman Street
A windowless midget of a cafe with food cooked to order on a grill out front. So small you've got to see it to believe it. Tucked behind the Happy Hour Bar.

ST. CROIX FALLS
St. Croix Cafe
103 South Washington Street
Sadly, a remodeling has erased the vintage character of the former Miller's Cafe, featured in the first edition. Mostly all homemade food, however.

Solon Springs
Prevost's Restaurant 🍽
11393 South Business 53
Opened in 1934, this longtime fixture has suffered with the opening of the new highway. Despite a really big sign placed near the highway people do not often drop off the highway onto Main Street. Slow down. Pull off the highway. Stop at Prevost's. Good food ahead.

Webster
Calico Kitchen Cafe and Catering
7428 Main Street
If the locals aren't at the cafe across the street, they're here.

Northeast

Presque Isle
Manitowish Waters
Land O'Lakes
51
45
17 Phelps
St. Germain
Eagle River
70
Woodruff
Minocqua
Sugar Camp
Three Lakes
Niagara
Lake Tomahawk
55
Rhinelander
8
Crandon
8
Tomahawk
Elcho
Wabeno
17
51
141
Merrill
Antigo
64
45
55
Pound
Peshtigo
Oconto Falls
Lena
Gillett
22
Wittenburg
29
Cecil
41
Shawano
Bonduel

NORTHEAST

ANTIGO
Dixie Lunch ▨ ☷
716 Fifth Avenue
(715) 623-4634
M–Sa 4:30 A.M.–11 P.M.; Su 4:30 A.M.–10 P.M.
Larry Ourada

The Ourada family has operated the Dixie Lunch for going on sixty years, the longest period of family ownership of any cafe in Wisconsin. Seventy-some years ago, before World War II, before the space race, before the Cold War, before computers, Ed Ourada was working at Stepanek's Bakery and thought it might just become his lifelong career. But military service intervened, and when he returned to Antigo, he wound up buying a little lunch counter from Frank Poulos. Ed's son, Larry, underscores "small" by quoting its corridor-like dimensions: "I mean it was only twelve feet by twenty-four feet."

Ed operated the lunch counter for two years before tearing it down and rebuilding it as the new and improved Dixie Lunch. He celebrated its grand opening on June 13, 1947, and with his brothers Rudy and George proudly posed for the photos that still hang on the wall. The three brothers were the sole employees, and in those early years they shared the cafe's $30,000 annual income.

The years passed, with the sturdy Formica and chrome furnishings withstanding continuous use and the changing fads in interior decorating. Ed married Georgian and together they raised Larry, who jokes, "I'm sure I was born in the back booth," and his sister, Sue. In 1996 Larry took over the Dixie Lunch and, feeling it was overdue for a remodel, got rid of the 1940s look. "We remodeled it top to bottom, front to back," he explains. The cafe was closed for ten days, with crews working around the clock. In came new tables, booths, banquettes, and two horseshoe counters. Ceramic floor tiles were laid and new wallpaper went up. When the doors opened to the new Dixie Lunch, "the customers loved it and business almost doubled," recalls Larry. In December 2001 readers of the *Antigo Journal* named the Dixie Lunch their top choice for dessert, coffee, and people watching.

This is a sure indication that, despite its updated look, the Dixie Lunch is still the great cafe it always has been. The food is just as good as I remember. I order a bowl of vegetable beef soup and a piece of Georgian's cottage cheese pie (because anything unusual is bound to be good), and then kick myself for not having made the plunge into one of the full meal daily specials. The Polish sausage and kraut is the top choice of the day for the regulars, who possess undaunting courage in their convictions by passing up the beef barbecue with potato salad. Since everything on the menu is homemade, any choice is pretty near a sure thing. But what really brings out the crowds is the pork hocks, sauerkraut, and dumplings—served every Tuesday since 1945. "We can never make enough," Larry says. And did I mention the real potatoes? You'll swoon over the real mashed, real fries, real hash browns, American fries, and boiled potatoes for salads.

Though they have retired, Ed and Georgian stay involved with the Dixie Lunch. Georgian is in the kitchen at four every morning preparing the day's baked goods, including today's selection of pies, one of which is cottage cheese and raisin. Served at the Dixie Lunch "since day one," it may be unusual to me, but with the regulars it is a steadfast favorite. Arriving at my table on an antique, turquoise-rimmed Pyrex plate with a gilt Hyatt logo, it has an interesting mixture of flavors and textures and reminds me of a slightly chewy cross between buttermilk pie and cheesecake.

Challenging Georgian's cottage cheese pie for the title of favorite treat at the Dixie Lunch are her kolaches, raisin rolls, and best-selling poppy seed rolls. You'll find a full run of Georgian's fresh baked goods only on Sundays, but serious breakfasters will be tickled to know that at the Dixie Lunch, breakfast is available all day. I recommend the pancakes, made in more varieties than at any other cafe in the state. But beware: you'll have a tough time choosing among buttermilk, blueberry, cinnamon spice, silver dollars, strawberry delight, apple, chocolate chip, peanut butter, banana (what? no peanut butter banana?), potato, and manhole cover pancakes.

After you've polished off your cakes, drop a penny in the vintage yellow and red scale promising "Your Wate and Fate. Character Readings. Your Future?" Ed bought the scale from the American Scale Manufacturing Company in 1951 for $175, with $10 down. Larry found the original receipt during the remodeling and marvels at what his dad must have been thinking to buy such a thing at such a cost. "It's really just a toy. I doubt Dad ever got his money back on that with the pennies that people put in it over the years." Nevertheless, the scale still works, even if you don't like the information it gives. It tells me that after nearly four months on the road, eating at every small town cafe in Wisconsin, I have gained twenty pounds. To test its judgment, I put in another penny. Twenty pounds again. And my fortune? The first one said, "You're the type to hold grudges. Be more forgiving." The second, "Your type needs praise and can't take criticism." Pretty true, I have to admit.

But I pass out praise and withhold criticism as well. And the Dixie Lunch is a stroke of excellent fortune waiting to be discovered. The menu cover, which boasts "Garden of Eatin'," doesn't lie.

CECIL
Rosie's Cecil Diner
212 North Warrington Avenue
(715) 745-2728
Summer: M–Th 6 A.M.–7 P.M.; F 6 A.M.–8 P.M.; Sa–Su 6 A.M.–7 P.M.
Winter: M–W 6 A.M.–2 P.M.; Th 6 A.M.–6 P.M.; F 6 A.M.–7 P.M.;
Sa–Su 6 A.M.–6 P.M.

Neil Albertson, owner
Tina Bratz, manager

For going on twenty years, the red-roofed restaurant across the highway from Lake Shawano and its summer cottages has become known for its good "plain food," such as fresh beef roasts, real mashed potatoes, all-you-can-eat potato pancakes, and Friday night fish fry and homemade strawberry jam. "The previous owners started with some extra fruit in the freezer, and now we make about one or two ten-pound batches of jam a week," manager Tina Bratz explains.

But it is the made-from-scratch pies that have made the Cecil Diner famous around these parts. Fruit pies are made with frozen fresh fruit rather than canned fillings, and together with banana cream, coconut cream, lemon meringue, graham cracker, and other specialties, the number of pies total ten per weekday and up to fifteen per day on the weekends. Slices of the day's pies are displayed in a glass case temptingly located in the center of the dining area, so you can pick out dessert even before sitting down with the menu.

Though she has been associated with the restaurant since her late mother, Rosie Alberston, bought it in 1994, Tina is still unable to explain the attraction most people have for pie. She is also hard pressed to explain just why great pie has the ability to elevate a cafe to the status of pie palace. "I don't eat pie," she says, "and I never really have." From informal surveys of her friends and nine years of observing her customers, Tina concludes that "pie is not a young person's thing." As if to confirm this, she confesses to developing a likeness for it as she gets older. "I'm starting to change," she says.

Tina far prefers making pie to eating it and is pleased to learn that I find her lemon meringue and graham cracker cream pies not just worth eating but worth eating *both* during the same visit. (I confess that the pie case in the center of the dining room encouraged my gluttony.) "I love baking pies," she enthuses. "I like creating a masterpiece so other people can enjoy it."

The Cecil Diner originated in 1985 when previous owners, Gordon and Muriel Parsons, converted an old root beer stand into a full restaurant.

Muriel's commitment to homemade everything quickly became known to the locals, tourists, and summer cottage owners, who often waited in line for the cafe to open. With such a loyal following, Tina's mother, Rosie, knew her own success would be assured if she didn't veer off the Parsonses' path. "She just carried on in the same vein," Tina explains.

Rosie passed away a few years ago, and since then Tina has run the business in memory of her mother. But, she admits, owning a restaurant was her mother's dream, not her own. Her dream is to be a paramedic, and until recently she made daily hundred-mile round trips between her Birnamwood home and the cafe in addition to attending school full time. "It's getting impossible to do both," she admits, but she is not yet ready to give up the cafe. "I'll keep going as long as I can. I'm told the average period of cafe ownership is two to three years, and I'm already beyond that. It's such hard work, and I don't think people really realize that. Mom did it out of love for the work and the people, and I'm doing it out of love for her."

CRANDON
Log Cabin Cafe 🍽
502 South Lake Avenue
(715) 478-3998
M–Sa 6 A.M.–8 P.M.; Su 6 A.M.–2 P.M.
Larry and Susan Palubicki

"My wife likes to cook all the time, so this is right up her alley," explains Larry Palubicki over a hot turkey sandwich brought by a waitress who tells him, "Your wife says you've got to eat." In July 1991 the Palubickis purchased the forty-year-old-and-then-some Log Cabin Cafe (it really is, from the outside, at least), on Crandon's main street. Susan Palubicki had managed the restaurant for a year after earning a degree in hospitality management and didn't need much convincing when the then-owner offered it for sale. "We had been thinking about buying a supper club but didn't want to get into the hassles of owning a bar," Larry explains. "Besides, supper club cooking and cafe cooking are really different. One is steaks, the other's cooking like at home."

Less than a year later, Larry left his job in the wood industry in order to help full time at the restaurant, greeting customers, doing the bookwork, grilling burgers, and supervising the hired help. He is surprised at how quickly he took to the restaurant, explaining that it is Susan, not himself, who brings professional experience, a natural love for cooking, and an outgoing nature to the Log Cabin. "I learned a lot about food," he explains, "and I learned that I really like running a restaurant. I was always really shy and didn't talk much to people."

His actions, however, don't mesh with his words. As we eat dinner together, Larry greets the locals by their first names as they enter and chats with regulars at the counter about their work, the weather, the local off-road car racing competitions.

"Does it ever bother you that everyone knows your business and that you know everyone else's?" I ask.

Larry smiles. "Excuse me?" he laughs. "This is Crandon. You've got to understand that these people all grew up here and have known me just about my whole life. It's the same way anywhere I go in town."

The food, I assure you, is not. The Log Cabin Cafe is known as the home of "A Working Man's Meal at a Working Man's Price," and the loggers and construction workers around these parts certainly agree. "They're hungry all the time, so we fill them up" with huge orders of real potatoes (hash browns, fries, mashed, baked, and every other way), home-cooked meats, liver and onions, hefty soups and chili, jumbo fresh meat burgers (try the Texas burger served open face on a bun with chili, grated cheese, and onion), and daily specials home-tested on famished teenage sons by Susan and her cooks and recreated in the back kitchen. Larry says, "Most of these daily specials come from the cooks, who say, 'We had this at home and it was really great. Let's try it here.' But we also ask the customers what they're hungry for. The loggers want a lot of stick-to-the-ribs stuff: biscuits and gravy, mashed potatoes and gravy, corned beef hash and meat for breakfast, stuff like that."

Ten years ago, the Log Cabin Cafe was perhaps the only cafe in Wisconsin serving biscuits and gravy—crumbled pork sausage in milk gravy served over baking powder biscuits. Because it is a traditional southern comfort food, I was surprised to find it so far up north. Its presence in Crandon was explainable, however. Kentucky migrants who came to work in the logging industry around 1900 introduced it. Now, it is standard fare across the state, but, ironically, it no longer has a permanent place on the Log Cabin's menu. "We serve it as a Friday breakfast special," Susan explains. "If we didn't have it as a treat, you couldn't get in here, it's so popular." I've never cared for biscuits and gravy, so I have to take her word for it.

Breakfast is "a really big deal," according to the Palubickis—and the breakfasts are also really big. The retired couple at the next table, visiting from Illinois, eye the passing plates heaped with hash browns, omelettes, and toast, and raise their eyebrows at each other in doubt. When the waitress stops to take their order, the husband asks, "Can we split one of those breakfasts? We're old and we don't eat much anymore. And we're on a fixed income." The wife laughs and playfully swats at his arm, telling the waitress, "He's kidding! But I don't think we each could eat a whole one."

Larry and Susan have heard it all before. They consider themselves blessed to have such faithful customers and excellent help, most of whom have been on board since they bought the place. Georgine, the longest employee at fifteen years, is "the life of the restaurant," according to Susan. Georgine takes plenty of guff from the regulars and isn't afraid to give it right back. "It isn't anything for her to say, 'Oh, get your own coffee. I'm busy right now,'" laughs Susan.

Georgine arrives at four thirty in the morning, letting the loggers in the back door for their wake-up coffee. When Susan comes in at five thirty, the loggers are still sitting at the counter, and Georgine has done all of the preparation. "All I have to do is start breaking eggs," Susan says. "She's the kind of worker everyone wants." If you're fortunate enough to have Georgine as your waitress, leave her a little extra with your tip. She deserves it.

EAGLE RIVER
Fay's Dinky Diner
121 South Railroad Street
(715) 479-5929
M closed; T–Su 5:30 A.M.–1 P.M.
Fay and Dale Hillner

Proud to have the "dinkiest diner in Wisconsin," Fay Hillner relaxes beside me at the counter after the last of her customers has left and entertains me with stories of the customers who fill the downtown lunch counter twenty people at a time. Fay's Dinky Diner is so dinky, she says, "if you come in a stranger, I guarantee you that in ten minutes you won't be a stranger any longer. We have a lot of fun in here."

The fun often extends out to the sidewalk, where people drink coffee while waiting for a seat to open up inside. The regulars know the system well enough to go inside and pour themselves a cup, but for others, Fay goes out with the coffee pot. This all might be just a bit disconcerting for the first-timer, but settle in and enjoy the hospitable quirkiness of the Dinky Diner. The food inside is worth the wait.

Founded in the 1940s by Lenny and Evonne Merkel, the Dinky Diner is just a tad younger than most of its loyal customers. Though it has been owned by a number of people over the years, none of them felt an overwhelming urge to remodel or expand. And thank goodness. The Dinky just wouldn't be the Dinky if it weren't so, well, dinky.

Fay has been at the helm for the past five years, but the sign advertising the previous owner, Don, still hangs over the sidewalk. That's because it's too hard to take down. Two names for the same diner don't confuse the locals, who know the place as Fay's palace of good home cooking. Fay doesn't bother with instants and premade anything, preferring to put her own hands to work peeling potatoes, mixing cookie dough, and preparing a variety of daily specials that rotate on a weekly basis. Wednesday is the busiest day, when she prepares fresh pan-fried chicken from the time she arrives in the early morning until the time the door closes at one o'clock. She typically fries enough chicken to fill forty orders—in a diner with only twenty seats, that's a lot of chicken—and frequently runs out.

Other top choices are Fay's skillets, hefty combinations of hash browns, fried eggs, and a variety of other mix-ins. The Northwoods Skillet, for example, features diced ham, mushrooms, onions, and cheddar or American cheese, while the Celtic Skillet combines corned beef hash, mushrooms, onion, and cheese. Fay makes both at the grill behind the counter, from where she and a single waitress manage the orders. It gets a little hectic at times, but Fay has the regulars well trained. "I've got the guys getting their own coffee, picking up their silverware, even taking their dirty dishes into the kitchen," she says. Cooperation has its rewards, even for the dogs the guys often leave waiting in the car. For the patient pooches, Fay keeps a plastic container of Ol' Roy dog bones by the front door.

EAGLE RIVER
Four Seasons Cafe and Deli
107 South Railroad Street
(715) 479-8499
May–August: M–Th 6 A.M.–7 P.M.; F–Sa 6 A.M.–2 P.M.; Su closed
September–April: M–F 6 A.M.–2 P.M.; Sa 7 A.M.–2 P.M.; Su closed
Elly and Jerry Mocello
The couple seated at the table in the center of the Four Seasons Cafe has been making the trip from their home in Joliet, Illinois, to Eagle River for fifteen years, and in all this time they have never, not once, tried the pasties, hefty beef and potato pies introduced to Wisconsin by lead miners from Cornwall—the original Badgers. The wife tells me that she has often thought about it, but when it comes right down to the minute the waitress writes their order on the ticket, she changes her mind and plays it safe by ordering a burger with chips. Knowing exactly what she is going to eat is no adventure, so she usually makes up for her lack of courage by ordering dessert, which she and her husband share. Today's choice is Elly Mocello's mixed berry pie, made with Door County cherries, blueberries, and rhubarb, about which she proclaims, "This berry berry pie is very, very good."

A few weeks before Halloween, the Four Seasons is decorated with plastic pumpkin lights in the front plate glass windows. Glossy paper pumpkins, witches, and goblins hang by strings from the ceiling. It is just before noon, and Elly comes out of the kitchen to greet me, nodding to the counter and saying, "Oh! You came at just the right time because the boys are beginning to line up." One older gentleman sits on a stool waiting for the others. In front of him, alternating sheets of green and yellow construction paper are taped to the vintage stainless steel splashboard quilted in a diamond pattern. On each sheet of paper is written the Green Bay Packers' weekly match-up for the season, with scores filled in for the few games already completed.

The football schedule stretches forward in great anticipation of the future, but inside the Four Seasons, time has pretty much stood still. The deep, narrow building built as a cafe about fifty years ago has not lost much of its original look. From time to time, one of the early waitresses will come in and share a story or two, as will the contractor who built the building of concrete block and brick. According to Elly, he put firecrackers in the walls on the theory that if the restaurant caught fire, the walls would get so hot that the exploding firecrackers would serve as a kind of fire alarm. I think it's a very blessed thing that his system has never had to be tested.

Far more likely to pass muster is Elly's home cooking. She jokingly refers to herself as "just the lowly cook," but there is nothing lowly about the real food she prepares daily in the rear kitchen. The special the day I stopped in was a Reuben sandwich made from slow-cooked corned beef. I passed on the Reuben but seized the opportunity to try the Irish vegetable soup made with crumbs from the roast, chopped cabbage, potatoes, carrots, and rutabagas. And, of course, I had to sample Elly's pasties, which led to the across-the-tables conversation with the couple from Joliet. They may not be daring enough to try the pasties, but you should not squander the opportunity. Of course, that means you may have to pass up any of Elly's other homemade specialties, including the hot beef sandwich or meat loaf—both served with real mashed potatoes, gravy, and a wiggly mound of bright Jell-O. Elly has a little fun with these blue plate specials by serving them on real blue plates, knowing that whatever she dreams up for the special on any given day will rarely be as popular as these old standbys. "I can never make enough roast beef and meat loaf," she says, shrugging her shoulders with bemusement.

Other favorites at the Four Seasons are the biscuits and gravy served on Fridays and Saturdays, the from-scratch buttermilk pancakes (especially those speckled with real Maine blueberries), and the house rox— seasoned red potatoes discovered by Jerry and Elly at a diner in Colorado and brought to Eagle River. "I make what we like," Elly says. "And it's nice that our customers have the same tastes."

GILLETT

OJ's Mid-Town Restaurant ⏺ 🍴

128 East Main Street

(920) 855-6395

M–F 6 A.M.–9 P.M.; Sa 6 A.M.–2 P.M.; Su closed

Owen and Joan Farrell

I was expected at OJ's Mid-Town Restaurant about ten but arrived an hour late because of a muffler mishap. Owen and Joan Farrell were both busy in the kitchen, grilling burgers and setting up plates of daily fish specials. "I'll wait as long as I have to," I tell their son, Jim, who took my order without writing it down. One look around OJ's Mid-Town and I knew I'd wait. One look at Joan's heavenly pies, and I knew I'd wait forever if I had to.

At the kitchen pass-through window, Jim explains to his dad that I want a plate of mashed potatoes covered with hot beef and gravy. (I never have understood why you need both bread and potatoes. Aren't they pretty much the same thing?) A man comes in and sits down beside me at the red counter, waiting for his take-out order of Alaskan walleye, coleslaw, and hash browns. "Are you from here?" I ask. "Green Bay," he says. "But I grew up here." A native moved away and come back, I thought. He qualifies. In the absence of the owners, always trust a loyal customer to tell you what you want to know.

"I graduated from here in 1941," he says. "And I know there was a restaurant here before then. Must have started sometime in the thirties, it'd be my guess. A classmate of mine, her dad ran it. . . . It hasn't technically changed much. . . . Same red counter and stools, same booths. I visit my mom at the nursing home just about every Friday. Before I leave I stop by here for an order of fish. I'll show it to you when it comes. I take it home and there's enough for two meals!"

He does and there is.

He pays his bill and leaves me alone with my huge mound of potatoes and enough beef and gravy for a famished farmhand.

Real potatoes, great gravy. By eleven thirty, the tables behind me are filled with retired couples, families, teenage girls, and women, with retired men strung out along the counter close to the kitchen window. When a place at the end becomes available, Jim picks up the silverware and plate belonging to the man next to me and asks, without waiting for an answer, "Do you want your regular place?" The man follows him to the end of the counter, where he sits with his lunch and the morning paper. "He always sits there," Joan explains. "He likes to read the paper. Every morning the first thing he turns to is Ann Landers."

Jim passes back and forth behind the counter between the kitchen window and the cash register, where women in business suits and heels wait for take-out orders of burgers and pieces of pie. Jim greets each one by name and makes small talk about summer activities. He is friendly and well-liked, a college student finishing up an education degree who lends an occasional helping hand at the family restaurant during the summer months. "You don't plan on taking over the restaurant someday?" I ask. "No, not hardly!" he laughs. "I can't cook. I make my own food but not anybody else's. I make too many mistakes.

"Dad's been cooking for years, since he was a teenager, I'd say," Jim continues. "He worked for Marc's Big Boy in Milwaukee before he decided he'd do just as well on his own. He does about 90 percent of the cooking. He comes in real early and doesn't leave until we close. He's here fifteen, sixteen hours. Mom, she makes all the pies. She looks through magazines and cookbooks, always looking for new ideas and something different."

As I scribble the last of his words in my notebook, he moves off down the counter to retrieve an order waiting in the kitchen window. The daily special board lists eleven desserts—all "something different"—which makes me recall advice I overheard at a cafe in the southwestern part of the state: "Anything out of the ordinary is bound to be good." Ordering presents a real predicament. Should I try the four-layer raspberry-walnut torte? The toffee mocha cheesecake? Millionaire pie? Chocolate eclair torte? Lemon angel pie? Banana cream pie? Fresh strawberry pie? Strawberry cheesecake? Custard pie? Pineapple upside-down cake?

Jim returns and innocently asks, "Can I get you anything else?"

"One of everything," I joke, waving at the pie case. Impulsively, because any measured judgment is impossible in the presence of such magnificent desserts, I order a piece of lemon angel pie, which Jim carefully cuts and transfers to a plate. I turn the plate in front of me, inspecting the piece before nibbling away at it layer by layer, downward from the real whipped cream topping, yellow lemon sauce, white creamy filling, and meringue crust.

It is beyond description. Extraordinarily, unbelievably good. In my opinion, Joan's pies are quite possibly the best in Wisconsin, especially on Fridays when she pulls out all the stops, all her magazines and cookbooks, and creates extra-special desserts found nowhere else. Later, when she is free in the kitchen, I ask her whether she considers baking as artistic expression. "For me it is, yes," she answers with a look on her face that asks, "How did you know?" It's no wonder, Joan. Your pies and other desserts are true masterpieces.

Proudly, Owen Farrell agrees. "We don't compare our product with anyone else's," he says. "That's something I was taught at Big Boy, and I've carried it here with me. If someone else says they have a good product, we go one step further. Our food isn't just as good as everyone else's. It's better."

Owen is confident in his success to spice up the traditional offerings with a bit of dash. He adds chili powder to meats and gravies the way most other cafe owners add salt and pepper, and the result is an unexpected splash of flavor and color. I have forgotten most of the other hot beef and meat loaf I have eaten, but Owen's holds its place in my memory along with a strong desire to return for more.

Owen and Joan are counting on just that. After being featured in the first edition of *Cafe Wisconsin* and later in *Wisconsin Trails* magazine, they sold the restaurant on contract in February 1998 in order to spend more time with their parents, who were living in Milwaukee, and three of their children who have moved away from home. For three years, the restaurant, known as the Mid-Town Family Restaurant, was under different ownership. But it was not the same place—it could never be without Owen and Joan at the helm—and the loyal customers drifted away. In May 2001 the bottom fell out of the deal and the Farrells got the restaurant back. "So many people were so excited that we were coming back," Joan remembers. "But it has been a struggle to get back the reputation we had. It was really heartbreaking at first, and all the kids came home and helped out."

The Farrells had to earn a new set of customers because while they were away, their old ones drifted off to new places and into new routines. Gradually, most came back to find a renewed Mid-Town, one perked up with a thorough cleaning, a new ceramic floor, and new additions to the menu, such as build-your-own pizza and hot sandwiches, including ham and cheese, Philly steak, and Bavarian made with corned beef, lettuce, tomatoes, and horseradish. And in their long familiar, long favored places are the old favorite menu items. Celebrate, fellow Wisconsinites! As Duncan Hines encouraged, shout the glad news to all your friends! Owen and Joan are back, and OJ's Mid-Town, anointed "Wisconsin's Definitive Diner" by *Wisconsin Trails* in 2002, is better than ever.

LENA
Graff's Restaurant ⦿
101 Rosera Street (Highway 141)
(920) 829-5243
M–Su 6:30 A.M.–7 P.M.
Linda and Donald Graff
Linda Graff pours herself a glass of ice water and leans against the counter, preparing to give me the next hour of her afternoon. She is clearly overjoyed that I have stopped to ask her about the history of Graff's Restaurant and

its role in the Lena community, and I'm glad that I've caught her at a slow time of the day. Only two coffee drinkers share the restaurant with us; wrapped up in their private conversation, they demand no attention from Linda and leave us to our friendly visit.

Linda and her husband, Don, a parochial school principal in Green Bay, always wanted to have their own food business ("but not a tavern"). They purchased the white clapboard restaurant twenty-five years ago, but its history in Lena goes back more than sixty years. Linda thinks it may have begun as a combination candy store and soda fountain. Linda marks the passing of her and Don's years of ownership by "the stages in people's lives. First they come in as couples, then as widows and widowers, and then they remarry and move away. There's always regret and sadness when someone moves away," she says. "You get to know people's lives."

Now a grandmother of three, Linda reflects on the enjoyable years she has spent running Lena's longtime cafe. Her three daughters, Nicole, Melisa, and Samantha, all worked in the family business. "We started them out at six and seven doing night chores, like washing the dishes and sweeping up," Linda recalls. By the time they were in high school, they were running the place on the rare occasions when Linda and Don took a day off. Linda emphasizes that Graff's Restaurant has always involved and depended on the entire Graff family. "The girls were always expected to contribute," she continues, "and were paid—not with a paycheck but with things they wanted, like a new bike. Everyone was made responsible for the family business. It was an excellent way to raise a family."

"Family" is also the word Linda uses to describe the men who "wait in the parking lot at five thirty for us to open for coffee." Gathered around the little "coffee table," the men share gossip, news, and postcards sent to the group by other members away on vacation. Often the group overflows to the counter, but when someone gets up to leave the coffee table, his seat is immediately filled. Although she has been observing the coffee group for the many years, Linda is still puzzled over why the men are compelled to gather every day for their morning ritual. She knows it isn't breakfast. Laughing, she recalls, "I used to make my husband coffee and breakfast once a week, but he'd stop here anyway on his way to work to get the day's gossip. He'd stop here with our two toddler daughters—they were one and two—on his way to the babysitter!"

The men's coffee klatch is something Graff's Restaurant shares in common with other cafes, but Linda notes several things that have occurred here that make Graff's Restaurant unique. One is the ghost lady. Linda says, "One time the old lady who rented the upstairs apartment hurt herself and went to live in the nursing home. One day we heard footsteps on the stairs and watched the door open at the exact same time during the day she always came down. That was weird, but we all saw it happen!"

And then there was the Christmas opening that wasn't. "One Christmas Eve the cleaning boy forgot to lock up, and customers came and went in and out of the restaurant. But we didn't lose anything. Not a thing was missing!"

Linda Graff tells fine stories. She's also a very fine cook. Graff's Restaurant is known for its homemade soups, pies, real mashed potatoes, fresh, hand-pattied burgers, and a variety of inventive daily specials, such as today's knockwurst, sauerkraut, and potato dumplings. In the past twenty-five years Linda has noted how "people's tastes have changed. There's a greater variety of food on the menu—more chicken, salads, less sweets. . . . We've adapted to changing health needs by adding a frozen yogurt machine, Egg Beaters, pasta salads, a fruit plate." Despite the changes, the emphasis on good home cooking remains. Linda says proudly, "We've never been tempted to change because we get so many compliments."

After twenty-five years, with their daughters grown and gone, Linda and Don anticipate the day in the near future when they will sell the restaurant and move nearer to their grandchildren. Linda hopes to resume the career in the medical field that she left to take over the restaurant, and to that end, she has taken a refresher courses in phlebotomy and is preparing for clinicals.

"I have really mixed emotions about selling the restaurant," she explains. "When do you stop? When do you say it's time to move on? It's been a really good thing, and I know I'll miss it and the people immensely."

MANITOWISH WATERS
Village Soda Grill
129 Highway W
(715) 543-8388
Summer: M–Sa 7 A.M.–8 P.M.; Su 7 A.M.–12 P.M.
Winter: M–Sa 7 A.M.–5 P.M.; Su 7 A.M.–12 P.M.
Nancy and Bill Crupi
You will find daily specials at the Village Soda Grill, but in this small northwoods town you can also find great hamburgers, malts and shakes made from the best ice cream in town, sandwiches, homemade soup, fresh-baked muffins and cookies, and pies. All this in a nonsmoking environment (a sign over the counter explains that smoking "makes the chipmunks wheeze"), plenty of hot coffee, and informed conversation perfectly seasoned with engaging wit.

The original Grill first opened for business sometime during the 1950s but burned down in the 1970s. Today's Grill, located at the south end of the town's minimall, is spacious but not too modern, sharing floor space with greeting cards, magazines, toiletries, and trinkety children's toys. I love the eclectic, odd little mix of necessities available for the tourists and year-round residents, who fill out the coffee drinkers from seven to eight o'clock and ten to noon on the rainy, mid-October morning that I drop in.

I'm thrilled to again find Pete Rasey, local jokester, athlete, true man of wisdom, and friend to all, holding court at the little table closest to the kitchen. In the first edition of *Cafe Wisconsin* I wrote about two of Pete's habits: rummaging for silver dollars in the till and collecting undershorts, which he showed off by pulling them above the waistband of his pants. (His wife, Sue, wags her finger at me and admonishes, "This time, no undershorts!") I considered him a charming example of small town eccentricity, which is certainly true, but not because he is dotty, as I might have led readers to think.

Pete is a highly intelligent man retired from the insurance business, with a hobby of meteorology and a passion for the silent sports. He's an active member of the local bicycling, kayaking, and cross-country skiing clubs and represents what the Manitowish Waters area has become: a retirement community for active, athletic senior citizens who enjoy the quiet and wilderness of the northwoods.

It's the reason Bill and Nancy Crupi came to own the Village Soda Grill. Many years ago, they'd purchased land in the area in anticipation of their own retirement. When the construction of their house was completed in 1993, they turned to each other and asked, "Why wait?" Three years later, they quit their corporate jobs in southern Wisconsin and bought the Soda Grill as a way to tide them over until true retirement age arrived. They had no previous experience running a restaurant, but when Bill saw the for sale ad for the Soda Grill in the local paper, he announced, "That's what I'd like to do." They knew immediately that they were home.

Says Nancy, "Owning the Soda Grill has introduced us to a lot of people. The northwoods attracts people just like us—people who like to relax but who like the active life. The people are very congenial. At first we thought we'd be outsiders, but the first day, people welcomed us. Factory workers, company CEOs, bank presidents—no one cares what you did in your past life."

What really matters in Manitowish Waters is how you use your current life. Nancy praises her customers and her staff for being committed participants in the large business of community and in the small business of restaurant ownership. "We could never have made it a success without customers like Pete and without our part-time employees, most of whom are retired ladies—there's Ruth, Darlene, Judy, Nancy—who want to work a little so they can be with their friends."

If Bill and Nancy first anticipated a retired life of solitude, as owners of the local eatery and gathering place they quickly discovered that was not going to happen. "The Soda Grill practically runs this town," Sue laughs. "We even put Pete on the Fourth of July float because we couldn't get there ourselves."

After eight years, Bill and Nancy are now ready for full retirement and are seeking to trade in kitchen work for days spent pedaling, paddling, and skiing with good friends. The Village Soda Grill is for sale.

MERRILL
Skipper's Restaurant
812 East First Street
(715) 536-9914
M closed; Tu–F 5 A.M.–2 P.M.; Sa 7 A.M.–2 P.M.; Su 8 A.M.–2 P.M.
Rick and Helen Scott
"Yeah, I'd say we're about the only one left in Merrill still into real home cooking: pies, soups, fresh meats," affirms Rick Scott, owner with his wife, Helen, of Skipper's, Merrill's landmark downtown restaurant since June 2002. Rick is reading for the first time the feature about Skipper's in the first edition of *Cafe Wisconsin*, which he had never before seen. He is a bit dubious of my claim to being a writer who is willing to write once again about Skipper's—free of charge—but is convinced the whole deal is legitimate by Danni, a waitress of twenty years. Danni pauses in the kitchen doorway framed in aged white oak and exclaims, "I know that book. We've had so much fun with it. We've had people bring it in and say their goal is to eat at every place in it."

"Every place?" I gasp.

"Yeah, and they've had us sign it, too. They say that's how they keep track of where they've been."

First opened as a restaurant in 1937, Skipper's gets its name from its original owner, who had the restaurant for almost forty-five years. He decorated the original eatery—not much more than a lunch counter—with a boating theme, including a captain's wheel, a boat helm in the basement, and other related items. The subsequent owners, Signa and Bob Lambrecht, from whom Rick and Helen bought the place, retained the name and the theme while expanding into the neighboring building, formerly a children's clothing store. Since the Scotts came on board, the sailing has been relatively ripple free. "We knew we didn't want to rock the boat," Rick says.

"We were taking on a successful restaurant with an established reputation, and it would have been foolish to make too many changes."

The Scotts stuck with the decor and the insistence on all home cooking, even continuing with some of the same recipes, especially Signa Lambrecht's trademark chicken dumpling soup. "Ninety-nine percent of everything we serve is homemade," attests Rick. "That means pies made from scratch, real mashed potatoes, and meats roasted right here. We have the best-tasting ham you're ever going to taste. We cook up green, cured hams that weigh at least twenty pounds each. We cook up many at a time because we can never have enough." A heap o' ham served with scalloped potatoes on vintage, turquoise-rimmed Buffalo china, at a table of equally vintage crushed-ice Formica tables, with a slice of cherry pie on the side. It doesn't get much better than that.

Ask any of the thousand-odd bicycle riders who make Skipper's a never-miss pit stop during the annual Great Annual Bicycle Adventure Along the Wisconsin River (GRABAAWR), held every June. I have ridden this weeklong tour many times, and, in fact, it was GRABAAWR that first introduced me to Skipper's in the early 1990s. Danni, the waitress, looks forward all year to the one day the cyclists swarm in like good-natured locusts on a holiday.

"I'll never forget the year they came in a cold, soaking rain. They were drenched, dirty, and miserable, and they sat in here most of the day. They just didn't want to go back out in it. We were doing their laundry, drying their clothes in the basement. There was a constant stream of bikers using the bathrooms, and they left baby powder all over our floors. We went through three huge pans of lasagna: as soon as one was out of the oven, another one went in. They gave us hugs when they left and said, 'Make sure you have lasagna for us next year!' That was so cool!"

Rick listens on with curiosity, preparing mentally for next June and his first encounter with the GRABAAWR cyclists, probably more than just a bit glad that his and Helen's first year started a blessed two weeks after the 2002 bike tour. The Scotts have months before the cyclists come again, and until then, they have many plans of their own to implement. This is a new Skipper's after all. Rick's assessment of Merrill's restaurant market showed potential in the areas of banquets, serving large groups, catering, and outdoor seating. "An outdoor cafe is something Merrill hasn't seen yet," Rick notes. He has also expanded the products available at Skipper's by adding hand-dipped chocolates made by Michael's Candies of Wausau.

MINOCQUA
Island Cafe ▐●▌
314 Oneida Street
(715) 356-6977
M–Su 6:30 A.M.–8 P.M.
George F. Callos Sr. and Crystal Callos

I first came to the Island Cafe years ago in search of the softball-size home-made muffins recommended to me by a bicyclist who discovered them one summer during a northwoods tour. Without the five-star recommendation I would have been sorely pressed to battle Minocqua's summer tourist crowd and plunk down the bill and odd change necessary to secure a muffin of my very own. But who could resist the bran, caramel, oat bran, cranberry nut, blueberry, poppy seed, banana nut, zucchini nut, and the mysterious "everything" muffins beckoning from the glass bakery case? I did! I opted for the bread pudding with brandy sauce and whipped cream made from Crystal Callos's own recipe.

The Island Cafe has changed considerably since my first visit, when it resembled a 1970s-era diner characterized by an orange counter, ceramic floor, counter stools, and vinyl-covered chairs. It now looks like an upscale European-style bistro—or should I say an Aegean island cafe? The Calloses are, after all, proudly Greek. Their redecorated Island Cafe—Minocqua is Wisconsin's Island City of the north—is absolutely gorgeous. Gone is the orange, replaced with a pleasant, softly tinted combination of tans and cream. The ceramic floor is laid out in alternating bands of tiles. Above, the heavy-textured plaster walls are stained and glazed with several hues of latte and mocha color. But what really makes the look is the painted murals of potted plants, flowering window boxes, and collections of gardening tools, gloves, and potting equipment.

Despite my ecstasy over the makeover, I have to admit I did miss the orange because it so defined the old Island Cafe for me. So I was pleased, and a bit amused because it is now so out of place, to discover remnants of the geometric orange-ish ceramic wall tile in the little hallway that leads to the rest rooms. Also missing was the large Greek flag, which, owner George Callos explains, "came down during the redecorating and just hasn't gone back up yet."

In 1970, after returning "from the city," owner George took over the cafe his father purchased in 1957. "In high school I had no interest in the restaurant, but I found I didn't like Milwaukee or Minneapolis and came back." George moved the original cafe to its present location in 1971 and found both success and satisfaction. Capitalizing on his Greek heritage, George hung the Greek flag I remember from my first visit on the restaurant's back wall and expanded his father's menu with additional ethnic specialties, such as the gyro sandwich and dinner, "a special blend of seasoned beef and lamb, sliced thin, served with tomato and cucumber sauce." The Greek offerings excited a traditional cafe menu distinguished by homemade quality and familiar, flavorful hot beef, turkey, pork, and meat loaf sandwiches, real Wisconsin mashed potatoes, soups, and pies.

Since my first visit, the menu, like the interior decorating, has undergone an uplifting makeover. Minocqua has become a major tourist destination for both outdoorsmen and power shoppers alike, and the successful menu reflects this seemingly incompatible mix. Alongside favorites like Mom used to make, you'll find a selection of espresso drinks, wine, and beer; vegetarian sandwich specials; an exquisite Norwegian salmon salad made with organic baby greens; pasta dishes; and stuffed shrimp, salmon, yellow fin tuna, and mahi mahi dinners (served only after five o'clock).

I would have loved to share one of George's delightfully fine meals, a lovely glass or two of wine, and warm conversation with close friends, but instead I was by myself and faced with a huge slab of Crystal's bread pudding. Sigh. The hazards of the job. The bread pudding and brandy sauce— as close to New Orleans as I think you'll get in northern Wisconsin—was served in a large white ceramic bowl whose rim was garnished with sliced strawberries, star fruit, and baby greens—all "glued" on by pillows of sticky nondairy whipped topping. The entire dessert was sprinkled with cinnamon and confectioner's sugar and was so beautiful I hesitated to ruin it by digging in my fork.

To be honest, both the dessert and its presentation are so far out of the norm for traditional small town cafes, I had to ask myself whether the Island Cafe had morphed into something else. It is on its way, certainly, but it hasn't yet completely severed its connections to what it began as. Hidden among the "irresistible Greek specialties," George's Sunday roast duck dinner, and other unexpectedly fine menu choices, you can still find a plate of real good old-fashioned hot beef or meat loaf. But don't hesitate to indulge yourself with something far less ordinary. There's plenty of meat loaf out there in Wisconsin's other small town cafes. (I'd start with the chili powder–infused meat loaf made by Owen Farrell at OJ's Mid-Town Cafe in Gillett.)

PRESQUE ISLE
Outpost Cafe
8279 Main Street
(715) 686-2193, (715) 686-7677
Memorial Day through Labor Day: M–Su 7:30 A.M.–2:30 P.M. and
5 P.M.–9 P.M.
Labor Day until Memorial Day: M–Th 7:30 A.M.–2:30 P.M.;
F 7:30 A.M.–2:30 P.M. and 5 P.M.–9 P.M.; Sa–Su 7:30 A.M.–2 P.M.
Call ahead for evening hours after Labor Day.
Terry and Kim Tassi

From my booth inside the Outpost Cafe, I watch owner Terry Tassi filling a cylindrical bird feeder beneath my window with millet. The late autumn view is worth capturing on canvas, even now when the neighboring wall-eye pond that typically fills the indentation in the earth is drained and dormant and the maples and other deciduous trees are long past their peak colors.

Created from a millpond in 1950, the walleye pond was drained by the DNR earlier this year as the first step in its complete restoration. By next year, Outpost diners will be able to look out on a shallow lake fringed with tall grasses and cattails. In winter, the walleye pond is a frozen surface ringed with a snowmobile trail dotted with tiny orange signs guiding the Arctic Cats through the northwoods. A loop off the trail leads directly to the lower entrance of the Outpost, where snowmobilers tether their machines before opening the door to the delicious warmth and food inside.

Terry and his wife, Kim, live in the house next door, where for many years they managed their construction company out of a home office. When the old village cafe burned to the ground, they took the opportunity to expand their holdings by buying the lot it stood on and the lot between it and their house. It wasn't long before Terry's nagging dream to operate his own restaurant had him thinking that the two lots would be suitable for a new cafe. The infernal nagging, together with the strong feeling that the "community really needed a restaurant," resulted in the stunning, handcrafted log building housing the Outpost Cafe.

"We had no restaurant background, but we were experienced eaters," recalls Kim with a wry laugh. "We hired the manager of the old cafe to get started, and she set the whole thing up. Because she had worked at the previous cafe, she knew what the locals liked."

With the operations of the restaurant in reliable hands, the Tassis turned to what they knew plenty about: the design and construction of the new building. At three thousand square feet, the building quickly altered "our whole vision of this place as a little cafe," says Kim. "It's much bigger, with more seating, than we ever envisioned. It's not really a cafe, but more of a restaurant."

The Outpost Cafe is certainly a hybrid place, both small town cafe and full-scale restaurant. Despite its size and its northwoods glamour, however, the Outpost offers to both a loyal local crowd and an itinerant tourist population a menu ranging from standard meat-and-potatoes fare to wine and local minibrews. Its emphasis on "everything homemade" and its role as a community center earn it a place in *Cafe Wisconsin*.

As I drove up the highway to Presque Isle, I caught a glimpse of the Outpost Cafe on the side of the road. My first impression was that it was a resort, and I thought, "This is no cafe." Pulling the heavy oak door open— its handle is a cluster of deer antlers—I marveled at the beauty of the rustic yellow pine building.

It is even more beautiful inside, capturing perfectly the mix of wilderness, history, and recreation that characterizes northern Wisconsin. The rounded sides of huge logs make up the wall surfaces, and the ceiling, trussed with log beams and heavy roof poles, lifts the dining space to the sky. Thick, sturdy pine booths with OUTPOST carved into the backs dwarf the average size diner. Above the booths and hanging throughout the dining room are chandeliers crafted of more deer antlers.

"Everyone asks about those," Kim says. "No one can believe that they're real." Real they are, and all made by Cripple Creek Antler Company of nearby Hazelhurst. Rounding out the decor are antique northwoods artifacts and taxidermied animals of all kinds—deer, fish, even a black bear dressed in a Halloween witch costume (his attire changes by the season).

The bear is not the only creature in Presque Isle who dresses up for Halloween. Terry and Kim celebrate the holiday by inviting area children to trick-or-treat at the Outpost. "Otherwise, kids up here don't have too much of an opportunity to trick-or-treat, and people living on the lakes don't get to see them or participate," Kim explains The adult locals come to the Outpost to pass out candy and view the costume parade, often staking out a booth or table beginning about four in the afternoon. Many wear costumes themselves, taking the lead of the waitresses, who often report for work dressed as ghosts, hobos, witches, and clowns.

By Halloween, the summer crush of tourists has disappeared, and the folks at the Outpost have settled into a relatively quiet life. "Summers are really crazy," Kim says. "People seem to really like us, and once they find us, they come back. Their friends send them here. People tell us, 'So and so told us to come over here.'"

If the people of Presque Isle are lucky, they get a few months to themselves between the start of school and the departure of summer tourists and the first heavy snow that brings the tourists back. But winter tourists aren't the same as summer tourists. They are not idlers, shoppers, or family groups. Instead, they are winter sportsmen and recreationists—ice fisherman, cross-country skiers, snowmobilers—who come seeking snow, and plenty of it.

"If it's a snowy winter, it can be almost as busy as summer. When we get snow, boom!, the snowmobilers are here. When we get a thaw, boom!, they're gone. They're all tuned to the weather station," Kim says.

They come north for the snow and miles of open land, and they come to the Outpost for the food. Winter and summer both, repeat diners at the Outpost know they might have to wait a bit for riches from the kitchen. These are the ones who know, as Kim says, "we're from scratch." For those who aren't privy to this knowledge, a sign in the dining room provides directions to alternative eating: "Directions for FAST FOOD & SERVICE / Perkins 28.12 miles South / McDonald's 33.48 miles South."

Breakfast, lunch, or dinner, I recommend that you stay and wait for the "from scratch." The chicken quesadilla that I ordered was hot and cheddar cheesy, as any decent Wisconsin quesadilla must be, and a light, refreshing alternative to burgers and meat, potatoes, and gravy meals. I also ordered a wedge of apple pie but, alas, had to forgo it because the pie was still in the oven. At one o'clock, the pies had all been eaten, and manager Don Psenicka had just whipped up a few more for the afternoon and evening. Bubbling hot from the oven, the Dutch apple pie Kim carried out to show me was a beauty. But I didn't take time for it to cool enough to prevent a taste from blistering the skin off the roof of my mouth.

Among the A-list menu offerings at the Outpost are the ten-inch pancakes, eggs Benedict, corned beef hash, and French toast made from homemade bread (also appearing in other forms and guises). As you might guess, breakfast is a crowd-pleaser for tourists and locals alike. I love watching tourists leisurely feast on breakfast as if it's going out of style, while the locals across the room sit back and chat over dry toast, coffee, and bowls of oatmeal. The vacationer indulges. The local shows measured restraint because he'll be back tomorrow and the next day and the next.

The Outpost excels with a continually updated menu featuring interesting sandwiches and specials available as "cook's choice" offerings Monday through Wednesday. Thursdays are set aside for chicken—either barbecued or batter fried—sided with coleslaw, real mashed potatoes and gravy, a vegetable, and a baked roll. Chicken is one of the best-sellers at the Outpost and is available by the piece or bucket for takeout. (If a picnic is part of your plans, don't overlook the barbecued riblets.) Fridays are reserved for the ritual fish fry, served with coleslaw, baked beans, a dinner roll, and choice of potato. "The Great Steak Cookout" is Saturday's treat. Choose from grilled rib eye, tenderloin, or center cut butt. By all means, don't miss Sunday's "roast night—just simple home cooking!" featuring old-time favorites: meat loaf, pot roast, and pork roast.

Pizza is available throughout the week, along with select wines and domestic and specialty beers. Local microbrews include Bell's Kalamazoo and South Shore, made in nearby Ashland. Other unexpected offerings include Gray's all natural sodas and a full ice cream parlor with a walk-up, take-out window.

RHINELANDER
Sportsman Cafe
230 Thayer Street
(715) 362-2100
M–Th 5 A.M.–7 P.M.; F 5 A.M.–8 P.M.; Sa 5 A.M.–2 P.M.; Su closed
Vicky and Jimi Richter
Located in the area of Rhinelander known as the Hollow, the Sportsman Cafe caters largely to the working class and local senior citizen population, particularly residents of the nearby senior apartments. Jimi Richter speaks fondly of his and his wife Vicky's elderly customers, who linger over daily and often twice-daily visits to their home away from home, and looks upon the entire cafe crowd as a kind of extended family. "If a regular doesn't come in when expected," he explains, "one of us will call or ask around to see if things are all right. Working here is a good way to keep an eye on the day-to-day workings of our small town."

Meals are made with the tastes of the older population in mind and include traditional favorites such as fresh burgers, Vicky's homemade soups, beef stew, and hot beef. I spent the first six years of my married life listening to my husband, Mark, promise me we'd someday stop at a small town Wisconsin cafe for hot beef. I had no idea what hot beef was; I imagined it was something like barbecued beef on a bun.

I finally ate my first one at the Sportsman Cafe in 1991, and, like Jane and Michael Stern, authors of *Roadfood,* I found it difficult to understand what all the commotion was about. Mashed potatoes and roast beef between two slices of bread all smothered in gravy? The Sportsman's version wasn't bad, and the gravy was tasty and made from the pan drippings, but I wasn't about to become a true connoisseur. I thought I'd leave that to other adventure eaters.

"Our hot beef is second to none," boasts Jimi. "We cook our own meat, make our own gravy."

"Real mashed potatoes?" I ask.

"Absolutely. Lumps included," he replies.

I'm convinced, so I order one—or rather a half of a whole because I've learned after ten years of experience that hot beefs across Wisconsin are generally lumberjack-sized portions. When my waitress lays down a platter of beef, potatoes, and gravy the size of a Green Bay Packer end zone, I try to correct her mistake. "Oh, there's no mistake," she laughs. "The funny thing is, he didn't quite get the half-size order." She stands for a few minutes to chat, observing my fussy little ritual of separating the two slices of white bread from the rest of the dish. "Is there something wrong?" she asks. (If I had a dollar for every time I was asked this question, I'd be rich.) I attempt to explain why I find bread and potatoes redundant, and she nods her head in sympathy. "Try to tell the old guys that," she murmurs softly.

Jimi and Vicky, their two daughters, one son, and an assortment of future children-in-law have operated the restaurant since 2001, but they all worked for Vicky's brother, the former owner, before that. When he got "pooped out and wanted to sell," explains Jimi, they were afraid of losing their jobs, so they bought the business. "It's almost all family working here. That means a lot of loyalty and commitment, but it also makes it hard when there's a family event of some kind. We shut down on those days, and we're closed on Sundays because that's God and family day."

Both Vicky and Jimi worked in restaurants all of their lives, longing for their own place while working for others. Jimi always thought he'd wind up with a supper club, but Vicky preferred the home-style cooking she learned from her mother. They place "a lot of emphasis on quality food and service" and find that to be the best form of advertising. "We don't have much money to advertise, but we don't need to," Jimi says. "We have a cheap menu full of good, real food."

You know you've stumbled into a good cafe when you see food service deliverymen eating at the counter. "We have delivery men for products we don't even use here," Jimi confides. "We also have the guys who service our equipment, and the morning mailman, who brings in our mail and stays for breakfast."

I, like them, am glad Jimi didn't get his supper club. The home-style cooking is a perfect match to the family dining room atmosphere that makes the Sportsman such a pleasure. What I really like about the cafe in the Hollow is its namesake 1950s vintage decor. Chrome stools covered with orange and avocado green vinyl march along three yellow horseshoe-shaped counters and down another separating the kitchen from the dining area, and heavy blond Buckstaff chairs are tucked under the vinyl tablecloth–covered wooden tables. Gone are the aging deer mounts and other hunting trophies

I remember from my first visit ("They'd collected a lot of dust and dirt over the years," Jimi tells me), replaced by a display of "Affordable Original Oil Paintings" by Jimi's cousin, local artist Bobbie Keso-Mode.

Located in the Hollow, the Sportsman Cafe may be at the bottom of Rhinelander, but it is far from the bottom of the locals' hearts. Like any truly good cafe, it is an important social center that sponsors and supports many community activities and events. Shelf space is set aside for the display of craft items sold by Homes Open Wide foster care and cookbooks sold as fundraisers for the local chapter of the Alzheimer's Association. Xeroxed wall posters promote the sale of raffle tickets for the Sugar Camp–Three Lakes youth football league and advertise other events and promotions. And a collection of local business cards pinned to the wall guide the curious onlooker—or anyone really looking for roofing and landscaping contractors, a tattoo artist, a home inspector, a pet groomer, and my favorite of them all: a "wife-to-rent. Does house cleaning, cooking, errands, and laundry."

ST. GERMAIN
Wolf Pack Cafe 8
426 Highway 70 East
(715) 479-8737
M 6 A.M.–1:45 P.M.; Tu closed; W–Su 6 A.M.–1:45 P.M.
Joe and Kathy Lass
In February 2000, only a month shy of their first anniversary as owners of the Wolf Pack Cafe, Joe and Kathy Lass unknowingly played host to two important diners. Stephanie Klett and Rick Rose of *Discover Wisconsin Radio* had been tipped off to the bounteous portions of outstanding home cooking and paid the Wolf Pack a visit, then followed up by naming the St. Germain cafe their restaurant of the month. "The Wolf Pack Cafe is fantastic," declared Klett. "Their food is absolutely delicious and you never go away feeling hungry. Rick was right when he said this is the place to go in St. Germain."

I can't agree more. Joe and Kathy have fashioned a winner out of the former Susan's St. Germain Cafe, featured in the first edition of *Cafe Wisconsin*, which they discovered one day with a for sale sign in the window. "We bought it right away," remembers Kathy, who had years of restaurant experience behind her.

Joe, however, was molded from other material. Concrete to be exact. He excelled in cooking at home for family and friends but in his professional life was a concrete worker. It may seem terribly ironic that he is now the cafe's head chef—not a mere cook but a chef. Yet Kathy explains, "It's not so strange as it seems. He uses a construction way of thinking when he cooks. A dish, like a building project, is made up of individual parts: meat, vegetables, herbs, that sort of thing."

Having purchased the cafe, the Lasses spent the first six months trying to get their bearings. They made an effort to eat at all of the area restaurants and decided early on that "the town needed home cooking." After giving the restaurant a thorough cleaning and a facelift with fresh paint, wolf-themed decorations, and new furnishings, they turned their attention to the menu.

Old-time favorites were enlivened with an extra bit of spice and pizzazz. The coleslaw has sunflower seeds, for example, and the Sunday morning perch, potatoes, and eggs is panfried in basil-infused olive oil. (The perch is also available blackened.) You'll find the tried and true at the Wolf Pack, but don't blind yourself to Joe's celebration of creative cooking, an innate talent until so recently hidden to all but his closest friends that even his own mom is surprised by his gift.

"Joe tries to bring cheflike cooking into the cafe at reasonable prices," Kathy says. "He's really good at creating his own thing. He just experiments, pulls things together—spices, flavors, textures, etcetera."

In the back kitchen, away from the crowd out front, Joe turns out refreshing favorites that keep the people coming back. His Cajun chowder with catfish is a best-seller, as is his Prairie Outlaw soup made with pork and potatoes. "He comes up with the soups, and we have to come up with the names," laughs Kathy. Other favorites include the pancakes ("People say they drive from Chicago and the first thing they want is a pancake"), homemade potato chips, and burgers made with fresh ground beef ordered from the local grocery every morning. The same beef goes into the "darn good soup" made with a "tomatoey" base and a variety of garden vegetables.

As Joe and Kathy's eight-hour workdays stretch into twelve and fourteen, they find rewards in the comments of their loyal customers, many of whom are warm-weather residents. Each October Kathy mourns the impending seasonal, southward migration of good friends who are closing up their summer places for the winter. "I hate this time of year," she says. "Everyone leaves us." She sends them off with a hug and kind words that anticipate their return in the spring. As the door closes behind him, a man calls out, "We'll be back. But what we'll eat until then is anybody's question."

Despite their winter loneliness, Joe and Kathy find the off-season to be a creative time. They have more time to experiment with their cooking and find the locals to be receptive to new foods. "Boredom is definitely not a problem," Kathy says. "I'd say winter is the time when Joe really gets creative and comes up with new ideas."

For her part, Kathy specializes in a mouth-watering variety of pies and other desserts on the daily menu board—an electric black sign glowing with items written in colored neon. She is also the "up front" one of the pair, greeting customers by name and knowing what they're hungry for without having to ask.

Even without the Wolf Pack Cafe's recognition by *Discover Wisconsin Radio*, Kathy knows it is a very special place, and she is proud of what she and Joe have created. "We travel across the country looking for cafes, and they're so hard to find. They're like a dying breed."

SUGAR CAMP
The Cookery
6694 Highway 17 North
(715) 272-1616
M–Th 6 A.M.–2 P.M.; F 6 A.M.–2 P.M. and 4:30 P.M.–8:30 P.M.;
Sa–Su 6 A.M.–2 P.M.
Lisa Jolin

Crystal at the Rhinelander Chamber of Commerce tipped me off to the Cookery in Sugar Camp. "Have I got a great one for you," she said when I asked about the cafes in the area. "I eat breakfast there every Saturday, and the food is the best." With that kind of ringing endorsement, I headed north and found a clean, trim little white houselike building across the highway from the new Sugar Camp elementary school. A flock of shiny new Harleys were lined up at the edge of the parking lot, and I couldn't help blinking my eyes with a sense of déjà vu. I'd walked into a scene not terribly unlike the Harley-Davidson calendar shot featuring Earl and Charlotte Bruinsma's cafe in Union Grove (see the entry for Callen's Restaurant).

The Harley riders were sipping ice water at the counter and visiting with owner Lisa Jolin, who was finalizing the last minute preparations for the Friday night fish fry, when I walked through the door. My déjà vu evaporated like exhaust at eighty miles an hour when I saw what Lisa had done to the place since my visit ten years earlier. Like so many other cafe owners, she started with a dream of running her own restaurant; bought a run-down, worn-out old place; and completely transformed it through scrubbing, remodeling, redecorating, revamping the menu, and adhering to her own ideas of home cooking with integrity. The Cookery in Sugar Camp is bright, pretty, and clean, and an altogether pleasant place to enjoy Saturday breakfast, Monday meat loaf, or, as I did, the Friday night fish fry.

At four thirty, the Cookery was just beginning to fill with early fish eaters confronting the very tough decision of how to accessorize the standard all-you-can-eat order of three pieces of lightly seasoned and breaded cod.

I studied the menu and debated: homemade clam chowder? Baked potato, fries, or potato pancakes? I was stymied. Sue, my waitress, gave me a few more minutes to mull it over. The problem was clearly endemic, as the couple at the next table faced the same hard choices. Sue solved the problem for both of us when she advised, "You can bake a potato at home, but you can't get potato pancakes." True. We both ordered the pancakes, deliciously crisp and hot, with bits of minced onion and served with applesauce.

"This is a good time to come because it's mostly locals," Lisa tells me when she pauses to chat. A family at the corner table up front feasts on fish and burgers—the adults siding with the fish, the kids with the familiar patty on a bun. Still, I am surprised to see how the kids relish the food, but why shouldn't they? It is darned good. The fish fry is a sizable meal, even if you choose not to make a glutton of yourself with the all-you-can-eat deal. "People tend to eat only one order," Lisa says. "Our portions are so big, they generally don't need to take advantage of it. There are a few regulars who order a couple more pieces, my husband included." I can eat only two of my pieces and feel terribly guilty for sending such delicious waste back to the kitchen. But I have to save room for lemon meringue pie, made by Lisa that morning at the request of one of the regulars.

"Glenn just had to have lemon meringue pie," I overhear Lisa tell Jamie, another loyal customer who has just negotiated a day next week for chicken rice soup. Jamie came four different times hoping her favorite soup would be on the menu, only to have to settle for something she didn't like quite as well. Lisa is happy to accommodate the passions of her customers, she points out to Jamie, but Fridays are always reserved for clam chowder. Chicken rice soup is a perfect choice for Monday. Jamie will be back, spoon in hand.

Lisa rotates daily specials throughout the week so that the meat loaf lovers know to come on Monday for their fix, spaghetti lovers on Wednesdays for theirs. Tuesdays are reserved for baked ham with pineapple and scalloped potatoes, and every Thursday, the roast beef, mashed potatoes, and gravy addicts get their fill. Lisa spreads her wings a bit on cook's choice Saturdays, but Sundays return to the traditional postchurch dinner of baked chicken. Throughout the week, you can always find liver served with onions and bacon, as well as chopped steak with sautéed onions and mushrooms—both entrees served with your choice of potato. (Remember: You can get a baked potato at home. Pick the potato pancakes.)

As I polish off the last crumbs of my pie, a man comes through the door and announces that a car in the parking lot has its lights on. It's mine. I say loudly enough for everyone in the cafe to hear, "It's okay. I'll be leaving in a few minutes." My neighbors at the next table and I pay our bills and walk out together. The woman and I pause to admire Lisa's Halloween decorations out front; behind a white picket fence is a cemetery with two limestone slabs for tombstones. One reads RIP. The other reads, "Here lies the last person who complained."

We laugh—there's certainly no need to complain about the food at the Cookery—and the woman touches me lightly on the arm. "I'm sure glad it doesn't say the person who said your lights are on!"

THREE LAKES
Cindy's Country Cafe ⦿
1672 Superior Street
(715) 546-3733
M–F 6 A.M.–2 P.M.; Sa 6 A.M.–1 P.M.; Su 7 A.M.–1 P.M.
Cindy and Ed Starke

Cindy and Ed Starke started coming to Three Lakes as summer tourists from their home in Peoria, Illinois, and loved it so much they made it their permanent home. Newly relocated, Cindy found work at the Copper Kettle restaurant, which she bought in 1987 and renamed. "Everyone in town knew me from my work in the cafe," she explains, so Cindy's Country Cafe, in a small twin-gabled purple building ("I thought I was buying cranberry-colored paint, but this what I got," explains Cindy) just south of the main business blocks, was quick to take hold in the community. "I count on the locals," Cindy notes. "The tourists are just an extra."

Close to fifty white ceramic coffee mugs hang on the peg rack behind the counter, representing "the locals who come in every day." Cindy has personalized each of the mugs with gold-lettered names and nicknames inscribed above cartoon characters and other sketches that suit the mugs' owners. "The customer gets a nickname and a picture that match their personal characteristics," Cindy explains. Ron, who owns the Sunset Resort, has a sunset on his mug, and Cher's mug has a scissors and comb because she's a hairdresser and owns the business across the street. Tom, the town chairman, is also represented on the mugs. "He's here at least twice a day," Cindy says. "We're like the adjunct town hall."

"I hope he's not violating any Open Door laws," I joke.

"Oh, no! Everyone's involved, and everyone's got a say!" she laughs.

Cindy supplies a great coffee klatch with even better coffee accompaniments: daily homemade bakery items, including bear claws, cinnamon rolls, kaiser rolls, cake doughnuts, and "yeast doughnuts on occasion." Seasonal lunch specials include summer salad plates and winter casseroles. A soup and sandwich special is available every day, along with regular menu items such as burgers and hot beef with mashed potatoes.

"The time has gone so fast. I'll be here seventeen years in May, and in all that time, it doesn't feel as if much has changed," Cindy says of her involvement with the cafe. Yet there have been changes, and Cindy recognizes them when she takes a few minutes to reflect. There is the purple paint that was supposed to be cranberry. The loss of many of her local customers because, she points out, "we're a community of mostly older people." A gift shop stocked with local crafts, knickknacks, stuffed animals, and copies of the Ladies' Auxiliary cookbook. And a shift in eating habits that has made breakfast the most popular meal of the day.

As with many other cafes throughout the state, Cindy acknowledges, "we're mainly a breakfast place now. The emphasis on breakfast has definitely increased. I think it's because it's a cheaper meal, and you can afford to take out the whole family where you can't always for dinner. It's really popular with tourists because they can come in, fill up, then head out on the boat for the day. They'll take a picnic with them and then be able to afford going out to dinner."

Among the popular breakfast choices at Cindy's Cafe are Belgian waffles and the breakfast special consisting of three pancakes (as big as the plate), choice of meat, juice, and coffee. "It's a big breakfast," notes Cindy, "but then there's always the people who add hash browns. I never have been able to figure out how they do it."

THREE LAKES
Kristine's Restaurant ❧
1802 Superior Street
(715) 546-3030
M–Tu 7 A.M.–2 P.M.; W closed; Th–Su 7 A.M.–2 P.M.
Kristine Bassett

In October 1991, after a decade as a professional cook, Kristine Bassett learned of the sale of the Alpine Haus restaurant in Three Lakes and went to take a look. She liked what she saw but thought she'd delay her decision until she came back from a Florida vacation just three days off. "I was there only a couple of days when my dad called and said if I wanted the restaurant, I'd better come home right away," she remembers. With deer hunting season looming, the owners wanted out immediately. Kristine flew back, signed the papers, and had five days to organize her business before the hunters arrived. "Fortunately," she says now, "we had a ton of snow right before opening weekend, which made deer hunting poor, and so I made it through just fine. People warned me against buying a restaurant in November. They thought I was crazy. They said I'd never make it through the winter. But snowmobile season jumped in right away and business never really slowed. I was really lucky."

Within a year of her first fateful day, Kristine was comfortably settled in with new kitchen equipment, a new menu, new employees, and old customers become new friends. Today, with the old Alpine Haus replaced by Kristine's Restaurant, she finds it hard to believe that so much time has passed.

"Has it been that long?" she asks incredulously as she ponders the changes at the restaurant, in the town of Three Lakes, and in the snowless winters that have pretty much brought an end to the reliable business of snowmobile fanatics.

"It used to be that we had twelve good weeks of snowmobiling, and the business would be just like summer," she says. "People would be lined up all day. But the past few winters have been pretty bleak. I think we're entering into a new period with winters just like it. The lack of snow is no longer a fluke."

A solution to withering winter tourism may lie in opening the snowless snowmobile trails, abandoned railroad corridors, and fire roads to all-terrain vehicles, which a few towns have embraced with profit and success. "If we don't come up with a solution for the poor winters, the locals are going to realize they won't have anywhere to eat," Kristine jokes. Laughing about the situation is a comfortable way to express real concerns and fears that are far from funny. Until a real solution is found, Kristine cuts back her winter hours to make ends meet.

This is a sad consequence for the regulars, who have to adjust their daily schedules accordingly—and who have to plan to cook for themselves an additional one or two days a week. For thirteen years they have been spoiled by the menu selections prepared by Kristine and her business partner, Jeff Frye. Both insist on "from scratch" cooking, running the gamut from familiar pies and soups to burgers and daily specials.

Even at that, as trained, professional cooks who view cooking as a form of creative expression, Kristine and Jeff's menu ideas often conflict with Wisconsin tradition. For example, they do not have hot beef as a regular menu item because Kristine prefers preparing it fresh as a daily special instead of having it continually on hand. "I'd rather have people really excited about it than come in and order it without seeing what else we have," she explains.

In this way and others, Kristine and Jeff encourage reflective, not rote, choices, and the regulars are now not only willing but eager to try Jeff's creations, especially his soups. "When we first started here," Kristine explains, "people wanted chicken noodle, beef noodle, vegetable beef. Now the more outlandish soup we try, the better it sells. Today we had Bavarian-style ham and dumpling, and we sold out right away. There's not a drop left. Jeff's soups are becoming so good, people are willing to try anything."

Other menu innovations at Kristine's Restaurant include hotdogs and hamburgers smothered in "Jeff's famous chili." Hamburgers in any variety are always best-sellers, particularly Kristine's famous "doggy burgers," which have been known to cause quite a fuss and can even bring the right parties near tears. "I don't know what it is about this place," Kristine laughs, "but I always see dogs waiting in pickup trucks for their owners. The regulars come in to eat, and before they leave, they'll order a hamburger patty for their dogs. We call them doggy burgers. My dad's dog whines if he forgets to bring him a burger. I'm not sure if that means we're better or worse cooks than we think!"

TOMAHAWK
The Hungry Bear
204 West Wisconsin Avenue
(715) 453-4707
M–F 5:30 A.M.–6:30 P.M.; Sa 5:30 A.M.–2 P.M.; Su 7 A.M.–11 A.M.
Randy and Ann Becker

Tomahawk's longtime downtown cafe, formerly LaNou's Restaurant, has always been a favorite of mine for its tradition of fine home cooking and exceptional vintage look, and I was looking forward to my visit because I could tell by the change in name that a new owner had come on board. On a cold day in late October, I pulled open the front door, noting with pleasure that the old white and green ceramic tile floor hadn't been covered in a push to modernize. But as my eyes swung upward to take in the aged quartersawn oak back bar inside the front door—thank goodness it also is still here—I gasped with surprise. There in the entrance facing me squarely was a taxidermied black bear reared on its back legs. The Hungry Bear, I thought. Of course.

I walked to the rear of the cafe where a handful of people clustered at the counter, caught between the morning coffee klatch and the lunch rush. The only waitress in sight was Sherry, and she nodded at a big, bearded man wearing a Harley T-shirt when I asked to see the owner. He's the owner?, I thought to myself. She must have been nodding to someone behind him in the kitchen. But it was the owner, Randy Becker, who looked up from the newspaper he was reading and began to tell me the story of how he made a career switch—one of the most unlikely of any cafe owner in the state.

Randy grew up in nearby Minocqua before moving west, where he became a professional big game hunter, leading clients into the deep wilds of Alaska and Canada to stalk moose, elk, grizzlies, and other coveted trophies. "I love hunting and fulfilled my dream of making a living with it,"

Randy explains, "but now it's a passion more than a dream." The dream was replaced with a new one: owning his own restaurant where he could continue to work one-on-one with people and pursue his interest in cooking. Many of his hunting buddies are surprised at the dramatic domestic turn in his life, sputtering out demanding questions such as, "You've done what!?" But to Randy and his wife, Ann, owning the Hungry Bear is just another aspect of a life lived well and with purpose.

During the past seven years following his return from the northwest, Randy became a devotee of the Corner Cafe next door, so when it came up for sale, he tried to buy it. But the deal fell through, and in frustration, he sat at the counter of LaNou's Restaurant—not far from the very spot he now occupies next to me—and moaned about his misfortune to owner Gene LaNou. LaNou offered to sell him his restaurant, and so "bing, bang, boom," the deal was made. Looking back on the sudden turn of events, Randy considers the purchase to have been a very fortunate one.

"I love the old oak, the floor, the high ceilings," he enthuses, "and I'd never trade them in for anything." Mix all of that with the mirrored oak back bar and the spine-straightening oak booths, loyal clientele, reputation for good home cooking, and Randy's growing collection of taxidermied animals and other hunting-related collectibles and you've got a one-of-a-kind cafe that stands out head and shoulders of a rearing black bear above the rest.

The namesake bear was the first to arrive, shot by Randy and a friend in the Chequamegon National Forest. He'd often eaten at a restaurant in Alaska named the Hungry Bear. Because it summed up both sides of his life—hunting and cooking—he borrowed the name for his own restaurant. Besides, Randy explains, "I love bears. I just love them." Gradually, more bears started coming, brought in as gifts from his customers. The owner of the antiques store across the street—appropriately named the Northern Bear Antique Mall—contributed a vintage print hanging on the wall. Seeing the bears, a couple recalled a pair of bears carved into a tree stump that had long been moldering in the garage. They cleaned up the woodcarving, put it in the back of the pickup, and carried it in. It now stands sentinel in the front window. Other smaller black bears—wooden cutouts and craft figures—are joining their bigger cousins on a continual basis.

Look for an assortment of other animals both real—taxidermied musky, deer, moose—and unreal, such as the exquisite, award-winning woodcarvings made by a local man. Randy carefully removes from its display on top of the ice machine a very detailed elk bucking a mountain lion. As Randy gently rotates the sculpture in his hands, the clean cuts of the carver's knife and his attention to accuracy, detail, and scale distinguish the piece as exceptional.

Come to the Hungry Bear to gawk, but come also to eat. (You can gawk some more while you're waiting for your food to come hot and fresh from the rear kitchen.) Randy credits his restaurant's success to his own passions for cooking and eating and to Pat Garreau, his "priceless cook." Randy knows what he likes, and he knows what you'll like too. For those with a bearlike appetite, he recommends the Grizzly Burger, a two-fisted-at-all-times eight-to nine-ounce saucer (patty is far too inadequate a word to describe this!) of fresh ground Black Angus beef sandwiched into a sourdough bun. Sided with a mound of real potato hash browns or American fries, or a bowl of slow-simmered soup, it will set you up for a week of hunting in the woods alongside Randy himself. He's heading out coon hunting tonight with his blue tick hounds. Care to go?

WITTENBERG
Gus and Ann's Restaurant ᵍ
101 Genesee Street (Highway 29)
(715) 253-6007
M–Su 6 A.M.–8 P.M.
Paul, Audrey, and Jenny Sikora

Pulling off Highway 29, I squeeze my budget-sized Mazda into one of three parking spaces left in the large lot adjacent to Gus and Ann's Restaurant, a fixture in Wittenberg since 1969. The car to the left is a late-model Fleetwood Cadillac; the car to the right, a new Lincoln Continental. My Mazda looks like a junkyard dog next to these purebreds, but it's not as bad as the mongrel pickup on the other side of the Lincoln. The cars in the parking lot describe Gus and Ann's pretty accurately: A combination down-home humble pie and classic, classy all-American best-seller.

I confess to having left out Gus and Ann's in the first edition of *Cafe Wisconsin*. That was a serious oversight because it is an exceptional home-cooking treasure. I did visit and eat there ten years ago, but because of its location at the intersection of two highways and about a mile from downtown Wittenberg, I interpreted Gus and Ann's as being a truck stop and not a small town cafe. I apologize to you, Gus and Ann, and to everyone who has made Gus and Ann's a regular stop for fries after school, hot beef during the drive between Minneapolis and Door County, and pie at any hour of the day.

Those who have been coming to Gus and Ann's for years may be surprised to learn that Gus and Ann Weller have retired from their namesake restaurant. The changeover to new owners Paul, Audrey, and Jenny

Sikora occurred quietly in 2002, after a month-long period of side-by-side apprenticeship with the Wellers. Paul had retired from his own tire business but quickly discovered retirement wasn't for him. He looked around for something to keep him busy and found Gus and Ann's. A savvy businessman, he knew a good thing and a smooth operation when he saw it. "You take something like this that works and you don't change it," he explains. "We have the same menu, same specials, same prices, same employees, even the same appearance."

Like Paul, Ann Weller isn't too sure that retirement is something she likes, although she is glad for the time it provides for visits with her sisters and children. The day I stopped in for a revisit, Gus was roofing a shed on his stepmother's farm, but Ann was in the kitchen for a lunchtime visit. "Retirement is an ongoing process," she tells me. "I miss the routine of knowing exactly what I'll be doing all day. I get up in the morning and ask myself, 'What should I do today?'"

In 1969 Gus and Ann bought a little combination roadside restaurant and gas station with a house out back. They lived in the house, and Ann operated the restaurant while Gus went to work each day for Marathon Electric. On weekends Gus manned the grill and kept the talk flowing up front. As the years passed, the Wellers expanded the restaurant in order to keep pace with its growing and widespread reputation for friendly, efficient service and homemade everything. In between the growth spurts, periodic remodeling kept everything clean and fresh. Says Ann, "We wore through two inlaid floors before we got smart and put down ceramic tile." A few years before they retired, the Wellers remodeled the entire cafe. The counter area received a facelift and new oak booths replaced the originals.

I love the booths, which are sturdy, thick, and blond—like stubby church pews. Sharing my booth with Ann, I apologize for my sin of first edition omission and am absolved. My penance? Ann is a saint and requires none. Instead, she takes my order for a bowl of vegetable beef soup and coleslaw and heads for the kitchen. I lean against the back of the booth and peruse the menu.

If there is indeed retribution for my sin, it must be that I can't sample everything on the menu. I would like to! One bowl of soup is not nearly enough to become well acquainted with Gus and Ann's. I wish I could eat a plate of hot roast beef, gravy, and mashed potatoes sandwiched between slices of snow white bread—a belly-bulging favorite that can be enjoyed every day of the week. Other days are reserved for rotating specials: oven-roasted corned beef and cabbage on Thursday, deep-fried cod on Friday, meat loaf on Saturday, and roast chicken on Sunday. Monday, Tuesday, and Wednesday are reserved for cook's choice specials.

If you don't find what you like on the daily specials board—and you must be pretty hard to please if that's the case—you won't err in ordering a burger. The Gus Burger is a flavorful fistful, invented by Gus himself, who took a jumbo beef patty and topped it with Swiss and American cheese, lettuce, tomato, and fried onion. Another burger that deserves its name is the Wittenburger, layered with Wisconsin cheese and crowned with famous sugar-cured, applewood-smoked Nueske bacon. Made just up the road, Nueske's bacon has been featured in *Cuisine* magazine and the *New York Times*. Even Gus and Ann's made the *Times*. The reporter included a line about his lunchtime BLT at "Wittenberg's main (and only) crossroads" diner.

Come to Gus and Ann's for hot beef, burgers, Nueske's bacon, or any of the great varieties of homemade soups. They're all satisfying sided with fresh-cut French fries or the homemade potato salad or coleslaw with sour cream dressing. A whole slough of baked goods—raised doughnuts, cherry turnovers, muffins—that vary by day and the baker's mood are unexpected treasure. Take a booth and take your fill. Just don't leave without a piece of pie or, in season, a hot apple dumpling.

Until her retirement, Ann made fourteen daily pies—two each of seven varieties. Audrey Sikora has since inherited the honor, working at Ann's elbow until she mastered the techniques, textures, and flavors. "I was worried that we'd get complaints," Paul Sikora says about the switch in pie bakers. "But no one said anything. Gus came in and had a piece and couldn't even tell."

The seven daily varieties of pie include custard, apple, banana cream, coconut cream, cherry, blueberry, and cranberry nut. Other varieties such as raspberry, blackberry, peach, and rhubarb are available in season. The pies are exceptional, boasts Paul Sikora, and are so popular that the "waitresses don't ask if you want pie. They ask, 'What kind of pie do you want?'"

Frequently, the pie of choice is cranberry walnut. Ann's sisters, Janice and Rosie (former owner of Allan and Rosie's Kitchen, now the Main Street Diner, in nearby Shawano), adapted a vinegar pie recipe by adding walnuts, and then Ann took it a step further by adding cranberries. "That pie has gone all over the country," Ann says proudly.

Despite my overwhelming fondness for pie, I opt for the apple dumpling, made fresh with Macintosh apples picked from trees on the family farm. In my opinion, there is no better apple for baking or eating than a crisp, squirty Macintosh. At Gus and Ann's, a peeled and cored whole Macintosh is packed with brown sugar, butter, and cinnamon and wrapped in a soft pastry crust. Baked in the oven until the apple softens and the sugar turns to syrup, the dumpling is served hot in a ceramic soup bowl. A whiff of it, a taste of it, evokes October trips to the apple orchard, black ribbon roads, fiery maples, and bracing prewinter air. If autumn in Wisconsin has a taste, it is Gus and Ann's apple dumplings. Load up the kids in the car and see for yourself.

WOODRUFF
Woods Cafe ⭐
903 First Avenue
(715) 356–3471
M–F 6 A.M.–3 P.M.; Sa 6 A.M.–2 P.M.; Su closed
Bob and Jeanne Michaelson

The Woods Cafe has been a part of Woodruff for around fifty years and a part of Jeanne Michaelson's family since October 1963, when her stepfather, Bill Waltich, bought the original Woods Cafe located next to the town theater. Bill, who worked as a chef at area resorts and at the Palmer House in Chicago, "was a legend restaurant man," says Jeanne. In 1985 when Jeanne's mother, Jo, and Bill wanted to retire, Jeanne explains, "the restaurant was offered to Bob and me first because my sisters already had jobs, and I'd been involved in the restaurant business." Until his death in September 2001, Bill was an almost daily visitor at the cafe where he had spent many years of his life. He is still there: in Jeanne's way of asking herself, "Is this the way Bill would have done it?"; in her loving memories; and in the "history washstand" against the back wall where she keeps a small photo album as tribute to a fine man.

Sharing the photo album with her customers who knew him, and with me who didn't, Jeanne presents images of Bill that convey his personality and his life. Here is Bill the family man, surrounded by children and grandchildren. Here is Bill as Santa Claus, as cafe owner, as friend. "He was the kind of guy who drives his pickup into the snow bank," Jeanne laughs softly as she points out a faded color photograph.

Jeanne had advised me to come to the cafe at nine in the morning, after the regular breakfasters and coffee drinkers had moved on, and she would have some time to spend with me. But this morning the cafe was busier than she anticipated, and as she got up to wait tables, she leaned over and whispered, "I told you it's unpredictable. Every day is different. You can never tell. It's like they all meet on the street corner and say, 'Let's go to the Woods.'"

She leaves me alone with the photo album. As I page through the images of Jeanne's family's past, I find my eyes becoming moist. The Christmas photos especially are like windows into my own childhood in the 1970s: the same hair styles, the same two-piece flannel pajamas, the same gifts, the same wood-look paneling on the family room walls, the same household furnishings.

I move on from the family album to other items displayed on the history washstand, including two other albums of photos depicting the daily antics and activities of the morning coffee group known as "the six o'clock gang," the other regulars, and the employees, which include Jeanne and Bob's children, Samantha and Matt. The photos testify to the importance of the cafe in the town's social life and also prove that despite the passage of years and beautiful new floor covering, the Woods Cafe hasn't changed so dramatically that you won't recognize it from the black and white photo of forty years ago. The walls have the same paneling, the counter the same white Formica top with blue starbursts, the chrome stools the same birch bases and black chrome feet.

And the same authentic home cooking. Bob chooses and cooks the daily meat, potatoes, and vegetable specials, which "depend on the weather or whatever he feels like making," according to Jeanne. Among the local and tourist crowd, favorites include roast beef and roast pork with real mashed potatoes, sirloin steak, liver and bacon, and chicken. The chicken noodle soup is delicious, with homemade noodles swimming in a sea of rich yellow broth thick with meat and celery. "People come for our homemade soups," notes Jeanne modestly. "They're about the best in the area from what I've heard."

The three diners at the next table have never before been to the Woods Cafe. They selected it as a place to meet because it was equal distance— about twenty miles—from each of their homes. They are pleasantly surprised by its cleanliness ("We're very proud of that," Jeanne notes. "The inspector was here last week and we had no violations—she said she just loves places like this.") and their huge breakfasts of hash browns, eggs, and cakes. They'll definitely be coming back—the next time with their husbands.

Jeanne has enough experience to know that they will indeed be back as they promise. Once people try the Woods Cafe, they usually become diehard fans. "People come in and say, 'It's just like home.'" Others drive past the main street eatery, heading for the fast and familiar food joints farther down the highway that are slowly converting Woodruff from the self-contained, self-sustaining small town it has been to a franchised vacation town with fewer and fewer owner-operated local eateries. But there are many tourists for whom a trip to Wisconsin's northwoods requires an adventure in local eating, and their comments in the guest book—found alongside the photo albums on the history washstand—are testimony to their epiphanies.

"Super place. Great Service. Very impressive," write Danny and Pat.

In a child's large-lettered printing, Caitlin says, "Food was Great! Thanks!"

Jessica, also a child, shares Caitlin's sentiment: "Great food loved it!"

Praise for the breakfasts comes from Audrey and Dan, evidently surprised to find "corned beef hash!" and Rick and Mindy, who are thrilled with the "great eggs and bacon!"

That the Woods Cafe is a gem among Wisconsin's small town cafes is known far and wide. Witness the guest book comments written by people from as far away as Zoetermeer, Holland, and Frankston, Australia. And just think: the three women in the table next to mine initially considered forty miles round trip to be a little too far to go for breakfast. Oh, but they'll be back.

· ·

Next Best Bets

Bonduel
Carol's Diner
237 South Cecil Street
Formerly the Golden Grill, Carol's Diner features pork hocks and sauerkraut every Monday. Broasted chicken and the homemade pies are other best-sellers.

Crandon
Hotel Crandon Cafe
200 North Lake Street
Slow-cooked real food in a rare old-time main street hotel with its own small restaurant. I love the huge cinnamon rolls.

Eagle River
Donna's Cafe
4356 East Wall Street
One of three hometown, home-cooking cafes in this northern town, Donna's is about one mile east of the downtown commercial hub—a kind of refuge from the omnipresent tourists.

Elcho
Koni K's Restaurant 🍽
N11204 Antigo Street (Highway 45)
Featured in the first edition, the former Connie's Cafe—once a one-room schoolhouse—has been torn down and replaced with this bigger than expected restaurant. Still the same reliable real food.

LAKE TOMAHAWK
Village Cafe
7249 Bradley Street (Highway 47)
The only small town cafe in Wisconsin with real cloth napkins and Rowe pottery lamps on the table.

LAND O'LAKES
Leif's Cafe
4187 Highway 8
A great breakfast cafe. Be prepared to wait for a table in the middle summer months.

MERRILL
Kozy Korner
427 Grand Avenue
This westside corner restaurant has been a local favorite for almost one hundred years. Cheap, mostly homemade eats, but avoid the frozen fruit pie.

NIAGARA
Jim's Restaurant
973 Main Street
Try the pasties, pastry-encased beef and vegetable pies introduced by the Cornish who settled the area.

OCONTO FALLS
Falls Family Restaurant
158 North Main Street
Fans of the Green Bay Packers—and I think that's everyone in this part of the state—will like this green and gold home-cooking restaurant.

PESHTIGO
Peshtigo Cafe
101 South Emery Street
A fine hometown cafe with good food and even better talk. My favorite line overheard from the five guys in the booth behind me: "Everyone has a foot in the grave and the other one on a banana peel."

PHELPS
Cozy Corner Cafe
2268 Highway 17
A favorite breakfast stop of the thousand or so cyclists doing the Great Annual Bicycle Adventure Along the Wisconsin River. If you are not a cyclist, avoid this place on the last Sunday in June.

POUND
Wilson's Cafe
4065 Highway 141
The fresh homemade cake doughnuts are unbelievably cheap at ten cents for unfrosted, fifteen cents for frosted. Sadly, a makeover erased the original 1940s look of the former Hut, featured in the first edition.

SHAWANO
Angie's Main Cafe
132 South Main Street
In the former Dehn's ice cream parlor, Angie's Main Cafe still has the feel of an old-time eatery. The swooping retro counter is the only place to breakfast on the pan-fried walleye and real potato hash browns and American fries. Add the homemade doughnuts on the side, and you'll be in heaven.

SHAWANO
The Main Street Diner
123 North Main Street
I was a bit disappointed here. Everything was homemade but not the consistent high quality I knew when the place was Allan and Rosie's Kitchen, featured in the first edition.

WABENO
Safari Cafe
4453 North Branch Road
Snowmobilers on the Snow Safari Trail will be happy to discover this cafe along the way. The Logger's Breakfast will keep you fueled for a good part of the day.

Central

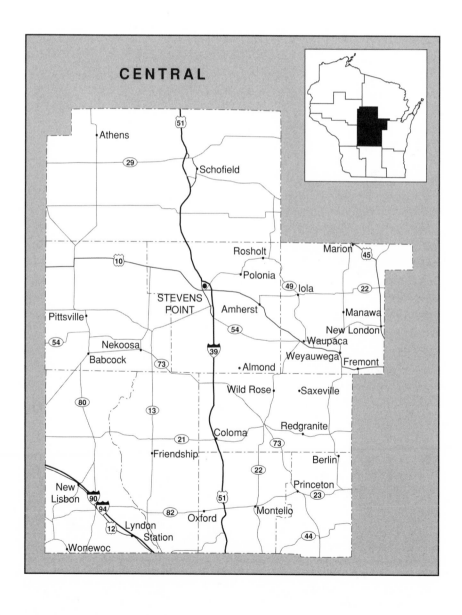

CENTRAL

Athens

29

Schofield

51

RoshOlt

Marion

45

Polonia

49 Iola

22

STEVENS
POINT

Amherst

Manawa

Pittsville

54

New London

54

Nekoosa

Waupaca

Babcock

73

Weyauwega

Fremont

39

Almond

Wild Rose

Saxeville

80

13

Coloma

Redgranite

21

73

Friendship

Berlin

22

New
Lisbon

90

Princeton

23

94

51

Montello

82

Oxford

12

Lyndon
Station

44

Wonewoc

ALMOND
Farm House Restaurant
150 Main Street
(715) 366-2141
M–Th 5:30 A.M.–7:30 P.M.; F 5:30 A.M.–8:30 P.M.;
Sa 5:30 A.M.–7:30 P.M.; Su closed
Cindy Laux

After graduating from culinary school, Cindy Laux worked as an executive chef, all the while harboring a deep-seated desire to own a little cafe where she could be her own boss and cook old-fashioned food to her heart's content. To that end, she opened a little place in Amherst and was content until the fateful day she wound up in Almond, lost while out looking for a rural property in which to set up housekeeping. She stopped for gas and directions at Almond's lone station and was surprised to discover that she knew the man working there. He told her the cafe up the street was for sale, she took a look at it, and lo and behold, two weeks later she was its owner.

"The first year was really rough," Cindy recalls. "This is a small community and the older people had a hard time getting to know me because I spent a lot of that first year in the kitchen." Although she had purchased an established business, it was closed when she bought it, requiring her to do extensive cleaning and redecorating, replace equipment and stock, train new staff, and establish new menu items and prices. She also had to relocate her family and educate her customers in her new ideas and ways.

Since then, the locals have become devoted regulars who cluster at the counter for breakfast and serve each other coffee when Cindy and her staff are busy. The Farm House has also been discovered by travelers, including this morning's Harley riders who make a weekly trip from Coloma, Princeton, and other nearby towns, and in winter, the snowmobilers who pull off the trail that runs alongside the restaurant.

In a town that boasts one gas station, three bars, four churches, and the two-day Tater Toot festival in late July, the Farm House Restaurant serves as social center, civic hall, and convenience store—since the lone grocery store closed a year ago. This is where the locals gather to discuss the latest news, where the Lions Club holds its meetings, and where those who have run short of life's staples—bread, milk, pop, candy—can make ends meet until the next trip into Stevens Point.

For those who require more substance to their eating, the Farm House doesn't disappoint. Cindy's culinary training is put to delicious use preparing "good down-home cooking," including daily specials, soups, pies, rolls, and pastries. Smack dab in the heart of Wisconsin's potato country, Cindy offers locally grown potatoes in a variety of guises: mashed, hash browns,

American fries, potato salad, you name it. "We couldn't get away with anything less," she says. Other homemade must-haves are hot beef ("What is it about hot beef?"), soups, taco salads with fresh deep-fried shells, and the Friday fish fry.

Cindy claims that her customers are "not a sweets crowd," but they do like her huge homemade cookies—M&M chocolate chip, chunky chocolate chip, and peanut butter—muffins, turnovers, pies, and both the hard and soft-serve ice cream. But day in and day out, weekdays and weekends, breakfast is the biggest meal at the Farm House. "It's really a big thing," Cindy says. "We sell a lot of omelettes, toast (be sure to request the homemade bread), and hash browns."

Four years after reopening Almond's only restaurant, Cindy has hit her stride. But it took awhile for her to understand her customers—and to circumvent their ways by outsmarting them. Cindy laughs when she remembers the day she discovered that chicken cordon bleu served with rice pilaf wasn't going to be the big seller that she anticipated. The first time it appeared as the daily special, she sold only two servings. She couldn't understand why it didn't sell because "it's exactly what they like: chicken, ham, and cheese. I can understand the rice—it's not mashed potatoes—but the chicken?"

The next time she offered it, she advertised not chicken cordon bleu with pilaf but stuffed chicken breast with rice and quickly sold out. "I just had to figure out what to call it!" she laughs.

The Farm House lives up to its name. In the ten years since my first visit, the place has been reinterpreted from a 1960s-era hotel diner to a country farmhouse, complete with a rocking chair–equipped front porch. Its interior decor is comfortable country, with burgundy wainscot, country print wallpaper, and lace curtains with checkered tiebacks. The tables are covered with farmyard print vinyl cloths, which Cindy rotates with seasonal themed prints throughout the year. I really like the Fiesta-look real china plates and bowls, and the complementary striped, real glass tumblers. They show a bit of class and stylish flair and are a welcome substitute for the typical and mundane white restaurant china and plastic glasses.

The farm theme is underscored by this poem by M. F. Power-Dixon on the menu's front cover:

> The Wisconsin Farmer
> Why would anyone live on a farm? My grandpa
> Once told me why: you wake up at dawn,
> Put the strong coffee on, and look out at a
> Bright morning sky!

You start chores early, work hard and long,
At planting or milking or such.
But at the day's end, when quiet has come,
You know you've seen God's perfect touch!

A farm may not be the only place to live,
to grow and die—
but my grandpa said, "It's the only place
I'd ever suggest you try!"

AMHERST
Amherst Cafe ⧉ ⧉
122 South Main Street
(715) 824-3112
M–Su 6 A.M.–7 P.M.
Diane Stroik

It is dark inside the Amherst Cafe when I arrive, and rain beats against the front window. A summer storm has knocked out the power, and Diane and a waitress are alone, waiting for the power to come back on. As Diane and I converse over the counter, a man and his five-year-old nephew come in looking for something to eat. When Austin, the boy, learns there is no food because there is no power, he suggests, "We could eat ice cream!"

As if on cue, a man enters carrying three cardboard tubs of ice cream for the freezer. The power is out, the freezer is off, and he brings ice cream.

Diane Stroik, owner of the Amherst Cafe since 1982, remembers eating ice cream as a child at the old Amherst Cafe while accompanying her parents on visits with hometown friends, but there was nothing in those childhood experiences that ever caused her to believe she would some-day own the place. Growing up in Milwaukee, she helped her parents in their tavern and then moved on to other restaurant work before proving that people do find their way back home. About twenty-five years ago, Diane moved to the Amherst area, following her parents who settled on the original family homestead. Under Diane's care, the Amherst Cafe has become one of Wisconsin's true gems, as is Diane herself. Be sure not to miss either one.

Diane's reputation for pie making extends far and wide around these parts. Travelers regularly drop off nearby Interstate 39 for a slice of her popular sour cream apple pie. Bicyclists lean their bikes against the front window and refuel for the return trip home. Out-of-town customers plan visits and call ahead to ensure that their favorite pie will be waiting for them to eat in or take out. "You know," Diane confesses, "I didn't start out making pies. I had a local lady, Helen, come in and bake all the pies, but when she died I had to learn how to make them."

For years Diane had the corner bakery make her baked goods, but when it went out of business, she had to be resourceful and find a way to replace the much-loved breads. The bakery gave her the sunflower bread recipe that had become synonymous with the cafe. She took it to Amherst Family Foods, and now its bakery makes it for her. Her meats, especially the sausage and thick-sliced bacon, are equally acclaimed. They come fresh from Waller's Meat Locker in nearby Nelsonville. Out-of-town customers are so impressed by the bacon, they often pay a visit to Waller's themselves. "I send customers—deer hunters mostly—to Waller's and they take bacon back with them to Milwaukee."

Nothing at the Amherst Cafe is run-of-the-mill, including the French fries, which are skin-on fresh. "You've got to have hot beefs and traditional menu items—if you want that, I've got it. But I get sick of making the same old things," Diane explains, "so I'm always trying to find something new. I bring back recipes from my travels. I went to New Orleans and had corn sausage soup and now when I make it, I have to call up the businesses and my regular customers to let them know it's on the menu." Other successful experiments include chicken cordon bleu, chicken chimichangas, and Polish chop suey—a combination of pork, sauerkraut, mushroom soup, and other ingredients. "My customers trust me when I say it's good, even if it looks funny," Diane laughs. "Sometimes I think I've brought a little culture to this town."

She also brings the town to the culture. Diane works as an outside representative for a travel agency and organizes trips for her customers and any of the locals who care to sign on. She loves to travel and is adventurous, having been to places as close as New York City and as far away as Italy. A rack of travel brochures is displayed under the sign "Cafe Travel," the name she has given her side business. In December 2002 she led a group of thirteen people, including eighty-seven-year-old Char—a "pistol of a woman"—to view Ground Zero. Char had announced, "If you ever go to New York, I want to go," so Diane organized the trip.

Diane's local customers think of her cafe as home and find it hard to leave, if even for an exciting trip to unknown lands. When she was closed for remodeling, she was constantly being asked when she'd reopen. One of her regulars was in the hospital at the time. When she visited him, he only wanted to talk about the cafe. "I miss the cafe," he told her. He was curious about the remodeling and couldn't wait to get back and have coffee with the guys.

"There's a real family feeling here," Diane agrees, "because the girls and customers are just like family." Photographs of the regulars from the past twenty-two years cover the walls. Some of the people are now gone, and from time to time, someone asks Diane if the photos shouldn't be removed. "Take them down?" she asks me. "I've got to keep them up now more than ever." A tear slides down her right cheek as she talks about the people she has loved and lost. Her mood lightens when she recalls a teenage employee who laughed to see her parents in the old photos. "Her brother was in a high chair, and she wasn't too far behind," Diane points out.

The cafe's homey feeling is inspired by personal touches, like the real maple syrup left under the counter by regulars who bring it from home for their morning pancakes. Diane offers quite a variety, including "gourmet" chocolate chip, pecan, blueberry, buckwheat, and blueberry buckwheat. "One morning, this guy came in and ordered the buckwheat pancakes," Diane remembers. "'I haven't had buckwheat pancakes since I was a kid.' He was so excited. After he finished them, he said, 'Now that I think of it, I remember that I didn't like them any more as a kid!'"

As Diane and I talk, the waitress mops the floor in the dark. Light is falling through the front window, creating a sheen on the wet floor. From where I am sitting, I can see that the mop has not missed a spot. Suddenly the lights flicker on, and the waitress blurts, "Oh, no! Now you can see all the dirty spots." Instantly, the lights go off, and the three of us stare at each other as if her words had conjured magic. Fifteen minutes later, still in the dark, Diane and I say goodbye. As I walk gingerly across the wet floor to the door, they wish me good luck. "I'll need it to get safely across in the dark," I reply—at the very moment the lights go back on. Again, we stare large-eyed and open-mouthed. And then we laugh with surprise and disbelief: light really can strike twice in the same place with the right words.

BABCOCK
Country Cafe 🍽
1699 Highway 80
(715) 884-2414
M–Sa 6 A.M.–6:30 P.M.; Su 7 A.M.–6:30 P.M.
Sherri Dessart
Located as it is in the heart of Wood County's cranberry country and not far from the Ocean Spray factory, the Country Cafe gives the tart little red berry and its dried and sweetened offspring, the craisin, a starring role. In the low-slung brown cafe with its sign on the roof promising GOOD FOOD, Sherri Dessart and her employees turn out shapely loaves of cranberry and craisin bread and flaky-crusted pies—cranberry nut, cranapple nut, and cranraspberry. They serve regular cafe meals too, including real potatoes and fresh meats and burgers, but at the Country Cafe, pie is the thing. If you're a

fan of the berry, you'll want to call ahead and order pies to take home, either in singles or by the dozen.

Twelve years ago, when her father convinced her to buy the cafe so she could live near him, Sherri knew she was also acquiring the previous owner's fame for cranberry pies. "Mrs. Peterson's pies" have gradually become a significant part of her business, much to Sherri's surprise because, she confesses, she doesn't like cranberries at all. She bakes pies for gift shops in Eagle River and Warrens. She also caters meals for the Wisconsin Department of Natural Resources and hosts groups touring the Ocean Spray factory. "I knew what I was getting into, but I never thought it would be so big," she says. "Some weeks we make 150 pies. Some weeks we make eight or ten. It all depends what's on the calendar."

Cranberry specialties may be the star at the Country Cafe, but the rest of Sherri's menu is no understudy. "We serve all homemade food," she promises, including fresh daily specials, soups, and a variety of noncranberry pies. The parking lot has ample space for adventure eaters with big rigs— whose cabs might feel a tad bit smaller after filling up on Sherri's home cooking.

BERLIN
Steele's Restaurant
117 West Huron Street
(920) 361-1276
M–Th 6 A.M.–2:30 P.M.; F 6 A.M.–2:30 P.M. and 4:30–8:30 P.M.; Sa 6 A.M.–2:30 P.M.; Su 6 A.M.–1:30 P.M.
Therese Lewallen, owner
Mary Jo Doro, manager
Passing through the front door of Steele's Restaurant in downtown Berlin is like walking through a time portal. You leave the main street with its late-nineteenth-century facades that have been remodeled and remuddled over the years, pull open the very heavy solid oak door, and return to the year 1937. Everything in Steele's is vintage and the real thing, from the black marble counter with red stools on steel posts to the oak booths with their own amber glass lamps, from the terrazzo floor to the beamed ceiling. Even the rectangular mirror on the back wall is original. Don't believe me? Check out the 1940s linen postcard that owner Therese Lewallen keeps in the glass case beneath the counter. The Steele's in it is precisely the Steele's you're in! It's amazing that nothing here has changed over the years.

Therese, manager Mary Jo Doro, and their staff are running to keep up with the unexpected deluge of lunchers, and I wait at the counter for my waitress and watch them. They are a well-oiled machine, today supplemented by Mary Jo's husband, Dan, and son, John, who have come in to help bus and set tables. The customers are patient and understanding, including a woman with two young children at the counter next to me waiting for a table to become available. Her daughter has double-jointed shoulders and drapes herself over the stool like a sideshow contortionist.

Laura, my waitress, stops to take my order. I've mistaken the stainless steel service counter for a soda fountain and order a chocolate Coke. "What's that?" Laura asks, and instead of confessing my blunder, I teach her how to make one using Hershey's syrup. "I've never heard of that before," Laura tells me as she finishes stirring the chocolate syrup and Coke with an iced-tea spoon. She has heard of the "new" Vanilla Coke being sold by Coca-Cola but has, ironically, never heard of the original soda fountain variety. She runs off to the kitchen to place my order: half a turkey sandwich on rye, a cup of homemade vegetable beef soup, and a side of homemade potato chips.

The food is unexpectedly good. My sandwich is fresh and simple; the soup hearty, flavorful, and full of chunky beef; the potato chips thick and crisp. There is no need for me to move on to pie because I know it is sure to be good. (My trip to the bathroom, which is as vintage as the cafe, took me past the refrigerator where the pies are kept. Bypass the frozen fruit pies and order the homemade cream, custard, and cream cheese varieties.) Although I linger over my chocolate Coke, it is easy to see that Therese will not be available to talk anytime soon, so I promise to return an hour later and wander down the street to Strong's Landing antique mall.

There I meet dealer Roger Daul, who also owns the Whiting, a bar on the opposite end of the street located in the historic Whiting Hotel building. Roger is proud of his bar and takes me there to show it off, opening the front door with his key because the business is not open during the day. He holds open the door. I walk through it and once again I am in the 1930s, this time thoroughly art moderne in appearance. Is all of Berlin a time portal to the past? I am amazed by the preservation of the two main street buildings—Steele's and the Whiting—especially that they are both vintage 1930s but so entirely different in their decor and mood. The Whiting is all neon and chrome in streamlined swoops and curves, very modern and upscale compared with Steele's. But like Steele's, it has miraculously escaped the years between then and now unscathed, unaltered, so that it is the historic past freeze-framed in the present.

Sterling Steele was born and raised in Ripon, moving to Berlin in the 1920s to open his first namesake restaurant. By 1937 he had moved into the present building, confident enough in his success to invest a considerable sum in its complete remodeling. He spared little expense, selecting materials of enduring quality, such as oak and marble, and hiring designers and craftsmen of considerable skill. Steele's was a classy joint and for a number of years served double duty as the Union bus depot. As the social center of Berlin, Steele's Restaurant kindled many a romance, including that of Therese Lewallen's own parents fifty-eight years ago.

Therese remembers coming to Steele's as a child with her parents and eight brothers and sisters, but she never would have guessed then that she'd own the place as an adult. "It just sort of happened," she explains. She had been working at a cafe across the street, eying the vacant Steele's, when it dawned on her that she might buy it. "It was pretty much a turnkey," she remembers of the day nine years ago when she became owner. "All it really needed was a good cleaning and we were ready. I left the door open the whole time and people were in and out all the time. Everyone was happy to see it reopened because it had always meant a lot to the whole town."

Although there were four other restaurants in downtown Berlin at the time and Therese found the going "tough the first couple of years," Steele's is once again on solid feet. The locals quickly discovered Therese's commitment to homemade most everything. It wasn't long before the tourists discovered it too. They came for the incredible food but didn't expect to be time travelers in the process. "I love to see people's faces as they walk through the door," laughs Therese. "They just can't believe it."

Therese features the kind of cooking she grew up with at home because it is "what I was taught" and because it is the same food she wants when she goes out to eat. "I want to know that people have cared and worked hard and made good food for me," she says. You will know this at Steele's. Among the favorite offerings are (you guessed it) the hot beef; chicken and turkey dinners; potato pancakes; almost everything on the Sunday breakfast menu, especially the breakfast strata—a baked egg, veggie, and meat dish; stuffed French toast; fresh seasonal fruit; and the from-scratch coffee cake. Steele's does not offer a daily full plate special because Therese feels there is enough variety of dinner-type selections on the menu. Instead, daily specials feature soup and sandwich combinations. If you're lucky enough to be there when homemade sloppy joes are available, you will be a happy time traveler indeed.

COLOMA
Royal Cafe ౿
Interstate 39 and Highway 21
(715) 228-2352
M–Th 6 A.M.–6 P.M.; F 6 A.M.–8 P.M.; Sa–Su 6 A.M.–6 P.M.
Mary and Chuck Becker

Established in 1951, the Royal Cafe once stood in downtown Coloma on the former route of Highway 21. When the new highway bypassed the town in 1986, then-owners Lucy Rowley and Joanna Sherman had the red box of a cafe moved up the hill to the intersection of Interstate 39 and Highway 21. "When the highway was rerouted," Jo had told me, "it became apparent that we needed to move too, in order to save the operation. The move was definitely the highlight of the area. People came out of their houses and stood watching the little red building move up the street."

The move was the right one. Since that time, the Royal Cafe has gone from diamond in the rough to sparkling red ruby. When Lucy and Jo sold out in 1999, Chuck and Mary Becker stepped in and brought the Royal into the twenty-first century by going back to the 1950s. They expanded and redecorated in a classic red and white diner theme, bringing in white chrome-legged tables and red vinyl dinette chairs; full-color pictures of Elvis; photos of vintage cars owned by local collectors; and a Rock-Ola jukebox. The retro look might be a new one, but nothing else at the Royal has changed. And it's a good thing. The Royal was a five-star cafe under Lucy and Jo and remains so under the Beckers.

Chuck is a native of Coloma, and Mary is not. Consequently, she is not Mary but rather "Chuckie Becker's Wife. I always will be," she laughs. Chuckie Becker's Wife, like many other cafe owners, is a wonder at successful multitasking. She runs the cafe with her best friend Tanya Burrows, is the mother of three school-age boys, and is also a licensed CPA who keeps the books for Chuck's real estate business. She often finds herself at the cafe at the end of the week, where she decompresses by making pies or the cafe's signature Yum-Yum Coffee Cake. "I enjoy it a lot, and it relaxes me," Mary explains. "It really de-stresses me, and it's a lot of fun. I don't see it as a job."

Mary and Tanya, who agreed to help out for two weeks then stayed on because she was having so much fun, are mothers to their own kids and family to many of their customers. They pamper and please their regulars, many of whom stop in two or more times a day. Tanya describes working at the Royal as "kind of like playing," yet she realizes the impact of the work on the community. Mary, Chuck, and their employees worry about the regulars if they don't show up and often call to see how they're doing.

The national disaster of September 11 proved the power and strength of community particularly well. Tanya, who was working that morning, recalls, "The people came to the restaurant to be together. They brought in their radios and sat and listened most of the day. They helped each other and us get through the day."

Many people predicted that the Royal Cafe would not survive the Beckers' changes. So many people had become accustomed to its cozy confines and long-established ways. But it quickly became apparent that the Beckers had no intention of making sweeping changes. They only intended to make the place bigger and brighter. Mary explains that throughout the remodeling, the restaurant never closed, and people felt like part of the entire process. "It was done with them right in the middle of it," she says. "We set the tables right down on the uncovered particle-board floor. Some of them thought that was just the best thing."

Despite the naysayers, the Royal Cafe still has its regulars—and a lot more of them. They quickly discovered that the Royal was their same beloved place under its fancy new clothes. Mary knew that you don't change a perfect thing, so she carried over the same winning menu items: the bread made by local Amish families, the tempting homemade pies, the Yum-Yum Coffee Cake, the real mashed potatoes, the huge pancakes. Despite the sure-fire selections—and you can't go wrong selecting anything at the Royal—it is that old Wisconsin standby, roast beef and gravy, that is the sure-fire, number one top seller.

If you are a connoisseur of roast beef, you must not miss the Royal Cafe, which offers it up in three carefully discernible differences. Pay close attention now. First, there is the hot roast beef sandwich consisting of homemade Amish bread, real mashed potatoes, and gravy. Second, there is the roast beef sandwich—distinguishable from the first offering because it comes hot *or* cold on regular (i.e., store-bought) bread, sans mashed potatoes and gravy. Third is the roast beef dinner. It is different from choices one and two because it consists of roast beef with the following sides: mashed potatoes (with gravy or butter), homemade bread and butter, vegetable of the day, and a salad of some sort. Such fine distinctions! And it's still just roast beef.

But very good roast beef. Mary selects quality cuts and seasons and bakes them until the meat falls in heaps of tasty shreds. The gravy is rich and homemade. Served together with home-style real mashed potatoes, you've got a meal fit for a Wisconsin farmer. None were at the Royal the evening I ate my hot beef sandwich, but Ron and Jen Wilke were there from a nearby town. We were the only three in the cafe with the exception of Marge, the one-woman staff, and since it was silly to sit there silent like church mice, we quickly launched into an animated conversation.

The Wilkes were on their way home from Adams, where they had picked up some siding for their outhouse—"the first thing we built together after we got married in 1962," laughed Jen. Feeling a bit peckish, they stopped at the Royal where Ron ordered a chocolate malt and Jen had the chicken dinner. They know their local restaurants quite well and offered me plenty of additional recommendations. After an hour, we said goodbye to Marge and convened at Ron and Jen's truck, where the siding was stretched out in all its glory. Fine siding, too. Just the thing for the outhouse of connubial bliss.

FREMONT
Wolf River Diner
306 West Main Street
(920) 446-3153
M–Su 5:30 A.M.–7 P.M.
Bob and Nance Klapper, owners
June Klapper Otto, manager

I was completely fooled by the green and ivory vintage look of the Wolf River Diner. I thought it was the genuine article, miraculously kept alive and mint despite the passage of time. The curved chrome legs of the dinette chairs still held their shine; the green vinyl seats are still supple and soft; the shamrock Formica table tops are unscarred; the padded banquettes squishy and comfy. "It's all new," confides June Otto.

The Wolf River Diner is a new theme restaurant that successfully captures the nostalgia of the 1950s roadside diner. Opened on Memorial Day weekend 1998, it replaces the old Wolf River drive-in operated first by June's grandparents, Bob and Jean Klapper, and then by her parents, Bob and Nance Klapper. As the business outgrew the small kitchen, they tore down the old restaurant and replaced it with a new brick building, then outfitted it with a collection of authentic 1950s memorabilia—stuff they'd saved from their own childhoods ("They never throw anything away," explains June)—and new reproductions of classic restaurant pieces.

The Klappers hired an interior decorator to take the restaurant back to the future, and the result is so authentic you too will be convinced the place is a miraculous holdout from the time of poodle skirts, vinyl record albums, and Elvis. Slide into one of the green padded booths and let your eyes wander over the artifacts prized by a generation of baby boomers. Over there is an old pair of roller skates—the kind you clamped on over your shoes and tightened with a metal key (even I had a pair of those)—and the transistor radio you held to your ear as you skated down the sidewalk. While Sis stayed at home playing Cootie and Bubby tinkered with

Tinker Toys, Big Brother took his best girl out dancing at the corner malt shop, plunking quarters into the Wurlitzer jukebox to hear such hits as "Yakety Yak" by the Coasters and "School Days" by Chuck Berry. At the Wolf River Diner you can feast your eyes on the past while feasting on a half-pound Big Bopper Burger and a Green River float.

"There's two places to Eat . . . at Home and Here," the menu boasts on its front cover. The fare is a combination of authentic, slow-cooked favorites and stuff like the "humongous fungus" portabella sandwich that the folks of the 1950s could never have imagined. Best-sellers include the Muddywaters—the traditional hot beef sandwich spiffed up with a clever name—and morning biscuits and gravy, which June calls "the cat's meow. We've got the best biscuits and gravy between here and Texas." The Highway 10 Pile-up is a popular choice for breakfast and is "made with everything but the kitchen sink. It's got hash browns, scrambled eggs, mushrooms, cheese, you name it," June says. A late night–early morning version is the Hangover, which June describes as a Highway 10 Pile-up in an omelette.

With ten years under her belt as manager of the Wolf River Diner and before that the drive-in, June knows the eating habits of her customers. "If it doesn't end in casserole or stew, they don't order it," she laughs. "Anything with cheese and gravy sells like hotcakes; they like it slopped all over on top. We're a gravy, cheesy kind of people, I guess." June estimates that more than 75 percent of them are tourists and travelers who have been coming for years "as part of tradition." Just this morning I had some guys in who stop every time they take a fishing vacation. They've been coming for twenty-five or thirty years." Others regularly make the drive from Oshkosh—a thirty-five-mile round trip—for the diner's chicken dumpling soup and strawberry shortcake. The chicken dumpling soup is rich and thick, with diced carrots, chunks of celery and celery tops, and dumplings like homemade noodles. A bowl of it with a chaser of strawberry shortcake—"You won't believe it til you see it!" the menu tempts—is the perfect midday summer meal.

June has been part of her family's restaurant since she was an infant put down for naps on the bread shelves ("I remember knees shuffling past," she says), yet she is surprised that she has become so enamored with the job. "Trained by a family collective," she enjoys the creative, people-oriented work that brings "instant job satisfaction, instant gratification on a minute-by-minute basis." She is involved with every aspect of the job, from making homemade bread and cinnamon rolls to scrubbing grease off the kitchen walls, and is now introducing her own children—daughter Brooklynn and son Brandon—to the family line of work. Proudly, she notes, "They're the fourth generation to be part of the restaurant. It's really a family affair."

IOLA
Crystal Cafe ⦿ 🍴
126 North Main Street
(715) 445-9227
M–Su 5:30 A.M.–7 P.M.
Judy Bolier

When owner Judy Bolier's mom, Ann Moerke, began commuting between
Stevens Point and Iola thirty-eight years ago to operate the Crystal Cafe,
there were still many older people who spoke Norwegian and asked for the
traditional foods from their homeland. Ann prepared graut—milk por-
ridge—and learned how to make the lutefisk and lefse served during the
Christmas season. "I'm not Norwegian," she told me ten years ago. "I'm
German. But there was such a strong Norwegian flavor in the town, I
figured I'd have to go along. I remember the old Norwegians sitting there
speaking Norwegian. They used to sit there eating sugar lumps we had in
bowls for coffee until the state said no."

Ann retired a few years ago at age eighty, having worked hard her
entire life, leaving Judy in charge of the very successful cafe that stands as
a landmark on Iola's main street. Judy's own daughter, Jennifer, works a
few times a week even though she has a full-time job in Stevens Point,
making her the third generation of Moerke women to have had a hand in
the business.

The legacy began in 1966 when Ann, recently widowed, was faced
with earning a living and providing for her six children. "I never went to
high school," she told me, "but started working in restaurants at sixteen. I
learned to cook on my own after I got married, and so I looked at the
world and thought, 'I could run a restaurant.' When I bought the Crystal
Cafe, it was a dive, a real junky place. I always had plans to change it, but
they came slowly as I could pay. At first Judy and I ran it ourselves. We
commuted three or four years from Stevens Point and then moved here. I
remember early on counting up the money at the end of the day and saying
to Judy, 'We had a really good day, Judy. We took in eighty-two dollars!'"

The cafe has come a long way since then. Now the social center of
Iola, the Crystal Cafe is bright and roomy, with cream-colored walls decorated with wooden rosemaled pieces and copperware. The Old World
warmth is further accentuated by the blue-checked vinyl tablecloths and
the use of Norwegian on the menu, which promises "all homemade cooking from scratch"—or *Hjem Laget Pai.*

Although Judy does little advertising, word-of-mouth recommendations and articles in various magazines and newspapers have brought in
flocks of adventure eaters and highway travelers from across the region.

Popularity leads to acclaim, and the Crystal Cafe has received numerous recognitions, including being voted the "Best hometown diner in Wisconsin" in 1996 by readers of *Wisconsin Trails* magazine. I've been in all the other cafes, and I have to admit the readers' choice is right on the mark. The piece of cherry I pie I consumed in very short order was hands down the best I've ever had. It was still warm from the oven, with a delicately browned crust subtle in flavor and perfectly flaky and a thick filling of fresh Door County cherries. As the T-shirts advertising the Iola Cafe say, the pie is to die for.

Since the early eighty-two-dollar days when Ann sold "a couple of hot beefs and maybe a few other things," the Crystal Cafe has become deservedly famous for a variety of homemade items. These include chicken dumpling soup, buttermilk pancakes, fresh roasted meats, hand-pattied burgers, homemade bread, pies, cookies, and Sunday morning cinnamon rolls. Judy is proud of everything served here. "It would be much easier to buy everything, but this is what I want. It would be cheaper and easier if we went to boxes and instants, but it wouldn't taste as good! You know the difference, then why not go to a chain restaurant?"

Ann rarely used a recipe for anything she made, and Judy follows suit today. Instead she relies on a "feel" method—"until it feels like such and such." Several years ago, the *Milwaukee Sentinel* requested the recipe for cinnamon rolls, but there was none to send. Ann said ten years ago, "A lot of the things I make, I make just by thinking them up. By inventing. The blueberry-cherry pie and raspberry-peach pie are top sellers. Do you think you could think up twenty pies a day? I get bored and make things up."

During the period of their ownership, Ann and Judy have noticed the disappearance of the old Norwegian ways and the increasing isolation of the elderly. For quite a few years, they hosted a "family" Christmas dinner at the cafe for seniors who were alone during the holidays. "It got smaller and smaller and finally stopped," Ann recalled ten years ago. "Before, people took care of the elderly, but now they put them into nursing homes." As in countless other cafes throughout the states, the elderly feel at home at the Crystal Cafe.

Says Judy, "We treat out customers like family. We have their coffee on the counter before they sit down, and we know their likes and dislikes—who prefers their eggs over easy, who likes their bacon crisp, who likes dry toast instead of buttered." Breakfast and lunch are the busiest times at the cafe, with the townspeople meeting to share the latest news, conduct business, strengthen friendships, and connect with people from surrounding towns who stop in while shopping, golfing, or bow hunting. "For a lot of people," Ann notes, "the cafe is truly their social center."

On June 20, 1999, a fire destroyed seven historic buildings on Iola's main street opposite the Crystal Cafe. It was a devastating loss to the small town, says Judy, and she didn't feel she could reopen the next day. But she did, and people flooded into the cafe, wanting to look at the charred mess across the street and talk about the fire. The day after was a time for people to express their grief and remember the people and businesses the buildings had housed during the past hundred or so years. The old buildings were replaced with new ones, but Iola doesn't look or feel the same. "Some people don't like them because they don't look old," Judy says. Still, the indefatigable spirit of the town lives on, thanks in large part to the Crystal Cafe.

LYNDON STATION
Sandy's Lyndo Inn and Cafe
111 East Flint Street
(608) 666-2045
M–Tu 6 A.M.–2 P.M.; W–Su 6 A.M.–8 P.M.
Sandra and Adam Trynzolyn

A funny thing happened on the way to the Lyndo Inn on a Saturday morning in July. I met several cyclists riding across America, got trapped in a traffic jam, stopped by a cop, and sidelined by a parade—all within eyeshot of the cafe.

"What's going on?" I asked the state trooper directing traffic.

"You mean, what did you stumble into? It's a parade."

Of course! Parkfest. Lyndon Station's big summer party. The Juneau County town of 474 people plays host to a two-hour parade, with enough units throwing candy to keep the kids happy until Halloween. Realizing I wasn't going to get anywhere fast, and knowing that I also wasn't going to have a productive visit with Sandy and Adam at the cafe, I scrunched down on the curb opposite the cafe and watched the parade. I saw the fire trucks roll by, listened to the tinny middle school band from nearby Mauston, and laughed at the lady dressed as the Statue of Liberty with a citronella torch in her right hand. Like the kids bouncing up and down beside me, I even caught a few Tootsie Pops and the real prize: a full-size Hershey bar with almonds.

When I finally sat down at the horseshoe-shaped counter of Sandy's Lyndo Inn a few days later, Adam Trynzolyn looked up from his plate of eggs and hash browns and chided, "You said you'd be here Sunday."

"I was here Saturday," I replied, "but couldn't get across the street."

Adam laughed, remembering what Saturday had brought down Lyndon Station's main street. He and Sandy have had a curbside view through the windows of the cafe since 1992, the year they purchased the

Lyndo Inn from previous owners Casey and Mary Koscal. For over fifty years, the white clapboard building at the corner of Highway 12 and Flint Street was owned and operated by Casey's sister, Martha Jorzak. The building itself was erected in a community raising bee in 1933 after the previous building on the site, the town's general store, burned to the ground.

You will want to linger in Sandy's Lyndo Inn to savor the atmosphere, the company, the food. Not much has changed over the years. The aging tin sign on the wood screen door has not been replaced; dropped panels have not obliterated the original tin ceiling; the old red Coca-Cola floor cooler has not been sold. Generations of customers—both local and distant—have passed through, made friends with first Martha, then Casey and Mary, and now Adam and Sandy, and left their comments in the guest book.

Among my favorites:

From Brian and Vera, snowmobiling on 1/20/95: "Great food! Best hot beef sandwich I've ever had. Friendly owner and friendly people! Guarantee we'll be back again!"

From Nancy, of Barron, Wisconsin, on 11/26/95: "When I was a child my family, then living near Chicago, vacationed in the Cumberland, Wisconsin, area. We always stopped in Lyndon Station at this cafe for breakfast! That was over twenty-five years ago! My last visit was when I was nine years old."

From Jack and Deb of Elgin, Illinois: "Good Meal—An evening finding Lyndon from County Rd H—no sign at HH and J to lead to Lyndon Station—so we got to 12/16 and found it the long way around. We recommend only that you serve frozen peas rather than canned."

Jack and Deb may not have been pleased with the peas, but locals and travelers alike agree that a meal at Sandy's Lyndo Inn is like Sunday dinner at Mom's. Among the favorites are hot beef, made with fresh roasted meat and real mashed potatoes, barbecue ribs, Friday's beer-battered fish, and burgers made from Black Angus beef. What's a burger without skin-on fries and a malt (a "real malt," my waitress points out) made with Morning Glory ice cream whirred in a green Hamilton Beach malt machine? The pie lover will be disappointed here, for the pie case is filled with commercial pies, but a variety of other desserts and Sandy's homemade cookies are always on the menu. One year, my friend Ken and I stopped while on the weeklong bicycle tour known as GRABAAWR and ate crunchy sugar cookies with abandon. We reached Lyndon Station early in the day after a competitive sprint from Mauston, and Sandy's fine cookies were just the power-packed fuel I needed to pedal the rest of the day's ride into Portage. Thanks, Sandy.

MANAWA
Gorman's Family Restaurant
310 South Bridge Street
(920) 596-2615
M closed; Tu–F 6 A.M.–2 P.M.; Sa 6 A.M.–1 P.M.; Su 7 A.M.–1 P.M.
Barb and Bob Gorman

Barb Gorman is just wrapping up the noon rush when I sit down at her counter for a chat. We don't get far before she is called into the kitchen, which allows me to join the four men shaking dice at the table behind me. I had heard the dice crackling on the table while Barb and I talked, and I was anxious to see what was going on. I drag a chair up to an unoccupied corner of their table, introduce myself, and boldly ask what they're playing.

Several days a week they are here—Tom, Dick, Harry, and Joe—enlivening their noon meal with a little chance and excitement. Two of them play their own version of the standard game of bar dice, also known as ship, captain, crew or 6-5-4. They shake and roll so rapidly that I cannot see the spots on the dice, but they do and know the status of the game at any given time despite the conversation that flows in and around it. They shake to see who pays the group's bill and who leaves the tip for the waitress. "We've kept informal track of the game from day to day, and it's amazing how it all evens out," I'm told.

Despite the noise and animation, the dice game appears to be oblivious to everyone else in Gorman's Family Restaurant. While the guys shake, rattle, and roll, an older man sits at the counter doing a crossword puzzle, drinking coffee out of his own Wile E. Coyote mug brought from home ("He thought my mugs weren't big enough," Barb explains), and a woman reads a paperback novel in a booth up front. Intently focused on their own diversions, the two pull themselves away from the community that they came to the cafe to absorb.

The good food is undoubtedly a diversion as well. Today's special of hearty beef stroganoff, garden fresh green beans, and a dinner roll is the perfect preamble to Barb's apple pie, which the teenage waitress enjoys at the counter with a heavenly roll of her eyes. Other consistent favorites are the Friday fish fry of hand-breaded perch, green pea soup, and the homemade baked goods, including bread. Be sure to request it for toast. Barb's vanilla torte especially is in demand for dessert. "They get really crabby if there's none in there," Barb says.

MONTELLO
Mary's Coffee Cup ¶●¶
15 Montello Street
(608) 297-7385
M–Su 5:30–2 P.M.
Mary and Mike Klug

In the kitchen at the back of Mary's Coffee Cup, Mary Klug fries eggs, bacon, and sausage for the breakfasters waiting at tables in the dining room. She is the only cook on duty this morning and can't leave the grill, so she motions for me to come in and talk while she works. I have never been invited into a kitchen before, and I eagerly seize the opportunity. I am constantly impressed with the multitasking of cafe owners, and I have a hard time taking notes while marveling at Mary's flurry of activity. I stand behind her, leaning against a stainless steel work counter, and peer into the plastic tub of cut boiled potatoes. They're real. As is everything else here.

As we talk, people come and go from the kitchen door, pausing to say hi to Mary and chat for a minute or two. Mary not only juggles three or four breakfast orders at a time, she can also carry on several conversations. For eleven years Mary has done the same, fulfilling a long-time dream of owning her own small town restaurant. Every weekday morning she arrives a half hour before the cafe's official five-thirty opening, turning on the grill, making the first pots of coffee, and preparing the day's soup, pies, and noon special. She is both cook and waitress until eight thirty, when a single employee comes on board. Stir and repeat five days a week, ten hours or more a day.

The rewards come in the form of close friendships with customers, especially the men in the daily coffee groups who become fixtures at the table in front of the artificial fireplace. Almost every morning they gather about six forty-five, staying for an hour or two. During this time, around this table, "all the fish are caught, all the deer are slain, and all the world's problems are solved." Left to themselves, the men discuss medical bills, medical practitioners, and medical problems. When I join them and ask why they continue to gather day after day, they joke:

"To get away from the wife. She'd put me to work."

"To see who's still around."

"We gotta be here or otherwise they'll talk about us. We gotta protect ourselves!"

As the years pass, members of the coffee group pass away and are replaced by others who carry on the comfortable ritual. Ten years after my first visit to Mary's Coffee Cup, I detect little change. The men are gathered around the same table. Mary's collection of salt and pepper shakers is still displayed on shelves throughout the cafe, the floor is still vinyl with a pattern of red brick. There are no new surprises here.

At least not to me. But to three Iowans passing through on their way to the Experimental Aircraft Association show in Oshkosh, the cafe is an eye-opening experience. "Those are the biggest pancakes I've ever seen," the man tells the waitress, handing her his empty plate. "That's because we never let you leave hungry," she replies. Leaning across the table to the two boys sitting there, the man raises his eyebrows with confirmation. "Didn't I tell you this would be a great place?"

NEKOOSA
Chong's Country Cafe
324 Market Street
(715) 886-3848
M–F 7 A.M.–7 P.M.; Sa 7 A.M.–1 P.M.; Su 8 A.M.–1 P.M.
Chong Jaggar
The men gathered for coffee at the counter of Chong's Country Cafe in downtown Nekoosa get up and leave en masse, leaving me and Leo Coulthard from Wisconsin Rapids as the sole occupants. Leo drops in about five or six times a week, usually on his way to or from the nearby casino, where he spends most of his time since his wife of fifty-seven years died in March. "I come here because they treat me nice, and because they treated my wife nice," he confides. To prove his point, he shows me a cream cheese container filled with Chong's homemade strawberry rhubarb jam. Across the lid is a piece of masking tape that reads "Leo." It's his own personal jam—his favorite. Chong makes it especially for him.

When she can spare a minute in the kitchen, Chong chats with us briefly at the booth we share. She once owned a restaurant in Stevens Point but sold it. "I was on my way to the casino," she explains with a slight shrug of the shoulders, "and I saw this for sale and bought it. I thought Nekoosa could use another restaurant. I guess I traded in my chips and gambled on this instead! Twelve years I've been here."

Chong's cafe is beautiful, filled with old wooden booths with their own decorative mirrors, lovely floral carpet, a vintage tin ceiling, and cornice molding. Unlike Unkie's Cafe next door, this is a woman's cafe, decorated with taste and flair. And, as Leo says, "It is clean, too. That's why I like it here."

Leo is a credible restaurant critic because he owns one himself. "I'm probably more critical than other people," he notes, "and know when they've made a mistake." He applauds Chong's efforts and praises her cooking, which includes everything from simple breakfasts to a tempting array of pies and other desserts. Today's list features lemon meringue, Dutch apple, rhubarb custard, pecan, and strawberry pie and strawberry shortcake—in pieces so perfect they'll have you, like Leo, coming back day after day for more.

NEKOOSA
Unkie's Diner
318 ¹/₂ Market Street
(715) 886-4590
M–Su 5:30 A.M.–8 P.M.
Corey Bagnowski

I ate baked chicken, dressing, mashed potatoes and gravy, and corn on Sunday afternoon at Unkie's Diner. I was the only stranger there and felt terribly out of place. Everyone else knew each other and passed conversation between tables, leaning out over the ends of booths to include even people sitting at the end of the room. To my left, a couple planned their wedding with the help of her mom and dad. In the adjoining dining room to my right, two women prepared for a baby shower that would take place later in the afternoon. This is interesting, I thought to myself. Two life rituals bookending the lives in the cafe.

When owner Corey Bagnowksi's mother, Rose, was pregnant with him, she worked at this very cafe. He worked here at age fourteen, then went on to spend several years with Kentucky Fried Chicken before becoming a truck driver. He thought he'd give running the cafe a try after it sat idle for four months, having closed with the departure of the previous owner. He gave it the name Unkie's after his own nickname, given him by his niece. Now he's everyone's uncle.

"He just more or less picked it up," says Rose proudly, pointing to the awards he has won despite having owned the cafe for only a few years. In 2001 the *Wisconsin Rapids Tribune* named Unkie's Diner Best Fish Fry. Readers were asked to call in and identify their favorite fish fry, and then the newspaper sent a five-person taste test crew to eat, evaluate, and rate the top fish fries. Coming out on top was Unkie's. "He was here only two months when he got the award," boasts Rose.

More recently, Unkie's placed second in the *Tribune's* taste test for burgers. Rose can't say exactly what makes Unkie's burgers so good but explains that they start out big—either one-third or one-half pounders— and stay big after cooking. Clearly, they don't leave much room for the many varieties of homemade desserts available at Unkie's. I followed up my chicken dinner with burgundy pie—blueberry, cherry, and cranberry filling in a pastry crust. It was acceptable but a bit glooey for my discriminating pie palate. I think I would have preferred the triple chocolate pie, spiced carrot cake, or peanut butter dessert.

NEW LISBON
Corner Cafe |●|
101 East Bridge Street
(608) 562-5445
M–Sa 5:30 A.M.–3 P.M.; Su closed
David and Heather (Oatsvall) Dahl
Heather (Oatsvall) Dahl's parents, Delbert and Kim Oatsvall, were operating the Corner Cafe, in the former post office building in downtown New Lisbon, the first time I stopped in for a visit. Heather was then twelve years old and away at camp, but her younger brother, Paul, then eight, was building card houses at the counter while Delbert tended the kitchen and Kim played the daily cribbage game with a handful of locals. Heather is now twenty-five, married, and mother of Ashlie. Paul has graduated high school and is looking forward to entering the National Guard. Delbert is now a minister. Kim ran the motel the family owned, and after it was sold she returned to the cafe to work for Heather.

"When I was a kid, I hated the restaurant," confides Heather. "I despised it. I didn't want anything to do with it. I resented that I didn't get to do kids' things. It took up a lot of my spare time. But when my parents decided to sell, I couldn't stand to watch anyone else run it. I mean, this is our family business. We built it up. My parents are very happy that I've taken it over."

Delbert remains "on staff as a consultant," but Heather clearly has found her own way. She is efficient and businesslike, yet takes a minute or two out from her work to greet people she knows well, having literally grown up alongside them. She brings coffee to tables before people sit down and places orders in the kitchen window as soon as people walk through the front door. As she scurries around the dining room serving people—she is the only one on duty—she walks into one man's seeing-eye dog and apologizes, "Sorry, Bailey," with as much affection and intimacy as she shows her customers.

"I love the restaurant now," she resumes. "It was my choice to take it on, and that's the difference. No one made me work. I determined to do it, and I'm not the kind of person to give up on things."

Like daughter, like father. Delbert and Kim Oatsvall were both working at a large Tomah supper club, resenting the fact that family time meant a few stray hours here and there. When the chief of police in Camp Douglas told them the Corner Cafe, closed for nearly two years, was available, they took a look. "The realtor tried to talk us out of it," Delbert recalled when we first met. "She told us we wouldn't want to look at it, and then after we did, she said we really shouldn't take it seriously. The place was filthy and needed lots of money."

"Delbert was competent and determined," Kim joined in. "And once he gets an idea, he's going to make it work."

Now in its second generation of family operation—and in its third because Ashlie helps out by busing tables and filling coffee filters—the Corner Cafe is an unqualified success. You can still find quality home cooking, community coffee groups such as the nine o'clock Back Room SOBs (the "Sweet Old Boys," Heather smiles), and authentic friendships strengthened by pranks and laughter. The menu features the regulars' favorite selections, such as Bob's By-Pass—hash browns topped with sausage, onions, green peppers, and two eggs—named for Bob, who always ordered this, and then had a by-pass operation. "They all joked that this caused his heart attack," explains Heather. Variations of this favorite heart-stopping breakfast are the Double By-Pass—Bob's By-Pass smothered in sausage gravy—and the Triple By-Pass—the double topped with shredded cheddar cheese. Please pass the nitroglycerin.

OXFORD
The Cafe
116 East Ormsby Street
(608) 586-4141
M closed; Tu–Sa 6:30 A.M.–2 P.M.; Su closed
Terry and Sherri Tellier
Sara Tellier has been crossing off the days on the July calendar one by one. With each X she is a little bit closer to the day the family will shut the door on the Cafe and head north for two weeks of vacation. She is now down to four hours and counting. Her mother, Sherri, floats through the kitchen door to the dining area with a singsong chant of "we're going on vacation." There is a lightness, almost a giddiness about the Telliers' anticipation of two weeks away from the Cafe, which has been the center of their life for the past twenty-two enjoyable and satisfying years. It is impossible not to note their excitement, and one of the regulars playfully picks at them: "You'll be sorry. While you're gone, we're gonna find a better restaurant."

Pat Schable, Terry's mom, bought the restaurant in 1983 "with the understanding that I'd be here two years, then my son would take it over." Terry did take it over, but Pat still lends a helping hand a few days a week and throughout the summer. In the kitchen, Terry prepares slow-cooked real food, such as scalloped potatoes and ham, lasagna, and daily soups, which Sherri dutifully logs into the notebooks she has been keeping since 1986. The notebooks come in handy when Terry is at a loss to come up with yet another creative daily special; looking back at past choices helps to solve the problem. "It's hard to think of different things to make," notes Sherri, who as the designated baker turns out "homemade everything except bread": pies, cinnamon rolls, turnovers, cakes, doughnuts. Other favorites at the Cafe include old-fashioned soda fountain treats like malts and sundaes made from hand-dipped ice cream.

The Cafe is an amalgamation of different decades of decorative elements, from the late-nineteenth-century Eastlake back bar salvaged from the local International Order of Oddfellows hall, to the birch paneling and avocado green vinyl flooring installed during the 1970s. No one is certain just how long the cafe has existed, but a black and white photo of Lydia's Cafe depicts it in the 1940s. Terry has been told that the entire block save the cafe was destroyed by fire and that the cafe remained open to feed the exhausted firefighters. Charlie, a wit drinking coffee at the counter, explains that the fire started in the shoe store. "Over a thousand soles were lost."

"You're such a stand-up comic," Terry retorts, "only you're sitting down!"

A round of pitiful groans fills the cafe. Sara rolls her eyes and announces, "We need a vacation!"

PITTSVILLE
Laura's Corner Cafe
5355 Second Avenue
(715) 884-2450
M–Tu 6 A.M.–7 P.M.; W 6 A.M.–3 P.M.; Th 6 A.M.–7 P.M.;
F 6 A.M.–8:30 P.M.; Sa–Su 6 A.M.–1 P.M.
Laura Zdun

At the exact geographic center of Wisconsin lie Pittsville and Laura's Corner Cafe, formerly the Little Bear Cafe featured in the first edition of *Cafe Wisconsin*. Laura Zdun had waitressed at the Little Bear, and when it came up for sale, she bought it. "I'd always wanted to try my own cafe," she explains. She enjoys the work and the people, but her children tell her to "sell it before you die, Mom, because we don't want it." Laura knows it's not for everyone, and she realizes the time will come when she'll want to move on to something else. "My goal is ten years."

When the former owners sold out in 1997, they took with them the namesake black bear and his friend, a taxidermied raccoon. For most of the people who return year after year on their way up north, the animals are lost friends who came to characterize the place. The kids especially wonder where they went. But Laura says, "That's about the only thing different here. That and the name. I just carried on as it was because you don't change a good thing." The chicken dumpling soup, huge omelettes, hash browns, two-inch-thick French toast, pies, and daily plate specials remain consistent favorites.

Five years into her ownership, Laura confesses that even she is surprised that she loves the work so much. "It's just a lot of fun," she says. Much of the daily fun comes from the antics of the guys who wind up in the Dog House, a wood cutout strung with gold hooks from which hang little white dogs, each labeled to represent one of the men. There are Fred, Carl, Bud, Erv, Ray, Bill, Rol, Tony, and LeRoy, who today occupies the hook in the doghouse doorway. "Every day they come in and sit at the counter drinking coffee," Laura explains. "And it isn't long before one of them says something or does something that lands them in the doghouse. It costs a quarter to get out, and the money goes to the end-of-the-year Christmas party."

Four out of seven times, it's Rol who winds up in the doghouse, but ninety-six-year-old Erv, a staunch Republican, often challenges him. Laura can't keep from laughing as she recalls some of Erv's more memorable jokes and quips. "Last year, Senator Feingold stopped in for breakfast. I told him, 'If you can get him to vote for you, I'll buy your breakfast.' You know what Erv said to that? 'Don't bother. I'm ninety-five years old and don't have a vote left in me!'"

POLONIA
Polonia Cafe
7419 Highway Z
(715) 592-4900
M closed; Tu–Th 7 A.M.–2 P.M.; F 7 A.M.–2 P.M. and 4:30–8 P.M.;
Sa–Su 7 am.–2 P.M.
Diane Dombrowski

"I love my cafe," enthuses Diane Dombrowksi as she takes a break from cleaning up after the day is over. She is sometimes surprised at just how much because in the beginning she was a bit unsure that she wanted to get involved. She had worked as a school cook but didn't have restaurant experience. When a local couple, Ken and Diane Kizewski, approached her about running a cafe that Ken would build, she decided to give it a try for one week. She immediately felt at home with her "cafe family," loved the experimentation and creativity that cafe cooking provided, and thrived on the organization and management that running a successful business required. Four years into her one-week experiment, Diane and her staff have a smooth running system and plenty of dedicated and supportive customers who return day after day for her menu that features homemade everything, including bread, muffins, and pies. Other favorites are the side pork ("like bacon except it's not smoked"), real mashed potatoes and gravy ("that's number one"), and the roasted meats bought fresh from Waller's in nearby Nelsonville.

The Polonia Cafe resembles a house from the outside. Built on the foundation of a former bank that was moved down the street, it has a refined newness that sets it apart from the great majority of small town cafes. And everything including the food is high quality and real: oak moldings, a working stone fireplace, and beautiful carpet. On the walls hang framed photos of historic Polonia and a sketch in ink on a coffee-stained paper napkin of one of the Catholic churches that dotted the nearby landscape.

"This guy sat at a table one morning and drew it," Diane explains. When the waitress went to clear the table, she gathered it up and asked, 'Is this yours, sir?' He said, 'It's yours,' and walked out. We don't know who he was, and he never came back. But he must have known that old church because his drawing looks just like the photograph.'"

REDGRANITE
Curve-In Cafe
1000 Bannerman Avenue
(920) 566-0188
M–Su 5:30 A.M.–8 P.M.
Pam and Byrdie Chamberlin

You can smell Fridays in Wisconsin. They smell like fried perch, cod, smelt, catfish, and any other variety of fish or other critters that live in lakes or the sea. At the Curve-In Cafe, Pam Chamberlin provides the requisite Friday fish, but takes into consideration those folks who gave up abstaining from flesh with Vatican II by offering three or four other daily specials. Today's hobo dinner—ground sirloin, cubed potatoes, carrots, and onion cooked in a foil packet (who remembers making this over the campfire?)— is a best-seller, as are the Italian sausage with creamed cucumber salad and pepper steak over rice. Good eating at the Curve-In Cafe is always a sure thing, but it can also be problematic: there's just way too much to choose from.

Witness today's dessert board boasting all homemade selections: blueberry cream, apple, cherry, blueberry, pumpkin, and pecan pies; bread pudding; and cheesecake with fruit topping. How can I possibly decide?

It's easy for ninety-one-year-old Elmer Swersinske ("That's German because of the *e*; if it were an *i*, I'd be Polish"), whom Pam points out as one of her regulars. Elmer and his daughter, Bev Colburn, make the ten-minute drive to Redgranite from their side-by-side homes near Berlin almost every day. And almost every day, Elmer orders hot beef with a side salad for roughage.

"What is it about hot beef that makes you eat it day after day?" I ask Elmer.

"It just agrees with me. I never cared much for chicken," he answers.

Bev is a little more philosophical, theorizing that the real mashed potatoes, shredded soft-cooked beef, and homemade gravy is "comfort food" because it recalls Sunday dinners at home with the family. She may be on to something because Elmer is preoccupied with family—or rather the loss of it. He tells me again and again about the death of his son in a car accident in the 1960s and of the recent loss of his wife. Elmer comes again and again to the Curve-In Cafe because he is part of the cafe's family. "I come here because everyone knows me and talks to me," he says.

Elmer is hard of hearing but easy of talking. He repeatedly asks me to speak up, and when he wants to know how I pronounce my name, I shout it across the table. We are sitting in a booth, and I am facing another booth in the corner of the dining room. When I say my name, the two men in the booth whip around with eyes like saucers. The one sitting back to back with Elmer, exclaims, "That's my name!"

I jump up from my seat next to Bev and say, "You're kidding!"

"No!" he says, "I'm Raatz," pronouncing his name as I had pronounced mine despite the difference in their spellings.

The five of us marvel at the coincidence. Russell Raatz lives in Redgranite, and, like Elmer, he is a regular at the Curve-In Cafe. "I come in two, three times a day," he says. "If I don't come in, I feel like I'm missing something." Of course, he knows Elmer and Bev. I'm the new one in the group, and he now knows me because we share the same name—and because I'm just nosy enough to have plopped myself down at Elmer and Bev's lunch table.

As Bev wraps up leftovers for her dog waiting in the car (a true doggy bag), Elmer gets up to say goodbye to his friends. I see him walk into the kitchen and give hugs and kisses to Pam, the cooks, the waitresses. He gives each of them a dollar—a tip—to thank them for all they do.

"That's Elmer," my waitress tells me. "He's our best customer and our best friend."

WAUPACA
Waupaca Cafe
107 West Fulton Street
(715) 258-9699
M–Th 5:30 A.M.–3 P.M.; F 5:30 A.M.–9 P.M.; Sa–Su 6 A.M.–2 P.M.
Jeff and Maureen Olson
The sign on the front of the Waupaca Cafe promises The Finest in Home Cooking, and it does not lie. The refrigerator case filled with beautiful handmade pies attests to the prowess of owners Jeff and Maureen Olson, who have made a career out of preparing traditional Wisconsin food in simple and pure ways. After polishing off bowls of Jeff's clam chowder and the best-selling "anything with mashed potatoes and gravy," customers have a hard time selecting the perfect piece of pie to round out their meal. It might be Dutch apple one day, pecan, coconut cream, or any other of a dozen varieties the next.

Jeff has been at the restaurant business since 1976, when he was a high school kid washing dishes alongside his mother, both of them part-time help. When the cafe came up for sale, they bought it. Jeff was only a high school student, and when most of his friends were still sound asleep, he'd unlock the door at four in the morning to prepare the day's baking before heading off to school. After his mother died in 1981, he faced long days on his own and remembers, "I started to hate it." He sold the restaurant in 1984 but kept a jealous and proprietary eye on it through a succession of different owners. "I was really disappointed in how run down it got, and even though it wasn't mine, I always felt like it was mine."

When the opportunity came in 1998 to buy back the cafe, Jeff did. His wife, Maureen—who as a sixteen-year-old employee quit on him during his first tenure as owner—and his two sons joined him. His old customers returned. Jeff is back home now, glad to be up to his elbows in pastry dough and mashed potatoes. "It's nice," he says. "It's very nice."

WONEWOC
Country Gals Cafe
215 Center Street
(608) 464-7277
M 6 A.M.–2 P.M.; Tu closed; W–Th 6 A.M.–2 P.M.; F 6 A.M.–8 P.M.; Sa 6 A.M.–2 P.M.; Su 6:30 A.M.–1 P.M.
Diane Hess and Nicole Jackson
It's late on Friday afternoon in September, and I am cutting cross-country between Baraboo and La Crosse. On the side of the road just outside of the Juneau County town of Wonewoc, a young man is sitting beside a

backpack. I stop and ask him if he wants a ride. "No, thanks," he replied. "I wanna walk." The joke is a common one, even though it becomes increasingly less funny the more you hear it.

There was no man, but I did indeed have my car set for Wonewoc, and it being about dinnertime on a Friday, I couldn't help but think fish fry. Since moving to Indiana thirteen years ago, I have had, from time to time, intense cravings for deep-fried cod come the end of the workweek. Early on in our transplantation, we hooked up with a midsummer, Friday night fish fry fundraiser put on by a rural volunteer fire department. In great anticipation, we headed out to the Wilbur fire station, a pole barn the size of a Hoosier basketball court. As the kids flocked to the huge red fire engine that had been moved out of the station house, the adults waited in the serving line. My first glimpse of the fish people were carrying on Styrofoam plates to the picnic tables made my heart sink. It wasn't beer-battered cod loins fried to a golden brown in a vat of hot oil, that's for sure. It was frozen minced fish squares served on a squishy white bread bun. Not fish and most certainly not a fish fry.

So, on a Friday night in Wonewoc, I happened to drop in at the Country Gals Cafe. Determined not to make a glutton of myself on the offerings, I admonished my waitress to bring only the half portion, which came with my choice of potatoes (I chose au gratin) and the salad bar. A little salad of iceberg lettuce, a tomato or two, and perhaps some shredded cheese sounded just fine as a pre-fish appetizer. I picked up my plate and headed into the adjoining dining room where the salad bar stretched out along the side wall like JV players on a bench.

My waitress did not sufficiently prepare me for the glory I saw there! She didn't tell me that owners Diane Hess and her daughter Nicole Jackson spend most of Thursday and Friday afternoons preparing salads for not only the Friday night fish fry but also the entire weekend. With gleeful abandon, I plunged in, building myself a lettuce salad topped not only with tomatoes, but also sliced cucumber, green pepper, mushrooms, hard-boiled egg bits, and cottage cheese. I took this plate to my table and then headed back for more: potato salad, coleslaw, pasta salad, pea salad, broccoli salad with raisins and bacon, taco salad, Waldorf salad, Jell-O, and fruit salad.

Did I say it was all homemade? There are no jars opened and dumped into this salad bar, which I hereby anoint the Wisconsin Queen.

By the time I got through with my rainbow of salads (and, I admit, a few second helpings), I was far less interested in the fish than when I walked through the door. Nevertheless, I took a deep breath and my first bite, and then continued until not a morsel was left. The loins were about the size of a bar of soap and so scrumptious that, like any glutton worth her weight, I ordered more. I decided to forego the au gratin potatoes to make room, but even at that, I practically rolled out of the Country Gals Cafe when I left. But not before having three pieces of irresistible pie—butterscotch, apple, and lemon meringue—packed for the road.

The lucky folks in the Wonewoc area have been treated to Diane Hess's magic in the kitchen for over twenty years, though Country Gals, located just a few blocks off the 400 State Trail, has been in existence for only the past four. Diane began her community cooking career in 1983 when she signed on to run the food concession at a local sale barn. She branched out ten years with a little chuckwagon she set up at area auctions, and in 1999 went into full bloom with the addition of the cafe. Since then she has successfully managed to do all three jobs at once with the help of her daughter, Nicole, her mom and expert pie baker, Edith Burkhalter, and her loyal and supportive staff. "There're days when it gets a bit too much," she admits, "but there's nothing else I'd rather do."

. . . .

NEXT BEST BETS

ATHENS
Athens Country Cafe
220 Alfred Street
A mom-and-daughter effort worth your attention.

FRIENDSHIP
Friendship Cafe
303 Main Street
Try the kolaches, jam-dolloped Czechoslovakian pastries.

MARION
Steve and Mary's Main Street Cafe
216 North Main Street
Watergate Cake was on the menu the day I dropped in for a bite to eat. When I asked what it was, my waitress wrote out the recipe on the back of my ticket. Combine two boxes of pistachio pudding with a box of white cake mix, a little oil, and eggs. Bake and frost with a mixture of Cool Whip and a third box of pudding. (Great for St. Patrick's Day, as I inadvertently found out.)

MONTELLO
Cafe Hilltop
125 Church Street (Highway 22)
An entertaining local crowd packed the place for Friday fish. My salmon patties were a delicious alternative to deep-fried cod.

New London
The Pantry
317 South Pearl Street
The Borden advertising mural on the side of the building proves this place has been here a long while. Don't pass up the pie.

Princeton
Country Cafe
428 West Water Street
You won't find turtle soup anywhere in the state but here. Available on Fridays, along with clam chowder and an unbeatable fish fry buffet complete with homemade desserts.

Redgranite
Warren's Family Restaurant
140 West Bannerman Avenue
A bit more upscale than the average small town cafe and with impressive home cooking. This restaurant was known for years as the Quarryside Diner; the red granite quarry, where the locals kids swim, is just out the back door.

Rosholt
Coffee Cup Restaurant
167 North Main Street
Home-cooking smells and tastes in this little box of a cafe, with one of the neatest vintage neon signs in Wisconsin.

Saxeville
Crossroads Cafe
Highways A and W
Sweet, eggy rhubarb custard filling in a frozen crust, but darned close to the real thing.

Schofield
Mom's Cafe
3406 Schofield Avenue
On any given Wednesday, there will be fifteen or so people who can't pass up the special of stewed chicken gizzards on rice. Other favorites on Mom's menu are hot beef, hot turkey, and hot pork sandwiches, homemade breads, soups, pies, and any type of casserole.

WAUPACA
Tooter's Place
1036 Royalton Street
Perched at the counter like a bird on a wire, you have a panoramic view of the
real potatoes being peeled by hand in the kitchen, the freshly frosted cake, and
the still-warm pies under the counter. What you see is what you get.

WEYAUWEGA
Pine Cafe
129 East Main Street
Breakfast only, Monday through Saturday, 6 to 10:30 A.M.

WILD ROSE
Chatter Box
457 Main Street
No engaging chatter in the box when I was here, but a nice piece of pie filled
with Maine blueberries. The short-cut frozen mixed vegetables used in the
chicken dumpling soup lent color but no flavor.

Chippewa Valley

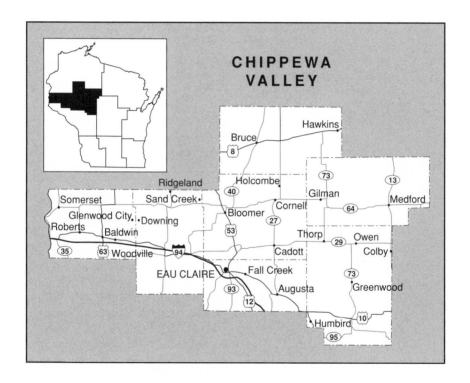

CHIPPEWA VALLEY

Hawkins
Bruce
8
Ridgeland
Holcombe
73
13
Somerset
Sand Creek
40
Gilman
Medford
Glenwood City
Downing
Bloomer
Cornell
64
Roberts
Baldwin
27
Thorp
Owen
53
29
35
63
Woodville
94
Cadott
Colby
EAU CLAIRE
Fall Creek
73
93
Augusta
Greenwood
12
Humbird
10
95

AUGUSTA
Red Dot Cafe 🍽
312 East Lincoln Street
(715) 286-2068
M–F 6 A.M.–7:30 P.M.; Sa 6 A.M.–4:30 P.M.; Su closed
Doris Krueger

Doris Krueger, owner of the Red Dot Cafe since 1975, still can't believe she turned cooking into a successful career. She laughs when she confides, "I never wanted to be a cook. I never wanted to get married and be a housewife and do housewife chores." As a child she spent more time helping her dad on his Augusta-area farm than she did working alongside her mother in the kitchen. Domesticity made few demands on her until, as a young wife living in Chicago, she began caring for her husband's elderly uncle. She remembers how "particular" the uncle was about where she was to buy certain cuts of meat, the best sausage, the freshest produce, and baked goods. "I'd say he was the one who taught me how to cook, how to shop for meats, cook a roast, and make gravy, that sort of thing," says Doris.

After the uncle died, Doris, her husband, and their children found their way back to Augusta, where Doris found part-time work at the Red Dot Cafe. Four months later when the restaurant came up for sale, the family bought it. Suddenly and quite unexpectedly, Doris had gone from a neophyte cook to a professional one. The uncle's favorite foods crept into the menu, and today Doris gives him credit for chocolate éclairs ("I make them every so often"), lemon meringue pie, chicken chow mein, Polish sausage and sauerkraut, and the Red Dot's cold plate—a selection of luncheon meats, cut vegetables, and homemade potato or macaroni salad. Still amused by the ironic course of events that has her looking forward to her thirtieth year of cafe ownership, Doris says, "I had no idea at first what all I was getting into. I started out doing everything myself: cooking, waitressing, bookwork. I built it up until I couldn't do it all myself anymore. He'd [the uncle] be pretty proud of me today, I think."

I ask Doris about her cafe's unusual name, one I hope leads to an interesting story.

She smiles and laughs, "I can't say why it was named that, but when I came the back wall was covered with red dots, and a sign on the roof had red dots on it. Even the curtains had red dots!" Doris gradually got rid of the red dots (leaving the ones on the menu cover and the asphalt pavement out front) and filled the front walls with a variety of signs with humorous sayings, such as: "PRICES SUBJECT TO CHANGE ACCORDING TO CUSTOMER'S ATTITUDE!"

But on my return visit in 2002, the signs themselves had been replaced by framed historic photographs of the Augusta area and a collection of brightly colored McDonald's Furbies, miniaturized versions of the interactive robotic toy. There were Furbies in the front windows, on the counter, over the kitchen window, and in the back room on the salad bar. "I brought in a few to entertain the kids," Doris explains, "and then everyone started bringing them in. One day a little girl counted them and we have just over two hundred. 'Do you know how to take care of them?' she asked. 'When they get dirty, you just lick'em clean!' We've got the Vikings playing the Packers on the salad bar." Sure enough, wrangling it out over the iceberg lettuce, cut veggies (including fresh tomatoes from the plot out front), and selection of homemade pasta salads are a team of purple Furbies and another team of green and yellow Furbies.

The Red Dot Cafe is popular for its Thursday fried chicken ("I'd walk over fire for her chicken," says a man at the community table), Friday secret recipe beer-battered cod, chicken dumpling soup made fresh every morning, and daily specials. The food is good, but the humor and high jinks are even better. Come to eat but spend some time absorbing the fun. On the wall over the counter is a clock labeled: "God's Time / Last of October–First of April." A second clock, set an hour later, is labeled: "Government Time / April 07–October 27."

Behind most of the fun lies Doris herself, but sometimes things have a way of backfiring. "We were in Florida for vacation and found some Sold signs. We bought a couple and for an April Fool's joke, I put them in the front window. You should have seen how upset people were! But the joke was really on me because a few days later I got an offer for the place! They couldn't come up with the financing, so I'm still here."

BALDWIN
Shelly's Northside Cafe
1040 Curtis Street
(715) 684-3037
M–Sa 5 A.M.–4 P.M.; Su closed
Shelly and Keith Tollefson
At Shelly's Northside Cafe I found what seemed like everyone in Baldwin eating lunch. "This is the place," my waitress Val told me. It definitely is. By twelve thirty, the daily special of barbecued ribs is already gone, and Val climbs up to write a new special on the board. Anyone coming late to Shelly's has to substitute beef tips in gravy for the ribs. But no one is complaining. They know everything at Shelly's is sure to be good.

Even Val's son, Caleb, and his two friends are sure of it. In summer, Caleb walks over to the cafe two or three times a week for lunch. Today he orders chicken strips and fries, and his friends—perhaps not as familiar with cafe food as he is—play it safe and get an order of fries and an order of bacon. That's lunch?

The tanned men at the center table know they'll need more than that to get them through their day working construction. They smoke cigarettes between forkfuls of mashed potatoes and gravy, talking loudly to each other and to men sitting across the room. Not only is Shelly's full, it is also very noisy.

People come and people go. Two elderly men get up and leave their place at the table to two men who have been waiting a few minutes. Three college-age girls enter and sit at the counter—reluctantly, but there are no other places available. Two travelers at the table behind me discuss the menu. I hear her say, "I'm not sure I want to eat here."

He says, "We can leave if you want to," but they stay and order breakfast. I want to lean over and reassure them, "This is the place."

Shelly Tollefson had worked in a number of area restaurants before the desire to get out on her own inspired her to sit down with Mel and Laurence Vier, under whose ownership the Northside Cafe was featured in the first edition of *Cafe Wisconsin*. "I'd never met her before," Shelly explains, "but I thought the first step was to talk to her about the restaurant." Mel was convinced that Shelly had the experience to succeed and, despite the bankruptcy of the intervening owner, Shelly has "turned it around and is doing well."

Mel agreed to work alongside Shelly for a few weeks until she was securely on her feet. After she and Laurence sold the restaurant, they traveled for a few years, sold their house, and downsized into a mobile home. "But I thought there has to be more than just sitting around," Mel says, so when the first weeks ended, she decided to stay on and wash dishes. "I love it. I'm here being part of the restaurant, seeing people, but I don't have any responsibility."

Instead, all of the responsibility falls on Shelly's sturdy shoulders. When the daily lunch special runs out, she scrambles to find another to feed the loyal lunch crowd. She relies on tried and true favorites, saying, "If it doesn't come with mashed potatoes, they won't eat it." Among the most requested items are biscuits and gravy—brought by Shelly from her previous job at a truck stop—and rhubarb pie. But Shelly also schedules and supervises the help, pays the bills, and maintains the aging building. Her initial investment was considerable and included adding on to the kitchen, installing an exhaust system, updating the building to meet current state codes, replacing the windows and siding, and redecorating. Now, seven years later, she is secure and confident in her decision.

Everyone crowded into the dining room testifies to that. Shelly's Northside Cafe is the place.

BLOOMER
Main Street Cafe 🍽
1418 Main Street
(715) 568-2233
M–Su 5 A.M.–9 P.M.
Donald Stoik

Born and raised in Bloomer, Donnie Stoik "got his feet wet" in the restaurant business at nearby supper clubs when he was nineteen. By the age of twenty-eight, in 1981, he was ready to step out on his own and discovered the Spanish-accented Matador restaurant, on Bloomer's Main Street, "for sale cheap. It was really a mess! Dirty. Needed remodeling and lots of cleaning. But I looked at it and knew what could be done. It's like when you go to an auction or a thrift sale and see a piece of junk and think, 'I know what can be done with it.' Buying it was totally spontaneous, and I think if I had waited I would have had a hundred people trying to convince me out of it."

Hiding under the Matador's black and white wall tiles and glaring fluorescent lights was Donnie's diamond in the rough. Authentic knotty pine paneling and cozy pine booths—each with its own overhead lamp— replaced the Mediterranean decor, and over the years, antique farm implements such as lanterns, tractor seats, and other miscellaneous pieces have found places on the walls. Everyone is happy with Donnie's makeover now, but Donnie remembers how the group of retired men who gathered in the Matador every day to play cards worried that he'd kick them out. "It didn't matter to me," he laughs. "I even went out and bought them a round table." A very small round table in the front window. Just "small" enough for nine or more men to bump knees and deal cards for an hour a day.

Not far from the Round Table, an inflatable Holstein cow suspended from the ceiling by a transparent thread bobs above the refrigerated pie case promoting the satisfying Wisconsin drink: real milk. "We sell a lot of cows throughout the year," Donnie laughs as he points out another floating in the adjacent dining room, converted from a section of the city's old movie theater. The cavorting Holsteins and the liberal use of the Real dairy seal on the colorful menu indicate Donnie's commitment to using only authentic dairy products—milk and cream, whipping cream, butter, cheese, sour cream, and ice cream. On his "brag wall" in the appended dining room, Donnie proudly displays his highly coveted award for being the 1987

Wisconsin's Dairy Best Restaurant of the Year and a plaque honoring him as the 1990 Dairy Products Promoter of the Year, along with many other local and state awards.

"You know," Donnie tells me, "the woman at the milk marketing board told me that out-of-state tourists know Wisconsin as the dairy state, and they have this image of Wisconsin restaurants serving only real milk, pots of cream on the table, real butter, things like that. That's what they expect, and that's exactly what we give them. Pies made with real cream, butter served on pancakes, free refills on milk, and all year long free ice cream with pie."

"Did you see our bumper sticker?" he asks as he slides one across the table. "It says, 'And don't forget to leave room for the pie.'" We like to say we have the best pie north of Highway 10. That's the highway that runs right through Osseo [famous for the Norske Nook and nationally acclaimed pies]. We're really famous for pies."

In 1992 Donnie added the stage and screen area of the former theater as a pie-only kitchen and since then it has doubled in size. The Main Street Cafe now produces well over fifteen hundred pies a week, sold both in the cafe and wholesale to area shops and restaurants. Donny leads me into the pie kitchen and points out the boxes, bags, and crates of supplies, pausing at the cooling counter to linger over fresh-baked Dutch apple, pecan, strawberry cream cheese, and blackberry cream cheese pies. "Last Thanksgiving, we made three thousand pies," he tells me proudly. "This year we expect to make five thousand. We'll run three eight-hour shifts twenty-four hours a day for the three days before Thanksgiving, with one person hauling pies between the shop and the stores." Donny wouldn't dream of missing the work and has already scheduled time off from his full-time job as a rural mail carrier.

Despite the availability of Main Street pies in area food stores, pie sales at the restaurant haven't fallen off. "People still go out to eat," Donny tells me. The best sellers are the "signature" raspberry cream cheese, pecan-caramel cream cheese, and caramel apple, with pumpkin and pumpkin cream cheese being top sellers during the Thanksgiving season. Donny has made pies such a large part of the business because "people are just fazed by something I thought was normal." He grew up eating pie as a regular part of family meals but realized that to most people, pie is a special, elusive treat. The Main Street menu itself reflects the types of foods Donny's Mom made for the family, with a slightly unusual twist. "I come from a supper club background, so that's why we offer prime rib and steak and lobster," Donny explains. "I noticed that people go out to eat at night, not just during the day, so we're open a little later and offer fancier dinners." Noon specials, served 11 A.M. to 2 P.M., seven days a week, are more traditional cafe offerings: chicken served with real mashed potatoes, vegetables, and gravy; Friday deep-fried or broiled fish; and on Wednesday, the Main Street's famous pork roast, potato dumplings, and sauerkraut. "There's a lot of old-time Germans around here who grew up on that," Donny explains. "Mom always made that at home when we were growing up."

When he was offered the opportunity to buy the entire theater building, Donny expanded not only the pie kitchen but the dining area as well. The Main Street Cafe now seats about two hundred people, with banquet-sized tables available for groups of twelve or more. Despite its size, Donny says, "We're still the same cafe. We've got the same menu, the same recipes, the same people in the kitchen."

To many people, the Main Street is actually a better cafe. One of the most appreciated improvements is its smoke-free policy. Donny notes a decrease in asthma-related problems among his employees, less odor absorption by foods, and a productive shift in his customer base. "We've gotten new customers who come in to eat. The smokers sat for hours drinking coffee. It's really so much nicer in here since we went smoke-free."

BRUCE
Katie's Cafe
706 North Main Street
(715) 868-1500
M–F 7 A.M.–7 P.M.; Sa–Su 8 A.M.–2 P.M.
Katie Verhagen

From the corner of the counter, a man swabbing egg yolk with homemade toasted bread supervises the comings and goings of the locals at Katie's Cafe. "How are you?" he asks a newly arrived couple. "Just fine, now that we got our restaurant back," the woman responds.

On December 29, 2001, Katie's Cafe and two neighboring businesses—a hardware store and a bowling alley—burned to the ground. "As I stood here and watched my restaurant burn to the ground, I decided right then and there I would rebuild," says Katie. "I love this place. It's my second home." For countless years a restaurant had stood on this site, including McDowell's Cafe, featured in the first *Cafe Wisconsin*, and the locals had become accustomed to gathering there and sharing the latest news and opinions. Katie did rebuild and reopen Katie's Cafe, and you—as well as the locals—will be very pleased she did.

It is a refreshing and fine thing to eat pancakes at the counter of the brand new, shiny clean cafe, surrounded with customers who know and love Katie and her food. They are convincing testimony to her earnest emphasis on homemade everything—from bread and other bakery items to meat loaf and other daily specials. And they should know. One of them is a former owner; another's wife was an owner before that; and yet another known as Goose, a former town board member (who did not vote for the construction of the new library, he is quick to point out), is a former owner of a cafe in a neighboring town. Restaurant men all, they know what they're talking about.

Katie worked in food service for twenty-five years before realizing she might as well earn the money herself instead of working for other people. Originally from Appleton, she had often visited friends in Bruce and eaten at the restaurant. "I always thought it was a gold mine of a place," she explains, "and when it came up for sale, I bought it." She was devastated when it was reduced to rubble but immediately located a local contractor who had just completed a renovation of the supper club he owned on a nearby lake. Her selection of quality, durable materials such as blond knotty pine for wall covering and ceramic tile for the floor is a convincing indication that she intends to be in Bruce for many years to come.

"A lot of people thought this place was too good for Bruce," she tells me. "They thought it was too fancy, but they don't give themselves enough credit. They deserve it." The new Katie's Cafe is not elaborate; it is plain and fancy, to borrow an Amish phrase. It is simple and clean, spacious and bright, with the crisp newness of a just-completed building. To soften the edge—and to soften Katie's heart—the locals soon christened the new cafe with gifts: replacements of the vintage kitchenware and other antique items that Katie had lost in the fire. Slowly the walls are filling with red-handled eggbeaters and steel graters, old stoneware crocks, baking pans, and other pieces that Katie had intended to pick up at auctions and flea markets. "They decorated it just the way I would have when I got around to it," she says. "They knew we had a lot of antiques, and every day they keep bringing in more."

Despite the brand new setting, up-to-date kitchen, and never-before-enjoyed equipment and accessories—"That pie case is a pretty nice thing," Goose says—the cafe remains at heart exactly what it was: a place to eat, talk, laugh, conduct business, and meet friends. During the months when the cafe was being rebuilt, the regulars had to adjust their daily schedules, with most choosing to eat at home rather than go out to another place. One day, Katie laughs, she was walking on the street when she heard her name being called. Inside their RV, across the street from the cafe, sat a local couple eating sandwiches. "You've got to get that place opened," they told her. "Without you, we have to make our own lunch!"

COLBY
Colby Cafe
100 West Clark Street
(715) 223-4006
M–Th 6 A.M.–6 P.M.; F 6 A.M.–8 P.M.; Sa 6 A.M.–2 P.M.; Su closed
Cyndi and Wayne Satonica
On July 13 I am in Colby attending a Christmas party at the Lions Club building.

The girl passing out door prize tickets wears a red felt cap that reads, "I believe in Santa Claus." In the corner is a decorated Christmas tree; icicle lights hang from the ceiling; green and red metallic ornaments reflect the couples on the dance floor below. It is Christmas in July—Cyndi Satonica's annual gift to her regulars, complete with piñatas and wrapped presents for the children, Christmas gift door prizes, and the Harmony Four polka band. (A bumper sticker on the leader's music stand reads, "Old musicians never die. They just decompose.")

Like so many other cafe owners, Cyndi always wanted a place of her own. She had worked for the Waffle House franchise and for several owners of small town cafes before she landed a job cooking at the Colby Cafe. When the owner wanted out, she stepped in and bought it. Fifteen years later, she and her restaurant play a major role in the lives of the locals, as well as truckers and travelers who routinely pass by. The couple on the dance floor attracting the most attention for their moves drove over from Owen. As a trucker, he has been stopping at the Colby Cafe for many years. "It's a great cafe," he tells me. "And we love to dance," she says.

Cyndi learned to cook as a child, experimenting first on the hired hands on her parents' farm, then moving on by age eleven to preparing entire meals for the family. A sickly child, she spent more time in the house than in the fields, and because her mother preferred fieldwork, the kitchen duties naturally fell to her. When she grew up, she continued on that path.

At the cafe, she prepares everything from scratch. Bread, cakes, pies, cinnamon rolls, caramel rolls, and other items round out the bakery requirements—and they make great door prizes at the Christmas party as well. As Cyndi's daughter, Nicolle, reads out numbers, Cyndi distributes blue gift certificates for homemade pies to those who raise their hands. When the certificates are all distributed, Nicolle announces, "For everyone who got pies, Mom's going to be gone next week. So don't come in unless you want me to make it." The crowd laughs as Cyndi blushes and comes back with a not altogether convincing, "She's really good."

The Colby Cafe is not particularly distinctive in its appearance. Housed in an old neighborhood grocery building at the corner of Highway 13 and Clark Street, the eatery is easy to pass by. From the highway heading south, watch for the RESTAURANT sign peaking out from the side of the overhanging awning. It is a hardworking building, filled with hardworking folks. The days before the Christmas party, Cyndi managed all of the everyday tasks plus took on more. She prepared gallons of coleslaw and pounds of hot turkey, pork, and beef for sandwiches to serve her guests at the party; cubed melons and cut vegetables for dipping; and picked up several marble sheet cakes from the local grocery.

Dressed in everything from black spike heels and silk dresses to hiking boots and cutoff jeans, Cyndi's guests pile the specially prepared food onto foam plates and cluster at cafeteria-style tables. A few dance to the music of the Harmony Four, but most prefer to sit and watch. One couple shares a dance or two with college-age grandsons and granddaughters. The mixing of generations is a pleasant thing to witness. But the great majority of partygoers are senior citizens, an age group that Cyndi estimates represents at least 90 percent of her regular customers. On this Christmas night in July, however, all are merry and gay, young again as they enjoy the music of the Harmony Four.

CORNELL
Stacker Cafe
609 Bridge Street
(715) 239-3636
M–Su 5:45 A.M.–9 P.M.
Paula and Ed Jenneman

"Anything different is bound to be good," I tell Paula Jenneman, owner of the Stacker Cafe, as I order a piece of sour cream peach pie to go with my lunch. I heard a woman say this about ground cherry pie at another cafe while researching the first *Cafe Wisconsin*. She was right—the ground cherry pie was excellent—and I have since taken her advice to heart.

I have sampled a lot of pies but never yet encountered sour cream peach. It is a deceptively simple single crust pie with a brown sugar crumb topping, baked in the oven yet served cold with a squirt of aerosol real dairy whipped cream. It is a refreshing touch of cool summer on a hot July day but would have been better made with fresh peaches instead of canned.

I do eat more than just pie—"one of the traveling eater's basic food groups," according to Jane and Michael Stern in *Blue Plate Specials and Blue Ribbon Chefs*. Paula's daily special offering of cheesy cauliflower soup and egg and ham salad sandwich, with my addition of potato salad, was also excellent. I have to admit, though, when I first read the special board and saw egg and ham salad sandwich, I was confused. I thought I had to choose between egg salad and ham salad, but Paula set me straight. It was an egg salad sandwich with bits of ham in it. So simple, so obvious, yet like the pie, I had never before encountered it.

The Stacker Cafe replaces the former Red's Garden Cafe on Cornell's Bridge Street, featured in the first edition of *Cafe Wisconsin*. Named after the world's only existent pulpwood stacker, located next to the Chippewa River, the cafe opened in 2000. Paula's first year was spent waiting tables, and then when the owners decided restaurant business wasn't for them, Paula bought it. She loves the new spin on restaurant work, which she has been doing for some ten years. "It's the most fun thing I've ever done," she enthuses. "It's like not having a job at all."

Many of Paula's loyal customers followed her when she left her previous employer, and many others have wandered in on their own and stayed. Still others, like the man enjoying the daily special of Salisbury steak in the front window, stop while in town visiting friends and relatives. He is not likely to ever come in again, yet he has words of praise for Paula. "That was mighty good. Just like home."

In fact, Paula tells me, many of the recipes used in the restaurant come from her family, including her mother's recipe for oatmeal raisin cookies and her grandmother's recipe for chocolate chip. Her customers become accustomed to everything homemade, and with twelve employees to help her, Paula serves food to keep them coming back. Among the favorites are pie and the homemade sourdough bread, soups, biscuits and gravy, liver and onions, ribs, and hot beef. "Our Friday night fish fry is a big thing, and so are our fresh potato pancakes," she says.

Pale yellow pine boards line the walls of the little cafe, and the wood floor and painted high back booths, wood tables, and chairs add to its old-timey, mellow mood. The booths are framed by what look like columns and gingerbread from a Queen Anne porch. Hand-painted signs on the bathroom doors read Lumberjacks and Lumberjills. On the walls, historic photos of Cornell depict street scenes, the old dam, and the namesake pulpwood stacker. Surrounded by history, Paula proudly points out something new: the Restaurant of the Month Award from *Discover Wisconsin Radio*, received in January 2001 "for exemplifying Wisconsin at its best." Paula had owned the cafe for less than a year when hosts Stephanie Klett and Rick Rose stopped by and fell in love with the peanut butter pie.

Cyclists on the Old Abe Trail connecting Cornell with Chippewa Falls will find the Stacker Cafe a well-earned reward for their miles. Watch for the sign on the trail directing you to the restaurant.

FALL CREEK
Village Haus
333 West Lincoln Avenue
(715) 877-2841
M–Th 6:30 A.M.–2 P.M.; F 6:30 A.M.–2 P.M. and until 8 P.M. during
school year for fish fry; Sa closed; Su 8 A.M.–1 P.M.
Sheri and Jim Coldwell
My mother-in-law, Eleanore, was with me the day I drove on county highways through rolling countryside to the village of Fall Creek looking for
the Village Haus cafe. As I typically do, I drove into the heart of the commercial area, which in Fall Creek is about a block long, and searched for
the cafe. I couldn't find it, so I headed west toward Eau Claire until I came
upon a sign by the side of the road that read: HAP B DAY / MIKE 59 MILT /
OPAL WENDY. This is it, I thought. The small town cafe. Where the community meets and celebrates.

"Birthday parties have become a tradition here," owner Sheri Coldwell
tells me. "Customers all pitch in for a gift and a card."

And truth be told, we weren't seated at the table five minutes before
a couple came in for lunch in honor of the wife's eighty-first birthday. I
didn't think to ask whether she was Opal or Wendy. They ordered "our
kind of salad," and were brought a huge chef's salad split in two. It was
overflowing with crisp fresh vegetables, including carrots, cucumber, broccoli, and ripe red tomatoes.

Everything at the Village Haus is homemade if not homegrown. Sheri
wouldn't have it any other way. She bakes her own bread, cookies, cinnamon rolls, and other treats ("pie is not a big thing here") and picks vegetables straight out of her one-acre garden. When she finds herself short
of seasonal produce, such as rhubarb, she asks for donations from area gar-
dens by putting a sign out on the road, and then treats her customers with
the results. The vegetables find their way into a variety of popular items,
including autumn squash stuffed with Italian sausage and tomatoes. "I sometimes send out postcards to people when I make it," Sheri says. "If I didn't,
I'd have a lot of people mad at me."

Other favorites at the Village Haus are the lumberjack omelette—
big enough to feed Paul Bunyan—and the pan-fried walleye and eggs breakfast. Sheri expands the "basic menu" with daily specials like stuffed cabbage and Irish stew, and a special cranberry nut pie made famous by Jim's
grandmother Josie Griswold, who once owned the cafe Mom's Country
Kitchen in Babcock.

Sheri was assistant manager at a bakery when she began to get the
itch to work for herself. Jim had worked at a restaurant in college, and with

their combined experience they began looking for a small restaurant to buy. In Fall Creek they found the perfect place—and got the motel to boot. "We started noticing that the motel was sometimes used for 'four-hour naps,' and we had kids and didn't think that was too good an idea." They broke through all the dividing walls and converted the motel into their home, all the while preserving the little cafe on the west end. The entire place has a funky vintage-motel-combination-grandma's-dining-room feel to it. It's way cool, decorated with a creative scattering of antiques, such as the quilt-style curtains at the front window, and children's artwork. The family portrait in crayon by one of Sheri's children contributes much to the homey, personal atmosphere. "I want people to come here and feel like they're sitting at the dining room table with family and friends."

That's exactly the way it felt when months later my sister, brother-in-law, and I returned to the Village Haus on a near-zero-degree Friday night. Two men in the back room talked across a table, their empty plates pushed aside to make way for elbows and forearms. Up front, a family of three (soon to be four by the size of the woman's belly) finished their dinner in front of a small color television tuned to *America's Funniest Home Videos*. On the coldest night of the year, with the three of us wearing our coats at the table to stay warm, their young son, quite oblivious to the cold, happily licked a chocolate ice cream bar.

The deep-fried cod was already gone by the time we arrived, so we happily substituted the pan-fried walleye filets. The special fish fry menu included salad, choice of potatoes, and "baked goods"—thick slices of home-made white bread spread with butter. On the side of the bread plate was a paper cup filled with a creamy white spread flecked with green. I was impressed with the sophisticated added touch of herb butter—until I tasted a bit on the tip of my knife and discovered tartar sauce! "It's a good thing you didn't spread it all over your bread," my sister and brother-in-law laughed.

Our large dinner salads were beautiful, made with an assortment of fresh, crisp greens, sliced cucumber with artistically peeled rinds, slices of Romano tomatoes, chopped celery, and green peas. "This is not your typical cafe salad," my sister noted, and she's right. A remarkable salad in a small town cafe is almost an anomaly. I was served a bowl of rusty iceberg lettuce with a few sorry tomato pieces so often during my Great Wisconsin Cafe Adventure that I nearly swore off cafe salads altogether.

Our waitress was attentive yet left us alone to enjoy our dinner. Just as my brother-in-law finished the last piece of my walleye, she brought over an unexpected plate of honey-walnut bars, part of the menu's promised "baked goods," which we easily polished off.

"What a great cafe!" my sister exclaimed as we climbed into the car for the trip back to Eau Claire. "What cafe includes dessert with your meal? It was just like home. No, it was a lot better than home!"

GLENWOOD CITY
Kate's Cafe
143 East Oak Street
(715) 265-7418
M–F 7 A.M.–4 P.M.; Sa–Su closed
Kate Platson-Phalin

The combination bakery-cafe is my favorite type of small town eatery, particularly on stormy summer days with black clouds roiling across the sky. In 1991 my then-four-year-old son, Peter, and I waited out the storm in the Midway Cafe. Today I am back, and it is raining again in Glenwood City. The cafe is no longer the Midway. Current owner Kate Platson-Phalin has renamed it after herself.

When I telephoned ahead to see if the cafe was still open, Kate's waitress, Rosie, informed me of the change. "It's even better than it was," she assured me, and advised me to "bring an appetite." Taking her at her word, I scheduled my visit for the first thing in the morning so I could have breakfast. I wasn't disappointed. The hand-cut cake doughnut and Rosie's Favorite Irish Potatoes—hash browns scrambled with egg and chopped onion—suited me well.

Despite the passage of time and change in ownership, the cafe looked pretty much as I remembered it. It has been repainted and redecorated with painted handsaws, sketches, and paintings done by Kate herself, who unknowingly left the items that remained benchmarks of my first visit: the high back booths and the vintage display rack of Kellogg's dry cereal. As I enjoyed homemade pie, Peter munched on dry frosted flakes ("Leave it to a kid to pass up homemade!" I wrote). I couldn't believe that the little boxes of frosted flakes were still there—or rather there again.

Kate grew up in Glenwood City and attended the local elementary school before her family moved to southern Wisconsin. Life took her many places and through many careers before depositing her once again in her hometown. She was a hairdresser, real estate student, bartender, RV park manager, and gaming industry worker in Las Vegas before she realized that she wanted to "move back home." Her parents and other relatives were still here, so she returned and purchased a full-scale restaurant just down the street, opening with the help of her sons, Robert and Jason. When the Midway Cafe came on the market, she made the switch to an easier workweek and a slightly different kind of cooking.

"I never dreamed I'd be here again," she laughs. She remembers coming to the cafe when she was a child and can close her eyes and see it again in her mind. Rummaging in the basement shortly after she bought it, she found pieces of the original curved counter and dragged them upstairs. A man eats breakfast at one of them as the other waits for the next group of coffee drinkers.

A wonderful cook and baker, Kate credits her Aunt Phyllis with teaching her how to bake. "Baking was a growing up thing," she explains—something she slowly developed by helping her mother, grandmother, and aunt in the kitchen. Kate acquired business skills at Southern Nevada Community College and in her many other careers, and today she successfully combines her family recipes with bookkeeping and management. And family is a key ingredient to her success. Her staff of three—Kate, daughter-in-law Carole, and Rosie—is supplemented by parents Bud and Rethia Platson, who help bus tables and wash dishes between visiting with old friends.

Kate is proud of the muffins, pies, cakes, cookies, doughnuts, sweet rolls, bread, and other bakery items made from scratch from family recipes. Against the rear wall is a 1920s-era, glass-fronted bakery case filled with Kate's temptations, and near the register, three glass jars filled with round cookies. "Baking is what I really like best," she says, but she also provides a menu of more hearty fare. Roasted meats, real mashed potatoes, burgers, and a list of daily specials will keep you going until dessert. The sweet rolls and caramel rolls are so big that most customers share one.

It is not easy to think up a new special every day, and sometimes Kate makes mistakes. "Carole makes this wonderful chicken garlic fettuccine. I like it best of anything she makes, and one day I decided to make it here. But people didn't get it. They just wouldn't order it. I sold a lot of burgers that day. Maybe I should have made it into a hot dish!"

"With cream of broccoli soup and crushed potato chips on top," I add, and we both have a hearty laugh. No respectable Wisconsin hot dish would be considered well dressed without them.

Despite the occasional misjudgment, Kate "sticks with my gut instinct about what sounds good" on any given day. Soup and chili are in demand year-round, as well as meat-and-potato meals. Her menu boasts "fresh homemade meals" every day, and she does not disappoint.

Kate has decorated the cafe with a collection of antique kitchen pieces: stoneware crocks, graniteware bowls, copper molds, green-handled utensils. It is not uncommon for customers to be heard saying, "I had one of those," she notes. Seeing things from the past often inspires them to dig through the barn for the old porcelain creamer that has been lying beneath the abandoned tires for years. In this way, Kate's Cafe has acquired many choice pieces, including a stovetop toaster, a Watkins egg separator, and a Coca-Cola tray used by the cafe's original owners. "It makes my customers feel they're part owners," she smiles.

GREENWOOD
Greenwood Family Restaurant
125 North Main Street
(715) 267-3133
M closed; Tu–Su 7 A.M.–7 P.M.
Ernesto and Linda Rodriguez
Ernesto and Linda Rodriguez, owners of Greenwood Family Restaurant since February 2001, were away on a shopping trip to Marshfield when I arrived at about three o'clock for a visit. Left behind to tend the store and answer my questions was Patty Bright, who cut me a piece of homemade carrot cake with cream cheese frosting and drew me a Pepsi. I was tired, and the sugar perked me up enough to carry on my half of the conversation. Patty ran through the basic information and then launched into a description of the activities of the men's daily coffee klatch. From seven to nine each morning the counter is filled with men. They talk, drink coffee, and shake dice in a leather, felt-lined cup to determine who will pick up the tab.

The game is similar to "poker with dice," explains Patty. One by one the men shake and pass the cup. The best roll means you're out—saved from paying the bill for that round. The rounds continue as men come and go, with winners receiving a chip good for a free cup of coffee. The chips are really little laminated green squares of paper on which are written Greenwood Family Restaurant in ballpoint pen. Chips are kept and later redeemed, usually by men who lose the dice shaking game. Sometimes in lieu of cash payment, Patty receives a handful of chips collected over a period of days or weeks.

While the men gather at the counter, the ladies prefer a table where they drink coffee and eat toast. Like clockwork, the "church ladies" arrive every day about nine, following morning mass. The days are so predictable, Patty says, they worry if someone doesn't show up when expected. Most of the regulars ward off the worry by letting the crew know if they'll be away on vacation or at an appointment.

Ernesto and Linda operated their own restaurant in Marshfield but were forced to close when the new bypass absorbed the building and lot. "We had to go out looking for another place," Linda remembers. "We looked all over. I hated this place when I first saw it because it was so small and cold. I couldn't see how it would do. But then I began to see what it could be, and we bought it. We closed down for five weeks and my brother Kevin—he's a contractor—did all the remodeling. Everyone was waiting for us to reopen. Our first day was a Tuesday, and that Friday there was a line out onto the street. I was frantic. I was running around this place like a cat on a hot tin roof."

They soon found that the locals like to eat early and get home to do the evening farm chores. As the days settled into a predictable pattern, Linda's blood pressure evened out and the grand-opening kinks disappeared. Their six-page menu includes traditional Wisconsin food—"We gotta have hot beef"—mixed with Italian, Greek, and authentic Mexican. Ernesto has a magic touch when it comes to cooking; he can taste something once and figure out how to make it. Everything he makes is from scratch, including the spaghetti sauce and specialty Mexican dishes served every Saturday night from four to seven.

I returned on a Saturday night for Ernesto's enchiladas. Served with rice and pico de gallo, the enchilada was big enough to provide me with three different meals. I ate about one quarter of it in the restaurant and the rest of it for lunch the following two days. It was wonderfully flavorful, from the filling of stewed chicken to the topping of special cheese purchased from a Mexican grocery. As chance would have it, Patty's parents ate at the next table, and even though her father is a big fellow, he too was unable to eat the whole thing. We both requested take-out boxes.

Of course, I had to save room for the fried ice cream, which Patty claims is the top-selling dessert at the restaurant—even more popular than pie. Ernesto takes vanilla ice cream and adds a sprinkling of raisins and shredded coconut, shapes it into a ball, and freezes it solid. Just before serving, he rolls the ball in a mixture of cornflakes, sugar, and cinnamon and dunks it into hot oil. Served with a couple of mounds of nondairy topping and a maraschino cherry, the ice cream is crunchy crusted on the outside and frozen on the inside. The taste, texture, and weirdness of the whole are beguiling.

The Mexican Saturdays are popular, especially with the area's Mexican migrants and senior citizens. This surprised me, but Linda theorizes that the older people are the ones who are familiar with Mexican food because they have traveled in that country. Patty's parents lived in California for many years; her father says, "I got kind of used to the food down there." Linda believes the younger generations are reluctant to try it because their idea of Mexican is Taco Bell or Taco John's. That's a shame because the real thing is found here, made by Ernesto and his two sons, Arturo and Ernesto Jr.

When Patty's parents leave, the parents of my waitress, Kim, replace them. Her mom eyes my dessert and asks, "Is that that fried ice cream?" I answer that it is and that she should try it. "I just might," she says. I am not convinced that she will. When Kim comes to take their order, she asks, "Are you going to try the Mexican tonight?" They're not. Her father orders broasted chicken. Her mother orders something equally American. (When she asks about the gyros, Kim responds, "Isn't that sheep meat?" Somehow seasoned lamb sounds much more appetizing.)

"I can tell when people walk in the door whether they're going to order Mexican," Linda says. "I'm not offended when they don't. Chances are they'll order broasted chicken or hot beef. Even though we have a hundred things on the menu, they'll always go for that."

HOLCOMBE
Lake Holcombe Cafe
4206 Irvine Avenue
(715) 595-4328
M 6 A.M.–2 P.M.; Tu closed; W–Sa 6 A.M.–2 P.M.; Su 6 A.M.–11 A.M.
Jeff and Ronda Gulich

On the Friday of Rock Fest northwest of Cadott, I find myself driving along Highway 27 to Holcombe. Not the wisest of choices, but I smirk at the cars tangled in traffic and the efforts of the locals to pull in some extra cash by holding thrift sales and selling bundles of firewood, bagged ice, and bottled water to Festers intent on seeing aging rock bands in the ninety-five-degree heat. I'd do the same if I lived anywhere near Cadott.

The traffic thins by the time I reach Cornell, and when I pull into the parking lot at the Lake Holcombe Cafe, I'd never guess anything out of the ordinary was occurring just a few miles away. The one college-age waitress inside is excited about the weekend event, however, and she eagerly tells me all about the music festival, where people camp out in designated sites and listen to the likes of Meatloaf and Creedence Clearwater Revisited from lawn chairs. "It's great," she tells me, but I am unconvinced. I decide I've got to stop by and check it out, but Jeff Gulich warns me that curiosity seekers are bound to be caught in traffic jams all afternoon and evening. I decide to let my opportunity pass.

Jeff is just closing up the cafe for the day, having escaped the onslaught of Festers by being just a little too far from the festival grounds. To his knowledge, none of the rock musicians have ever stopped in for breakfast, but he confesses that he probably wouldn't recognize them if they had. It's a shame that they came so far without making a visit to the Lake Holcombe Cafe. The music world is ripe for another prize song like "Alice's Restaurant."

Six days a week since 1991, Jeff and Ronda Gulich have slipped through the doorway joining their house and cafe and served breakfast to the people of Holcombe. They bought the restaurant from Jeff's parents after Ronda's job "went south" and she didn't follow. "We never thought about running a restaurant," explains Ronda, "but one day I said, 'Why don't we . . .?' and he said yes, and here we are."

The family doubled with the addition of two children—eleven-year-old Chloe and nine-year-old Tanner—and grew again and again to include all of the cafe's regular customers. "They really are like family to us," Ronda says. The Gulichs throw several parties a year to which everyone is invited. They include a Green Party on St. Patrick's Day ("One lady is English and didn't think much of the Irish, so we called it a Green Party," explains Ronda), a summer picnic at the park, and a Christmas trim-the-tree party. A potluck dinner follows the two or three occasions each year that the morning coffee crowd picks up trash along a two-mile stretch of Highway 27 as part of the Adopt-a-Highway program. The gatherings include games and prizes, Wisconsin lottery scratch-off tickets, and gift exchanges for added fun.

A community dining room, the Lake Holcombe Cafe is popular with all ages, from the sixth grade boys who ask their parents to take them there so they can have Ronda's homemade coleslaw to the senior citizens who gather daily to drink coffee and talk. Most of the regulars are natives of the Holcombe area, but others are retired folks from the Twin Cities who bought lake houses and wound up staying year-round. "One couple from Minnesota settled here in part because of the cafe," Ronda says. "They were looking for certain things in a retirement home, and they found them all in Holcombe. They're regulars now and come in almost every day." Still other regulars are seasonal homeowners or guests at the area's resorts. Each May, Jeff and Ronda anticipate their arrival as long-lost friends returning home for a visit. "If they don't come, or come late, we really miss them," she says.

The role of cafe owner has many demands and expectations. Ronda sends many get well and sympathy cards to customers and their family members throughout the year, and is often among the very first people in the community to learn of an illness or death. She keeps tabs on everyone's health ("That reminds me, one of our customers had an angiogram today, and I have to send a card"), vacation plans, and the status of children or grandchildren. She laughs when she explains that the cafe is often perceived to be the community information center. People call to ask about fire, police, and ambulance sirens; the schedule for local events; weather forecasts; or the location of a cheap motel. "We're the chamber of commerce of Holcombe, I guess."

But foremost among the variety of roles that Jeff and Ronda play is that of cook. Their customers wouldn't be so loyal, so much like family, if the food weren't so down-home good. Ronda relies on family recipes and the occasional help of her mother to keep her extended family well fed and happy. Breakfast is the largest meal of the day—especially on weekends—with Jeff producing countless omelettes, pancakes, and eggs at the grill. Ronda is in the kitchen early every morning preparing homemade soups, daily specials, and desserts, including her popular bread pudding and pie. The day before my visit, she picked raspberries from her mom's bushes and baked them into a pie. It is too runny to serve as wedges on a plate, so Jeff spoons it into bowls and plops on a dab of Cool Whip. Rechristened with a variety of names—raspberry shortcake, upside-down pie, cobbler—it is scrumptious and garden fresh despite its underdoneness, the undeniable mark of homemade.

RIDGELAND
Dairyland Cafe 🍽
125 Diamond Street
(715) 949-1985
M 6:30 A.M.–4 P.M.; Tu 6:30 A.M.–8 P.M.; W–F 6:30 A.M.–4 P.M.;
Sa 6:30 A.M.–3 P.M.; Su closed
Darlene and Steven Miller
I recognize both the Dairyland Cafe and owner Darlene Miller on my return visit, ten years after my first. Not much has changed. The turn-of-the-century pink cafe is now covered with gray vinyl, and the pink booths are now green. Lillie Miller, who worked at the cafe off and on for fifty years, has retired to nurse her aching knees and ankles. Lolita, who with her husband purchased the cafe in 1936, is now in a nursing home. But let me back up.

On my first visit, I was late for my two o'clock appointment at the Dairyland Cafe, and I tried to recoup lost time by speeding along the county roads connecting Chetek with the Dunn County village of Ridgeland. When I pulled into the old downtown, my heart sank at the sight of cars lining the street. Surely, I thought, the cafe must be packed with late lunch eaters. I cautiously opened the door and found Darlene and Lillie tabulating the day's collection of orders. The drivers of all the vehicles must have been in the three taverns squeezed nearly side-by-side on Diamond Street.

Despite their combined fifty-eight years of first-hand knowledge and experience, Darlene and Lillie dodged my questions about the Dairyland Cafe, instead referring me to Lolita, the previous owner, who was due any minute for her daily visit over afternoon coffee. As Lolita settled into a booth, Lillie brought her coffee and a homemade pumpkin bar. Lolita began her story.

Her earliest memory of the old cafe was as a young girl visiting her aunt and uncle in the boardinghouse they operated in the same building, probably the oldest building existing in Ridgeland today. "This was when the salesmen came in on the railroad and stayed overnight at the boarding-house," she told me. "My aunt fed them all in the dining room at the back of the boardinghouse, the men on one side of the table and the women on the other. They weren't permitted to mingle in those days."

A staircase that climbed to the second-story rooms separated the front room, now the Dairyland's dining area. The staircase encouraged further separation of the sexes, with the men congregating over beer or liquor at the bar on one side of the room, and the ladies meeting for coffee and sandwiches at tables on the other.

Sometime before Lolita and her husband bought the cafe in 1936, it was known as Sam's Cafe. When Darlene had the cafe's counter (the original men's bar) removed to make way for more tables, she found tiny silver coins good for "5¢ in trade" at Sam's Cafe. She assumes they were used as food tokens, given to patrons to be redeemed for hot beef, a piece of pie, or a cup of coffee. In 1936 Lolita and her husband tore out the center stair-case and completely remodeled the building.

"That was the good old days," she told me, recalling Saturday night dances at the hall up the street that brought scores of people into town. "Some Saturday nights we stayed open until two or three in the morning. People would stop in after dances for a soda or ice cream. Some nights we never got to bed at all. Most nights we stayed open until ten or eleven. We had to wait for the railroad men to come into town, because when they got here the first place they came was in here for a cup of coffee.

"We used to sell hot beef with two scoops of mashed potatoes and coffee for thirty-five cents. A piece of pie cost five cents and a malted milk twenty-five cents. That's why we had to stay thirteen and a half years!" she laughs. "To make some money! My husband used to say we never had enough money to get out of Ridgeland."

In 1949 the Dairyland Cafe passed into other hands, eventually be-coming the property of Donna and Wilbur Miller, Darlene's in-laws. Darlene worked for Donna and Wilbur ten years before her mother-in-law asked her if she'd like to buy it. Owning the Dairyland had never really occurred to Darlene, but she says she felt an obligation, a commitment to both her in-laws and the town, to carry on the old cafe. "I didn't want to see it close down," she says. "It's been here so long it would have been sad to see it end."

Today, several features of the old cafe reveal its age: the upright Coca-Cola floor cooler, the ice cream freezer behind the counter, the painted booths—each with its own brass coat hook and gray cracked-ice Formica top—the cupboards in the kitchen. The Dairyland has indeed survived.

Hot beef no longer sells for thirty-five cents, but the prices at the Dairyland are low, and the food is authentic and deliberately prepared. Darlene and her staff make slow-simmered soups, cinnamon rolls and old-fashioned doughnuts, fresh pie, cookies and desserts, roasted meats and gravy, real mashed potatoes, and a variety of daily specials. Despite the variety of selections, however, Darlene notes that the most popular dish is still roast beef and mashed potatoes. As if on cue, the man in the booth behind us says to the waitress, "I guess I'll have roast beef." Did he make even a cursory scan of the menu?

Darlene does note several changes over the past ten years, and foremost is that her customer base is changing. "The older men and women have passed away," she says, "and the younger people don't drink coffee and sit around and talk. I've traded in the coffee drinkers for eaters. Also, a lot of the smaller farmers are gone, and the big ones that replaced them are too busy to come in." As the population of Ridgeland ages, Darlene has moved into serving the county senior meals three times a week.

It is still too early to tell what the future will bring, but if the kids and young adults who have not grown up on traditional Wisconsin food do not begin to seek it in cafes, the cafes themselves might become obsolete—or the meat-and-potatoes meals will be replaced by hamburgers, French fries, and other foods popular with the younger generations.

ROBERTS
Roberts Cafe 🍽
208 West Main Street
(715) 749-3133
M–Th 6 A.M.–3 P.M.; F 6 A.M.–8 P.M.; Sa 7 A.M.–1 P.M.; Su closed
Dawn French
At the end of the day, Darlene Dunn, owner Dawn French's mom, smokes a cigarette at the end of the counter, keeping an eye on three boys outside the front window. They look in, gesturing to each other and shaking their heads before they summon up the courage to come through the door and ask for glasses of ice water. Overnight, the temperature has dropped almost twenty degrees, and it is no longer stifling hot. Just why the boys want the water is unsure, but Darlene suspects they are playing a game of dare.

By the looks of the place, the Roberts Cafe has served the people of the little St. Croix County town—Wisconsin's Good Neighbor of the

Northwest—for years. A couple of historic photographs over the side booths depict the cafe "then," and a survey of the place "now" reveals few changes. Peer under the counter and notice how it's made with rustic log end posts and a corrugated log face just like in the photos. The brown tweed counter top is worn on the edges and in splotches across the surface where count-less elbows and coffee cups have rubbed off the color. The vinyl stool seats and the booths are worn, cracked and split from generations of use.

Some things change and others stay the same. Previous owner Donna French is retired, having passed the cafe on in 1996 to Dawn, her longtime employee and daughter-in-law. Despite the cafe's change in name, Dawn and her staff continue to make simple foods entirely from scratch, includ-ing cake doughnuts served with their holes, meat loaf and spaghetti, and a memorable Friday night fish fry featuring battered Icelandic cod from a secret recipe that draws people from as far away as the Twin Cities. The little cafe has gotten so much busier in recent months that the real mashed potatoes have been replaced with instant ("We can't keep up. We go through a hundred pounds of potatoes a week and can't peel them all," Darlene says). Likewise the homemade bread. But don't bemoan the loss. There is plenty more good food to warrant a trek to Roberts, including a bottom-less cup of coffee for fifty cents, malts served with the silver mixing cup, and my favorite butterscotch pie.

SAND CREEK
Sand Creek Cafe and Bakery 🍽 ⅄
Main Street (Highway I)
(715) 658-1335
M–Sa 7:30 A.M.–7:30 P.M.; Su 9 A.M.–3 P.M.
Cecelia Cruse
"I see you survived your trip down the Red Cedar," Cece Cruse greeted me for the second time in less than a week. The Saturday before, my brother and sisters and their families and I had been paddling canoes down the Red Cedar River when I realized we would be passing right behind the Sand Creek Cafe. It was toward the end of a very hot July day, and no one needed too much persuading to stop for Cece's chocolate malts. So we pulled up the canoes to the river's edge and hiked through the long grasses to the top of the riverbank. My brother, Tom, sighted the rear roof of the cafe, and we followed him past a van with the license plate CC CAFE and through the door into the dark, cool inside.

Four-year-old Robby and older sister Madeline plopped down at the red counter and began to spin on the stools. There's something about kids and stools! The waitress scooped Gustafson's ice cream into five sizable stainless steel cups and whirred in milk, liquid malt, and flavoring to make our treats. Robby loved the chocolate malt he shared with his mom and mooched more from my cup.

I have remembered the Sand Creek Cafe as the Place with Those Great Malts ever since the Saturday afternoon many years ago when Scott Wilson led a group of Eau Claire pie riders there. In our tight-fitting black shorts and tutti-frutti jerseys (Cece says, "I can always tell the bikers by their Lycra"), we made quite a scene sitting in the center of the small cafe at two tables we pulled together. An older, toothless gentleman at the counter found us particularly fascinating and stared half-smiling and unblinking until we left.

Sand Creek, a sleepy little village straddling the Red Cedar River, is surely out of your way on your way anywhere, but the rustic 1920s-era Sand Creek Cafe is worth any detour. In 1976, on a visit to the area from her home in Minneapolis, Cece fell in love with the cafe's splendid oak-mirrored back bar salvaged from a turn-of-the-century Chicago ice cream parlor. "The cafe was for sale," she explains, "so I bought it." Her move to Sand Creek brought her home. She had grown up on a farm about five miles north of the village and remembers coming to the cafe a few times as a child. "We stopped for an ice cream cone or a root beer float when we'd come into town. I never thought then that it would be a part of my life."

Built in 1927 as Hansen's Confectionary and Restaurant, the Sand Creek Cafe is frozen in time. Walk through the front door, and you'll feel as though you've passed through a time portal. Eye the back bar, the red Formica-topped counter and matching stools, the beaded board ceiling and wood floor, and the large collection of antiques before taking a seat. Bev Borgen, the Sand Creek postmaster tells a great story about the day her cousin and two sons visited from Virginia Beach. The boys looked over the antique cafe and whispered to their mom, "Do you think it's safe to eat here?" "They were city kids and never had seen anything like it," Bev explains. "Their mom said, 'It's perfectly safe. It's the real thing.'"

As is the food. Everything here is made from scratch. You won't go wrong closing your eyes and running your finger down the menu, ordering whatever item it stops at. Go ahead. Try the hash browns, made by frying shredded real potatoes in their skins in real butter. Mine came with two scrambled eggs and wheat toast with Cece's homemade strawberry-rhubarb jam. The from-scratch baked goods—always a reliable measure of a cafe's quality—include long johns, chocolate cake doughnuts (more on them below), cookies, cakes, brownies, and other selections are "more popular than pie." According to Cece, "Pie is no big deal here." The noon specials, including today's roast beef, real mashed potatoes, and gravy, are hearty and home cooked, but Cece warns they're typically gone before two o'clock. If you miss dinner, go straight on to dessert. Order a malt.

Twenty-eight years after she bought the cafe, Cece finds the job "getting easier every day." She credits her sister, Alice Motzer, with much of the success. "Alice started working for me in 1976 while she was still in high school," Cece says. "She is a people person, great with decorating—it's her taxidermy on the walls—and my main cook and baker. She keeps customers returning." Jim Nelson came to work in the kitchen after a tough skiing accident in 1995; he gradually took over all of Cece's share of the baking and cleaning. "Since 1995, my locals don't let Jim leave unless the showcase is stocked with 'Jim Doughnuts.' Alice and I don't even try to make them anymore. Jim's chocolate fry cakes are the best." I've had them, and they are.

Having discovered the five-star atmosphere and food, the bicyclists make repeat trips over the Dunn County hills to the Sand Creek Cafe, where their getups still amuse the locals. Paddlers on the Red Cedar are less likely to wander in, especially in the absence of Cece's boat dock, which washed away last summer and is yet to be replaced. The boat dock came in handy for the tubers who rent inner tubes from Cece and float down the river. There are two or three good put-in and take-out points above and below Sand Creek, making for a lazy, drifting day on the shallow river.

SOMERSET
Anne's Cafe
260 Main Street
(715) 247-5240
M–Su 7 A.M.–4 P.M.
Nicki Rhodes

Dee Foster, who recently sold Anne's Cafe to her right-hand gal, Nicki Rhodes, finishes doing dishes in the back kitchen and sits down opposite me in the booth. "I was one of the original members of the Elvis fan club," she explains as she gestures to the Elvis items hanging on the walls of the one-room dining area. There are Elvis photos, posters, album covers, knick-knacks, clocks. There once was a personally signed photograph, but it was stolen. After that, Dee took down all of the really valuable items. "The sad thing is the kids we think took it probably have no idea of its value," says Dee. Elvis is no longer a sexy object of undying devotion as he was in Dee's youth. Music fans today are more likely to pay allegiance to the regional and smaller national groups, like the Grateful Dead wannabes who are playing this weekend at nearby Float-Rite Park.

Dee has lived through the late 1960s and 1970s at Anne's Cafe, and is now seeing "new hippies and flower children all over again." The Dead Heads who have come to Somerset for the concert have also found Anne's Cafe, the only place in town where you can order a decent breakfast. "They're a strange crowd," reports Nicki, when she shows Dee a roll of bathroom towels that someone has cut up. Never before have the rest room towels been vandalized.

In 1964, Dee's mother, Anna Belisle, now ninety-three, bought her son's TV shop and opened the little cafe. Four years later, after being injured in a fall, Anna sold the cafe to Dee. "My husband had just been accepted into officer's school," she recalls, "when Mom called and asked me if I'd be interested in the restaurant. We decided to come to Somerset." Her husband worked alongside her until the cafe was paid off, then joined the highway patrol. He died early, and with Anna's help Dee supported herself and her children with the cafe.

Dee, Nicki, and their customers call Anna "Grandma," and she is a fixture at the restaurant where she bakes pies and many other foods. A few months ago, she broke her hip and had to recover in a nursing home. Asked by the staff what she missed most while in the home, she replied, "I miss peeling potatoes at the restaurant." They gave her potatoes to peel. They also let her make a pie.

From the windows of Anne's Cafe Anna, Dee, and Nicki have witnessed the passing years. On my first visit years ago, Dee's son Chris was a high school kid waiting tables and collecting upwards of sixty-five dollars on summer Saturdays in tips. Today he is a graduate of Brown Institute and a "computer whiz." He no longer works at the restaurant. Dee herself has recently retired and turned over the restaurant to Nicki.

Despite the passage of time, however, Nicki believes that "nothing much has changed." The Elvis collection on the walls remains the same. The same orange booths fill with regulars. A line still forms on the sidewalk out front every Saturday. The menu hasn't changed. "All the items are the same," Nicki notes. "I'm not a creature that likes change. I'm not." Besides, the locals like what she offers: plenty of homemade soups, Anna's from-scratch pies, and hot beef with real mashed potatoes. "I eat hot beefs everywhere I go," she says without apologizing, "and I have to admit these are the best ones I've ever had."

Like Anna and Dee before her, Nicki puts the meaning in "real home cooking." She goes one step further than most cafe owners by making her own jams and jellies with fruit—rhubarb, raspberries, strawberries—from her own garden. Her garden vegetables also go into soups, cabbage rolls, and stuffed green peppers. "Nothing comes out of a can around here," she asserts, including the apples from a friend's trees that are baked into autumn pies. At Christmas, Nicki makes cookies and hand-dipped chocolates and throws a party for everyone who walks in.

The sign in front of Anne's Cafe reads, "Enjoy a homemade meal." I guarantee you will.

. . . .

Next Best Bets

Cadott
DJ's Restaurant
Highway 27 and County X
Inside an Amoco station but definitely the local hangout, and the food is worth stopping for if your belly's a-rumblin' on Highway 29 or 27.

Downing
Downing Cafe
306 Main Street
Funky location in the basement of the Downing Civic Hall and memorable cooking make this cafe a best bet. Try the graham cracker cream pie, which has attained considerable notoriety courtesy of *Blue Plate Specials and Blue Ribbon Chefs* by Jane and Michael Stern.

Gilman
Kountry Kettle
240 West Main Street
Modest, steady and true, and the pulse of this little farming community.

Hawkins
Whispering Pines Restaurant
718 Ellingson Avenue
The Whispering Pines was a cozy small cafe ten years ago, but under new owners Robert and Melissa Kosmonos it has become a cozy expanded restaurant. A former owner of a Chicago construction company, Robert prepares home-style offerings based heavily on the Lithuanian traditions of his heritage. That includes plenty of real cream, bacon grease, and spices. On any given day you might find a special of Polish sausage and sauerkraut, meat loaf, or cabbage rolls. The move from construction to cooking is not as incongruous as it seems. "Both are about building from the bottom up," Robert explains.

Humbird
Tourist Haven
N2994 Highway 12
Looks like a tavern but tastes just like a real home-cookin' cafe. Ignore the beer posters and vodka lemonade sign over the malt machine and order breakfast or lunch. The pancakes are delicious. Cafe hours are 8 A.M.–2 P.M.

MEDFORD
Barb's Cozy Kitchen
145 South Eighth Street
Equally popular with the locals and travelers on the direct route between Marshfield and towns Up North, Barb's Cozy Kitchen offers a variety of traditional Wisconsin foods and refreshing alternatives to satisfy just about everyone.

OWEN
Cozy Corner Cafe
136 Central Avenue
Red apples are the decorative motif in this Owen County cafe where the farmers and their wives hover over plates of hot beef and burgers during the noon hour. My taco salad was a pleasure on a hot July day.

THORP
Dairy Bar Cafe
221 North Washington Street
In 1999 Leon Pawlak closed the Dairy Bar after forty-three years of ownership. One of my top choices in the original *Cafe Wisconsin*, the cafe was reopened under new ownership in March 2003. Definitely worth a try.

WOODVILLE
Woodville Cafe
120 South Main Street
You can't miss here for a pick-me-up to or from the Twin Cities.

Mississippi River Valley

MISSISSIPPI RIVER VALLEY

Spring Valley

29

63

Durand

10

Eleva Osseo

Mondovi

Pepin

Nelson

93

94

35 Independence

Hixton

Whitehall

12

Alma

Arcadia

Blair

Black River Falls

95

Ettrick

Fountain City Galesville

54 Melrose

21

Trempealeau

53

Tomah

90

LA CROSSE

162

27

14

61

ALMA
Alma Hotel
201 North Main Street
(608) 685-3380
M–Su 6 A.M.–2 P.M. and 5 P.M.–8 P.M.
Ellen Dierauer

The spacious dining room of the Alma Hotel is semidark and nearly vacant at one in the afternoon. Sitting alone at a square table, I order the roast pork dinner, wondering as I do just how big the portion will be. Two elderly ladies sharing a table in the front window confirm my suspicions that it will be far more than I can eat. "I just love potatoes and gravy," one of them exclaims. "I'm taking this home, and I'll have enough for three more meals."

Their conversation swings from topic to topic until it settles on favorite childhood games, like bingo and Monopoly. Both women are old enough to remember when both games were new. Bingo, I overhear, was invented in 1929 and first called Beano because beans were used to cover the called numbers. Monopoly was introduced during the Depression, when people who had no money were obsessed with making some, if even in a board game. "I was born in 1924," the quieter woman says. "I can remember a friend who got a Monopoly game for Christmas. We'd set it up, and the games would last for days."

The flood of distant memories evoked by a hot pork dinner at the Alma Hotel is understandable when you consider that the place is history itself. An old black and white photo postcard from the early 1900s depicts the sturdy brick Union House, a combination hotel-bar-cafe and the precursor to the present day Alma Hotel. A horse and wagon and the man driving them are stopped on the dirt streets out front; behind them, a wood sidewalk snakes along Main Street, providing townsfolk and travelers with dry and clean access to the inside. Behind the Union House, a woman can be seen hanging laundry—perhaps the bedclothes from the hotel.

The years brought changes as the Union House evolved into the Alma Hotel. A previous owner installed synthetic brick panels and aluminum siding over the real brick exterior walls and hung paneling—now painted—on the interior plaster walls. But there is enough evidence of the past scattered here and there to provide a feel of it. If you were the man or woman in the photograph, you'd probably recognize the bar—which also doubled as the lobby—coffee shop, dining room, and the staircase to the rooms upstairs.

As the women at the corner table launch into other memories, my waitress places a basket of sliced bread, dinner rolls, and foil-wrapped butter pats on my table. A few minutes later, my plate of roast pork arrives, accessorized with a mound of real mashed potatoes, gravy, and little avocado green peas. Just as I suspected! There must be a pound of thickly cut pork in front of me, far more than I can possibly eat, even without saving room for apple pie.

Answering my questions about good home cooking, the waitress extols the Alma Hotel's "homemade everything," pointing out cookies and doughnuts in glass storage jars and cut pies with pieces missing on the counter. "Pies are a must-have item," she says. Today's pies include real apple, coconut custard, and fresh rhubarb, but by this time of day there is little left. A taste test isn't necessary. I can tell with a glance they're the real thing: no aluminum foil pans, perfectly molded frozen crusts, or gooey canned filling. The Alma Hotel gets an A+ for pie, but you'll want to get there before five for the best selection.

Famous for its broasted chicken served every Thursday, the Alma Hotel supplements a variety of daily specials with roast beef, pork, or ham dinners, including real mashed potatoes and gravy from meat drippings. The barbecued ribs special and Friday night fish fry ("a real tradition") attract large numbers of locals and tourists and, in season, also hunters and fishermen. My waitress warns, "The hotel's booked two years in advance for the deer hunting and fishing openers. We open at four in the morning then, but the deer hunters and fishermen don't think that's early enough."

Owner Ellen Dierauer ("I'm a deer every hour") and her twenty-five employees face each hunting season, each fishing opener with bravery. Ellen knows the extra work that will be required to keep the three-businesses-in-one operation running efficiently. She relies on years of past experience shared by the previous owners before they stepped down and left Ellen on her own. That was in 1999. November 1999 to be more precise. Hunting season 1999 to be exact.

"I opened on a Thursday," Ellen remembers, "and the following Monday the exhaust fan died." Despite a subpar kitchen, a hotel full of hungry hunters, and new responsibilities, Ellen rebounded with the help of the previous owners, who drove all the way to St. Cloud, Minnesota, to bring back a suitable fan substitute. The first-year mishaps, which also included the death of the walk-in cooler compressor on Christmas Eve, are not-so-long-removed memories. Ellen manages a wry smile when she thinks of them, but is not yet able to laugh. "It's hard to keep things running without a hitch," she says, ticking off various aspects of the job: building and equipment maintenance, bookkeeping, staff management, cleaning, cooking, serving, running the hotel and bar.

The daughter of area farmers, Ellen graduated from Alma High School and then went on to UW–Stout, where she picked up a degree in business. She'd wanted to run a restaurant as early as childhood, but, she says, "I never envisioned a seven-days-a-week-three-meals-a-day kind of place. Growing up, it was either stay on the farm or get off the farm. Now I see I just chose another farm. There's no less amount of work being a restaurant owner."

ARCADIA
Kozy Kitchen
105 Main Street
(608) 323-7455
M–F 6 A.M.–8:30 P.M.; Sa 6 A.M.–1 P.M.; Su 8 A.M.–11 A.M.
Renee Brueggen

A reliable sign that you've stumbled into a cafe worth eating at are posters hanging on the wall that promote local fundraisers, high school sports teams, festivals ranging from the annual tractor pull to the town carnival, and the business-card advertisements of area well drillers, used car salesmen, and dog groomers. You know the cafe is a central gathering spot in the community when the owner allows a wall or two to serve as the town crier.

This pretty much sums up the Kozy Kitchen, owned since 1996 by Renee Brueggen. The locals can refer to the wall inside the entrance to find out whether this Friday's football game is home or away or to find a novel way to supply the family table with a Thanksgiving turkey. Saints Peter and Paul Catholic School has just the answer in its annual Poultry Fest and bingo auction. "Win all your poultry and meat needs for the holidays," promises the Poultry Fest poster. Turkeys, ducks, hams, and steaks—Saints Peter and Paul has them all.

A native of Arcadia, Renee was working as the office manager for her parents' business when she was bitten by the bug to run her own restaurant. She had worked at the local root beer stand as a teenager and was interested in buying it, thinking that its seasonal hours would fit in alongside her office job. But, she notes, "it wasn't for sale." One day her dad, a daily member of the coffee group at the Wagon Wheel Cafe, announced that the business was for sale. Renee took a look, liked what she saw, and traded in the soft-serve machine for a full kitchen and grill and adopted a new name for the old cafe. "I really like what I do," Renee says enthusiastically. "It suits my lifestyle. I like being in the public, and there's something new every day."

Bright and colorful with teal and white floor tiles and teal and salmon banquettes, the Kozy Kitchen is popular with the local coffee drinkers, who gather without fail every morning at six and again at midmorning and midafternoon. The day just isn't right without the ritual dice shaking that accompanies the countless cups of coffee, a tradition Renee inherited from the previous owner. "They wouldn't miss a day," she laughs. "Even my dad's still one of them."

They come for coffee and the clatter of dice, but they also come for the real food made by scratch in the back kitchen by Renee and her staff. "We have the standard stuff—meat, potatoes, and vegetables, mainly— but we try to be creative. We've certainly learned that you can't get too wild, or they won't eat it." One of the flops Renee remembers is her tortilla soup, which the regulars rejected in favor of the tried and true. "We sell a heckuva lot of burgers," she says. "And almost every day we sell out of our dinner special."

At the Kozy Kitchen you'll find real mashed potatoes, pies made fresh every morning, and a variety of baked goods from the bakery right next door. Most days the noon special will be something you're familiar with, but if by chance you wander in on a day Renee is being creative, take heed of the sign on the wall: "Today's Menu—Two Choices / Take It or Leave It!"

ARCADIA
Mary Kay's Kitchen 🍴
327 West Main Street
(608) 323-3535
M 5:30 A.M.–5 P.M.; Tu–Th 5:30 A.M.–7 P.M.; F 5:30 A.M.–8 P.M.;
Sa–Su closed
Mary Kay Hagen
On the west end of Arcadia's main street you will find Mary Kay's Kitchen, a 1960s-ish cafe with homelike appeal, complete with cozy booths and a long counter inviting newspaper readers and coffee drinkers. Taking a minute out from preparing breakfasts, Mary Kay Hagen reflects, "I've owned it for nineteen years, but worked here for seventeen years before that. A long time ago it used to be a dairy. They used to bottle milk in back."

Effervescent and outgoing, Mary Kay laughs loudly and easily as she points out the "reserved" tables around her cafe—there is the Thomas table close to the stove, over there the four-person coffee table that enlarges every morning between seven and eight to accommodate the eight or ten men who show up for the coffee klatch. Mary Kay considers the significance of this traditional gathering of mostly retired men and says, "I'd say it's an outlet to let steam off, get their frustrations out. It's like old times, a bunch of old guys together talking—not gossip really, but world matters, the weather." National and world politics, health issues—particularly Medicare and other insurance matters—local news, sports, reminiscences, Mary Kay's food. These are the topics that concern the men who fill Mary Kay's Kitchen every morning and sometimes again in late afternoon.

A hot cup of "great coffee" priced at two bits, a friendly visit with Mary Kay, and a piece of "real crust" pie to roll on the tongue have brought the man at the counter all the way from his home in Independence. "I like real crust," he confides. "Mary Kay makes pie worth driving for." And she does. One-sixth of any of the eight daily pies, including but not limited to lemon meringue, strawberry, pumpkin, butterscotch, cherry, apple, banana cream, chocolate, and coconut cream can be yours for a mere buck and half. That leaves you money to spend on the real potato daily specials, such as today's chicken fried steak served with gravy and vegetables. And you'll still have money left over from a five-dollar bill to leave a tip. But dig into your pocket for a little more. Mary Kay's good home cooking is worth it.

BLACK RIVER FALLS
Country Cafe
18 Main Street
(715) 284-1636
M–Sa 6 A.M.–3 P.M.; Su closed
Mark and Laura Chrest
After he graduated from the local high school, Mark Chrest high-tailed it out of Black River Falls for Milwaukee, where he earned his white cap as a sous-chef and practiced his art in fine dining establishments. He and his wife, Laura, a native of the big city on the lake, were back in his hometown visiting friends when their life made a sudden change. "My friend told me the old Avalon was for sale, and we took a look," Mark recalls. That was in 1996, and they have been in business for themselves ever since.

Mark remembers the old Avalon, the local eatery and popular hangout where the kids met to eat fries and drink Cokes, and the adjacent Hotel Bar. Both are long gone, transformed into the Country Cafe first by Jack and Darlene McPeak, under whose ownership the cafe was featured in the first edition of *Cafe Wisconsin*, and again by Mark and Laura. The only thing that remains the same is the name. Gone is the McPeaks' country-decorated restaurant filled with family keepsakes, antiques, and Winnebago split ash baskets. Gone too are the Winnebago woman making fry bread in the kitchen window and other nostalgic representations of the past.

The Chrests' Country Cafe is classy and simple. Mark and Laura have pared down the decor to a pleasing combination of forest green carpet and vanilla plaster walls above beaded board wainscot. Clean and clutter-free, the two dining rooms invite people to enjoy a sandwich alone over a paperback book, as does the lady in the booth opposite mine, or with friends. Though reinterpreted yet again, the former Avalon and Hotel Bar are far from erased. There is still a flavor of the past in the oak booths with real brass rails on the backs, the high ceilings, the deep dining room, and the glass storefront.

While I wait for Mark to finish up in the kitchen so we can chat, I order half a turkey sandwich and a bowl of ham and corn chowder. My waitress asks to look at my old copy of *Cafe Wisconsin*, and she and the other waitresses cluster around it. "We've never seen this before," one tells me, as they page through the book, stopping to read about cafes they are familiar with.

When my soup and sandwich appear in the kitchen pass-through window, my waitress leaves the book to the others and brings them to me. I am expecting a turkey sandwich made with deli-style meat. Instead, between diagonally cut slices of homemade white bread I am surprised to find sliced, fresh-roasted turkey breast. And it doesn't stop there. The real turkey is layered with curly leaf lettuce, a slice of tomato, and real mayonnaise—far more than I anticipated. One bite and I am transported to Thanksgiving afternoon and sandwiches made with leftover turkey and dinner rolls. If I had known I'd get a sandwich like this, I would have ordered a whole one. The ham and corn chowder has stiff competition, but it rises to the challenge and is both flavorful and satisfying, a perfect accompaniment to a delicious sandwich.

Mark appears in front of me wearing white pants, a white shirt, and a white chef's cap. "You are the only cafe owner I have met in the entire state who dresses like a chef," I tell him. Mark *is* a chef who just happens to run a small town cafe, and though he serves up plenty of small town traditional favorites, he also spreads his culinary wings "every once in a while. I usually throw in a couple of new things but kind of keep to the meat and potatoes thing," he says. Some of the more unusual things he has tried, like salmon, have stuck, but others, like gourmet-type salads, come and go. Laughing, Mark notes, "Things like toasted pine nuts are kind of unknown here."

Even with the many changes, the Country Cafe remains a local hangout where tourists and natives mingle. When he is not in the kitchen, Mark greets his customers by name and carries on brief conversations about children, grandchildren, vacation plans. Tourists who are led to the Country Cafe by advertisements at campgrounds and hotels are encouraged to order this or that—just as I am urged to try Laura's cherry pie, which, Mark claims, "is to die for."

Always a sucker for good pie, I eye Laura's pie in the three-tier pie case on the counter. It looks as good as Mark promises, so I order a piece. Sweet-sour Montmorency cherries—I'd bet money that they are Wisconsin's own Door County cherries—are enveloped between crispy sheets of pastry fluted at the edges to seal in the cherries and their juice. The top crust is sprinkled with oversize crystals of white sugar that add an extra crunch. Laura's pie is superb, but is it better than the cherry pie at Iola's Crystal Cafe? Try both and let me know what you think.

BLAIR
CJ's Cafe
116 ½ North Gilbert Street
(608) 989-2820
M–W 8:30 A.M.–7 P.M.; Th 8:30 A.M.–8 P.M.; F 8 A.M.–9 P.M.; Sa 8:30
A.M.–7 P.M.; Su closed
Sherry and John Rawson
There is no more reliable test for the quality of a cafe's cooking than a well-stocked bakery case, but you mustn't be fooled by baked goods that start life as frozen prepared dough. The proof is in the pudding, they say, and at CJ's Cafe, that pudding is homemade. "Do it yourself" is owner Sherry Rawson's motto.

"As long as I'm here, it will never change. I don't think the world needs instant food, and we don't either. I will never use instant mashed potatoes or boxed pudding. It's homemade all the way," asserts Sherry.

In CJ's bakery case, you will find a vast array of cakes, cookies, bars, muffins, sweet rolls, and other tempting treats all made by Sherry and her aunt Karen. Fresh and orphaned day-old choices share space with candy bars, Blow Pops, Starburst, and other packaged candy, but I don't know why. Why would anyone choose these when they could have cake spread with labor-intensive seven-minute frosting made by cooking egg whites into a divinity-like confection? When they could have chocolate chip, peanut butter, oatmeal raisin, or date-filled cookies?

The baked goods in CJ's case are no mere run-of-the-mill variety. One look and you'll know that someone has gone to a whole lot of work to make you happy. And no less so themselves.

Sherry Rawson has been feeding the people of Blair and beyond for eight years. She'd always loved to cook, and when the previous owner closed up the cafe, she was encouraged to take it over. The building had been emptied and was being used by the area's Amish for religious services, so when she finally found the courage to act, she had to rebuild the cafe from the ground up. "It all just fell into place," she recalls. "It's like it was meant to be."

She found the booths and other equipment at an Arcadia bakery that was closing up, and her friends and relatives chipped in to help out.

Sherry describes herself as being by nature very quiet and shy. "It wouldn't have been hard for me to stay at home and hide," she says. "Now I can talk to people. Now I can look into people for honesty. The cafe really opened me up a lot and taught me a lot about the world."

Among the cherished lessons she has learned are how to know people by listening to their stories about their lives and the past. "They tell me their stories about growing up, about what it was like living in Blair long ago. Some people come every day, so I learn about their illnesses. They're just like your family. They take care of you, and we take care of them. It's about taking care of people."

Going beyond mere cooking and baking, the work of a cafe owner like Sherry includes taking meals to homebound customers, playing mother to teenage employees (and her own three daughters), and assessing which people are truly in need from those who are just taking advantage of her generosity. For example, she is willing to extend a line of credit or offer a free meal to those who are genuinely down on their luck, but to others with cash in their pockets but coldness in their hearts, she offers only an empty plate. "They think that I'm a business owner, then I'm rich. They try to get something for nothing but don't see how hard I work. How hard we all work."

Working and playing go hand in hand at CJs Cafe. There is plenty of fun shared with the regulars, who participate in birthday drawings and weekly drawings for a complimentary Friday night fish fry. The coffee groups keep the place giggling, laughing, and guffawing with talk, quips, and practical jokes. And all of the customers keep the place decorated with Holstein cows in various shapes.

"They bring me gifts—cow stuff—when they go someplace," Sherry explains with a wave of her hand over the cafe's collection. "I've got figurines, salt and pepper shakers, signs, just all kinds of stuff."

My favorite is the plaque of a cow's rear end that reads: "Come & Smell our Dairy-Air."

ELEVA
Pammy K's
130 Mondovi Street
(715) 287-3226
M–Th 6 A.M.–7 P.M.; F 6 A.M.–9 P.M.; Sa 6 A.M.–3 P.M.; Su 8 A.M.–2 P.M.
Pamela Rud
The afternoon coffee group at Pammy K's is passing a card around for signatures before sending it to the widow of a member who has recently

passed away. He is sadly missed because here everyone has a part to play. Some are jokesters, some are storytellers, some are listeners, and when someone steps out for a minute or a day, everyone else knows he'll be back. To face the future without one of your pals is bleak, but the coffee drinkers will gamely carry on.

Pamela Rud, also know as Pammy K, a nickname bestowed by her son, has a soft spot for all of her customers, but especially the members of the coffee group. Between them there is a friendly banter, part gruff affection and old-boy boisterousness on their side, daughterly attentiveness on hers. She is young enough to be their daughter, yet she is also a mother of sorts. She watches over their diets, their comings and goings, their health, and selects and buys the card when a missing member must be remembered.

Pam has been a part of the men's lives for more than twenty-five years. She worked twenty years for the cafe's previous owners before deciding she might just as well work for herself. When the opportunity came in 1997, she seized it. She bought the white vinyl-clad cafe, then known as the Cardinal Cafe, and set about making it her own. She was inspired by the example of her grandmother, the longtime owner of the former Grace's Cafe in Mondovi. "Grandma Grace was well known, well liked and well loved," she explains. "I started working for her when I was eleven. People still remember her, so I use her name in my ads: 'Continuing Grandma Grace's ways.' I do the same kind of recipes Grandma did."

Pammy K's specializes in all homemade food, including specials and desserts. "I make the kind of stuff that appeals to me," Pam says. "Just good old hearty, filling food." Hers is the kind of food that inspires Eau Claire bicyclists to make forty-mile-round-trip weekend jaunts for pancakes or pie or, in some cases, dry wheat toast and coffee. Hunters, too, have found Pammy K's to be a key element to an eventful weekend. On the day after the opening of the 2002 bow-hunting season, "the boys from Eau Claire" credited Pammy K's with their success at shooting a five-point buck with an eighteen-inch spread. "Another job well done for Team Mossy Oak!" they wrote in the guest book. "Breakfast is key to a good day of hunting. None better than Pammy K's!"

Pam trims out her namesake cafe with an ever-changing array of decorations. "Even people in a small town need a change once in a while," she explains. The day I stopped, the cafe was in an autumn mood, with green and white checked tablecloths covered with clear plastic and matching curtain at the window. Silk strands of autumn leaves were woven around the curtain rod, and in the corner, a silk fig tree was decorated with white lights and apples. The decor impressed Carlyle and Ruth, a Fort Myers couple, who praised the "wonderful food and even better decorations" in the guest book.

The casual, cozy cafe reflects Pam's aim to make it a welcome place that celebrates friendships and the Eleva community. "Sit, Relax, Gossip" a sign on the wall encourages. Pam provides material under the tablecloth covers for those who have trouble striking up a conversation with their neighbors at the next table. Under the cover on your table, you might find copies of newspaper articles about the Norwegian Lutheran Church or Eleva's first general store. Other tables have copies of old advertisements and photographs. At Pammy K's, there's always something interesting to talk about. Even if you're not from the community, you'll be welcomed back by the folks and the menu, which reads: "Please come again, the coffee's always hot—And see what's cooking in Pammy K's cooking pot!"

HIXTON
Hixton Cafe ⦿
133 East Main Street
(715) 963-4031
M–F 6:30 A.M.–4 P.M.; Sa 6:30 A.M.–2 P.M.; Su closed
Patricia and Richard Lohmar

Ten years ago, the Hixton Cafe was just closing when I stepped through the door and met Kathy Lohmar saying goodbye to the last of her customers. Locking the front door behind him, she joined me at the counter and began what would become a three-hour discussion about the Lohmar family's cafe. Halfway into our conversation, it was clear that Kathy wasn't going to return home at the expected time, so she called her father, Richard, to tell him about my visit and her delay, and he quickly put aside his supper and came down to the cafe to join us. It was nearly seven o'clock when I finally left the Hixton Cafe, and all I had eaten was one of Patricia Lohmar's delicious homemade doughnuts. But I knew that the Hixton Cafe—and my visit with the storytelling Lohmars—would rank high on my list of Wisconsin favorites.

The Lohmar family—parents Richard and Patricia, daughters Kathy and Maggie, and son Rick—came from Illinois in 1979 in pursuit of Patricia's dream of owning her own restaurant. Settling in the Norwegian-dominated Hixton area, the Lohmars purchased the modest red cafe, now surrounded by a number of antique shops on Hixton's main street. The cafe was established about 1900, or at least "longer ago than anyone around here can remember," according to Kathy, who is now married and no longer lives in Hixton. Hints of its original grandeur remain in the handsome, marble-topped back bar, half of a matching set that once included a soda fountain. Years ago the pair was separated and the soda fountain wound up in Chicago. "One day a man stopped in and stared at the back bar. He just sat there and studied it, and then offered to buy it. It turns out he had the matching soda fountain!" Kathy explained. "But Mom wouldn't sell it."

"It's pretty much Mom's restaurant," Kathy continued, as she went through the menu pointing out homemade items: cake doughnuts and raised doughnuts, cookies, sweet rolls, secret recipe pies, Wednesday's baked fish and Thursday's baked chicken dinners, soups and "cook's choice mysteries." Richard, a printer who lends a hand at the restaurant when necessary, agreed and laughed, "Customers will come in and ask who's cooking, me or Pat, and then decide whether they'll have food on the grill or the daily special! But usually you just see a customer coming in and can start cooking before they even order. You just know what they always order. You can be back in the kitchen and see an order and know just whose it is."

The regulars—mostly men—come in sometimes two or three times a day, beginning with the workingmen's morning coffee klatch about seven fifteen and the retirees' coffee klatch, which meets between eight and nine. ("The men are so much worse than the women," said Richard.) Crowded around "the Men's Table, where all the major decisions of the world and this town are decided," the two groups of men shake dice to determine who pays the coffee tab, sometimes moving on to bigger stakes like doughnuts. By the time the coffee klatches convene again in the afternoon, the stakes are bigger yet, with winners of meals or kitties of quarters determined by the luckiest throw of the dice.

Over the years of their cafe ownership, the Lohmars and the descendants of the original Norwegian settlers have come to know each other on intimate terms. But although the Lohmars are now firmly embedded in the Hixton community, they found "it took a while to be accepted. It was a slow, gradual process," said Richard. "Because we came from Illinois, we don't have a history. We don't have an extended family in the area. After twenty-three years here, we're just becoming insiders. When we lived on the farm—we live in town now—and people asked where we lived, I had to tell them the name of the original owner of our farm." Laughing, he said, "I had to go back four generations to let them know where we lived!"

The outsider-insider difference provides fodder for ethnic Ole and Lena jokes, anecdotes about the locals (like the time several years ago when Ole's Belgians got loose and tore off through town), and gag gifts to the regulars at birthdays and Christmas. Kathy laughed about the year the Lohmar family put their heads together and concocted their own versions of Christmas gifts commonly given by practical-minded Scandinavians shivering through Wisconsin winters. The Norwegian hand-warmer was a naked Barbie doll with batteries attached; the Norwegian flashlight, a toilet paper tube with matches glued to the end; and the Norwegian coffee mug, a cup from the cafe filled with dark brown mud, properly thawed.

The success of the Lohmars' practical jokes and good-natured teasing is a sure indication they have established a solid relationship with the Hixton natives based on mutual trust and respect. In its simplest expression, this relationship is demonstrated by Pat's willingness to extend credit to regulars who discover they've left their money at home or for other reasons can't immediately pay off their tab. In its fullest expression, the Lohmars' relationship with the community leads to what both Richard and Kathy regard as one of the cafe's most important roles in the community, what Kathy called "the community health watch." This consists of "taking care of the local elderly by keeping an eye on their health, the homebound and the others who come in."

"If a regular customer doesn't come in for several days," Richard explained, "Patricia will call them to see if they're okay. We keep a watch on the regulars, and if they're acting abnormal, we'll send out feelers to the county nurse, relatives, or close friends of the customer. That way we take care of them. It's one of our ways of paying them back for everything they do for us during the year because without them, we wouldn't be here."

In the absence of her children, who have grown up and moved away, Patricia has relied on Kim Sebron, a waitress who has worked at the cafe for the past ten years. "My daughter hasn't been with me for a long time, and Kim stepped in and took her place. She's real ornery," Patricia says. Kim laughs to hear her and replies, with Lohmar-influenced humor, "The guys, they like to be abused."

INDEPENDENCE
Carolyn's Coffee Shop 🍽
23716 Washington Street
(715) 985-3434
M closed; Tu–F 6 A.M.–1:30 P.M.; Sa 6–12 P.M.; Su closed
Carolyn Elstad

Carolyn Elstad's day begins at four o'clock in the morning when she comes down from her upstairs apartment to roll out piecrusts and prepare fillings, bake bread and cakes, and set kettles of soup to simmering on back burners. By the time of my visit, she is already eleven hours into a seventeen-hour workday. Waiting for her to put the noon-hour rush to bed, I watch as she cleans up the restaurant in preparation for the afternoon customers. She takes the plastic letters spelling out MUSHROOM STEAK from the daily special board, gathers up the money from the till, and prepares a deposit for the bank. "I'll be back in a few minutes," she tells me. With a bowl of southern chicken vegetable soup (a lot like gumbo, which I love), I settle back into my booth and wait.

The Coffee Shop, housed in a turn-of-the-century retail building, has long been an Independence gathering spot. Decorated now in printed wallboard and artificial brick, the high-ceilinged, deep restaurant has a comfortable lived-in look. Wooden tables and chairs fill the front half of the glass-fronted dining room, and in the back, two short counters face each other, separated by a glass floor case filled with baked goods and topped with the cash register. Another glass case is filled with homemade pie: banana cream, apple, pumpkin, rhubarb, walnut, chocolate, coconut, and blueberry cheesecake. I choose the chocolate and nibble at it until Carolyn's return.

"I used to own a cafe in Mondovi," she explains, "but I sold it. I was looking for a regular nine-to-five job and ended up going to school. Eventually I got a job in an office, just the thing I had been hoping for. I tell you, I just about went bananas in an office all day! So, I started looking around for a restaurant again and bought this one."

Clearly, Carolyn has found her niche. Under her ownership, the Coffee Shop has become a favorite place for home cooking, especially stir-fries ("popular with the ladies"), noon specials ("that's what the men order"), pies, and baked goods. The food is so good that Carolyn counts among her regular customers people from as far away as Eau Claire, Mondovi, and Winona, Minnesota.

Carolyn's out-of-towners may come once every few weeks, but the locals dependably fill the Coffee Shop every day. Without their friendship and support Carolyn doubts she would have survived the sudden death of her husband, Paul, ten years ago "They held me together," she says. His death tore a hole in her life, but Carolyn finds comfort and relief in the regularity and routine of daily business—the food, the early risings, the predictable comings and goings of customers—that tell her life does, after all, go on. There is laughter, too, when she looks about the cafe and sees Paul's handiwork, like the swivel lamp clamped to the booth closest to the kitchen, along the far wall.

"There was this old guy who used to come in early for coffee and to read the paper," Carolyn explains. "Sometimes he was outside waiting for me to come down at four thirty. (We open at six.) He'd sit here in the dark, wouldn't turn the overhead light on because people'd think we were open. The swivel lamp was Paul's idea. That old guy sat at his table, turned on the lamp, and read his paper.

"There's another guy waits here in the dark for a ride to work. And I've got construction workers and other workers who come in the back door before I open looking for breakfast. If I'm not up, they'll holler upstairs to get me up, get me moving. They keep me going, especially when the going gets tough."

MELROSE
L & M Cafe ⬤ ⸖
415 South Washington Street
(608) 488-2611
M 5 A.M.–3 P.M.; Tu–Th 5 A.M.–6:30 P.M.; F–Sa 5 A.M.–9 P.M.; Su 6 A.M.–1 P.M.
Martha Rommel

Martha Rommel spreads a Friday and Saturday night all-you-can-eat buffet at the L & M Cafe that will make your knees tremble with anticipation and your eyes grow ten times bigger than your stomach. This kind of food, and this quantity, is guaranteed to make pigs of us all, so be sure to wear elastic waistbands and belts with a few holes to spare.

You'll need more than one plate to move through the line-up, starting with salads of all kinds: tossed lettuce, coleslaw, cottage cheese, macaroni, fruit-filled Jell-O, and broccoli and cauliflower and peas. Then on to the fresh-baked white and cracked wheat dinner rolls and butter, real mashed potatoes, baked potatoes, French fries and American fries, and a selection of vegetables.

Take another plate and pile on the fish, broasted chicken, and some of the finest barbecued ribs you'll find anywhere in the state of Wisconsin. And then come back and do it again as often as you like.

But be forewarned: there's more coming the next morning if you care to stop by. Saturday and Sunday mornings, the L & M Cafe spreads out the breakfast offerings like jelly on toast. Bacon, sausage, ham, eggs of all varieties, potato rounds, pancakes (including blueberry) as big as a plate, French toast, biscuits and gravy. If you've saved room from the previous night, you just might be able to eat your fill. Around here, the folks know good eating and plenty of it.

Though all the stops are pulled out on weekends, every day at the L & M Cafe is a celebration of good Wisconsin home cooking and above all a tribute to Martha, her in-laws and former owners Lyle and Mardie Rommel, and the rest of her staff, who make it all, all by themselves.

Both natives of Melrose, Lyle and Mardie were dairy farmers and dabbled in hobby businesses—ceramics for Mardie and food concessions at auctions for both of them—before becoming full-fledged restaurateurs in 1987 with their purchase of the old Rose Cafe on Main Street in Melrose. Valuable practical experience came from feeding a family of six children and operating their mobile chuck wagon. Restaurant ownership was a new challenge, however, first met with massive remodeling. The Rommels enlarged the original existing cafe by tearing out the tavern in the front part of the building and adding more dining. Mardie laughs when she recalls how she and Lyle had to retrieve the original counter and matching vinyl and chrome stools from behind a wall. She says, "The previous owner took out the counter, but the people complained, and we put it back."

The locals might complain about some things, but the cooking is definitely not one of them (other than the buffet-binge groans about having eaten too much). This is why they cheered when Martha bought the place in December 2001. They knew everything would continue virtually unchanged, and so it has.

"The only thing we changed was to go to nonsmoking," says Martha, who has worked at the restaurant for twenty-three years all told, fifteen for Lyle and Mardie. All told, four generations of Rommels have been feeding and befriending the people of Melrose and beyond. Mardie, and her mother before her, worked at the restaurant while it was still the Rose Cafe, and now Martha's daughter, Dorothy, works at the L & M, too.

Mardie makes homemade cinnamon rolls, cake doughnuts—or "fry cakes"—and raised doughnuts, muffins, cookies, and other baked goods, in addition to "about three" pies per day. Lyle's gifts to the eating public include "the meats": chicken; pork roasts; beef roasts (to the tune of forty pounds per week); ribs and fish which he seasons, sauces, and bakes for daily specials, parties, and banquets; and the incredible all-you-can-eat Friday and Saturday night buffets that "people from all around come for." The rest of the week features rotating daily specials—Tuesday tacos, Wednesday broasted chicken, Thursday burgers—mixed in with best-loved favorites like roast pork and roast beef dinners.

"We cook what everyone wants," Martha explains. "It seems you can never have too much roast beef. And we cook just like the way we cook at home. Everyone's watching, so everything we make is homemade."

MONDOVI
Blondie's Diner III
104 South Eau Claire Street
(715) 926-3456
M–Th 5:30 A.M.–8 P.M.; F 5:30 A.M.–9 P.M.; Sa 5:30 A.M.–3 P.M.;
Su 7 A.M.–2 P.M.
Jill Poeschel
The Buffalo County town of Mondovi has had a cafe or two on Main Street for many years, and quite a few of them have been truly memorable.

This is why I am glad to pass on the good news: Blondie's is back for a third go-around. Begun as a traditional small town cafe over twenty years ago by Barb Meistad, who does indeed have blonde hair, Blondie's went through two incarnations and two locations before settling back onto the main block of the commercial district.

In August 2002 Jill Poeschel bought the business from Barb's son, Randy, and then hired Barb to help her. "I come with the business," Barb explains with a smile. Jill and Barb have worked together for many years, so despite the changes in ownership and location, nothing has really changed at all. A new look, yes, but the same real food and the same regulars, who have easily adjusted to each move, settling into their preferred spaces at the counter and the front coffee tables complete with leather dice cups.

It is Ash Wednesday, and I have already had a jam-packed day when I fall into Blondie's at five. I grab the first available seat and realize within minutes that I'm a direct hit for every blast of snow-filled air that rushes in with the opening of the door. With my eyes fixed on the daily menu board, I move closer to the wall. My decision is made by the time I sit down, and when my waitress comes, I quickly order the burger and cup of chili special. The cafe is nearly filled with people, and most of them—like me—have forgotten all about the ashes on their foreheads. It's the beginning of Lent, and we should be swearing off burgers for the fish nugget basket. Oh, we Catholics of short-lived conviction.

Lenten fasting is also far from our minds. I keep my eye on the last three pieces of luscious-looking lemon meringue pie, interspersed in the pie case with pieces of apple crumb, pumpkin, and rhubarb. Odd that the lemon meringue is in a graham cracker crust, I think to myself. I'm calculating my odds on whether the lemon meringue will still be available by the time I finish my burger and chili when a woman walks in and orders two of the three pieces to go. The odds have shrunk considerably. Within two minutes, the last piece is whisked out of the case and carried to a side table. My window of opportunity opened, let in a freezing blast, and then slammed shut.

Barb laughs when I tell her what has happened. "That graham cracker pie is a real favorite around here," she explains.

"Graham cracker pie?" I sputter. I thought it was lemon meringue. That explains the unconventional crust.

I've had graham cracker pie—vanilla pudding in a graham cracker crust, usually topped with Cool Whip or some other ever-last nondairy whipped topping. Personally, I don't understand its popularity. It's a simple, nothing-special sweet treat that anybody can make. Give me a pie that requires a special knack, an intricate balance of ingredients and an experienced hand with a pastry tool and rolling pin, and I'm in pie heaven. Give me apple, lemon meringue, pumpkin, or rhubarb and I'll extol virtues and wax poetical. The same inspiration just doesn't come with graham cracker pie.

With dessert no longer on my mind, I turn my attention to supper. My burger has the shape of a flower—a sure sign that it's made from fresh, hand-pattied beef. This is no frozen hockey puck–style patty thrown on the grill to melt and cook at the same time. The quality bun is thoughtfully buttered and grilled, and a squirt of ketchup and a couple of pickle slices add just the color and additional flavor a good burger requires. The chili, served in a small ceramic cup with a handle, is a Blondie's best-seller, with chunks of crumbled ground beef grown soft from simmering all day in the crock.

In its robust plaid wallpaper and lemon yellow booths, Blondie's is pretty to look at, but there is real substance here as well. The food is down-home and authentic. Witness the pies in the case, the homemade chocolate chip cookies and cake doughnuts in jars behind the counter. Take a peek, as I did, into the kitchen and notice the huge bricks of real Wisconsin butter alongside the spitting grill. There is no yellow-orange, simulated butter–flavored, spray-on-the-grill-and-grease-it-up gook used here. Blondie's sticks tight to its Dairyland roots. I give it my real seal of approval.

OSSEO
Norske Nook 🍽 ⛾
13804 West Seventh Street
(715) 597-3069
M–Sa 5:30 A.M.–9:30 P.M.; Su 8 A.M.–8 P.M.
Jerry Bechard

Thirteen years after purchasing the Norske Nook from founder Helen Myhre, owner Jerry Bechard is still filled with excitement and wonder. He and Amy Arnevik, his regional manager, have just returned from the 2003 Great American Pie Festival in Celebration, Florida, where the Nook's banana cream pie received a Super Gourmet rating and a first place blue ribbon. The pie competition is a way to keep the work fun and rewarding, Jerry says. Next year they'll send some of the restaurant's regular pie bakers, who'll get the chance to test their creations against big-name commercial outfits like Baker's Square, Mrs. Smith's, and Sara Lee.

Undoubtedly Wisconsin's most celebrated hometown cafe, the Norske Nook in downtown Osseo began its unique climb to fame back in 1977 when Jane and Michael Stern featured it in *Roadfood*, a directory to the best regional eateries found along American interstates and major highways. The Nook and its founder and owner at the time, "pie lady" Helen Myhre, went on to be featured in regional, national, even international newspapers and magazines, on the *David Letterman* and *Today* television programs, and in additional books by the Sterns. Heaps of awards followed. You can peruse them for yourself when you visit the Nook. And you will visit the Nook. Tens of thousands of people a year do.

In 1990, after seventeen years of business, Helen Myhre sold the Nook, as it is affectionately termed by the locals and other devotees, to Jerry and retired to write a cookbook and nurse her ailing knees. Jerry grew up in Chippewa County but was working in Colorado when he began casting about for a ticket to bring him back home. He was looking for police work when he found Helen's for sale ad in the newspaper.

"It was really a fluke that I saw the ad for the Norske Nook," he explains. "Helen had many offers and hand-picked me. I'm really lucky. I think she realized I had the drive to carry it on and that I was going to be in there working right alongside the employees, leading by example."

Jerry gets a thrill watching people from around the country drop by for a piece of pie, but it excites him even more that "people are really catching on to our meals." I confess I've always thought of the Nook as a pie place, but since I stopped by late in the afternoon, I decided to stay for supper. My neighbor at the next table (a grizzled local farmer wearing denims and a seed cap) ordered the hot pork sandwich, and because he did, I followed suit, topping mine off, of course, with a piece of chocolate mousse pie. Both the sandwich and the pie, which melted on my tongue like whipped butter, were immense and delicious. And while my neighbor and I ate ours, a fellow from Washington sat down nearby and ordered the same.

At the Nook, it is not unusual to find a local customer from across the street sharing a bite to eat with a stranger from across the country. During the summer, tourists flock in at an amazing rate ("You'd be surprised at how many are carrying *Roadfood*," Jerry exclaims), sometimes causing waits out on the sidewalk up to a half hour long. If you're in a hurry, you'll want to try out one of the eateries along the interstate. But if it's the Nook phenomenon you want to experience, waiting for a table is part of it. Spend the time crossing out states in the license plate game that's been keeping the kids busy since you left home. You'll find cars from just about everywhere clogging Osseo's downtown streets.

Without the summer tourists, many of whom arrive on the three to four bus tours that stop each week, the Nook would be any other small town cafe. Their presence changes things, such as the routines of the locals, who adjust to their numbers by coming in earlier in the morning and later at night; the workload, which rises from 50 daily specials to 120, from 50 daily pies to 150; and the restaurant itself, which was moved into the present building from its original location across the street in 1994.

Yet despite the new building and burdens (and the blessings) of the tourist trade, the Norske Nook remains a cozy, small town cafe. Service is friendly and prompt, conversation flows freely, the food is homemade and hearty, the walls decorated with local artwork: rosemaled woodenware, a mural of a Norwegian fjord and peasant woman, and paintings by Jerry's friend Mark Horton, who painted the cafe on the cover of this book.

Before moving to Eau Claire, Mark had his studio over the original Nook, which is now the Norske Nook Kaffe Hus og Gave Butikk. You can't read Norwegian? Relax. The former cafe is now filled with a variety of Scandinavian gifts and books, including Dala horses, sweaters by Dale of Norway, linens and paper goods, children's stories by Maj Lindman and Astrid Lindgren, as well as a wide assortment of other books.

"People tell us how glad they are to find some of these things, especially the books," Jerry says. Other popular items available at both the Gave Buttik and the Norske Nook restaurant are Scandinavian food items like lefse; potato pancake, potato dumpling, and Swedish pancake mixes; and lingonberry jam.

Under Jerry's ownership, the Norske Nook enterprise has expanded in many directions. In addition to the retail gift shop, two more restaurants were established in Rice Lake and Hayward. They help to relieve some of the pressure from seasonal tourism that the original Nook experiences while at the same time providing a gathering place for the locals. Out of all these successes, however, Jerry is perhaps most proud of the Nook's role in giving back to the communities in which it is located. Among the many awards and recognitions pinned to the Wall of Fame in the Osseo restaurant are plaques acknowledging the Nook's support of the Osseo Optimist Club, the Osseo-Fairchild youth baseball program, and the Osseo-Fairchild school district.

"The Norske Nook is part of this town," explains Jerry.

Guided by this principle of participation for mutual benefit, Jerry has also implemented a continuing education scholarship for returning employees. To be eligible, an employee must work a qualifying number of hours through the summer and be nominated by his or her manager. One recipient is selected each summer.

"I went with this because I wanted to establish a return corps of experienced workers, and I wanted to return to the community what it has given to us."

SPRING VALLEY
Deb's Country Inn
S214 McKay Avenue
(715) 778-5789
M–F 6 A.M.–4 P.M.; Sa 7 A.M.–1 P.M.; Su closed
Deb Zimmerman

It is a raw, wintry day in late October when I stop at Deb's Country Inn in downtown Spring Valley. Some months ago, another cafe owner in a nearby town, a former employee of Deb's now out on her own, praised the food and the atmosphere. With a recommendation like that, I figured I couldn't go wrong at Deb's.

The outside air was smoky and smelled like a summer cookout, but even at that I was unprepared for the daily special written on the board on an inside wall: grilled sirloin *or* chicken with onions and mushrooms, baked potato, and cheesy broccoli and cauliflower soup.

"We've got the grill going outside," my waitress told me. "That's pretty ambitious for a day like this."

I had to agree. Having a smaller appetite than a full meat and potatoes meal and wanting to spare the cook from going out in the wintry weather, I opted for a petite burger—half the standard eight-ounce burger. I spiffed it up a bit by requesting lettuce, tomato, onion slices, and mayonnaise.

"So what you want is a petite California burger," my waitress confirmed. Exactly. A petite California burger. I added curly fries and a Coke, inspired by the cafe's accumulation of Coca-Cola collectibles.

Several years ago, owner Deb Zimmerman set out a couple of Coke bottles for display, unaware of exactly what this would lead to. It wasn't long before her customers were bringing in other Coke items for her collection. She laughs when she remembers, "I didn't have a collection. They made one for me!" Today, there are vintage Coke cans, paperweights, salt and pepper shakers, bottles, a Coca-Cola Barbie, tins, miniatures, and countless other Coke items throughout the cafe. Look up. You will even find a wallpaper border of reprints of vintage ads.

Swiveling in my chair to see all the Coke items, I spot something even more interesting: Deb's collection of vintage coffee tins. Packed onto two shelves, the display of tins reads like a who's who of coffee brands. As a girl brought up around the mainline brands such as Maxwell House and Folgers, and later Sanka and Taster's Choice, I found the names on the tins homey yet exotic. A few inspired a smile. Over there is Flame Room coffee, over here Cup-o-Cheer. Some of the others include Red Owl, Red Rooster, Wish-Bone, Radiant Roast, and None-Such.

Deb's Country Inn is so packed with old and new that there is plenty of gawking to keep you busy between ordering and eating. Don't miss the old tin tourist sign over the door advertising Crystal Cave, the largest cave in the Midwest, located just outside Spring Valley. To keep the cafe filled and to satisfy their never-quelled curiosity, Deb and her husband haunt antique shops, flea markets, and junk stores in search of Coke items, coffee cans, and pieces of local interest. They were shopping in Illinois when Deb found the Crystal Cave sign.

"I was in one room, and my husband was in another when I found it," she say. "My heart just about stopped when I saw it hanging on the wall. I couldn't find my husband fast enough. We were just meant to bring it home, I guess."

I spot my waitress carrying a plate with a burger and curly fries. I am stunned when she stops at my table. I thought I'd ordered the petite California burger! She assures me that it *is* a petite—half of the regular sized burger. Even at that, it is plenty generous in size. The skin-on fries were crisp and lightly browned, without seasoning or salt, and the burger was an over-the-top delight with a buttered bakery bun and plenty of "California" accoutrements.

For more than seventy years, the people of Spring Valley have been dining at the downtown eatery long known as Thompson's Cafe. Deb herself has been here nineteen years. Despite this, she sometimes wonders just how much the place is actually hers, since her customers have a way of taking over the decorating, the menu, the community table. At this hour, the lunch rush has ended and Deb has time to chat a little with the people gathered around the round oak pedestal table known as the Round Table. Even if they weren't seated there, you would know the community table by its proximity to the serve-yourself coffeepot and its lazy Susan stocked with napkins, seasonings and condiments, and the leather dice cup.

Every day around this table, the men shake dice to see who will pay for rounds of coffee, or who will win fabulous prizes—maybe a meal, maybe a quarter. Others look on, sharing the talk and the fun. No one is excluded or exempt from teasing unless they choose to be.

No one in the cafe, including me, can ignore the friendly ribbing of one woman whose parking skills leave much to be desired. "You hit the curb yesterday," the people at the Round Table jibe. "Today you're about two feet away. Are you gonna take a taxi here tomorrow?"

"Just you wait! Tomorrow I'll park perfectly," she retorts.

Brought by taxi or driving herself, she'll be back. They'll all be back. They've got a place reserved for them at the Round Table.

TREMPEALEAU
Wildflower Cafe
11364 Main Street
(608) 534-6866
M–Su 6 A.M.–1:30 P.M.
Sharon and Tom Kupietz

A block off the Mississippi River in downtown Trempealeau, the Wildflower Cafe is a bustling place over the noon hour. Just ask Dean Mewhorter (his business card introduces him as the White Tornado, musician of Old Time, Country, Variety, and Gospel), who minutes ago came in for his daily lunch only to find none of his usual companions. It is the last Monday in October, the traditional day to fall back. Laughing at himself, he says, "I turned back the clocks upstairs but not downstairs. I looked up and saw eleven thirty, so I came in for lunch."

It is only ten thirty and Dean is an hour early for the lunch prepared and served through Trempealeau County's program on aging. A central location in the southern part of the county, the Wildflower Cafe has served an average of thirty meals per day to seniors for the past four years. Verneille Hunter has been the chief volunteer all of this time, and she and her small staff of three or four other women ready the dining area for the day's meal. Vinyl tablecloths with autumn scenes are spread over the tables, the knives, forks, and spoons are wrapped in paper napkins, and the coffee cups are set out. The women are nearly ready for the day's seniors who, unlike Dean, have remembered to set all of their clocks back an hour.

Every day, Verneille explains, "We get a lot of widowers. There's fewer widows because they're more inclined to cook for themselves."

"Sometimes," she adds coyly, "there's some matchmaking going on."

Sharon and Tom Kupietz, owners of the Wildflower Cafe since 1999, work with the county agent to develop balanced and healthful meals for the seniors. Most days, the senior meal is the same as the home-cooked daily special Sharon and Tom offer to their regular customers.

Don't make the mistake of equating senior meals with bland, mushy institutional food. There is no fear of encountering it here. Everything served at the Wildflower is made from scratch in the back kitchen. The seniors and the regulars alike have come to expect nothing but homemade, from the crusty bread to real mashed potatoes, soups, and a changing variety of plate specials and baked goods.

Tourists following the Mississippi or using the Great River State Trail will be glad to learn that Trempealeau is home to a nice little cafe, for there aren't many worth stopping at along Wisconsin's southwestern boundary. The trail can be mighty long and wearisome for cyclists who have no hope of finding a good sandwich or piece of pie. Cheer up! The Wildflower Cafe has pie worth pedaling for, and in enough daily varieties to satisfy everyone in your group. Little stokers and bugger passengers make chocolate cream their top choice, with moms and dads opting for the fruit varieties. Other favorites for all ages and physiques include the peanut butter silk and seasonal pies like rhubarb and pumpkin.

. . . .

Next Best Bets

Blair
Dawn's Home Cooking
106 South Urberg Avenue
Tempting desserts and solicitous help in an expansive cafe.

Durand
Durand Diner and Bar
307 West Main Street
My first ever taste of corned beef hash at this mainstay on Main Street left me thinking there's got to be more to it than this.

Ettrick
Coffee Cup Cafe
22801 South Main
This farmer's favorite—and one of mine as well—recently changed hands. But a good cafe has forward momentum and the Coffee Cup will surely roll on down a bumpless road.

Fountain City
Bluff View Cafe
Highway 35
Between the Great River and the Great River Road, this cafe has a bulletin board with the state's largest collection of local business cards. The UPS man eats here, and that's a testimony as good as it gets.

Galesville
Garden of Eatin'
19847 East Gale Avenue
The garden has a few weeds—the hot beef doesn't meet my high demands for Wisconsinites' favorite menu item—but is generally in full bloom.

NELSON
Beth's Twin Bluffs
S286 State Road 35
With a large dining room, Beth's is more restaurant than cafe, but it does have home cooking and pies worth driving for. Popular with day trippers out of the Twin Cities and motorcyclists following the mighty Mississippi. Don't miss the Nelson Cheese Factory just down the road.

PEPIN
Ralph's Bar and Mary's Kitchen
206 Lake Street
A burger and soup's the ticket at this combination drinkery and eatery.

TOMAH
Ted's Corner Cafe
1120 Superior Avenue
Mickey Mouse pancakes are favorites with the kids, and the hot beef is worth a return trip.

WHITEHALL
City Cafe ¶●¶
1510 Main Street
This cavernous cafe once had a bowling alley in the basement. The usual pin-striped counter is a recycled lane. You'll roll a perfect game any day of the week with the slow-cooked casseroles and meats, all variety of baked goods, even homemade salad dressings.

Southwest

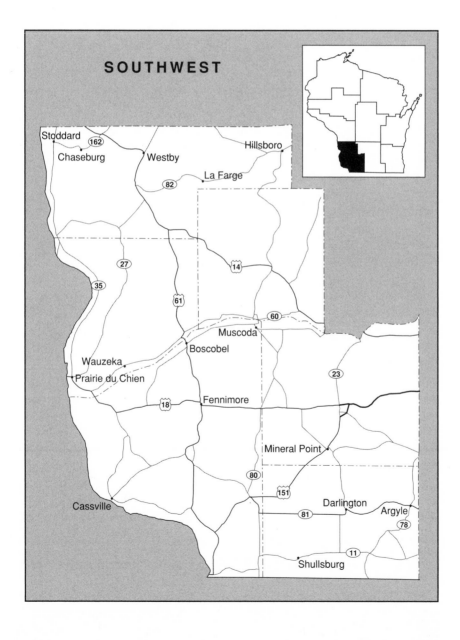

ARGYLE
Irma's Kitchen 🍽
318 Milwaukee Street
(608) 543-3703
M–Sa 6:30 A.M.–3 P.M.; Su closed
Joyce Flanagan and Patty Noble

Traveling west on Green County Highway C toward Argyle, I found a mailbox that looked like a Swiss chalet. Personalized mailboxes are some of my favorite things, and I carry a camera in the glove compartment to take pictures of any I find. I parked the car on the gravel shoulder and walked across the road for my picture. And there I met Ernest Steinmann, maker of the little Swiss chalet designed for mail and the inhabitant of the matching Swiss chalet designed for humans. "If you're headed into Argyle," he advised when he found out what I was up to, "you'd better stop at Irma's Kitchen." I was, so I did.

I can say without hesitation that Irma Collins, namesake of the Argyle cafe now owned and operated by daughters Joyce Flanagan and Patty Noble, makes the best cake doughnuts anywhere between the Mississippi and Lake Michigan. Practically greaseless, perfectly fresh, unadulterated with sugar or frosting and with the most delicate hint of nutmeg, these doughnuts begged to be tucked into a wax-coated sack and taken along with me for the day. Just what was I doing with three take-out doughnuts, as if I didn't eat enough food at the ten or twelve cafes I visited each day? But that's what good home cooking does to a person, and I doubted I'd ever pass through Argyle again. Thanks, Irma.

I was smitten with the doughnuts, but my four-year-old neighbor at the counter, Ashley, was just as sold on the toast and jelly. The elderly gentleman on my right sided with me, however, and ordered a doughnut and a cup of coffee with a sugar cookie chaser. Irma's is known for its tempting baked goods—doughnuts, sweet rolls, cookies, and above all, pies. Irma's pies, like the doughnuts, are positively poetic.

For twenty-nine years, the good people of Argyle have been spoiled by not only the great home cooking at Irma's Cafe but also the camaraderie and conversation. Two old gents at the table behind me discuss the upcoming lutefisk dinner put on by the Utica Lutheran Church. "When I was a kid," one says, "I wouldn't eat lutefisk for all the money in the world. Now I pay to eat it!"

The early morning breakfast talk competes with the collection of little plaques over the counter, with pithy sayings such as: "THE LORD GIVETH / THE GOVERNMENT TAKETH AWAY" and "PUSH BUTTON FOR SERVICE / If no one answers— / Get it yourself!"

"Oh, those old things," Patty tells me, "they've been here for what seems like forever." I can't help but wonder if she means the men or the plaques. Two years ago, Patty and Joyce took over the restaurant when their mother retired. Retirement may not be a wholly appropriate word because Irma continues to bake all of the pies and—praise the Lord!—the doughnuts.

"We'll always think of the restaurant as hers," says Patty. "We do everything just the same as Mom did. She passed on all of the recipes to us. All but the doughnuts. She says she's taking that one to her grave."

I'm sure I'm not the only one who hopes Irma is immortal.

BOSCOBEL
Unique Cafe 🍽 ⚲
1100 Wisconsin Avenue
(608) 375-4465
M–Th 6 A.M.–7 P.M.; F 6 A.M.–8 P.M.; Sa 6 A.M.–4 P.M.; Su 6 A.M.–2 P.M.
Doyle and Nancy Lewis
When he was a boy (and more recently than that), Doyle Lewis liked to prowl in aging dumps for old bottles and other discarded collectibles. His wife, Nancy, often wishes he weren't so prodigious a collector, but she puts up with the boxes and boxes of antique bottles stored upstairs on the second floor of the Unique Cafe she and Doyle own. "He's always collected old things," she says. "His interest has really developed since coming here and redoing the inside."

Many of the items Doyle salvaged from rubbish heaps appear as decorations throughout the spacious, high-ceilinged cafe. On the large range hood is his collection of multicolored Veedol, Wolf's Head, Ajax, and other brands of oil cans ("Who but Doyle Lewis would see art in motor oil cans?" the menu cover asks). On a shelf on the side wall are children's toy tractors, reapers, combines, and trucks, some on loan from a Milwaukee man who felt Doyle needed them for his display. In the glass floor case under the register are old toys—a jack-in-the-box, Dial typewriter, cars, marbles—and, of course, more bottles, some from long-closed area breweries and others commemorating historic events. Steel signs in high-gloss colors advertise Buckeye root beer and John Deere farm equipment, and above the door, mounted very, very securely, hangs a giant, red Mobil Pegasus.

"People know what's in here," Doyle says as his eyes sweep the room. "They know what's been added, when something's been moved. It might look like a disorganized mess to some people, but a lot of people know just what's here."

The same goes for Doyle's Packers Room in the basement, used for private parties and meetings of Boscobel civic groups. Filled with an assortment of green and gold Packer collectibles, the room is popular with "out of town, out of state, and out of country" visitors who marvel at the intensity of Doyle's devotion to the football team. "But it's not just me," he explains. "The Packers Room represents everyone."

Doyle's antiques and Packer collections contribute much to the nostalgic flavor of the Unique Cafe, moved in 1968 from its original location next to a drugstore a few doors away. (A police officer on hand for the three fifteen coffee klatch remembers helping to wheel the counter up the street.) Now housed in Boscobel's oldest limestone building, built from hand-hewn blocks in 1869, the Unique Cafe replaces the former Pipkin State Bank upstairs (once known as the Bird's Eye View of Boscobel) and a combined general merchandise/hardware store downstairs.

Doyle and Nancy became owners of the Unique Cafe in 1982 when they purchased the business from Doyle's mother, who owned a cafe in Soldiers Grove before that town was swallowed up by the Kickapoo River. When Soldiers Grove was relocated to higher ground, the state of Wisconsin reestablished Doyle's mother's business in Boscobel's Unique Cafe. Her new business was never a great success, however, because, Doyle explains, "this cafe was so much bigger, the town was so much bigger, that the work got to be too much for her."

Having worked in a large Sauk City restaurant for several years, Doyle and Nancy came to Boscobel to take over the restaurant from his mother. He and Nancy made many changes: enlarging the cafe by tearing down a center wall and adding more tables and booths, refurbishing the kitchen, adding air conditioning. "We were naive when we bought this," Nancy says. "We never realized how much work it needed. We've been here twenty years and we're still not there. It's been a really big sacrifice. We haven't been able to buy a house. We haven't had kids."

Other changes included establishing new "food traditions" based on conscientious, homemade quality. "Mom's place was kind of a greasy spoon type place," Doyle explains. "The only thing we continued was the hot beefs and the large pancakes."

"I wanted small ones," laughs Nancy, "but the customers insisted on large pancakes! From the beginning, we've refused to use mixes or instant mashed potatoes. Home cooking isn't that much more work, and it's cheaper than mixes. I don't have to pay myself to do it! Besides, we want to hear the people say how good it is. And when you're used to doing it, it's easy."

Among the "easy food traditions" at the Unique Cafe are Nancy's homemade pies, especially the sour cream raisin (made on Fridays) and the

Unique cream, a vanilla pudding filled with coconut and sliced bananas and topped with meringue. Sweet tooths will also swoon at homemade doughnuts, cinnamon and caramel rolls, cookies, and malts made in a newly refinished green Hamilton Beach machine from real ice cream scooped from the "working" soda fountain. Those more inclined to beef than bon-bons will appreciate the oversized burgers on fresh-baked buns and fresh-roasted meats and homemade gravies. For veggie lovers and waistline watchers, Nancy packs a salad bar to overflowing with crisp fixings and her own potato, pasta, and vegetable salads, "and of course Jell-O. It's a real comfort food. You've got to have green Jell-O and marshmallows. I like to throw everything in it, give it some substance."

Nancy can have the green Jell-O. I'll take pie. I remember the first time I stopped at the Unique Cafe in 1989 as one of hundreds of GRABAAWR cyclists. Climbing up the ridges south of the Wisconsin River, I began to dream about homemade pie. When I dropped out of the hills into downtown Boscobel and saw the bikes leaning against the outside of the Unique Cafe, I knew I'd found the place. Even day-old, the peanut butter pie was the stuff of dreams.

The next year we again pedaled into downtown Boscobel, this time in a chilling, miserable rain. The Unique Cafe was crowded and steamy with dripping cyclists hovering over bowls of soup and cups of hot coffee. I ordered a grilled ham and cheese sandwich—hot and melty, with a slice of ham as thick as my finger—and a huge wedge of sour cream raisin pie. We ate and ate, thinking we'd wait out the rain in the Lewises' cafe. But the sun came out earlier than expected, and we climbed our way into coulee country with painfully full bellies.

Nancy and Doyle remember those visits too, and all the others every year since. "One of the highlights of our year is the day hundreds of cyclists come into town," Doyle says. "They pack this place and really have us running. One year it was raining and we had cold, wet cyclists staying here for a couple of hours. They come every year and call ahead to let us know they're coming, so we haven't run out of food yet. It's been pretty close some years, though!"

CHASEBURG
DeGarmo's Tippy Toe Inn
307 Depot Street
(608) 483-2119
M–Th 6 A.M.–1 P.M.; F 6 A.M.–1 P.M. and 5 P.M.–9:30 P.M.; Sa 7 A.M.–1 P.M.; Su 7 A.M.–12 P.M.
Linda and Marv DeGarmo

My La Crosse friend Eric led a peloton of fellow bicyclists up coulees and down to the Tippy Toe Inn one morning for breakfast. The food was so good, he told me, that he wouldn't hesitate to do it again. That's a pretty convincing endorsement for the Tippy Toe, which by its name alone would have misled me into thinking it was a tavern. So, on a blustery October morning I drove south out of La Crosse, hugging the Mississippi River, to the tiny hillside village of Chaseburg.

At the Tippy Toe Inn I found Linda DeGarmo frying eggs at the huge stainless grill in the kitchen. She laughed when I confessed my doubts about the place on account of its name.

"The name's a joke," she says. "Years ago when it first opened, some-one came up with the name because 'you tippy toe in and stagger out,'" she said. "And it stuck. It's been the Tippy Toe Inn ever since."

Sixty years ago, the Tippy Toe Inn was born as a tavern. Linda says the old-timers remember the basement being dug out with shovels. The railroad came through Chaseburg back then, and the engineer would stop the train so the crew could get out and eat. Over the years, as the food portion of the business grew, the Tippy Toe became known as much as a restaurant as a bar. "It's always been known for good food. It has a good reputation," Linda says.

It was in part its reputation that led Linda and her husband, Marvin, to buy the Tippy Toe Inn in 2000. "Chaseburg has five bars—you can see that Chaseburg isn't a big town—and we felt we really needed a cafe. So we bought it with the intention of running it as a restaurant."

In the summer of 2002, the DeGarmos doubled the size of the Tippy Toe Inn by enlarging the kitchen and adding a nonsmoking dining room. The new addition reflects Marvin's passion for stock car racing—he is both a fan and a racer himself—with finish flag checked tablecloths and walls filled with awards, posters, and assorted memorabilia, including a car hood in memory of racing great Dale Earnhardt. The old Tippy Toe with its characteristic tavern look is just on the other side of the wall.

A native of Chaseburg, Linda remembers as a teenager going to the Tippy Toe with her sister for sandwiches and pop. Though it was a local hangout, the Tippy Toe was frowned upon by her Norwegian grandmother, an immigrant at age sixteen, who disapproved of the beer drinking and card playing that went on there. What she would say about Linda's ownership of the Tippy Toe is uncertain, but she'd no doubt be proud of its evolution into a family eatery with a commitment to home cooking.

"We have everything real here," Linda says. "We don't use margarine. We don't use instants. We even just started handling decaf!"

The Tippy Toe excels at breakfast, which packs the place with local farmers, truckers, and others—including bicyclists from La Crosse—requiring a belly full to start the day. Eggs and toast, eggs and hash browns, eggs and a slab of meat—all are popular at the Tippy Toe. The stuffed hash browns filled with chopped green pepper, onions, ham, and Swiss cheese are a best-seller. Linda calls the stuffed hash browns a potato omelette.

Later in the day, both at noon and in the evening, the Tippy Toe fills with people hungry for the kind of food they no longer make at home for themselves: real mashed potatoes, slow-simmered soups, roasted meats and gravy, and pies and other desserts. The hot beef sandwich is always a best seller, but the regulars also go for the mushroom Swiss burger, the pasta offerings available every Monday night, and the steak fry offered on the fourth Saturday of each month. The place is generally packed for the Friday night fish fry, leaving little room for the area Amish who, Linda reports, are "pretty shy about coming in and prefer to order take-out. They take a fork to eat it on the way home. If they wait to eat it until they get home, it's cold."

LA FARGE
Chatterbox Cafe
110 Main Street
(608) 625-4040
M–Sa 6:30 A.M.–8 P.M.; Su 7 A.M.–2 P.M.
Danny and Nancy Green

Danny Green is away from the Chatterbox Cafe, attending parents day at his son's school. While other dads talk about their jobs doing road construction, farming, or other manly work, Danny shares his day-to-day experiences manning the kitchen in La Farge's cafe. His wife, Nancy, tells me, "The previous owner told us people in a small town don't want to see a man in the kitchen. That lasted about a month." Now, the only person they want back there is Danny himself.

A year ago, Danny was just like the other dads at parents day. A boy growing up on a farm in the vicinity of a small town like La Farge, Danny trod likely paths to the adult world of employment. He served a stint in the military and then parlayed his experience into a job as a heavy equipment mechanic—a reasonable compromise to his youthful dream of being an auto mechanic. As his three children grew older, however, Nancy says he felt the need to "have something for the future." As it turns out, the future was in the past: in his great passion for cooking that took root and was fostered by his mother back on the farm.

"Cooking and mechanics, it's the same thing," observes Nancy. "It's about creating things. About taking different parts and assembling them into a motor or a casserole or soup."

It's this sentiment that ensures only home cooking will come from Danny's kitchen. Danny Green loves to think up new foods, prepare them, and serve them. "He doesn't use cookbooks or recipes so to say," Nancy points out. "What he makes is what he makes up."

That is not to say that old standby favorites are unknown at the Chatterbox. Danny and Nancy couldn't let a day pass without his well-loved chili, which sells at an average of two gallons a day, even in the dead-heat of summer. The locals' collective mood can be gauged by the size of bowl they request. Today is a salad bowl day—cold and wet, gloomy and gray—that demands a hefty helping of chili. "There's some days we just can't have enough chili," Nancy points out.

Other favorites, like chicken noodle soup and Tater Tot hotdish, are childhood comforts. "We used to feed Tater Tot hotdish to the babies instead of rice cereal. We'd add formula to the casserole and blend it in the blender," recalls Nancy. The days of bottle and spoon-feeding are decades in the past for most of the Chatterbox regulars, but a hot mound of ground beef, mixed vegetables, and Tater Tots baked together with cream of mushroom soup still does wonders to soothe the ache of an empty belly.

Home recipes, home favorites—the food at the Chatterbox is as real as it gets. "If it's not home cooking, it's not served here," Danny promises. Top off the Tater Tot hotdish with a wedge of deep-dish, real apple pie made by a local Amish woman from Danny's foster mother's recipe. "She bought Mom's cookbooks and recipes at the sale," he explains, "but it never dawned on me that the pies are Mom's."

Danny and Nancy's confidence and success belie the fact that, at the time of my visit, they have been on the job for only one month. They have settled in comfortably after that first day, when the previous owner opened, got them started, and then left them to finish and close up the old main street restaurant made out of a Quonset hut. With interior side walls that curve upward to the ceiling, its origins are unmistakable, no matter how much past owners tried to disguise it by laying up a brick false front on which can still be read the cafe's long-ago name: BAND BOX CAFE.

Inside, the Chatterbox Cafe, which seats about forty people, has a wonderful postwar look, with vintage green floor tiles, wood chairs and tables, a huge Kelvinator ice cream freezer, and, behind the counter, a Multimix malt machine. As owners came and went, they tried to bring the place into current time by hanging fresh wallpaper and coating everything with another layer of paint, but thankfully, no one had enough money for a complete makeover. The Chatterbox Cafe has a patina of age and authenticity that matches its food. Come for both, but be prepared to wait. "It may take a little while longer to get your food," Nancy advises. "Real food takes time."

MINERAL POINT
Red Rooster Cafe 🍽
158 High Street
(608) 987-9936
Summer: M–Su 5 A.M.–7 P.M.
Winter: M–Su 5 A.M.–5 P.M.
Helena Lawinger and Patti McKinley

Mineral Point is the center of Wisconsin's Cornish country, settled as early as 1830 by lead miners from Cornwall, England, who built homes of the native yellow stone and baked pasties—seasoned beef, potatoes, rutabaga, and onions wrapped in pastry—on their hearths. When the area's lead, copper, and zinc mines stopped producing, the Cornish people left or lingered, their houses slowly decaying with hard wear and neglect.

In 1935 Robert Neal and Edgar Hellum purchased an old stone house (and later its neighbors) and set about restoring it. They christened it Pendarvis. They began serving Cornish teas and pastries to visitors attracted to the nostalgic charm of streets such as Shake Rag and Jail Alley, gradually expanding their menu to include pasties and other Cornish specialties. In 1937 Duncan Hines, who was seeking unusual regional eateries for his gustatory guidebook, *Adventures in Good Eating*, visited them. Hines was thrilled with the saffron cake, clotted cream, plum preserves, and pasty served at Pendarvis House, and in his 1937 and 1939 issues he encouraged adventure eaters to stop for a visit.

Pendarvis House, now a state historic site, no longer serves food, but you can still find Cornish delights at the Red Rooster Cafe on High Street, owned since 1972 by Helena Lawinger and her daughter, Patti McKinley, who joined her in 1981. Patti says tourists frequently have to be told what a pasty is, but once they try them, they come back, sometimes filling empty coolers so they can enjoy pasties at home throughout the year. "Other people come down from Pendarvis where they're explained," she notes.

Served with a side of fresh salad—my choices were coleslaw, macaroni salad, or Jell-O—the pasties at the Red Rooster are filling, just as they ought to be: a meal to tide a lead miner over a thirteen-hour workday. Made with cube steak ("the better the meat, the better the pasty," Helena says) and available either in the traditional pastry pocket or layered in a baking pan, the Red Rooster's pasty is most popular with the tourists and other out-of-town visitors. "Local people eat it some," Helena notes.

The plump pasties don't leave modern day folks much room for dessert, but loosen your belt a notch in order to sample a piece of figgyhobbin, a rich, raisin and walnut-filled pastry covered with thick caramel sauce and whipped cream, or a piece of fresh fruit homemade pie. Having eyed mine with increasing curiosity, the two ladies at the table behind me split a piece of figgyhobbin, moaning with delight at each bite.

Helena, Patti says, has a gift for cooking. "She can taste food and copy it. People are all the time asking us for recipes, but she doesn't use any. It's just a little of this, a little of that." Though the conservative nature of Wisconsin cafe food is often limiting, Helena satisfies her creative impulses by eating out at other restaurants, trying different foods, and bringing new ideas back to the Red Rooster's kitchen to try on the locals. During a trip through the South, for example, Helena discovered biscuits and gravy, now a popular Wednesday breakfast feature. "We sell out right away," Helena notes.

While Duncan Hines's volumes of *Adventures in Good Eating* have long been banished to dark, dusty library archives, more recent writers have ventured to the Mineral Point restaurant filled with roosters ("Mom's always collected roosters," Patti says, "but the wallpaper took forever to find") and sung its praises. In the 1980s the Red Rooster and its humble meat pie was featured in the "Secret Snacker" segment of *P.M. Magazine,* the *New York Times,* and the *Chicago Tribune.* In 1998 the Red Rooster won Best Pasty recognition by the readers of *Wisconsin Trails* magazine and was named one of the top ten dining places in the state. In August 2001 *Discover Wisconsin Radio* honored the Red Rooster as Restaurant of the Month.

All that matters little to the locals, however, who treat fame like a next-door neighbor. Every day—just as they always have—they face each other across the horseshoe-shaped counter for coffee and chatter. "When we bought this place," Patti recalls, "the counter used to be real long and faced the wall. Dad moved it to the center of the room and made it U-shaped. He made it a locals' counter." Others settle into their "reserved" tables along the side wall, under old black and white photos of Mineral Point, or the "locals' booth" set out with a red candle and a special ashtray for an older gentleman who likes it best.

Over the years, Patti says, "we've seen lots of customers pass away. When you see them every day, you miss them. They tell you about their lives, and you really get to know them." When Helena and Patti celebrated their thirtieth anniversary, photographs of regular customers were pinned to the bulletin board near the front door. Dressed in Santa suits, decked out in parade regalia, and captured at their card-playing, breakfast-eating, coffee-klatching best, they tell the story of the Red Rooster. Fame be darned. They're still just hometown folks.

STODDARD
Mamie's Cafe
122 South Main Street
(608) 457-2777
M–Th 6 A.M.–4 P.M.; F 6 A.M.–8 P.M.; Sa 7 A.M.–4 P.M.; Su 7 A.M.–2 P.M.
Tom Ristow and Karen Loomis
Snow is falling in gloppy white flakes the March morning I drive south out of La Crosse in search of Mamie's Cafe, recommended to me by a group of southern Minnesota cyclists. The village of Stoddard is stretched out along both sides of the highway like beads on a string, but there are few pearls among the handful of buildings built cheap and easy between this century and the beginning of the last. Yet Stoddard is undergoing a kind of renaissance built on the hope that it could be a stop and shop town for tourists trolling the river highway.

If any place in Stoddard is worth stopping for, it is Mamie's Cafe—the only cafe on Wisconsin's Great River Road between Prairie du Chien and La Crosse. Unlike pseudo-country gift shops selling highly fragranced candles and the latest fad in collectibles, Mamie's is just the kind of genuine small town place tourists are hoping to find. Tucked into a little building with yellow siding—the town's former video store—the cafe features authentic home-style food worth driving for.

Just ask my table partner, trucker Steve Schmitz from nearby La Crosse, who has been crisscrossing the Upper Midwest for going on twenty-seven years. Heading south on the Great River Road with a load, he began to feel the familiar gnawing that signaled it was time for breakfast. Up ahead he spotted cars parked along the curb, a pretty reliable sign, in his book, of either a darn decent cafe or a tavern. Hoping for the former, he downshifted and crawled through Stoddard, spotting the green awning with the words Mamie's Cafe. "I drove past the place while I was looking for it," he relates, "then I backed up the truck to get back."

Mamie's Cafe was filled with breakfasters of all shapes and sizes when I wandered in with morning hunger, and co-owner Tom Ristow looked puzzled as to where he might seat me. Steve saved the day by offering to share his table, and I seized the opportunity to meet someone new.

Good choice, too. Steve is an expert on small town cafes, having stopped at hundreds during the course of his trucking career.

"You just never forget the good ones," he says. "Number one, it's the food. I gotta have home-cooked, what-I-like meals. Number two, it's the people. They treat you like family."

At Mamie's Cafe, Tom's mom is your mom. He and Karen named the cafe in her honor, even though Mom's real name is Rose Norby. She became Mamie years ago when her oldest daughter couldn't quite say Mommy. In any case, Mamie's is a good, down-home, familial name for a cafe that promises the "best darn good cookin' around." Steve Schmitz is convinced of that. His plate of fried eggs, hash browns, sausage, and toast was so good, he'll be back. And with prices significantly lower than most he encounters on the road, he'll be back as often as his trucking routes allow.

Mamie's menu has pretty standard fare—burgers, soups, meat and potatoes daily specials—but there are a few surprises. Capitalizing on their location beside the Mighty Mississippi, Tom and Karen offer the "fisherman's brown bag special," consisting of a cold sandwich, chips, cole-slaw, and a cookie. Sick of ham and cheese? Try the bologna, peanut butter and jelly, or braunschweiger sandwiches. I can promise you're not going to find braunschweiger—it was called mushy meat in my family when I was growing up—anywhere else in Wisconsin.

WAUZEKA
Hayseed Cafe
206 Front Street
(608) 875-5611
M closed; Tu–Sa 6 A.M.–8 P.M.; Su 8 A.M.–2 P.M.
Corliss "Corky" Mead and Beth Groom
On a summer day not long ago, neighbors Corky Mead and Beth Groom decided to combine their two yard sales into one. Corky made macaroni salad for lunch and shared it with Beth.

"It was the best macaroni salad I ever had," remembers Beth. "I said, 'It's so good, you should sell it.' And she said, 'I always wanted to run a restaurant.'"

As it turned out, Corky and Beth shared a dream. With each other's support and that of their contractor husbands, they turned Wauzeka's homely funeral parlor into a fashionable, friendly cafe. During the three months the transformation was in the works, many of the local people dropped in to check its progress. "They were shocked because they knew it was a funeral home," Corky says. Beth and Corky are proud to show doubters their collection of "before" and "during" photographs. The "after" views are the cafe itself.

"The first time we looked at the funeral home, we could see it," Beth says. "We just told our husbands what we wanted." What they saw is what you get: a clean, bright, and warm interior featuring a counter made of weathered barn boards and wood booths in the front windows. The former funeral home's showing room is now a spacious side dining room that is filled on Friday nights with fans of the Hayseed's cod loins and bluegill filets, which Corky and Beth hand-dip in beer batter before deep frying.

The cafe's rustic, country appearance is right in sync with Corky and Beth's choice of names for it. "We wanted a name that reflected the country theme," Corky says. "We wanted something that reflected the area's alfalfa farming." They considered a handful before settling on the Hayseed Cafe and a logo that shows a wagon heaped with hay and pulled by two horses wearing hats. "That pretty much sums up what we're about," says Beth.

The Hayseed Cafe has been open only a few years. From the beginning Beth and Corky made a commitment to home cooking. Says Beth, "Everything that's feasible to make homemade we do." This means fresh baked goods made from favorite recipes used at home—including coffee cake, muffins, cinnamon rolls, cookies, and honey-oatmeal bread used for French toast—real mashed potatoes, Corky's life-changing macaroni salad, even slow roasted meats that Corky seasons to perfection. "She rubs spices into roasts like she's powdering a baby," points out Beth.

Full of good ideas, a love for cooking and creative energy, Corky and Beth are discovering day by day that though they're the cafe's owners, they're not really the ones in charge. "Every day brings constant adjustments," notes Corky. Like the day a busload of women showed up hungry for pie, only there wasn't a pie in the place.

"We'd only been open a few weeks, and we hadn't yet got the system down enough to make pie," Beth remembers. "They all settled on ice cream. The next time they came, we had pie—apple, cherry, and blueberry—but what did they want? They all wanted ice cream! Every day it's clear. What we do in the future will be dictated by what our customers do, and what they want."

WESTBY
Borgen's Norwegian Cafe and Bakery ◉ ▋
109 South Main Street
(608) 634-3516
April–December: M–Su 5:30 A.M.–6 P.M.
January–March: M–Th 5 A.M.–6 P.M.; F 5 A.M.–8 P.M.;
Sa–Su 5:30 A.M.–6 P.M.
Donna and LeRoy "Perk" Perkins
First opened in 1904 by Norwegian immigrants Engebert and Anna Borgen as a combination tavern, cafe, and tobacco store, Borgen's Norwegian Cafe and Bakery, purchased by Perk and Donna Perkins in 1973, is known state-wide (and beyond) as the home of great home cooking and even better baking. Ten years ago in Vilas County, a state trooper who pulled me over for speeding rhapsodized about the real mashed potato noon plate specials. In Baraboo a pair of truckers praised the endless Friday night smorgasbord, and in Wisconsin Dells, a couple following the "cafe trail" in southwestern Wisconsin swooned over the caramel-pecan rolls, "real scratch" pies, and coffee. My waitress agrees that "people come from all over" to sample the extraordinary cooking and proudly adds, "We're pretty well known even in Norway."

To accommodate the overflow of locals, tourists, businessmen, and troopers and the demand for banquets, parties, and receptions, the Perkinses bought the neighboring building a number of years ago. The back half is a gift shop selling Norwegian collectibles and Amish furniture, crafts, candies, and other foods made by the area's Amish. The front half is filled with tables and chairs—and a great glass box containing three life-size mannequins wearing Norwegian festive costumes, or *bunad,* from the district of Gudbrandsdalen. I mention this because not only are the bunad worth seeing but the sight of people in a glass box may startle you. The people are not real. The bunad are.

Donna and Perk ordered the bunad from a seamstress in Norway, a friend of a local woman. The arrival of the completed bunad was greatly anticipated, but after a few years passed, Donna and Perk began to feel they had been cheated. "Then they arrived piece by piece," remembers Donna. "We got a package addressed, 'Please take to chef in Westby.' Another package arrived at the school bus station in Westby." Grateful that the costumes had at long last arrived, the Perkinses carefully dressed their mannequins and encased them in the great glass box. That was many years ago, and the bunad are still as fresh and clean as the day they arrived in Westby.

Despite the availability of the spacious side dining room (or perhaps they are uncomfortable with the people in the great glass box), the locals tend to stick to their "coffee break corner" in the cafe's original room. "That corner's filled all day," laugh the waitresses gathered with me at the counter for a chat between orders. "See, somebody hung a sign on the wall above the table."

"COFFEE BREAK 9:00–5:00 DAILY."

"The men come and go like ants on a hill!" a waitress tells me. "There's more bull spread at that table than most of the farms around here. If you believe everything they say, well!"

The truth may be exaggerated and reshaped in the coffee break corner, but the tales I've heard about the food at Borgen's are true enough. Roast beef, Norwegian meatballs, chicken, and the ever-changing daily specials based on meat, real mashed potatoes and gravy, and vegetables require heavy decision-making Monday through Thursday, but on Friday everyone agrees on Borgen's famous smorgasbord, served from 11 A.M. to 8 P.M. Built around oven-baked chicken, Norwegian meatballs, and traditional end-of-the-workweek fish, the smorgasbord includes a cornucopia of home-cooked accompaniments: a bar with twelve varieties of salad; baked, mashed, or French-fried potatoes; dinner rolls, and a variety of vegetables.

Added by the Perkinses in 1973, the bakery, whose motto is "Where Pies Я Us," makes up the other half of Borgen's Norwegian Cafe and Bakery. It features a gamut of baked goods, from Norwegian treats like fattimand, sandbakels, and lefse (available during the Christmas season and as special orders year-round) to caramel and pecan rolls, crusty homemade white and wheat bread, doughnuts, cheesecake and real-crust, seasonal real fruit and cream pies to the tune of twenty per day. The baked goods are available both off the menu and as take-out items from the table in the center of the cafe's main dining room, but you'll want to come early in the day because by noon the table is pretty picked over. If you come too late and find the coconut cream pie you counted on sold out, compromise with the banana, sour cream raisin, chocolate, lemon meringue, pumpkin, Hershey-almond, graham cracker cream, apple, or seasonal strawberry or peach glazed. Whew! Borgen's bakers have a pie repertoire of over fifty varieties, so you're bound to find something worth swooning over.

The pies are made by Donna's mother, Alice Amundson, and Audrey Slack, both of whom have worked at the cafe since the fall of 1973. Donna takes me back to the kitchen to meet Alice, whose hands are covered with apple pieces dredged in a sugar-flour mixture. At the counter beside her, Donna's father, Elmer, is at work making rolled and cut sugar cookies in the shape of pumpkins. In his eighties, he is well—and happily—into a second career.

Donna explains, "He sold the farm and just about went crazy at home with nothing to do. He came in to drink coffee twice a day. Dad drove Mom to work, and then he'd go to our house and clean and iron clothes. Then he started baking here, helping out Mom by making cookies, mixing batter, making doughnuts and sweet rolls. One day, after helping to make several double-batches of doughnuts, Dad said, 'If you see me rolling down Main Street like a doughnut, you'll know I turned into one!'"

Despite his light-hearted complaints, Elmer enjoyed the baking so much, he stayed. "They just have a routine," Donna says. "They work together like a well-oiled machine."

Next Best Bets

Boscobel
Home Town Cafe
928 Wisconsin Avenue
The latecomer on Boscobel's main street, this cafe has stiff competition. Worth a try, but my loyalty to the Unique Cafe just can't be swayed.

Boscobel
The Vale Inn
813 Wisconsin Avenue
Beef stew over biscuits was just the ticket for a rainy and cold October day described as "damned damp" by a white-haired gent. A plaque over the counter reads: "The only thing more overrated than natural childbirth is the joy of owning your own business."

Cassville
Rivers Cafe
115 East Amelia Street
After your trip into the past at nearby Stonefield Village, take comfort in the present with an old-fashioned bowl of homemade soup.

Darlington
The Towne House
232 Main Street
Try as I would, I just couldn't finish the gigantic piece of coconut cream pie that was placed in front of me. And it was so good.

Fennimore
Our Little Restaurant and Bakery
940 Lincoln Street

Fresh baked goods of all varieties—including pie. My burger on a buttered, toasted homemade roll was as good as it gets, and I loved sharing the cafeteria-style tables with the locals. This relatively new cafe deserves return visits.

Hillsboro
Country Style Cookin' Restaurant |●|
824 East Water Street

Bypass the old stand-by selections at this coulee country favorite and dive into a bowl of out-of-the-ordinary shuleke—Czechoslovakian chicken dumpling soup. If it's Thursday, opt for the corned beef and cabbage.

Muscoda
Mary's Sunrise Cafe
132 North Iowa Street

My view of the old-timers straddling the chrome stools at the counter looked just like a photograph.

Prairie du Chien
Hungry House Cafe |●|
531 North Marquette Road

When the original *Cafe Wisconsin* came out in 1993, the Hungry House was a hole-in-the-wall downtown cafe. It has moved to the highway and expanded out of the cafe category, but stop in and see the full-scale family restaurant it has become. The food is still genuine and home cooked.

Shullsburg
Miner Alley Restaurant
133 West Water Street

Filled with an impressive collection of local high school sports memorabilia—red and white Shullsburg Miners uniforms, vintage letter sweaters, old leather baseball gloves, and sepia-toned photographs. There's no better display of local pride anywhere in the state. The menu is a cross between a traditional cafe and a burger joint.

Wauzeka
Wauzeka Family Cafe
102 South Business Street

Steady and true, and the longtime town hall for the local farmers and their wives.

South Central

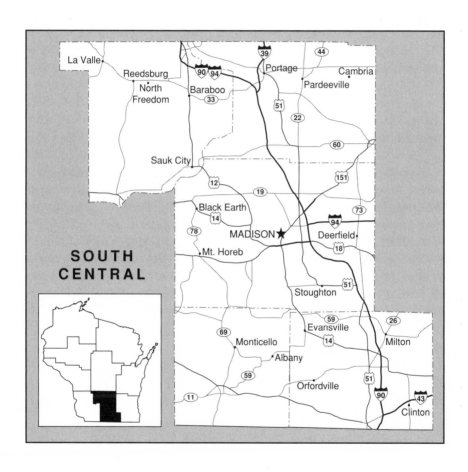

La Valle

Reedsburg

North Freedom

Baraboo 33

Sauk City

Black Earth 14

78

MADISON ★

Mt. Horeb

Portage

90 94

39

44

Cambria

Pardeeville

51

22

60

151

19

73

94

Deerfield

18

Stoughton 51

SOUTH CENTRAL

69

Monticello

Albany

59

11

59

Evansville

14

26

Milton

Orfordville 51

90

43

Clinton

12

ALBANY

Edgewater Cafe

101 North Water Street

(608) 862-3396

M–Th 6 A.M.–4 P.M.; F 6 A.M.–8 P.M.; Sa 6 A.M.–4 P.M.; Su 6 A.M.–1 P.M.

Terry and Roberta O'Bel

An amazing thing about the Edgewater Cafe is the transformation it has undergone since my first visit in 1992. It has improved considerably and is now one I heartily recommend to all adventure eaters. Terry and Roberta O'Bel were dairy farmers when Roberta decided to take over the restaurant. Terry soon followed, giving up the farm and enrolling in baking school. The beautiful pies and other baked goods, including "from-scratch bread," cakes, cookies, even cream puffs, are all products of Terry's hands. Between the two of them, everything made at the Edgewater Cafe is the real thing. "Everything here is made from scratch," explains Terry. "We don't use frozen potatoes or hash browns. We peel the real things ourselves. I won't fix something for someone else that I wouldn't eat," explains Roberta.

Every morning at five, Roberta goes down to the cafe, where she puts on a pot of coffee and turns on the grill. At five twenty, forty minutes before the cafe officially opens, the very early coffee drinkers arrive. They help themselves to coffee—setting additional pots to brew if necessary— and drink themselves awake before heading off to work. While the O'Bels prepare the daily soups and specials, the second shift of coffee drinkers gather around the community table, where they pass a few hours over talk and coffee. The group is fluid and changing; as men get up to leave, their places are quickly filled with newcomers. "Everyone pretty much knows who sits where," Roberta says.

Despite the unwavering loyalty of the locals, Roberta estimates that almost 75 percent of her customers make the trip from Freeport (Illinois), Brodhead, Janesville, and Madison. The Edgewater is certainly a destination cafe, one of those seven calendar dreams described by William Least Heat-Moon in *Blue Highways*. The cooking is authentic and true, as is the atmosphere. I especially like the old hardwood floor that was uncovered and restored after the carpet was removed, and the Howdy Doody and Bozo dolls supervising the comings and goings of the regulars from their perch on a shelf behind the counter.

BARABOO
Teri's Restaurant 🍽️
111 Fourth Street
(608) 356-5647
M–F 6 A.M.–3 P.M.; Sa 6 A.M.–11 A.M.; Su closed
Teri Scott

At three o'clock, with her restaurant closed and the day's work behind her, Teri Scott settles into a booth with a glass of Pepsi and announces, "I'm a dying breed. That's what people tell me. Ninety percent of what I serve here is made from scratch. That's the way I've always done it. I grew up in a family of eleven kids, so fixing supper was always a big thing."

The reputation of Teri's café is built on her luscious pies, which fill the glass case above the counter every morning but by closing time have disappeared. Teri likes to "putz" with pie, creating varieties such as cookies and cream and chocolate peanut butter to accompany more traditional cream and two-crust fruit pies. She also makes a sinful chocolate-almond torte, decadently rich and served in pieces large enough to split with a friend but much too good to split honestly.

Soups and daily specials, such as meat loaf and goulash, attract a loyal crowd, as do the homemade pancakes—the blueberry ones are packed with berries—and other breakfast items. When I stopped for breakfast the next day, Teri's was filled with locals swabbing egg yolks off their plates with toast, catching up on the latest news, spreading gossip, and trading jokes. "I see the same people every morning," Teri says. "I may not remember their names, but I sure know what they order." (And she does. I'd told her I'd stop for blueberry pancakes, and she knew I was up front when she saw my order.)

Out of the family kitchen and into restaurant work at the age of sixteen, Teri soon discovered that growing up as one of eleven kids was the perfect preparation for success in a small town cafe. From her mom she learned how to prepare the "down to earth" foods the customers want. From her brothers and sister she learned how to take "zingers" and give them back. "The customers want to come in here and have fun," she explains. "They want to have us send zingers back over the counter. Sometimes, though, apologies have to be made the next day."

Teri's "family" is now considerably larger than the one in which she grew up and includes a mixture of the Baraboo retired and business communities. She estimates that at least 70 percent of her customers—a majority of them men—come in at least three times a week. With nearly everyone, she says, "it's a first-name basis, a real personal thing."

The businessmen require a bit less mothering than the retired gentlemen, quite a few of whom are widowed or alone because of other circumstances. Quick to laugh and with a generous heart, Teri tends her customers as skillfully as she tends the kitchen, supervising the diets of those with special health problems, checking up on regulars whose absences are unexpected and unexplained, and providing balanced, home-cooked meals for men who would otherwise "eat out of a can." "I like to be important to people," Teri explains. "I don't think anyone else sees these people daily like I do. Bars used to do the babysitting, but now it's cafes—for at least the past thirty-five years or so. In Chicago, you don't know your neighbor and don't care. But in Baraboo, you know who did what when and why. It's not snoopiness. It's just the way we grew up, a genuine caring."

The past ten years have had their high and low points for Teri. She was divorced and remarried a man she met at her counter. He died and left her a widow. Through it all, the cafe and her customers have been the anchor that kept her from going adrift. She is now looking toward retirement and has the restaurant up for sale. She realizes she will miss the rhythm of the work and the camaraderie of friends, but she is ready to move on to new experiences that will guide her life as a single woman.

BLACK EARTH
Lunch Bucket Cafe 🍽
1204 Mills Street
(608) 767-3750
M closed; Tu–F 5:30 A.M.–3 P.M.; Sa 6 A.M.–11 A.M.; Su 7 A.M.–11 A.M.
Barb Paar
Barb Paar, owner of the Lunch Bucket Cafe since 1988, refers all questions of history to Roy Sarbacker, who grew up in Black Earth, retired as the town postmaster, and now stops at the cafe three times a day for coffee, cards, and meals. According to Roy, the building now occupied by one half of the Lunch Bucket was a combined clothing and general store around the turn of the century. In 1920 a drugstore moved in, and fifteen years later a pink marble soda fountain—now the counter—was shipped from St. Louis and installed along the south wall. By 1940 the pharmacy had closed and, Roy says, "two guys from Rice Lake bought the place and made it into a kind of teen hangout, with booths and pinball machines. It's been a full cafe for about nineteen or twenty years.

"It's been a hangout for me since high school, you might say," continues Roy, who arrives about five thirty every day for breakfast with the "early coffee klatch" made up of "about five to seven retired guys—sixty-five, seventy-five, eighty-five—and usually two women."

"Five thirty?" I ask. "Isn't that kind of early?"

"I used to work at the post office early and have always gotten up early," Roy replies. "There's another group of younger fellows comes in at five thirty too, and I guess if they can, we can. Then after we leave another group comes in and talks about sporting and hunting. But that's not things we talk about. We're trying to straighten out the world!"

Roy returns at about nine, when he joins friends for midmorning coffee and a hand of cards, and again about two thirty, meeting friends for coffee and talk. The social world of Barb's cafe is a satisfactory substitute for the continuous interaction with the community provided by Roy's postal job but displaced by his retirement. Speaking for others as well as himself, Roy says, "I don't know where I'd be if this cafe weren't here. It's kind of the center of the community."

At the center of the center is Barb Paar, who, like Teri Scott in Baraboo, has been recently widowed. For years, Barb cooked at an area nightclub, dreaming of someday owning her own restaurant. She says, "We always talked about moving north and buying a resort. Lawrence would run the resort, and I would run the dining part of it. After we bought this, he'd say, 'Well, you got your restaurant, but I still don't have my resort.'"

She whisks an egg and milk in a bowl for French toast, then dips thick Texas-style bread into it before dropping it on the sizzling grill behind the counter. "Lots of people tried to get a restaurant going here but never put their heart into it. I decided, 'Okay, this is it,' and made it a success. But the best compliment I've had was unintended. One day I overheard one of the guys say, 'Well! Black Earth's finally got a restaurant!' That's when I knew I was doing everything right."

In 1998 the readers of the local newspaper, the Black Earth *News-Sickle-Arrow*, concurred by voting for Barb and the Lunch Bucket in six different categories: Best Fish Fry, Best Lunch, Best Coffee, Best Breakfast, Best Diner/Cafe, and Best Businesswoman. What more bests are there to win?

At a breakneck pace, Barb prepares breakfast orders at the grill all the while talking with me. I scribble notes as fast as I can but can't match her egg whisking, hash brown frying, and pancake making. With a plastic mustard bottle filled with thinned batter, Barb makes a curving smile and two round, hollow eyes on the hot grill. When they're brown, she spoons pancake batter over them to fill in the face, and when bubbles appear at the edges, she flips the pancake over to reveal a smiley face. Every pancake that leaves the grill looks just like it, except at Christmas when Barb makes trees, Valentine's Day when she makes hearts, and Easter when she makes rabbits. She calls them "designer pancakes." Although I didn't order one, Barb flips the smiley pancake on a plate and hands it to me over the counter.

Laughing, she says, "A seven-year-old boy came in with his family last week and had a face pancake. He ate it all, but he wouldn't eat the eyes because they looked too much like 'cataracts.'"

Barb's success with the Lunch Bucket has led to the addition of a side dining room, more storage room, and a walk-in freezer that she is proud to show me. (As she swings open the heavy insulated door, I think of Lucy Ricardo and wonder if we'll be trapped inside.) "There were so many people standing in line on Friday nights that we had to get bigger or lose business," she explains. Since then, Black Earth has grown and seen more restaurants move in, so the extra dining room is rarely filled. Barb has had the Lunch Bucket on the market since Lawrence died, and so far has had no takers. She wonders if the extra dining room may now be a liability instead of an asset.

From her vantage point behind the counter, Barb has witnessed other changes that have marked the past ten years, especially the loss of many of her older customers. When they pass away, they leave a part of themselves behind: a favorite menu item that acquires their name, a joke or story, and, in the case, of Irv Simley, a collection of handmade craft items below the cash register. Take a look under there. You'll see jokes made of wood, such as the bean spoon with tiny pegs like a ladder for the "little farts" to climb up out of the beans. There's also a portable washer and dryer consisting of a washer and clothespin attached to a piece of wood.

Barb is deservedly proud of the success she has had with the Lunch Bucket. She's proud of the fact that she has the only Lunch Bucket Cafe in the state of Wisconsin, a name "that gets right to the heart of the matter." (Still, she laughs, "Some guy once called up and asked if the name meant we packed lunches!" They do. It's called take-out.) She also is proud, and somewhat dumbfounded, by the inclusion of her cafe in *Outsider* magazine's recent feature on the Baraboo area.

As eleven o'clock approaches, Barb readies the grill for the switchover from pancakes and eggs to burgers and fries. One of her regular customers stops at the counter to pay his bill and tells her, "The breakfast was superb."

"I know! It always is!" Barb replies. Turning to me she laughs, "I've got my lunch cook saying that now, too!"

CAMBRIA
Leystra's Venture Restaurant 🍽 ☻
126 West Edgewater Street
(608) 348-5886
M–Th 5:30 A.M.–5:30 P.M.; F 5:30 A.M.–7 P.M.; Sa 5:30 A.M.–1 P.M.;
Su closed
Evelyn Leystra

In Cambria, a town in northeast Columbia County settled by the Welsh, Evelyn Leystra has decorated her thirty-one-year-old restaurant to reflect her family's Dutch heritage. Outside, Holland blue vinyl siding covers the corner cafe, and shutters decorated with bright painted tulips trim the windows. Inside a collection of beautiful Delft plates with windmill scenes hangs on the fresh white walls ("They're real Delft but I bought them at a Dutch restaurant in Cedar Grove," smiles Evelyn) and the wainscot is decorated with delicate stenciling of tulips and garlands. Her choice of decor is a deliberate expression of her heritage and that of her late husband, Sam. "My father and mother, and Sam's, too, came from Holland. I like tulips, windmills, that sort of thing," Evelyn explains.

When Sam died in 1993, Evelyn wondered if she could manage the restaurant without him. But since they converted a teen center into the family-oriented eatery in 1972, it has been a Leystra family venture. "These girls are my daughters," Evelyn tells me, nodding toward the kitchen where her daughters Mary, Barbara, and Kathy are working. "We've had the same crew since 1972, and only one isn't family. People who haven't been here in a few years can find the same waitresses."

Evelyn measures her years of cafe ownership by stability and consistency, and also by change in the family and family farms. She used to enjoy the days when mothers and their young children came in, but they have been replaced with working moms and latchkey kids who don't have time for good home cooking at the town cafe. "The farming picture has changed so much, too," she says. "The small farm doesn't exist anymore. They're all *big* farms now, and the farmer doesn't have time to come in for dinner."

Because her daughters are not interested in owning the cafe, Evelyn anticipates the day she will sell out and retire. Before that happens, you must drive out to Cambria, a village filled with lovingly tended Victorian homes built on the edge of the hills like a Welsh mining town. The menu at Leystra's Venture includes no Dutch foods (and no Welsh foods either) but plenty of Wisconsin down-home cooking. Fresh baked bread is cut into slices for toast and sandwiches; daily specials are built around the traditional farmer's meal of meat and potatoes; and homemade soups thaw winter cold and chase away the chill of a late summer rain. As drops splash against the window, I enjoy a warm piece of blueberry crunch pie. There were four varieties of pie on the menu, but Evelyn recommended the blueberry because she had eaten half a piece and found it so good she was tempted to eat the other half as well. With a recommendation like that, how could I refuse the blueberry? I ate the whole piece.

When Evelyn retires, the Leystra family's venture will continue with son Jim's restaurant of the same name in Sauk City (see the listing on page 208).

CLINTON
Clinton Kitchen ▮●▮ ☗
239 Allen Street
(608) 676-4461
M–Th 5 A.M.–7 P.M.; F 5 A.M.–8 P.M.; Sa 5 A.M.–3 P.M.; Su closed
Connie and Jim Farrell
The Clinton Kitchen has butterscotch pie and homemade doughnuts so good that I knew immediately it had to be featured in *Cafe Wisconsin*. Owners Connie and Jim Farrell weren't in the afternoon I first stopped by, but one of their nephews was. He offered to lead me to the real estate office where his grandmother and Connie's mother, Lois Kroeze, worked. She'd tell me what I wanted to know, he said. She'd owned the cafe for thirty-one years before selling it to Connie.

"That's right," Lois laughs after I'm seated in a chair at the antique oak table in her office. "I was retired two weeks and had to have something to do, so I came to work here. I missed the people contact." She has since retired from real estate and is back to working part time at the cafe.

In 1968 her late mother-in-law, Johanna Kroeze Schryvers, was working at Ma's Country Kitchen when the business went up for sale. Johanna was worried she'd lose her job, so she convinced Lois to buy the restaurant and keep her on. "I didn't know ups or downs about a restaurant," Lois says. "Johanna taught me how to cook. She stayed on about ten years, and after that I was on my own with the same employees."

Ma's Country Kitchen had established a tradition of good home cooking, and Lois found it easy to carry on in the same way, as Connie does today. When a national franchise sent a "nasty letter" about the trademarked last half of the cafe's name, Lois relates, the Kroezes' attorney "wrote back and said they were privileged to share a name with us because the food was so good. She didn't think the franchise's food could be so good!" Nevertheless, Ma's Country Kitchen was rechristened the Clinton Kitchen.

A change of location followed the change of name when the original Ma's was destroyed by fire. The fire was on a Saturday and on Sunday the motorcycle shop in the next block had a for sale sign in the front window. "We never thought about not reopening," Lois says. "Clinton needed a restaurant with real good home cooking. So many people came there to eat and meet."

Times haven't changed much since the reopening of the Clinton Kitchen. The morning coffee klatch has changed members, but it still meets regularly every day "to solve the problems of the world." Saturday mornings the Breakfast Club of retired men meets to do the same thing, as do the Maple Street Neighbors. The Power and Light Guys meet weekdays over the noon hour and start shaking dice as soon as they arrive. Lois laughs, "You can't hardly get their orders they're so busy worrying about what's being played."

Connie Farrell recognizes Lois's stories about the regulars the next morning when we meet in the Clinton Kitchen over doughnuts and coffee, and she provides a few of her own dredged up by her and her sisters in preparation for our visit. "There was the time Grandma [Johanna] once locked one of the regular men in the storeroom," she laughs, "and he got back at her by taking all the labels off the cans! And another guy kept ordering things 'on a cart,' so one time his food came out to him on a toy sleigh!"

Lots of laughter gets spread around the hometown cafe, but serious business—especially the cooking—goes on there too. "We have basic American cuisine," Connie notes. "Our calling card is our roast beef—that's always a daily special—and our pies."

A soup and sandwich special and one or more daily plate specials are run alongside the roast beef, served with homemade gravy spooned over bread and real mashed potatoes. Chicken and biscuits are available every Wednesday; every Friday from four thirty to eight o'clock you'll find an all-you-can-eat fish buffet, including potato pancakes and chicken. "That's stand-in-line usually," Connie warns. "Some people come all the way from Rockford, Illinois."

Other popular main-meal items include the taco, grilled chicken, and Italian chicken pasta salads; ham and corn fritters; and a variety of homemade soups—fresh tomato in summer, split pea, clam chowder, cream of broccoli, cream of vegetable, cheese, and many others. Goodies—doughnuts, bran muffins, and pies—are made fresh every morning. Connie recommends the best-selling coconut cream, sour cream raisin, Dutch apple, and graham cracker cream pies, but I'll stand by the butterscotch topped with fluffy meringue. It introduced me to Lois and Connie and put the Clinton Kitchen on the adventure eater's map.

MILTON
Squeeze Inn
105 Merchant Row
(608) 868-5966
M–Th 5 A.M.–5 P.M.; F 5 A.M.–8 P.M.; Sa 5 A.M.–12 P.M.; Su closed
Deb Hantke

I had trouble finding the Squeeze Inn because I was looking for it in the wrong place. The address is Milton, so I confidently drove into the downtown commercial area fronting the park and began looking for the correct street sign. There was no Merchant Row to be found. I drove west past the high school, which was just letting out, and when I got to farmland, I knew I'd gone too far. I turned north, then east on Highway 59 until I encountered another old commercial district. How could a town the size of Milton have a downtown and an uptown, I wondered.

The answer is simple. It doesn't. The parkside downtown belongs to Milton. The second downtown belongs to Milton Junction, found on the detailed map in the *Wisconsin Atlas and Gazetteer* but not on the state road map. Though it has a Milton address, the Squeeze Inn is on the main street—the aptly named Merchant Row—of Milton Junction.

Owner Deb Hantke laughs at my story and is sympathetic to my plight, but, she tells me, few people actually come in search of the Squeeze Inn. Most of her customers already know where it is. They remember when the little building was part of the lumberyard and after that an office for a car dealership. Its previous uses explain its rather strange location compared to the other buildings on Merchant Row. "It kind of looks like it's in the middle of the street," notes Deb matter-of-factly.

At twenty-five or twenty-six seats, the Squeeze Inn is not the tiniest cafe in Wisconsin, a title reserved for Fay's Dinky Diner in Eagle River. But it is still "small—very small," according to Deb. It is dominated by a red horseshoe-shaped counter that seats ten people, twice the number of the "five-woman show" that keeps the little place humming. The counter is the most popular place for a cup of coffee, a plate of hot beef, and a visit with friends because its shape makes it possible to carry on a conversation with each of the ten people gathered at it. Across from me sits Deb. Next to me sit Fred and Jerry. At the curved end sits one of Deb's young waitresses, who has come in on her day off for a burger and fries. Everybody's involved in my conversation with Deb. And everybody has something to say.

Jerry describes the Squeeze Inn as "a real family restaurant. Deb claims them all." That includes her teenage help and the "older kids" who concoct elaborate practical jokes, such as the day they talked Deb into the bathroom by convincing her it had a leak, and then cocooned her in Silly String when she came out the door. "They were paying me back for spraying them with a can of whipped cream," she laughs as she passes photographs the men took. "I told them, 'If you don't be quiet, you're going to get it.' They keep coming after me—like the day they brought in a rubber spider."

The practical jokes are lovingly plotted by the farmers gathered at three "trouble tables," which fill as much for laughter and fun as for Deb's "homemade everything." Deb bought the Squeeze Inn in 1998, having never set foot in the place. "I'd heard about it," she says, "but I'd never eaten there." From the very first day, she made a commitment to making everything from scratch. "I just wanted to do my own thing," she explains, despite the encouragement of food salesmen to try prepackaged convenience items. "It might be easier," she says, "but it won't be as good."

Deb's devotion to home cooking is definitely her customers' boon. She peels and boils real potatoes for hash browns, potato pancakes, potato salad, and mashed side dishes. Other celebrated menu items include Wednesday's hot beef and hot pork sandwiches, soups, and Deb's baked goods, including the favorite apple and Dutch apple pie made with Granny Smith apples. "I can never make that often enough," she says. It being Wednesday, and me being on a crusade to figure out the Wisconsin obsession with hot beef, I asked my waitress to bring me a half-order, which even at half-size was far more than I could eat. Deb watched me sweep the gravy off the top slice of bread, then push the bread to the side of the plate before sampling the roast beef filling. I always bypass the bread in favor of the mashed potatoes—especially when they're real—because I consider the bread to be silly. Aren't bread and potatoes pretty much the same thing?

"Is there something wrong with the hot beef?" she asks, puzzled at my behavior.

Embarrassed to be so exposed, I assure her that the hot beef is wonderful, even if my careful dissection has her thinking I think otherwise. It is darned good hot beef—but I am not yet convinced that hot beef is the be-all and end-all of Wisconsin cafe cooking. Hot beef as good as Deb's moves me closer, however. I'll keep at it.

While I'm pondering the matter, you ponder Deb's menu, whose cover features a drawing of a chicken eating bacon and eggs. A balloon puts these words into his mouth: "DON'T SQUAWK ABOUT THE ROOM!" The back cover asks coffee drinkers, "Need a coffee refill? Just Ask! A Smidge, A Dribble, A Dab, A Splash, A Half, A Stop!!, A This Much [using forefinger and thumb], A Half a Cup, A Cup, A Touch, A That's Plenty, A Little More, A Drizzle, A $1/4$ Cup, A Full Cup, A Tad, A Sip, A Gulp, A Enough to Wake Me Up, A Shot, A Squirt, A JustAlittle Bit, A Whoa, A One More for the Road, A Little Cup."

MONTICELLO
M & M Cafe
126 North Main Street
(608) 938-4890
M–F 6:00 A.M.–2 P.M.; Sa 7 A.M.–2 P.M.; Su closed
Mike and Mary Davis

Though they were not here ten years ago when their cafe, then the Midway Lunch, was featured in the first edition of *Cafe Wisconsin*, Mike and Mary Davis greet me like a long lost friend when I introduce myself and my mission. "We love your book," exclaims Mary. "We've had many customers bring it in, and we think it's just a fun thing."

We settle into one of the original wood booths, and as I dive into a piece of Amish cream pie—the only pie of this kind to be found in Wisconsin—I ask Mary where on earth she uncovered the recipe. I am familiar with it because years ago I introduced it to my family's Thanksgiving dinner, where it quickly took its yearly place alongside the mincemeat and pumpkin pies. Consisting of little more than heavy cream, sugar, and a few tablespoons of flour baked into a one-crust pie, the dessert is an unlikely and unusual sweet treat and a favorite of mine. And it's so easy to make. (The hardest part is getting the pie pan full of syrupy cream into the oven without spilling it and making a sticky mess.)

Mary found the recipe for Amish cream pie in the *Wisconsin State Journal* and in a cookbook by Marcia Adams celebrating Amish heritage. But both she and Mike make cookbook reading a course requirement for Restaurant Ownership 101, in which they enrolled in 1993. They had each reached a midlife crisis, Mary says, she with her job in a medical lab and he in his ownership of a Freeport, Illinois, shoe store, which fell victim to malls and discount stores. "We were so unhappy with what we were doing that anything seemed better," Mary explains. They saw a for sale ad for the Midway Lunch in the newspaper and thought, "How hard can it be to run a cafe?"

"We thought about it for a few weeks, but whatever problem one of us thought of, the other one had already solved." The couple signed on the sales contract's dotted line and moved to Monticello, where they were fortunate to be guided through the first trying months by the previous owner's "number one gal. She stayed with us and helped us out. She knew everyone in town—who's related to whom—and with her help, we made a good transition," Mary remembers.

Mary grew up in a family of ten children and soon discovered that "cafe cooking was family cooking on a bigger scale." Like kids around the family table, her customers quickly let her know what they liked and didn't like. "I found out right away that they didn't like frozen soups," Mary laughs. The customers had become accustomed to the way the previous owners did things and didn't allow Mike and Mary to lower the standards. That meant not substituting frozen soups for homemade, or replacing the boiled and shredded real-potato hash browns with dehydrated or frozen. As a result, everything (save the instant mashed potatoes, the Davises' one concession to premade) is just the way Mom made it at home in the family kitchen.

Mike and Mary prepare a monthly calendar listing all of the daily specials, which a postscript warns are "subject to availability and the whims of the chef." Favorites include kalberwurst (veal and milk sausage), any of the hearty homemade soups, the Reuben sandwiches and bison burgers, Mexican lasagna, beef stew, and ham balls and noodles, which are so popular that Mary has to "send a ham ball alert out to New Glarus." The baked goods—awesome muffins, pies, and desserts—are also top sellers. "I no more than make the Amish cream pie than it is gone," Mary says. It's so popular, in fact, that customers call ahead to reserve a piece. I enjoy my own—the last piece of the day—much more knowing how close I came to missing out on it entirely.

The M & M Cafe, decorated with a collection of Americana items and M&M collectibles brought in by customers, began life about seventy years ago as Jimmie's Hamburgers, a little roadside burger joint owned by Jimmie Laub, also known as Jimmie the Greek. "Old Jimmie, he had it about forty-two years," Leon Gempeler told me in 1992. "Started as a tiny newsstand, shoeshine stand, selling candy and tobacco. Then he expanded into a grill. He was famous for his round steak burgers."

Today's version of Jimmie's Hamburgers looks a lot like it did toward the end of Jimmie's ownership, despite the replacement Formica on the counter and table tops that replaced the original, worn out terrazzo-look surfaces. The boxy cream building an easy few blocks off the popular Sugar River bike trail is trimmed in fresh red paint, with red neon letters reading EAT hanging over the boxed-in entrance.

Inside, four old oak booths, each with its own brass coat hook, are lined up against the front windows to catch the overflow from the counter. Each booth has an overhead light and a recessed cubbyhole holding the napkin dispenser, salt and pepper shaker, and a glass sugar canister. Actually, nearly everything at the M & M Cafe is antique, from the counter to the glass-fronted candy case at the end of the counter to the antique ice-pack refrigerator and the mirror-fronted Your Weight and Fortune scale by the front door.

Mike and Mary Davis wouldn't have it any other way.

MT. HOREB
Schubert's Old-Fashioned Cafe and Bakery ⑩
128 East Main Street
(608) 437-3393
M–Su 7 A.M.–8 P.M.
Gerry Schubert

In 1980, when Gerry Schubert purchased the 1907-vintage bakery-restaurant on Mt. Horeb's main street "for a very summy price," people asked him not to change a single thing. They liked the original high-backed oak booths, the soaring pressed tin ceiling, the soda fountain and full front windows, even the tiny rest rooms at the top of a sagging flight of stairs. The out-of-towners, especially, were concerned they'd never find another place similar to it. "This really is a very unique cafe," Gerry believes. "I doubt there's many like it around."

For nearly fifty years, Mt. Horeb's original main street eatery was known as Olsen's Restaurant, a combination cafe-bakery–soda fountain that served the townspeople and area farmers. Jane and Michael Stern extolled its virtues in the first revised edition of *Roadfood* (1980) when it was known as Goble's Restaurant. Roy Tvedt, one of six coffee klatchers in residence around a table in the center of the crowded restaurant, remembers, "My sister worked here in 1922. It used to have a liquor bar in back where the booths are now. You used to be able to get all-you-can-eat chicken gizzards Saturday nights for a quarter. I could eat seven, eight, nine of 'em. I was a young fellow then, you know, so I could eat anything.

"I can remember when my dad would come in on horseback—he'd come in a sleigh in winter—and have a malt at the counter. It was the thing to do. A malt in those days cost fifteen cents. You could get a malt and a hamburger for a quarter.

"There used to be a guy named Fritz who worked here. He used to throw ice cubes up in the air and catch them in a glass behind him. I remember he'd stand at the front, take a doughnut out of the case, and throw it down the counter to the customer who ordered it. Nothing like that goes on anymore, though."

By the 1950s, Roy guesses, Olsen's Restaurant had earned a reputation for its delicious baked goods, and tourists regularly drove out from Madison for home-cooked dinners and loaves of bread. In 1960 John F. Kennedy's campaign appearance upstairs in the Ivy Room placed Olsen's Restaurant on the front page of newspapers and, from there, the travel itineraries of Wisconsin adventure eaters. In the early 1970s Mt. Horeb began to capitalize on its Norwegian heritage, drawing thousands of tourists a year to its Nordic-themed main street. And there, in the middle of town, looking pretty nearly as it did when it opened, stood Olsen's Restaurant—known then as Goble's, after the new owner.

Gradually, Mt. Horeb's tourists displaced much of the restaurant's local business, and today Gerry estimates they make up about 60 percent of his customers. "If it weren't for the west side of Madison," he says, "I don't think I'd be here at all." With children in tow, the tourists pile into the tables and booths lining the inside wall, gawking at the restaurant's period decor and examining the menu. "A lot of people like to see the local cafe," Gerry observes, "because it's not something they know. A cafe is small, with cute little tables and booths and a counter. A cafe serves good food and is friendly, noisy, you know. But the tourists come here and want privacy, so they take the booths first and the tables when the booths are filled. They almost never sit at the counter. The counter is for people who are alone, like the man there now: the architect in town who sits at the counter every day. Every day but Sunday."

Parties of tourists take up tables and booths, leaning in close together and speaking in loud voices to hear themselves over the surrounding chatter and clatter. They point here and there—at the fluted tulip glasses on a shelf over the malt machine, at the table heaped with baked goods inside the front door—pleased at finding some obscure pieces of a past with which they're only vaguely familiar. At the counter, the architect shares space with two cyclists wearing fluorescent green jerseys and black Lycra shorts. And in the center of the cafe, at a table surrounded by tourists, sits Roy Tvedt, his nephew Dean Tvedt, Amos Moen, and Jim and Violet Gilbertson—"the typical coffee klatch," Gerry points out.

Although the regulars have no serious gripes about the tourists, Roy explains, "they sometimes make it hard for us to get our regular table.

"Someone usually comes in a little early and stakes out a table in back. We all like to have our backs against the wall. Some of those Swiss who come up from New Glarus can't be trusted! Every day it seems we have to move a little farther up front. I figure pretty soon we'll be out on the sidewalk!"

The spokesman of the group, Roy has been coming first to Olsen's Restaurant, then Goble's, and now Schubert's two times a day since the 1950s, after he retired from the Mobil station he owned on the corner and stopped driving school buses. His nephew Dean is "a Norwegian from Door County." Amos Moen's wife, Verna, has worked at the restaurant over twenty years. Jim Gilbertson is a friend who drove school buses with Roy. Violet is his wife. "We come every day to solve the problems of the world," Roy explains. "If we don't get 'em sorted out, we come back the next day and go at it again."

Gerry notes that Roy's present coffee group is typical for today, but he remembers when groups used to include as many as twenty-five "old-timers."

"When there were no other restaurants in Mt. Horeb, this place was uncontrollable," he says. "The locals had no other place to go, and they'd sit here for hours drinking coffee and flipping coins."

Though Gerry doesn't mention it, coin flipping is still a popular pastime. "Sure, we flip coins," Roy says. "That's the highlight of the day to get some moneybag to pay! We stuck the hardware store owner one morning for nine cups of coffee. One guy even made a sign saying he was the winner of buying the most cups—hung it on the mirror."

The local humor and high jinks at Schubert's are just icing on the cake—and doughnuts, sweet rolls, brownies, and other bakery treats that fill the same case at the front of the cafe that Fritz threw doughnuts from years ago. The tourists don't come to hear Roy's stories or Norwegian jokes. (By the way, have you heard the one about the penny-pinching Swedes who decided to save money by building a bridge in the desert instead of over the river where it was needed? When the time came to move it, they couldn't get the Norwegian fishermen off.)

The tourists come here to eat. Specialties at Schubert's include Cornish pasties—a Thursday tradition for many years, but now served every day—hot beef, homemade soups and daily specials, pies and baked goods, especially a sweet, delicately flavored Swedish rye bread that, Roy claims, is "known far and wide." Gerry's son, Jim, oversees the kitchen operations and acts as "chief coordinator."

"He's the chef," Gerry explains, "but I have a hard time with that. We go places and see guys in white coats and caps, and the food is usually not as good as here."

You'll likely agree.

Note: A serious fire in the summer of 2002 closed Schubert's for a period of extensive remodeling. As the mess was cleaned up, hidden features such as a row of interior windows were revealed and restored. The restaurant "will be even more vintage than before," Gerry told me in May 2003. "We were able to salvage all of the oak booths and had them refinished, but we couldn't save the wood floor. We're having ceramic tile laid instead." What about the food? Gerry knows it's best not to change a good thing, so the menu will be pretty much the same as before—including the famous Swedish rye bread, lefse, baked goods, and traditional meals built around mashed potatoes and gravy and good meats.

NORTH FREEDOM
Carol's Railroad Inn Cafe
104 East Walnut Street
(608) 522-4485
M–Th 6 A.M.–2 P.M.; F 6 A.M.–2 P.M. and 4 P.M.–8 P.M.;
Sa–Su 6 A.M.–2 P.M.
Billie Clendenning

As testimony to Billie Clendenning's good cooking, local regular Keith Bender stands away from the counter and shows me the profile of his belly. "I used to be skinny," he says, running his hand along the edge of the protrusion. He wears a red T-shirt advertising Applebee's, the restaurant chain, which he got from a friend who deals in liquidated merchandise. Billie and I tease him about divided loyalties. He responds by saying, "If she'd buy me a T-shirt, I'd wear it. She's a real asset to us."

Billie recently purchased the Railroad Inn, just a block away from the Mid-Continent Railroad Museum, from her mother, Carol Clendenning, who operated the cafe since 1992. When Carol came as a stranger to the area, she knew no one and very little about operating a restaurant. She had just been divorced and was persuaded by a friend, the owner of an area restaurant, to get started by running a small cafe. "I told her okay if it had an apartment and a garage," remembers Carol. When her friend found the Railroad Inn, closed and vacant, with an apartment above, Carol entered into a new life.

By the looks of the Railroad Inn, you would never guess that Carol hasn't spent a lifetime here. The place is genuinely historic, with a layering of time and things that belie Carol's years of occupancy but speak volumes of the community's high regard for her. She began claiming the cafe as her own by painting and hanging wallpaper, making the few changes she could on a small budget. She moved in a small green and cream enameled cookstove and a few other things she had collected, and then opened the doors. Once the locals became friends, they started bringing things to decorate the restaurant. The cafe has one of the largest collections of antique green kitchenware—enamelware, ceramics, glassware, wood-handled pieces—and related items that I have ever seen. Of course, there are also plenty of trains.

While you're waiting for your food, swivel around on your green milk can stool and study the contents of the cafe for thirty seconds, then shut your eyes and try to recall what you have seen. The green items include wire whisks, a cup rack, match holder, funnels, rolling pins, knives, pastry cutters, potato mashers, egg beaters, sieves, sifters, colanders, measuring cups, food choppers, coffeepots, cookie cutters, doughnut cutters, cookie jars, nut grinders, paper towel rack, thermometers, brushes, a Hamilton Beach malt machine, McCoy mixing bowl, Niloak vase, cream separator in the front window, glass pitcher, a scale, measuring scoops, can opener, deviled egg plate, spatulas, cake plate, and much more. Go ahead, you try it. When you're done with the green stuff, move on to the trains. Don't forget the old-time popcorn poppers on the wall over the counter.

"Everything has a story behind it," Carol says. The Railroad Inn's regulars have found most of the items at flea markets, yard sales, auctions, and closets and garages at home. A great collection encourages additions, and other pieces have come in packages from people who stopped once while traveling through or while visiting the railroad museum.

"One day this artist from Indiana came in and saw the trains. He asked if I'd like to have a couple of his prints, and he went out and got them out of the trunk. I thought they looked familiar. Later I dug my plates out of the closet, and sure enough, several of them were by him." The artist's prints and collector plates now hang on the cafe's walls. Another addition of five color photographs of historic train engines were mailed to Carol by a man who had taken them while on vacation. The letter accompanying the photos explained that he thought she just might like them for the cafe.

The railroad theme extends to the menu with the Brakeman hamburger, Cowcatcher cheeseburger, and Handcar double cheeseburger. Other sandwiches include the Caboose hotdog and the Conductor BLT. For breakfast, you can have any number of Boxcar specials, including the Whistle Stop omelette; the Hobo omelette (with everything on it); and the Engine #2 omelette, made with a filling of jelly. Breakfast is the biggest meal of the day at the Railroad Inn, but there is plenty to eat later as well. Liver and onions, meat loaf, real mashed potatoes, soups, and some pies, including the current favorites, butterscotch cream and key lime, keep Billie's customers coming back.

It's not often that they need coaxing, but when they do, Billie's nephew Braydon and his friend Beth, who provides most of the colored drawings hanging beneath the daily specials board, found a novel way of directing them to the Railroad Inn. One day they spent several hours drawing footprints on the sidewalk with colored chalk. "Looking for good food?" they wrote. In the next block they wrote, "Try the Railroad Inn. You'll be glad you did." Carol laughs when she tells this story, remembering how the woman who owned the ice cream shop asked to be included in their sidewalk advertising. "If you're advertising good food," Carol says, "you can't go wrong in North Freedom."

ORFORDVILLE
K's Outback Cafe
313 West Brodhead Street
(608) 879-2716
M–Th 6 A.M.–7 P.M.; F 6 A.M.–8 P.M.; Sa 6 A.M.–2 P.M.;
Su 6 A.M.–11 A.M.
Kay and Gordon Nelson

At eight thirty in the morning, a light snowfall is dusting the streets of Orfordville, putting the finishing touches on the heavy, wet accumulation that appeared overnight. As I turn onto the street that leads to K's Outback Cafe, I see cars and pickup trucks clustered out front for nearly a block in either direction. I laugh to myself. Despite the weather—or rather because of it—K's Outback is filled with breakfasters and coffee drinkers. Owner Kay Nelson knows the phenomenon well. "The worse the weather, the more people are here. It's like they've got to prove to everyone they can get out of the driveway."

Fueled on a plateful of Kay's biscuits and gravy—crumbled pork sausage in milk gravy over baking powder biscuits—one gentleman pulls his jacket collar snug around his neck and his cap a little farther down to cover his ears. Opening the door to a blast of cold he utters the common Wisconsin winter lament, "I just finished shoveling my driveway, and now I have to do it all over again."

Several years ago, Kay Nelson was working in the restaurant business, as she has since the age of twelve, when she realized that all of her hard work wasn't laying the groundwork for a worry-free retirement. "You work so hard in this business that you may as well work for yourself," she explains. She gathered up her family and shared her idea: she'd run a restaurant of her own where everything would be homemade. "I told them that in order to make it a success, I had to make it my priority. My family agreed with me and let me make my dream come true."

In 1997 she bought Orfordville's only cafe, and on a shoestring budget and with plenty of imagination and hard work she converted it into K's Outback Cafe. Don't be surprised by the name. There is no Australian food served here. Rather the name refers to the cafe's location "out back" of Orfordville, along the railroad tracks and just down the road from the Farm-City grain elevator. The location is handy for farmers doing business at Farm-City, as well as truckers traveling the nearby highways and engineers and other workers on the train. "They pull the train up alongside the cafe and jump out to eat," Kay says.

People who travel roads and rails for a living could eat anywhere, so their choice in a cafe is always a reliable sign that something pretty special is going on in the kitchen. Kay has stuck by her commitment to home cooking and dishes up everything from homemade bread to real potato hash browns. Everything in between is just as fresh, just as real.

Kay says, "All my ingredients are the freshest I can get, and I do everything myself. I chop up the onions and the green pepper and sauté them with a little crunch. Sometimes people say to me, 'These vegetables aren't done.' They want them so they're mush. They're used to things being canned or frozen. But I won't use anything but fresh."

My plate of shredded real potato hash browns grilled with onion and green pepper was just as she promised. Topped with a melted slice of real Swiss cheese (as opposed to the plastic, processed variety), it was a real pleaser—and real huge. I couldn't finish either it or the from-scratch buttermilk pancake I ordered to go with it. It's always a shame to throw away such wonderful food, but at the risk of packing on the pounds, I opted to send what I couldn't eat back to the kitchen.

I had to reassure Kay that this was not a negative reflection on her cooking. Just like the pizza critic in the film *Mystic Pizza*, I can tell award-winning food with just one bite. And sometimes, it takes just one look. When food looks as good as Kay's, the taste can't be far behind. Kay nods in agreement. "Presentation is a top priority. It has to look good before it tastes good. I wouldn't serve anything I wouldn't eat myself."

Every day Kay offers at least four or five specials designed and portioned with all sizes of appetites in mind. Two full plate, meat and potatoes choices are paired with burger and soup and sandwich combinations. Today's two dinner specials are pot roast, potatoes, and carrots served with soup or a salad and a hot roast turkey sandwich served with dressing and mashed potatoes and homemade gravy. "Yesterday I roasted two twenty-pound turkeys and served a full turkey dinner as a special," Kay explains. "What was left over went into today's hot turkey sandwich. Anything left after today will go into soup."

Should pot roast or turkey not tickle their palates, Kay's customers can also choose among today's other specials: a beef cheddar-melt with fries or a chicken salad or ham salad sandwich served with soup. There is no easy choice at Kay's because even the soup comes in multiple varieties. How would you decide among ham and cabbage, cheesy cauliflower, and chili?

If you think Kay's daily specials board presents a dilemma in ordering, keep the regular menu closed. Confronted with the variety of choices inside, you might be completely flummoxed. Among the regulars' consistent favorites between the menu's covers is the Outback Breakfast, a heart-stopping concoction of hash browns, eggs, and green pepper crowned with a biscuit over which is poured sausage gravy. "Sometimes they'll add a pancake or a cinnamon roll," Kay says with disbelief even yet. The cinnamon rolls, like the white, wheat, and raisin bread, are homemade. Be sure to request your sandwiches on "home" to get the good stuff.

Just as she decorates the cafe with plastic window decals and brightly colored paper cutouts for each holiday ("The people just love it!"), Kay adjusts the menu to the season, with lighter fare—stuffed tomatoes and cantaloupe, potato and pasta salads—reserved for hot weather. Bagels and fresh fruit are also popular during the summer months. Sensitive to the change in temperatures and the whims of her customers' tastes, Kay credits her grandmother with teaching her how to cook. "She taught me the old-school ways, like how to make chicken and turkey gravy by adding a can of evaporated milk. It makes it so smooth. She also taught me how to make tomato soup. You add a small amount of sugar to cut the acid of the tomatoes."

When I comment that the only tomato soup I make is Campbell's, Kay wrinkles up her nose in disgust. "That's not tomato soup. I don't serve anything I don't make. These people here are real food, meat and potatoes type. They want good down-home cooking, good service, and good conversation. They like what I make. They're satisfied."

PARDEEVILLE
O'Brien's Restaurant 🍽
133 North Main Street
(608) 429-2332
M–Sa 6 A.M.–2 P.M.; Su 7 A.M.–12 P.M.
Lisa O'Brien

I love O'Brien's Restaurant, with its wood-framed front display windows, sloping floor, vintage painted wood booths, and cracked-ice Formica table tops (mine has the name Harold scratched into the surface) that date back to its 1940s origins as Tillie Alexander's cafe. For the past twenty years it has been owned by Lisa O'Brien, who grew up in her parents' Webster supper club, where she learned to make the real, slow-cooked foods that tease customers into coming back again and again for more.

In response to other restaurants that have been moving into Pardeeville since O'Brien's was featured in the first edition of *Cafe Wisconsin*, however, Lisa has cut back her menu to mostly breakfast, burgers, sandwiches, and soups. "It doesn't make sense for me to compete with them," she explains, "so I just stick to a few things and continue to make everything fresh from scratch."

Breakfast is the big meal of the day at O'Brien's and features a variety of omelettes, potatoes, eggs, meats (including homemade corned beef hash), toast, and coffee. Burgers are the stars at noon; they come fresh and thick and make the perfect accompaniments to the real old-fashioned shakes and malts made in antique Hamilton Beach electric machines. The malt powder comes out of an equally antique Carnation dispenser so unusual that people frequently ask to buy it.

Now, I love a good malt as much as anyone who calls Wisconsin home, but why pass up the chance at sweet potato pie? That's what was written on the daily specials board the day I stopped by.

"Why?" I ask, surprised to find a southern specialty this far north.

"There's a story," Lisa says. "I had a lady who worked for me from Texas, and she said, 'Honey, there's nothin' better than sweet potato pie.' So I tried it, and it was good, but nothing is better than a good apple pie." Lisa is always on the lookout for something new to make—and in many cases, her something new is really something old. She experiments with recipes in an old farm cookbook and has even made elderberry-apple pie. But apple pie notwithstanding, the hands-down favorite pies at O'Brien's are lemon meringue and pumpkin.

PORTAGE
Portage Cafe 🍽
111 West Cook Street
(608) 742-4005
M–Sa 5 A.M.–2 P.M.; Su closed
Dennis Starr

At seven in the morning at the Portage Cafe, the regulars are strung out along the orange counter like birds on a telephone line. Under their watchful gaze, owner Dennis Starr fries bacon and eggs on the grill, trading quips back and forth over the counter.

"How long has there been a restaurant here?" he asks.

"When did this open as a restaurant?" Dennis tries again.

"I didn't know that it did!" Looking at me and gesturing at Dennis, the neighbor says, "Did you know he's the real dummy around here? He was standing behind the door when they were passing out brains, and he thought they said 'trains.'"

An insult—or is it?—comes immediately from Jim Humphrey. "I've been eating here twenty-four years, and I'm still here!"

About sixty years ago, the Portage Cafe was established in an old A&P grocery store that had gone out of business. Today it is nostalgically decorated with food tins that the A&P might have had on its shelves, plus an assortment of other antiques: a child's wooden sled, a crate from Portage's old Eulberg Brewery, and old table radio. ("The radio plays," jokes Dennis, "but it only plays the older music.") An old black and white Frank Sinatra movie plays on the wall-mounted television, underscoring Dennis's interest in "old stuff." "I feel at home with it," he says.

Dennis was working in the lumber industry and ready for a change when the Portage Cafe came up for sale in 1979. "I ate a lot. That's the only experience I had! I had to learn everything on my own," he explains. He soon discovered that there were few tricks to the restaurant trade, and only one rule: "Just do it the way the customers want." That means a lot of "basic, just regular everyday, stuff-you-eat-at-home food."

In the past ten years, the regular daily specials—scalloped potatoes and ham on Mondays, spaghetti on Wednesdays, liver and onions on Thursdays—have given way to lighter fare, mostly soup and sandwiches. Dennis explains that more women are working downtown than before, and they tend to eat differently than men. As the noon meal decreases in size, the breakfast trade has become greater. "We sell a lot of breakfasts. More people are coming out for breakfast and eating more than before," Dennis observes.

Jim Humphrey, downing the last of his eggs, agrees. He also swears that no one makes pie as good as Dennis. He's eaten pie at the Norske Nook ("In high school, we used to drive to Osseo for pie just for kicks") and other area cafes famous for pie, but raves about only one: Dennis's southwestern apple pie with chopped jalapeños. "He found it in a cookbook, made it, and everyone liked it. I brought some to work and everybody wanted more," he enthuses. I was out of luck the day I dropped in. The only pie on the menu board was coconut cream. Too bad, so sad.

The Portage Cafe is a great place for food and an even better place for entertainment, especially when the resident wits are stretching the truth and trading insults. (Jim says his brother-in-law, an artist in New York City, never misses a morning when he's here visiting.) On his way out, an older fellow stops at the register to pay for his oatmeal and toast and asks, "Where're the fish biting today?"

"Right next to my boat," answers a man in Levi's Dockers.

"Yeah, wherever you snag it, that is!"

"You wouldn't believe the kind of stuff that I have to put up with here," Dennis moans good-naturedly. "Like every morning the electrical contractors sit in their booth lining up jobs for the day. Once they wanted more coffee and called the waitress on the cellular phone! Sometimes I ask myself why I put up with all this! But it's fun. The people are fun. That's probably why I'm still around."

REEDSBURG
Greenwood's Cafe ⦿
116 South Walnut Street
(608) 524-6203
M–Th 6 A.M.–3 P.M.; F 6 A.M.–8 P.M.; Sa 6:30 A.M.–2 P.M.;
Su 7:30 A.M.–2 P.M.
Jim and Joy Greenwood, owners
Mark Greenwood, manager

The "braggart's board" near the front door of Greenwood's Cafe is filled with color photographs of the regulars' prize catches, both big bucks and monster fish. My waitress, Earlene, tells me with a smile, "If there's a photograph, we're more likely to believe it."

The braggart's board is a perfect addition to the restaurant's northwoods theme, which was influenced by Mark Greenwood's passion for the outdoors. The upper walls are covered with wallpaper in a birch bark pattern so authentic looking I had to run my hand over it to be sure it wasn't the real thing. (I'm a real toucher and often get scolded by attendants in museums. To me, touching is truth.) The successful look combines the vintage features of the cafe with familiar tokens of the outdoors, including birch twig candles, bear figures, miniature pine trees, and a wallpaper border reminiscent of a Thomas Kinkade painting, with a rustic lakeshore cabin, its windows glowing with yellow light, and a canoe pulled safely onto shore. Adding even more magical charm to the carefully created interior are Jim Greenwood's hand-stamped menu covers, each one different from the next ("He's big into scrapbooking and stuff," explains Earlene). Mine has a farm scene backlit by a yellow-orange sunset.

In its attentive and tasteful decorating, Greenwood's Cafe is in a league shared by very few other cafes. The typical Wisconsin small town cafe is characterized by low-budget, do-it-yourself Menards-inspired decorating whose central ingredient is wood-look or floral printed paneling, which, when glued to a wall, can hide flaws or irregularities. Since most cafes are housed in older buildings with a multitude of age-related problems—sagging floors, cracked walls, faulty previous remodeling—paneling, as well as a fresh coat of paint, dropped ceilings, and floor coverings, is regarded as a great cover-up. But nothing substitutes for quality material and workmanship and artful presentation—not in interior decorating and not in cooking.

Freshly redecorated, with a perky green and white striped awning over the front window, Greenwood's Cafe is an altogether pleasant place to be. You will want to linger here, savoring the northwoods sights, the yeasty smell of dinner rolls rising in the kitchen, and the tastes of familiar food conscientiously prepared by Mark, Jim, and Joy Greenwood. Thirty-two years ago, Jim and Joy sold their Montana restaurant and headed home to Reedsburg, where they found the Walnut Street Cafe up for sale. Thousands of daily specials later, Greenwood's Cafe has become a popular eating and meeting place for the locals and not-so-locals who regularly make the drive over the Baraboo hills for the predictably good fare.

Every day, Jim, Joy, and Mark prepare daily specials, like today's choice of chicken and rice casserole or scalloped potatoes and ham, along with two steaming kettles of soup and freshly made pies and other desserts. Joy cites the Friday fish fry featuring hand-battered Icelandic cod as one of the cafe's main draws, along with the popular Sunday dinners that have after-church crowds coming from nearby towns. Roast turkey and dressing ("the whole thing, just like Thanksgiving") and roast chicken and dressing are available every Sunday, with a third special changing from week to week. Dessert is included, but you will be hard-pressed to choose from a luscious list like today's that includes pumpkin, blackberry, rhubarb custard, lemon meringue, graham cracker, Dutch apple, coconut cream, bread pudding, or chocolate pudding. She who hesitates is lost—or orders two pieces, as I did. I wouldn't want to influence your decision by confiding my choices, but I will reassure you that I did have lunch first. I had a bowl of vegetable beef soup and found it to be as impressive as Mark's decorating. I'll definitely be back.

SAUK CITY
Leystra's Venture Restaurant
200 Phillips Boulevard (Highway 12)
(608) 643-2004
M–Th 6 A.M.–8 P.M.; F 6 A.M.–9 P.M.; Sa–Su 6 A.M.–8 P.M.
Jim and Janine Leystra
Jim Leystra enjoyed canoeing the Wisconsin River as a boy, often taking out in the town of Sauk City where an interesting old yellow building known then as the Swistyle Dairy Bar caught his eye. In 1981, when Jim decided that he liked the restaurant business well enough to get into it himself—well, lo and behold, the yellow stone building came up for sale, and he became its owner.

Until that fateful day, Jim had been working as a salesman who spent five days out of seven on the road. "I ate all my meals in restaurants, and one day I thought, 'If this is all the better they can do, I can make money at this,'" he remembers. He took the lead of his parents, Sam and Evelyn Leystra, who, when Jim was eighteen, traded in the family farm for a restaurant of their own—the original Leystra's Venture in Cambria (see listing in this chapter)—and began his own venture in the restaurant business.

The people of Sauk City (and plenty more at that) are mighty glad he did. For the past twenty-two years, Leystra's Venture has "been serving the good taste of Wisconsin" with home cooking as good as Mom's. Evelyn, that is. The Sauk City restaurant is known for "the largest selection of homemade pies in the area," fresh baked white and wheat bread, and, in keeping with the Swistyle tradition, an old-style soda fountain serving up old-fashioned sodas, malts, sundaes, banana splits, parfaits, and shortcakes. Don't overlook the nine or ten daily dinner specials in your rush to get to dessert. Fair warning: you may not have room for dessert at all if you select any of the specials available the day I stopped in for breakfast. I vetoed the biscuits and gravy breakfast special in favor of scrambled eggs and bacon, toasted homemade bread, and some of the best hash browns I've ever had. Hash browns fried in real Wisconsin butter just can't be beat. Since it was already eleven o'clock, many of the other customers were opting for a choice of specials that included spaghetti, lasagna, chuck roast, roast beef, hot beef, beef barley soup with roast beef sandwich, German or regular potato salad with roast beef sandwich, mushroom Swiss burger with fries and coleslaw, or chili in a bread bowl.

Whether it's ground, chucked, roasted, hot, souped, sliced, chilied, or fixed any other way, there's no doubt that beef is tops in the Badger state!

Leystra's Venture is a restaurant good enough to be your sole reason for traveling to Sauk City. Yet you may be interested to know that Sauk City was the home of August Derleth, a prolific writer who died in 1971. Leystra's Venture celebrates the association with Augie's Room, a separate dining room filled with photos, news clippings, and other Derleth memorabilia. The main dining room also serves as a local history museum with displays of street scenes, business advertisements, and other views of Sauk City's past.

STOUGHTON
Koffee Kup ︎❙ ႘
355 East Main Street
(608) 873-6717
M–Sa 5 A.M.–8 P.M.; Su 5 A.M.–2 P.M.
Kendall and Trish Gulseth
For more than a hundred years the good people of Stoughton and many surrounding communities have eaten at the Koffee Kup, the oldest restaurant in town. (The Ks, explains owner Kendall Gulseth, are from the Norwegian settlers' spelling for coffee.) During all those long years, the little restaurant has been periodically updated but not too significantly altered. There's a lot of historical integrity and charm to the place, but that often fails as a magnet for drawing people in off the main street. "Outside, the

front of the restaurant hasn't changed much since it opened," Kendall says. "Some people don't like it. They see it and drive on. It doesn't look attractive to them, and they think it's not a good place to eat."

Kendall has plans to remodel the façade to resemble the other historic commercial buildings on Stoughton's main street, but until then—and only after the city replaces the street and sidewalk out front—the old look will remain. It has become a signature of the Koffee Kup, as much as the flower boxes filled with geraniums and the classic Mountain Dew sign hanging off the front of the building.

"The Pepsi man wanted to replace the sign with one for Diet Pepsi, but I said, 'It's a landmark.' They don't make Mountain Dew signs anymore." The sign talk reminds me of the observation of my son, Peter, who as an astute four-year-old accompanying me on my first food foray across Wisconsin in 1991, told me, "You know, Mom, it's easy to find a small town cafe. You just look for the pop sign hanging over the sidewalk." Yes, the Mountain Dew sign has got to stay.

And so must you. Don't make the terrible mistake of letting the Koffee Kup's exterior appearance persuade you to drive on by. Park the car—or lean your bike up against the front window—go inside, and take a seat at the counter. Look up: the dropped panels were removed to expose the original molded tin ceiling twelve feet overhead. Look down: the old flooring was replaced with stone-look vinyl squares. Look all around: the walls are synthetic brick rusticated with swaths of rough plaster and paint—because, Kendall explains, the old brick wall he hoped to find behind the old wall cladding didn't exist. While you're feasting on the Koffee Kup's new look, don't miss the Koffee Kup treat board, a remnant from the good old days and wise testimony to your decision to stay:

Koffee Kup Treats

Strawberry shortcake	Pecan pie
Apple Crisp	str-rhubarb
Bread Pudding ☺♥	apple
Brownies—frosted with nuts	cherry
carrot cake	pumpkin
Fry cakes (donuts)	blueberry
cinnamon rolls—large or small	peach
Rootbeer Float	choc cream
Shakes or Malts—choc, strawberry,	coc cream
passion fruit	lemon merg
Sundaes—cookie or brownie, strawberry,	Heath crunch
Hot Fudge, or Choc	Banana Cream Pie

The well-loved Koffee Kup Treats are made by Kendall's wife, Trish, who adds to the already impressive list over ten dozen chocolate chip cookies a week—all in urgent and constant demand by the regulars. I'm head over heels for Trish's handiwork, but my undying devotion undoubtedly belongs to the fabulous fry cakes, or doughnuts, made from a recipe handed down from Kendall's Norwegian great-grandmother. They are oversized and dense, almost breakfast in themselves, and made fresh per order with a crunchy glaze of hot oil encasing the yellow cake.

Trish's Koffee Kup Treats set a precedent for from-scratch production that nearly everything else at the Koffee Kup handily meets. Peeling potatoes over a plastic garbage container, Kendall says, "We try to keep everything old hometown. You can go anywhere to eat, but we want you to come here." Hot dishes, Norwegian meatballs, meat loaf, hot beef, and lots of real potatoes are the favorites at the Koffee Kup, but Kendall likes to offer alternatives to traditional Wisconsin cafe food. "Sometimes it feels like I'm in a rut. I'm always trying to look for something a little different," he says. The three to four different soups he makes every day are a good opportunity to spread his culinary wings, and he comes up with pleasing concoctions: cheeseburger, cordon bleu, gold soup.

"Gold soup?" I ask.

"Yep. You just add fourteen carrots! Ah, a joke. Now I feel better! Here's a couple more soup jokes if you want them. The trick to making navy bean soup is to add only 239 beans. If you add one more, it makes it 240. 'Too farty.' And how about this? 'How do you make kidney soup? Boil the piss out of it!'"

I groan with tired amusement.

Kendall regards cafe cooking as simple in itself, but it gets difficult when his regulars demand things just the way each of them likes. "Breakfast, for example, is pretty simple," he laughs, "but they'll say, 'Give me two eggs over easy medium, bacon well done but not crisp, American fries burnt, toast medium.' Don't think the customers don't run this place! I used to think it would be nice to go into business for myself, be my own boss. Now I've got five hundred bosses out there."

Despite its five hundred bosses, whose input influences everything from the cafe's look to its hours and menu, the Koffee Kup is a family-run business. Kendall and Trish's children, Sara and Adam, "earn a little paycheck" by being involved in the restaurant "whether they want to or not." Open seven days a week, with extra hours thrown in to accommodate the after-hours appetites of people attending shows at the restored opera house next door—watch for the growing collection of photos autographed by the likes of the Glenn Miller Band—there are plenty of opportunities for Sara and Adam to make spending money. With the city of Stoughton restoring its historic main street and promoting itself as a tourist destination, Kendall sees a lot of new directions the restaurant could take. "I have a lot of ideas, but I can't do everything because there's only so much time in a day. There's only so many years in a lifetime."

· ·

Next Best Bets

Baraboo
Jen's Alpine Cafe & Soup Kitchen
117 Fourth Street
An antique eatery decked out in vintage high-backed oak booths that make the perfect place to dine on inventive soups, scrumptious pie, and other old- and new-fashioned fresh fare.

Deerfield
Whitetail Cafe
15 North Main Street
Clean, pert, fresh—with food to match.

Evansville
Village Square Family Restaurant
5 West Main Street
Fairly diverse menu as small town cafes go. Try the Swedish pancakes, but skip the canned blueberry filling as an extra.

La Valle
Granny's Pantry Restaurant
205 West Main Street
Just off the 400 Trail and next to the old feed mill, which has been converted into an antiques market. Known for its home cooking, but I'm not convinced by the hot beef.

Portage
Gramma's Corner Cafe
100 East Cook Street
A vintage old-time look complements Gramma's real basic foods: mashed potatoes with lumps, potato pancakes with applesauce, biscuits and gravy people drive miles for. It's not uncommon for the daily plate special to come with Jell-O for dessert.

Southeast

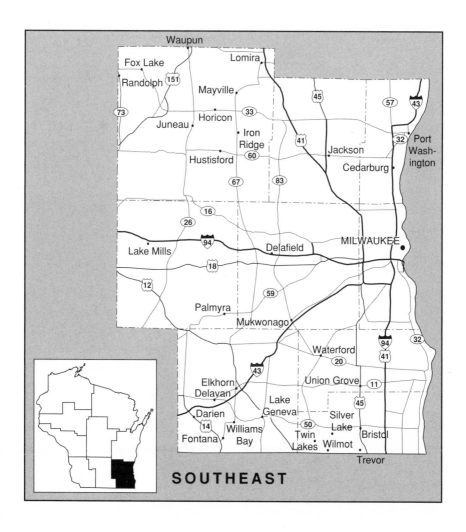

Waupun

Fox Lake
Lomira

Randolph (151)
Mayville

(73)
Horicon (33)
(45)
(57) (43)

Juneau
(41)
(32) Port
Wash-
ington

Iron
Ridge
(60)
Jackson

Hustisford
Cedarburg

(67) (83)

(16)

(26)
(94)
Lake Mills
Delafield
MILWAUKEE

(18)

(12)
(59)

Palmyra

Mukwonago

Waterford
(94) (32)
(20)
(41)

Elkhorn
Delavan
(43)
Union Grove (11)

Darien
Lake
Geneva
(45)

(14)
Williams
(50)
Silver
Lake

Fontana
Bay
Twin
Lakes
Wilmot
Bristol

Trevor

SOUTHEAST

CEDARBURG
Cedarburg Coffee Pot
W61 N514 Washington Avenue
(262) 377-1202
M–Su 5 A.M.–10 P.M.
Peter Demopoulos

Hanging on the wall over my small table in the Cedarburg Coffee Pot is a photograph of Peter Demopoulos in his native Greek village of Pyrgos. The sixteen-year-old boy stands behind a pushcart partially filled with a variety of fruit. The life of a fruit peddler is what Peter gave up when he immigrated to America in 1971. Today he sits across the table from me and relates the story of his Horatio Alger–like success.

With a promise of a job paying fifty dollars a week pumping gas, Peter left Greece for America, where he settled in Milwaukee and soon landed a job as a dishwasher in a relative's restaurant. In a few years he had worked his way into the kitchen and decided he was ready to be out on his own. He found a rundown little restaurant on Brady Street and put down as collateral his treasured 1970 GTO Judge. For the first year or two, he worked nearly around the clock, preparing food in the kitchen and sleeping there on a cot. In 1991 he sold the restaurant and bought the shopworn Coffee Pot Cafe in Cedarburg, bringing along a color photograph of the GTO Judge—which hangs in the rear dining room—as a tribute to his success.

Peter is friendly, handsome, and very tan from working on his beef cattle farm in nearby Belgium. "I get up early and run the farm, then come in here," he explains. "This afternoon I'm going home to cut hay." He raises about three hundred head of Black Angus and Maine Anjou and is heavily involved with the local 4-H program. Peter is just one man—just "one short Greek," in the words of the late Mike Royko, *Chicago Tribune* columnist—but he manages to accomplish more in a day—and in a lifetime—than a dozen other men.

"I like what I'm doing. I like people. I don't want to sit at a desk," Peter says. "And I'm used to working hard. Some people see troubles. I see opportunities."

Where other people would have seen in the previous Coffee Pot a cafe long past its prime, Peter saw a "gold mine." He had been eyeing it for some time before he succeeded in purchasing it. "I loved this small town, this unique town. It's in such a beautiful area." The town of Cedarburg is a charming historic village about four miles west of Lake Michigan, an easy bike ride from the Milwaukee area or West Bend.

My friend Kine points out that is also about halfway between the two cities, which makes the Coffee Pot a great meeting place for transacting a variety of business. It has also been recognized by readers of the *Milwaukee Journal Sentinel* as the best place to listen in on local gossip.

The Coffee Pot's history began long before Peter arrived on the scene. In the 1920s, Peter says, it was a house whose occupants prepared food and sold it on the sidewalk to passersby. In time, a small diner with grill was added onto the front of the house; this became the Coffee Pot, operated by the occupants of the house. If you stand across the street and look at the Coffee Pot it becomes clear: Peter's rear dining room is actually housed in a late nineteenth-century Queen Anne–style cottage whose fish-scaled gable can be seen protruding from the flat roof of the diner. "Sure, it's easier to tear down than to patch here and there," Peter says, "but the historical issue made me want to work with what's here."

Working within a high set of personal standards, Peter is both preservationist and darned good cook. At the Coffee Pot you'll find an array of homemade daily specials, breakfast items, and sandwiches and burgers. Peter believes in the quality of handmade and serves up fresh-baked bread and cinnamon rolls, slow-simmered soups, and real mashed potatoes. "It's got be fresh. It's got to be tasty. Cooking is an art. Eating is a pleasure," asserts Peter. About the only thing that is not prepared from scratch in the kitchen are the pies and other desserts, which come from an area bakery.

Another philosophy that guides Peter is the belief that the Coffee Pot is successful because he is there every day working alongside his employees. "I work with them. I cook. I bus tables. I do everything. It's important for people to see me and know me because this restaurant is me. It's my life."

DELAFIELD
Lumber Inn
617 Wells Street
(262) 646-8988
M 6 A.M.–2 P.M.; Tu–F 6 A.M.–3 P.M.; Sa 6 A.M.–2 P.M.; Su 7 A.M.–2 P.M.
Raul Perez

A plaque hanging near the grill in the Lumber Inn reads "IF YOU DON'T LIKE MY COOKING, LOWER YOUR STANDARDS," but I guarantee you'll have few complaints with the food at this restaurant built on the site of the former Cooper and Utter lumberyard by Dave and Shar Huebner in 1983. The man next to me at the counter, an out-of-town regular from Manitowoc, describes the fare as "old-time farm food: basically eggs, potatoes, and meat."

He's right. There's plenty of that here. The breakfast plates have brawny names like Buck Saw Special and Carpenters' Canadian Bacon Special, consisting of sirloin steaks or seasoned ham and lumberjack portions of fried potatoes, eggs, and toast. On the lighter side, my blueberry pancakes, brought from the kitchen by a waitress wearing a canvas nail pouch, were loaded with berries and just perfect for holding me until lunch.

If you stop by a little later in the day, you'll find slow-simmered soups, fresh daily specials, and nearly a dozen different pies, cobblers, and cheesecakes made from scratch by Shar. She and Dave sold the restaurant in March 2002 to Raul Perez, who capably trods the culinary path set down by the Huebners. But Shar loves to bake and has stayed on to the great delight and benefit of the Lumber Inn's customers. A dessert board near the cash register keeps you informed of what's still available; the day I stopped by, the selections filled it from top to bottom. A warning to husbands led the list: "Women who cook and wash the dishes should be given these three wishes: a grateful husband, a kiss on the cheek, and a piece of Shar's pie at least once a week!"

Raul brings twenty years of restaurant experience with him from Milwaukee. He moved to the United States from Mexico in 1985 when he was seventeen years old and soon discovered a passion for cooking. The dream of having his own restaurant became a reality when he found the Lumber Inn, a place with a great reputation. He worked alongside the Huebners for a month before closing on the restaurant, and since that time has "just been carrying on. You don't want to change a good thing," he explains. He has interjected a few of his own touches, however. On Mondays he prepares authentic Mexican specials, such as today's chicken tostada. He has also added popular requests, like the mushroom and Swiss burger, and is proud of his corned beef hash. When I wrinkle my nose, he laughs, "I see you're not a corned beef hash person."

Raul is a youthful, friendly man who, only three months into his ownership, has a warm, easy rapport with his customers. "He is a great boss," confides my waitress, and I have no doubt that he is. He was a bit worried about how he would fit into the small town crowd—"My biggest fear was being new and being a Mexican"—but the transition from the Huebners' ownership to his own went very smoothly. Raul explains that his customers like to eat, and he provides them with his best cooking. If the regulars don't find what they want on the menu, they ask for it. Raul complies, preparing today's special split pea soup and strawberry pie, for example. Each day, more and more of the immediate and distant community rediscover the Lumber Inn and become part of Raul's loyal following.

The Lumber Inn reflects the history of its site with a "modern woodmen" decorating scheme. The walls are hung with antique logging equipment, carpenters' tools, and artifacts from the old lumber company. When customers started bringing in pieces of their own to display, the walls began filling up with bucksaws and calipers, augers and gauges, yard rules and carpenters' pencils. Don't miss the lumber company's Fairbanks scale, once used to weigh train carloads of coal and corn, now displayed in the front window.

FOX LAKE
The Chalet
814 West State Street
(920) 928-2425
M–Su 5 A.M.–2 P.M.; also F 4 P.M.–8 P.M.
Jim and Diane Zindars

Diane Zindars is baking a cake for the next day when I stop in for a visit just ten minutes before she closes up the Chalet, a former drive-in about a half-mile outside Fox Lake. It's been another busy day, but she generously stays to chat about life at the center of the Fox Lake community.

Jim and Diane Zindars owned a bowling alley and sandwich shop in nearby Juneau when they began to realize that the late nights and the business didn't suit a family with two small children. About the same time, they sold their cottage on Fox Lake and purchased the Chalet, operating both it and their Juneau business before selling the latter. Eight years later, Jim has discovered a previously unknown talent: he is a great cook.

"Jim absolutely loves to cook," Diane says. "But when we bought the place, he didn't know how to cook at all. Our plan was that I would cook, and he'd work out front. Now he does all of the cooking, and I wait tables. But I remember the first year or two. I was here working and he was at home with the girls. One day my daughter came to me and said, 'I'm sick of having cereal for breakfast.' I said, 'Talk to your dad; have him make you an egg.' And she had to show him how to cook an egg because he didn't know how to do it! This week Jim's out, and I have to cook. I'm getting a lot of comments like, 'Gotta get out the Rolaids!'"

Despite the joking, the Zindarses' regulars have no complaints about the from-scratch cooking at the Chalet. Together, Jim and Diane produce daily specials ranging from meat loaf to Salisbury steak, daily soups, homemade bread, real mashed potatoes ("We have a lot of farmers, and they like their potatoes"), and a variety of homemade desserts. The breakfasts are especially popular, in part because the portions are oversized. "Our pancakes are huge," Diane warns. "A guy just ate three of them of them for the first time."

Today, Jim's secret is out and known to both the locals and the travelers who regularly fill the counter and small dining room for weekend breakfast. It is not uncommon to wait an hour for your meal, Diane says.

The locals know this and come prepared to spend the time visiting with friends, but travelers are often impatient and leave without sampling either the conversation or the cooking. Some who do stay come back, often becoming regulars themselves. "We have one woman who comes from Portage," Diane says. "One day she stopped while on her way to work, and now she comes in all the time because she's gotten to know the people."

The men's coffee group stretched out along the counter debates "everything important in the world" each morning. Summer topics center on golf, the stock market, and fishing, with the football pool and high school basketball being the most popular winter talk. Winter is also the true test of customer loyalty, and Diane is amazed at the fortitude and durability of the locals. "In winter, they have to prove they can come in," she smiles. "We had this one couple who had been married for sixty-five years. One day, the weather was just terrible—snow and ice and cold. We didn't expect anyone to be in at all, but here they come through the door. At their age, they should hardly have been driving at all, let alone on a day like that."

The folks at the Chalet are "just like one big extended family," according to Diane. If someone needs help, they all offer assistance. If it is busy in the restaurant, customers will drive out to the Zindarses' home, pick up the girls, and bring them back to the restaurant. At ages thirteen and fifteen, they are happy to work or not work, Diane notes, but they also have developed a sense of pride about the family's restaurant. When they go to other restaurants, they make comparisons and note differences. "We went to Florida and ate at a restaurant," says Diane, "and my daughter said, 'Listen. It's so quiet in here.' No one knew anyone. Our restaurant is loud and friendly because our customers feel they own the place."

HUSTISFORD
Joan's Country Cookin'
469 East Rubicon Street
(920) 349-3511
M–Sa 5:30 A.M.–2 P.M.; Su closed
Joan Nehls

For a day and a half I have been crisscrossing Dodge County on back roads, spotting black and yellow signs advertising Todd Nehls for Sheriff. When I shake hands with Joan Nehls over the counter of the cafe she has owned since 1984, I blurt out, "Is this campaign headquarters?" She gives me a blank look and suddenly breaks into a smile. "This is it. Campaign headquarters. Where everything important happens."

Joan's stepson Todd is the sheriff candidate. Her husband, Edwin, a former Dodge County sheriff and now the state commander of the VFW, is just leaving for the veterans' state convention in Milwaukee. Joan gives him a loving kiss and turns to take her place behind the counter. From here she can talk to her customers and tend the grill, which is busy this morning browning hash browns and frying eggs. Joan's Country Cookin' is a popular breakfast place with the locals, who, Joan says, "love their eggs and omelettes. Breakfast here is a good way to start the day."

Joan is bubbly and energetic and launches into stories—one after the other—of her regulars who come in for breakfast and get talking so much they forget to pay their bill. Some stay for hours, beginning with breakfast and talking right through the morning until it's time for lunch. The regulars are so predictable that Joan and her right-hand woman, Bonnie, can begin preparing their food as soon as they walk through the door. "If someone doesn't come in, we worry. Sometimes they let us know ahead of time that they'll be gone, but if someone doesn't come in when they're expected, then we give them a call or send someone to look after them."

A retired couple gets up from their table and waits to pay their bill at the counter. Joan asks, "What are you going to do today?"

"I'm going to take her down to Potawatomi and do some gambling," he says.

"Oh, sure!" his wife retorts. "I didn't bring any money."

When Bonnie gives the woman her change, she says, "Here you go. This should do it."

"Could you give that to me in quarters?" the woman quips.

Instead of plunking quarters into the slot machines at the casino, the woman tries her luck with a raffle ticket, a fundraiser for the Hustisford fire department. The winning ticket is worth a thousand dollars in cash. Another area fire department—an orange, misspelled poster identifies it as the Neosho Fire & Resue—is raffling off a 2003 Harley Road King, but the woman prefers cash to the motorcycle. "We're having a hard time selling the Harley tickets," Joan says.

The tickets might be a hard sell, but Joan's real country cookin' sure isn't. "I wake up at four every morning and meditate about what I'm going to fix that day," says Joan. "Everything is homemade: baked chicken, roasted meats. Everything is from scratch—no cans of soup or anything. I always use fresh vegetables from my garden in the back. I use no canned anything."

Joan grew up on a farm and ate mostly meat and potatoes meals, so this is the kind of meals she prepares at the cafe. She prepares daily specials such as spaghetti and meatballs, roast beef, and meat loaf and serves only real potatoes. "Mashed potatoes, hash browns, American fries. I feel I might as well use my time while I'm here," she says. "I even put potato skins in my mashed potatoes because the food salesman tried to sell me potato skins. I said, 'Potato skins? Why would I want to buy them?' 'To put in your mashed potatoes,' he said. And I thought, heck, I've got potato skins—I've been throwing them away—and so I put them in." Other real food specialties include pies made with handpicked apples, raspberries, and other fruit; turnovers; cinnamon rolls; banana bread, and other baked goods. Among the desserts, the Bonnie Delight is a favorite. Bonnie created it one day by combining a chocolate brownie with vanilla ice cream, chocolate sauce, real whipped cream from nearby Radloff Dairy, and a maraschino cherry.

When Joan bought the former White Top restaurant in 1984, she had just been widowed and thought it would be good way to support herself and her children. "It was just natural instinct," she explains. "I love work, I love people." The restaurant has been an excellent way to increase her number of friends, and she counts many out-of-towners among her most loyal. "I have a lot of people come all the way from Milwaukee. I have groups of motorcyclists and bicyclists coming on weekends. Usually the girls see them coming, and we run back and get the hash browns going. I had thousands of motorcyclists come last summer. They called ahead, and that's a good thing or we would have run out of food. They're excellent eaters."

JUNEAU
Oak Street Cafe ☟
130 East Oak Street
(920) 386-2966
M 5 A.M.–3 P.M.; Tu–F 5 A.M.–8 P.M.; Sa 6 A.M.–8 P.M.; Su 7 A.M.–7 P.M.
Diane Moulai and Santo Pulvino
The sign overhanging the sidewalk out front of the Oak Street Cafe depicts a cartoon granny whipping up homemade goodies. Diane Moulai is often teased about being the granny on the sign because she is herself a grandmother, but she is far from being gray haired and withered. And it's a good thing because I'd like to think she'll be in the kitchen for many years to come.

Three years ago, Diane was working for the bus company in Milwaukee when her partner, Santo, lost his job. They looked everywhere for another one and decided, finally, that a little motel would be the perfect solution to their problems. Diane had it all planned out: she would clean the motel rooms in the morning and work at the bus company in the evenings, and Santo would manage and maintain the motel. The only problem was, there was no motel to be bought. So they began considering other options, including the possibility of running a small restaurant. For two weeks they saw an ad for a cafe in Dodge County—"Where's Dodge County?"—and one morning, in near desperation, Diane called the listing realtor for information.

"Do you know where Juneau is?" he asked.

"Sure," she bluffed.

"The first thing I did was go out and buy a Wisconsin map," she remembers. Her naïveté still makes her laugh. "Then I woke up Santo and said, 'We have to go to Juneau to look at a restaurant.' He looked at me like I was crazy and said, 'Where?' And here we are."

For one year Diane and Santo operated the restaurant under its former name—Rita's Country Restaurant, which under the previous owner was featured in the first edition of *Cafe Wisconsin*—then renamed it to reflect its new ownership. "From the beginning I had intentions of home cooking because you can't buy customers," Diane explains. She developed a passion for cooking as a very young girl working beside her mother in the kitchen. When she was in first or second grade, her mother was reading aloud the ingredients required for a recipe she was making. When Diane heard her say soda, she climbed the attic steps and retrieved a bottle of soda pop. When she was not too much older, she spent hours looking for new recipes to try, poring over cookbooks the way other girls read fiction. By the time she was fifteen, she was preparing meals for her widowed grandfather. "I was always looking for new ideas," she says.

Diane's interest in food as a medium through which to express artistic creativity is parlayed into remarkably good eating at the Oak Street Cafe. She makes gorgeous pies completely from scratch, including a mile-high lemon meringue prepared for the jurors participating in a trial in the courthouse across the street. It is a beautiful sight, with its mound of lightly browned meringue and evenly crimped crust, and I wish the pie weren't reserved for other eaters. It is cooling on the counter, set off by itself from the other gorgeous pies in the refrigerator case behind the counter. From my stool, I hungrily eye the lovely creations behind the glass. There are fruit pies stuffed full of fresh blueberries and cherries, a rhubarb pie with a checkerboard lattice top, a Mounds bar cake, and strawberry schaum torte.

Of all the decadent desserts Diane makes, the strawberry schaum torte is her customers' favorite. "The sheriff's department says I'm the schaum torte queen," she claims. "I have people who will call up, and if we don't have schaum torte, they won't have anything," she says. She serves me a piece on a plate and asks, "What do you think?" I poke my fork through the fresh strawberries on top, down through the middle layer of cream cheese, miniature marshmallows and whipped cream, and into the baked meringue base. What do I think? It is divine, heavenly. It so good, I can't stop eating. It is strawberries on a cloud.

I have been hunting cafes for two weeks when I find Diane and Santo's Oak Street Cafe. It is the first truly exceptional cafe of my journey, and my spirits are buoyed at last. Many cafe owners had justified their shortcuts in the kitchen, claiming no one was making real mashed potatoes anymore or baking their own bread or rolling out their own pie crusts, until I was nearly convinced that William Least Heat-Moon's legendary seven-calendar cafes might no longer be found in Wisconsin. But Diane and Santo have restored my faith. Their strawberry schaum torte is my Eucharistic wafer.

Their ministry to those of faltering faith is not limited to dessert. Diane and Santo serve up generous portions of homemade bread, rolls, buns and pastries; fresh and inventive soups (Diane confesses that her liver dumpling soup was a flop with the regulars); casseroles; and meat and real potatoes main dishes. Santo dips into his Italian heritage to create pasta specialties with from-scratch tomato-based sauces. An obscure favorite is his breakfast spaghetti, which debuted at the first New Year's Day "Pasta Bowl." A spoof of football bowl games, the party thrown for the regular customers was such a success that it is destined to become an annual event.

LAKE MILLS
Cafe on the Park
131 North Main Street
(920) 648-2915
M–Sa 5 A.M.–3 P.M.; Su 7 A.M.–3 P.M.
Clyde and Debbie Hady, owners
Heather Blomgren and Jamie Thom, managers
As the American Legion sets up a large party tent in the grassy park across the street and puts the other final touches on the upcoming weekend festival, Cheryl Gard eats a grilled cheese sandwich and fries at the Cafe on the Park. She comes in a couple of times a week instead of messing up the pots and pans at home during the few hours she has between her two jobs. "I can get a good home-cooked meal, and big portions, too," she explains. "I drove out to Oregon on vacation and ate at a lot of restaurants, and am I ever glad to be back home and at my favorite ones."

The restaurant has been in Lake Mills for many years—at least since the 1930s by the looks of the vintage art deco interior. It has a gawky kind of pyramidal tower on top, which explains why it was once known as the Pyramid. If you hold up your hand to block out the tower, the current name becomes much more suitable. Go inside. The Cafe on the Park is beautiful. Painted moldings around the doors and windows are carved with tulips, vines, and geometric patterns, and walls are decorated with peach wainscoting and cream paint. Peach tables topped with green paper placemats coordinate with floral-patterned booths. Over them, suspended from the ceiling by brass chains, hang the original green glass lamps. Lush, patterned emerald carpet anchors the entire scene.

But all of this is merely framework to the cafe's magnificent vintage marble counter pieced with gray, white, and black tiles and edged with green. This counter is the kind you only find behind ropes in museum exhibits, where mannequins in flapper dresses and zoot suits sip plastic Cokes. So, if there's an empty stool or two, don't miss the chance to rest your elbows on the cold, glassy marble. And while you're there, reliving the beauty of the 1920s, take a look at the extensive menu. Time travel makes a person hungry.

At Cafe on the Park, you'll find good home cooking in a gourmet setting. Managers Heather Blomgren and Jamie Thom produce a steady stream of homemade soups and traditional Wisconsin daily specials—meat loaf, ham and scalloped potatoes, Salisbury steak—from the back kitchen. Among the most popular menu items are the breakfast skillets made by layering eggs and hash browns with vegetables, cheese, meats, and other ingredients. "They're a meal in themselves," says Cheryl.

LOMIRA
Susie's Home Cooking
1007 Church Street
(920) 269-7229
M–Th 6 A.M.–8 P.M.; F 6 A.M.–9 P.M.; Sa 6 A.M.–8 P.M.; Su 7 A.M.–2 P.M.
Susie and Jim Bisek

I drag into Lomira tired, hungry, and sweaty after getting to the last two cafes after they've closed for the day. I'm ready to eat not merely good food but exceptional food, and I'm not disappointed with what I find at Susie's Home Cooking, recommended by a cafe owner featured in the first edition of *Cafe Wisconsin*. The menu lists a variety of familiar offerings, plus some refreshing alternatives. I order the seafood salad (I'm craving fresh, raw vegetables) and a slice of apple pie—but first take a trip past the pie case to verify that it is indeed made from scratch as the menu promises. It is, as is everything else in the refrigerated case, including carrot cake, turtle cheesecake, old-fashioned bread pudding, and today's special cream puffs.

The cafe is almost empty, with no regular customers in their familiar places when I arrive. Also absent are Susie and Jim Bisek, owners since 1991, and I am at a loss because there's no one who can tell me about Susie's. Across the dining room, two women seated in a booth look over their menus, which are filled with a tempting selection of salads, sandwiches, burgers, and full meals. The board near the counter lists additional daily specials, making the decision about what to have for lunch doubly difficult. The women have not been here before, and they quiz the waitress about what is homemade and what is not. "Everything's homemade," she assures them. Surprised and pleased that they have unknowingly stumbled into a five-star small town restaurant, they confidently order sandwiches and pie and lean back to soak up the air conditioning.

Susie's Home Cooking has the clean, fresh, contemporary feel of a suburban restaurant. Teal and gray are dominant colors and a refreshing alternative to the browns, oranges, and avocados that tend to characterize many other cafes, whose owners cannot afford a major overhaul. The waitresses wear identical uniforms consisting of black pants or shorts topped with blue and red striped shirts with a Susie's logo over the pocket. There are indications, too, that Susie's is a very popular place: a hostess stand near the entrance with a pad of paper for writing down names; a sign that reads "Please Wait to be Seated," and Visa/MasterCard decals on the glass front door. I'm glad I'm here when it's slow, so I can linger over my food, eavesdrop on conversations across the room, and meet any regulars who might happen to come in.

Like Ray, who eats at Susie's several times a week. He sits at a booth along the side wall, eating a plate of hot beef and reading the newspaper. Most days he comes alone, but sometimes he arranges to meet friends or his sister for lunch or dinner. Ray says, "They've got a pretty big menu here," and recommends the meat loaf and the hotdogs.

"Hotdogs?" I ask, a bit surprised.

"I love the hotdogs," he confirms. "But you've got to be very fussy if you can't find something you like at Susie's."

MUKWONAGO
Little Babe's Cafe
507 Main Street, Suite 100
(262) 363-0663
M–Sa 5 A.M.–8 P.M.; Su 5 A.M.–1 P.M.
Lin McConnell and Missy Ramsdall
A sign on the door of the women's room at Little Babe's Cafe, located in a new mini mall in uptown Mukwonago, reads: "I am woman. I am invincible. I am tired." My sentiments exactly. I have been on the road in search of Wisconsin's best small town cafes for just two weeks (with fourteen more to go) in crazy June weather ranging from fifty to one hundred degrees. I have driven over a thousand miles. I have slept on the ground every night. I have eaten heedlessly and much too often. I am tired.

Throwing any lingering concerns about my diet to the wind, I find a piece of co-owner Missy Ramsdall's decadent, calorie-laden French silk pie to be the perfect antidote to my road-weariness. It restores both my energy and my mood. Neither Missy nor Lin McConnell is in—one is at home resting from a broken arm, the other for an upcoming surgery—so I approach the coffee group at the round table behind the counter, pull out a chair, and with my first question become one of the gang.

No better champions of Missy's and Lin's efforts could be found anywhere in Mukwonago than around the coffee table. "This is the best place to eat in town," I'm told. "It's better than home."

Lin and Missy, best friends for over twenty years, met in 1979 when both were waitressing at a local restaurant. When the business changed hands, "the girls" decided it was time to break out on their own. With the support of the community, they began buying restaurant equipment and storing it away until a suitable place could be found. Two years later, their chance came. "They were scared to death," says Shirley of the coffee group, "but we promised we'd support them."

With an emphasis on homemade American food, the girls quickly attracted a loyal and committed following. In doing so, they became part of a loving extended family. When Missy and Lin recently celebrated their anniversary, their customers gave them a bouquet of roses. And when a customer entered hospice care, the entire staff expressed concern by sending her a bouquet of flowers. Shirley says, "There's a lot of camaraderie and love that comes through this place." Bob concurs. "We think of them just like they're our own kids."

Nearly every day the gang meets at the round coffee table. They call each other up and make plans about going down to "the girls'" and then arrive one by one or in couples. Their loyalty is rewarded by menu selections named after them, listed on the menu under the heading Special Breakfast Requests. There is Rick's southern style biscuits and gravy, Al's eggs Benedict, Tom's vegetarian skillet, Ralph's Polish sausage, and Chatterton's scrambler.

The cafe's unusual name refers to Lin and Missy themselves. Bob explains that Lin is very short and has the nickname Little One. Missy is Babe. Together they are Little Babe's.

PORT WASHINGTON
Harry's Restaurant
128 North Franklin Street
(262) 284-2861
M–Su 5:30 A.M.–7:30 P.M.
Dale and Bertie Mahal

"I know that book," says Bertie Mahal when I introduce myself as the author of *Cafe Wisconsin*. "One of my out-of-town customers brought it in and wanted to know why we weren't in it." Mea culpa. Harry's Restaurant should have been in it, and I don't know how I missed it. It's there, right on the main street of historic downtown Port Washington, just as plain as day—and it has been for more than sixty years. Plenty of other people have found it, as evidenced by the guest book on the counter. I feel a bit ashamed and foolish when I read that even Patrice from Paris, France, has found it. She wrote, "Very best breakfast of the Northern Hemisphere!"

My teenage waitress, who will be attending UW–Milwaukee this fall to study creative writing, has never read the comments in the guest book, and I admonish her, an aspiring writer. There is much to be learned from guest books, and they should be mandatory reading for all adventure eaters. How about this entry recently left by Alma: "I was hired by 'Harry' 63 years ago because I was a 'Blue-eyed Blonde' and he thought the truck drivers would like a little 'variety' with their meals! When it was closing time I peeled a peck of potatoes and put them in cold water for the next day and also some onions and *pa* didn't like smelling onions all nite! *Harry* was always nice to us waitresses. I had to walk home to the West Side of P.W. and sometimes the police would take me home which pa did not like cause he thought the neighbors might think I was arrested!"

Harry Burton opened a little sandwich restaurant across the street in 1936, moving to larger quarters—the current location—in the 1940s. As business grew, he bought the neighboring beauty shop and broke through the shared wall to create a large dining area. He lined the walls with knotty pine—now burnished to a deep honey color—and dotted the floor with tables and chairs. When you step from the sidewalk through the corner door, you enter the original Harry's at this location. Sit in one of the side booths facing the lakefront and watch the marina activity through the windows to your left and the coffee drinkers gathered at the counter to your right. You'll be entertained for hours.

In 1978, after forty-two years, Harry sold the business. His widow, Mabel, still owns the building and lives upstairs; she comes down every day to visit friends and eat dinner. The Mahals—Dale and Bertie—bought the place in 1990 after Bertie survived a life-changing bout with cancer.

She had worked in the medical field and knew she didn't want to go back to that. One day she and her sister were lunching at Harry's when the owner indicated she would like to sell it. Although she had no experience in restaurants, Bertie decided she wanted it. Dale agreed and gave up his position as vice president of an advertising agency to become co-owner. "Here I am, a former executive," he observes. "Let me tell you, busing tables and washing dishes puts everything in perspective."

Now into their fifteenth year, Dale and Bertie are involved with every aspect of the job, from cooking to cleaning the rest rooms. Their willingness to roll up their sleeves and plunge into work up to their elbows sets a good example for their employees. "We've been blessed to have so many good, reliable, and honest people working for us," observes Bertie. "It's comforting to know they treat the business and its customers with respect." The Mahals hire many high school students and have found that those who excel in school—academically or athletically—tend to make better workers because they are more disciplined. "They show up on time and are prepared to work," Dale notes. "We've been fortunate to be able to hire and retain many good young people over the years, as long as we've been willing and able to work around their school schedules.

"We love to hear people say they've had a pleasant dining experience and the food was good and reasonably priced," he continues. "But it's even more reassuring to hear people say their service was exceptional—not just good. We have quite a few people—cooks and servers—who do an excellent job. Some of our young people have a lot to learn, but they're not without quality mentors in every position."

Bertie emphasizes, "It's so important that we spend time here, doing anything that needs doing." Over the years, their responsibilities have diversified to include not only operating the restaurant but also selling fishing licenses—"We used to sell more than any other place in Ozaukee County"—and comforting traumatized sailors. One year during the Clipper Cup sailboat race between Michigan and Port Washington, a storm blew the sailors off course. It also caused a major power outage in Port Washington, which Dale and Bertie waited out in the cafe. About eight in the evening the power came back on and the Mahals prepared to leave for home. But then the sailors started dragging in, soaking wet and distraught from their experience with the storm. "We stayed open until midnight feeding them until we ran out of food. We were doing their laundry in the basement. It really was a night to remember," Dale recalls.

Major storms notwithstanding, Dale describes his business as "very weather dependent." When the weather is bad, there are fewer travelers and tourists. Bad weather doesn't prevent the locals from coming in, however; at five thirty they are lined up on the sidewalk waiting for Harry's to open for the day. "They are not weather dependent," Dale says wryly. "On Sundays, it is really quite comical," Bertie adds. "After church, people go from table to table visiting. There is typically a line out front all morning."

The locals make up the church crowd, the morning coffee group, the daily lunchers, the "business mucky mucks and blue collar workers," and the investors who gather to discuss the stock market. Bertie subscribes to the *Wall Street Journal* especially for them; also found at the counter every day are copies of the local newspaper, *USA Today*, and the *Milwaukee Journal Sentinel*, which makes the crowd at Harry's very well read compared to those at most other cafes. The quality of a cafe can be rated by the number of newspaper boxes on the sidewalk out front. Harry's is a four-newspaper-box cafe—a pretty fine one indeed.

Breakfast is the largest meal of the day, with the trademark skillets— hash browns scrambled together with eggs and other ingredients—being a favorite choice of locals and out-of-towners alike. Writes an anonymous diner in the guest book: "Lovely breakfast, so friendly! Coming back over and over."

"Our high is 240 dozen eggs in a single week," Bertie says, "and on our busiest Sundays, we'll use sixty dozen eggs." Bertie and Dale are also proud of the Jewish coffee cake, the recipe for which was passed down from Harry himself. Other specialties on "the ordinary small town menu" are the homemade bread, daily specials and soups, and desserts. About the only thing not prepared from scratch is the mashed potatoes, but "they're as close as you can get," Bertie assures.

RANDOLPH
Denise's Cafe 🍽
163 Stark Avenue
(920) 326-3535
M–Th 4:30 A.M.–4 P.M.; F 4:30 A.M.–7 P.M.; Sa 4:30 A.M.–4 P.M.; Su closed
Denise J. Fischer
After graduation from high school, Denise Fischer stayed in her hometown of Randolph and got a job waitressing at the cafe she now owns. "There was nothing else to do," she explains, "so I just sort of fell into restaurants. I was working here and the other cafe in town came up for grabs, so I bought it. All I needed was a thousand dollars for rent and food. It just kind of took off."

Denise didn't know much about cooking when she bought her first cafe in 1986. She could make breakfasts and burgers on the grill but had to rely on an older woman to teach her how to roast meats and make gravies, soups, pies, and baked goods like bread and sweet rolls. "Younger women no longer know how to cook," Denise believes. "Older women have more experience, more wisdom. She was a very wise woman. Without her—well, a lot of people didn't think I could make it. I was just a waitress. I was just an average person. But I had to do it. I had to learn."

Eighteen years later, Denise is now an accomplished cook. Every day she and her crew prepare a meat and potatoes–based noon special—"We're a very big meat and potatoes town"—featuring real mashed potatoes, gravy from pan drippings, vegetables or fruit, and a slice of homemade bread. Denise's Cafe also features homemade buttermilk pancakes, hand-pattied burgers served on bakery buns, cookies, and lovely cream and fruit pies. After a week and a half of cafe hunting in southeastern Wisconsin, I finally found pie worth eating at Denise's Cafe. My slice of lemon meringue was rich and tasty. (My first choice, the strawberry cream, was already gone.) The filling had lumps, but I didn't mind; they were a sure sign it was homemade.

In the ten years since my first visit, Denise has redecorated the restaurant—to my great disappointment. Gone is its vintage art deco look. Gone is the Paint-O-Whirl patterned linoleum floor tiles, the square pine tables with straight-backed chairs, the old-timey counter, and the oh-so-cool back bar. Nestled in my high-back walnut booth—thank goodness they're still here—I scan the updated surroundings. The authentic historic items have been replaced with copies of photos of historic Randolph. My favorite is a 1940s interior shot of Wandreis Cafe ("Where the Elite Meet to Eat") showing the vintage accoutrements that are now missing. Two other photos depict the building in late-nineteenth-century appearance and after the art deco–era remodeling that covered the façade with colored opaque glass panels.

Digging in the basement during the remodeling, Denise found many of the old restaurant items, including menus and sundae dishes, now displayed on shelves throughout the cafe. The two stools at the short counter are originals, showing up in the Wandreis photo. Denise's attention to the past is further reflected in her own commitment to the cafe and her community. Looking back over the past eighteen years, she says, "I knew I was going to be here awhile because I grew up in Randolph and knew everyone, and everyone knew me. We're in this together. I can't imagine doing anything else because I've been working in restaurants my whole life. And I love my job, I really do."

SILVER LAKE
Silver Lake Grill
107 Cogswell Drive
(262) 889-4727
M closed; Tu–Th 7 A.M.–3 P.M.; F 7 A.M.–9 P.M.; Sa–Su 7 A.M.–3 P.M.
Debra Scully

In this business, I eat a lot of chicken noodle soup. There is bad soup and there is good soup. Bad soup is bright yellow—a sure sign of powdered broth mix—with bits of processed chicken bobbing around in a sea of over-cooked carrots and mushy noodles. (If it looks and tastes like Campbell's, you know you've found it.) Good soup is Debra Scully's: nearly clear real broth with crunchy-crisp carrots and celery, bits of chicken picked from bones, and al dente egg noodles, thick and firm. Ask her younger son, Ben, who devours three helpings while we talk over the counter, sucking up the dregs of each cup with a hollow plastic coffee stirrer.

Debra's Silver Lake Grill, the latest manifestation of a decades-old lakeside business, had been open only a few weeks when I stopped by in June 2002, but it had all of the signs of future success. It is clean and fresh, with a completely remodeled interior and a funky vintage neon sign at the edge of the parking lot that reminds you this place has some age on it. Originally built in the 1950s, the Silver Lake Grill has been operated by several different owners. The first owner, who raised four kids in the upstairs apartment, is one of Debra's end-of-week regulars. "She'd heard what I was doing and came in to check it out. Now she comes back every Friday."

Debra previously owned a restaurant just over the Wisconsin-Illinois border, but she lived in Silver Lake and wanted to spend more time there as her kids entered school. "I had a well-oiled machine there," she notes, "and I didn't know whether I should take the chance" by giving it up for a place in Silver Lake. But when the old Grill came up for sale, Debra bought it. "We started small, replacing stuff in the kitchen, and then found ourselves in the middle of a major remodel." The dream to open a little restaurant in Silver Lake became a nightmare, but Debra powered on. The locals were excited and anticipated great things. Debra did not disappoint.

"My food salesman keeps asking me why I want to make everything myself," she says. "He wants to sell me packaged this, packaged that. But I have a restaurant because I love to cook. That's why I got into this business. Anyone can go out and buy it." This sentiment translates to delicious homemade soups, breads, sandwiches, and desserts. For the time being, however, Debra is unable to bake what she'd like because the oven she bought refuses to work. This is one of the kinks in the new system that Debra is still working out, and she looks forward to the day she can pull golden, steaming loaves of bread from the oven. Until then, Debra satisfies her customers with a variety of home-cooked food, including the popular breakfast skillets, sandwiches, and other grill foods. Today's breakfast special, the "small mess," a concoction of scrambled eggs, real potatoes, sausage, green peppers, onions, and cheese, is served until close. Today's noon specials include chicken noodle soup, Caesar salad, and hot beef. The desserts are fresh strawberry shortcake and chocolate mousse pie. I, for one, can't wait to see what additional treats Debra has cooked up for the oven.

TWIN LAKES
Manny's Snack Shack
404 South Lake Avenue
(262) 877-4442
M–F 6 A.M.–2 P.M.; Sa–Su 6 A.M.–3 P.M.
Manny and April Valerin
"I've been here six years in this beautiful town," Manny Valerin says over his shoulder as he fries eggs with his right hand and stirs pancake batter with his left. At the grill behind the counter, Manny is the master of his universe, framed by the walls of the Snack Shack. It is a universe you will want to visit again and again.

I clearly remember being in the Snack Shack when researching the original *Cafe Wisconsin* ten years ago. I remember driving along the lakeshore and coming upon the little corner restaurant, going in, and snooping around. But I left empty handed and unimpressed. Back ten years later, I find the Snack Shack hopping with activity from the all-morning coffee group, other locals in for breakfast, father Ivan and son Ivan at the counter, and the Tuesday morning bike riders from McHenry, Illinois.

Manny is busy when I arrive about nine fifteen, so I sit at the counter with Ivan and Ivan. They live on a farm near the Illinois border and are gearing up for their annual country music festival. A breakfast regular, big Ivan reports with the surety of a man who knows that Manny "serves the finest breakfast in town, bar none." As little Ivan dives into his three-egg omelette (his favorite breakfast order), big Ivan says, "I can't tell you how many times I walk in and the waitress puts a platter in front of me, and I say, 'Okay, that's what I'm having today.'"

As Manny tends the grill within earshot of the two Ivans and me, little Ivan announces that he can't eat all of his omelette.

"You're wasting food," points out big Ivan. "There's starving kids in Costa Rica who'd give anything to eat your leftovers."

"You better believe it," Manny turns to tell him. "I took my kids to the islands and showed them what it was like. They saw but it went in one eye and out the other."

Life in Wisconsin suits Manny, a native Costa Rican. He and his wife, April, and two children moved to Twin Lakes from nearby Lake Geneva when they purchased the Snack Shop in 1996, and since that time, home has been an apartment above the business. A thorough updating in 1997 resulted in the Snack Shack winning the Twin Lakes New Look Award, but much more than the looks is new. It has a new round table for the coffee group, a new menu, a new clientele, a new man at the grill.

Part-time police officer Gary Hamachek extends a hand and sits down beside me at the counter. "This has always been a busy place in summer," he says. "Winters are a lot slower. It's primarily a local group anymore because the population doesn't swell like it used to. Most of the houses around the lake are primary homes now, where they used to be secondary homes." Gary invites me to join the rest of the locals at the coffee table, and I meet Russ, who has been in Twin Lakes "only forty-four years" and his wife, Nancy, a Twin Lakes native. Connie is there too, just as she is every morning. She no longer drives because of poor eyesight, but someone picks her up and takes her home so she can socialize every morning. "I told them I wouldn't be able to come anymore," she explains, "but they said, 'Oh we'll find a way for you to come. We'll pick you up.'"

The coffee group is fluid and continuous, occupying the table from about nine to eleven thirty every morning. Nancy explains that Manny had been here only about a month when he observed that the locals were gathering for coffee at another restaurant. Nancy told him he'd have to get a round table if he wanted them there, so he went out and bought one and placed it in the front window. They've been meeting daily ever since. "At a round table, there's always room for one more," Nancy says. "You can always scoot over and get another chair in."

"Here come the bikers," she notes as she looks out the window. Like clockwork, the riders from Wonder Lake, Illinois, start arriving and dismounting, leaning their bicycles against the front window. They come every Thursday at ten, riding the fifteen miles from home to the Snack Shack to refuel on eggs and bacon and French toast made with sliced cinnamon rolls before heading back home. Mostly senior citizens, they represent an alternative lifestyle to the stationary coffee drinkers at the round table. They are a coffee group on the move.

Manny serves up a great breakfast—it's perhaps the busiest meal of the day—but also features a variety of midday offerings, including salads, soups, sandwiches, and plate specials. A full range of ice cream treats keeps the sweets-eaters happy.

UNION GROVE
Callen's Restaurant ⦿
1027 Main Street
(262) 878-1150
M–Th 6:30 A.M.–7 P.M.; F 6:30 A.M.–3 P.M.; Sa 7 A.M.–3 P.M.; Su closed
Earl and Charlotte Bruinsma

In 1957, after working in his aunt's Union Grove restaurant and spending some time driving cattle trailers, Earl Bruinsma was approached by the owner of Callen's Restaurant and asked if he'd like to buy it. Some thirty-five years later, in 1992, he sat beside me at the counter and laughed, "The guy I bought it from lives in Indianapolis now, and a few weeks ago he stopped by and apologized for sticking me with it all these years! But I kind of liked restaurant work. I got in it for the long haul." Earl and his wife, Charlotte, claim the longest period of cafe ownership—forty-four years—by the same owner.

From the large porcelain and neon sign hanging on the front of the building ("the best thing I ever bought for the place," Earl says) to the elbow-worn, wood-look counter and tables, Callen's Restaurant still looks pretty much the way it did when Earl and Charlotte took over. Practically minded, they've never seen the need to update things because "stainless steel just doesn't wear out. Wood doesn't wear out. All we've had to do is just wash and clean and leave things the way they are."

The restaurant's mid-twentieth-century stainless steel look mixes with the Old World of the Bruinsmas' Dutch heritage—betokened by an assortment of blue and white Delft pieces—and Earl's fondness for Moline miniatures, which fill the front windows. Once serious and avid collectors of Red Wing pottery, the Bruinsmas recently sold off most of their collection.

The antique collectors' concern for authenticity, quality, and tradition carries over into the Bruinsmas' kitchen, where "everything's homemade." "Homemade is kind of a lost art," Earl believes. "It's a shame. It's sad. It really is." Earl and Charlotte bypass the displays of instant and processed foods at food shows and continue to mash potatoes, roll out piecrusts, and prepare soups with their own hands. Homemade is "a personal thing, a personal choice I make for my customers," Earl explains. "I always say that instant is a dirty word." Moreover, homemade is a well-established tradition at Callen's Restaurant. "When I bought this place out," continues Earl, "I just kind of stayed with the same things, the tried and true. Now I've been here too long to change."

Earl advertises his restaurant locally on church bulletins and in high school sports schedules, relying on word-of-mouth promotion and his location on a frequently used northbound highway out of the Chicago area to bring in business. Many of his regular customers come from nearby Racine and Kenosha, fleeing westward in advance of the swarm of impersonal franchises crowding I-94. "People come here because we're still basically the old-style homemade food," Earl believes. "And the prices. I don't have to charge $3.75 for a hamburger with lettuce and tomato on it like my big city competitors. Here you can see where your food is coming from and where it's going. You can see your food made on the grill right out front, behind the counter. And we have a real homey atmosphere, treat everyone on a one-on-one basis. They're not a number. I like to know my people."

In the ten years since my first visit, Earl and Charlotte have slowed down only a little. They have cut back their hours and enjoy evenings to themselves. But Earl is not yet ready to retire. "I want to do something," he says. "Going upstairs and sitting with my remote control doesn't interest me at all." After forty-seven years in the business, Earl continues to find things that convince him he is still on the right track.

"A couple of years ago, these two guys came in and sat in the front window. They didn't say a word, didn't say boo or why. A couple of weeks later, I get a call from Harley-Davidson, and they want to use my cafe in a photo shoot. I say sure, come on out. They were here a whole afternoon—over four hours!"

The result was hundreds of used plate negatives, from which one photograph was used in the 2000 Harley-Davidson parts catalogue and featured on the February page of the 2001 Harley calendar. A lineup of new Harleys stands parked at the curb. The camera is looking through the front window bathed in yellow light, with an old-timer sipping a cup of coffee at the end of the counter. It is a great shot. It is a great cafe. Don't miss it.

WILLIAMS BAY
Daddy Maxwell's Artic Circle Diner 🍽 ✌

150 Elkhorn Road
(262) 245-5757
M–Th 6 A.M.–3 P.M.; F 6 A.M.–8 P.M.; Sa 6 P.M.–3P.M.; Su 6 A.M.–1 P.M.
Marshall and Janette Maxwell

Daddy Maxwell's Artic Circle Diner has the longest name of any Wisconsin cafe. It also has the funkiest look: kind of an igloo with windows—an example of mid-twentieth-century popular architecture that gave us taco shops shaped like sombreros and restaurants shaped like coffee cups. I love this kind of roadside attraction for its whimsy and delight.

Built some sixty years ago, the Arctic Circle began life as a walk-up hamburger joint. When Marshall Maxwell discovered it for sale in 1987, it was just a summer place and not yet a local hangout. "I'd been working as a chef in Door County when I heard this place was for sale," Marshall explained on my first visit. "I came down to take a look and bought it cheap with plans to expand. I didn't know it would go. I was just ready to get out on my own and took the chance."

In 1989, after two good years of year-round local support, Marshall and Janette remodeled the Artic Circle. First, they moved the kitchen out of the igloo and into a newly built addition, part of which became a new eating area lined with booths and a counter. Then they converted the old walk-up igloo into a fashionable dining room. Now decorated in icy pale green and pink, the igloo is an unusual and therefore popular place to eat, especially with the summer residents and tourists. The local and area morning regulars prefer the new eating area, however. It's not as formal, and the arrangement of the booths and counter makes it possible to include all its occupants in conversation. The day I dropped in, a birthday party for two employees was just beginning. Two beautifully decorated fresh fruit whipped cream cakes sat on the counter, with wrapped gifts nearby.

In the seventeen years that Marshall and Janette have been in business, the Arctic Circle has become very popular. The food here is a delight—mostly the same things you find in cafes all over Wisconsin but with the creative flair of a former chef. Marshall explains that cooking food gets monotonous, but he also finds "cooking this type of food to be somewhat satisfying. I like to experiment with foods and try to create something different out of the same. Like one day we took our French pancakes and made a French pancake Monte Cristo by adding ham and Swiss cheese. Or we make French toast with cinnamon in the egg mixture or with different kinds of breads, like raisin swirl or mueslix. Trying something different, or trying to make things other people don't have, keeps it from being boring."

Creating new menus keeps things fresh and exciting. The locals are often surprised to discover their favorite dishes have been named after them. Enjoying lunch with his daughter and wife at the table next to mine is the namesake of the Davis-Smavis, a portabella steak marinated in teriyaki sauce, grilled, and served with Muenster cheese, onion, grilled tomato, and dijonnaise sauce on a moxie roll. "I'm in here all the time and have it quite often," he explains. "It's one of those small town things, you know." Other menu items are accompanied by parenthetical comments so there's no mistaking just who's fond of Marshall's creations. For example, there are the traditional Wisconsin brats (Doo-Wayne's addiction), Swedish pancakes topped with lingonberries (Cindy's, Rich's, and Judy's sweet tooth fix), strawberry or warm peach French batter pancakes (Hank's favorite, along with a million more who walk from Fontana).

The food at the Artic Circle—"Everything's homemade," Janette says matter-of-factly—is worth walking any distance. Add to it a generous helping of camaraderie and quick wits, and you have a great meal topped with great listening.

A woman at the counter picking up a take-out order is waiting for the cashier to figure what she owes. A regular eating lunch and reading the newspaper at the counter can't resist leaning in to look at the bill and offer a bit of advice to the cashier. The cashier playfully swats at him with the order pad, telling him, "You're not helping!" To the waiting woman she apologizes, "It's not always like this."

As the woman takes in the repartee between the man and the cashier, arms loaded with take-out boxes, her face changes from confused to bemused. With just a trace of irritation over the delay, she feigns leaving. Turning toward the door, she looks over her shoulder and sends a zinger of her own in the direction of the cashier. "I'll come back in August to see if you've got it yet."

While at the cash register paying your own bill, be sure to notice the many gifts that Marshall and Janette have received from customers during their years in business. This is always the mark of a great cafe because it shows the strength of mutual respect and friendship. On the Pepsi dispenser are two hand-carved wooden figures. One is Janette. The other is Marshall wearing a chef's cap. At the end of the shelf are other figures brought back from customers' vacations, and throughout the cafe photographs of the regulars and a portrait of Marshall and Janette hang on the walls.

WILMOT
Wilmot Cafe 🍽
Highways C and W
(262) 862-6662
M–Su 6 A.M.–2P.M.
Mark Badtke and Tom Badtke

I had a hard time getting to Wilmot because of road construction and wound up in Illinois a few times before finding the small crossroads town and the shopworn Wilmot Cafe. I'd heard tasty rumors about the German apple pancakes served there and had to sample one for myself. At the olive green counter, two teenaged sisters bickered good-naturedly about life at home, conscious that they were on public display. A retired man next to me at the counter kicked dirt around under his stool, left from some earlier customer's boots. "Do you think you're gonna be able to eat that whole thing?" he asked when my waitress brought me the platter-sized pancake.

I have to admit that my intention was merely to taste the apple-laden pancake. I was over halfway through, however, when my waitress paused beside me with an order in both hands and whispered, "So, what do you think?"

"I think I'll have to eat the whole thing," I laughed. It was absolutely impossible to stop eating the marvelous concoction.

Russell Badtke brought the German apple pancake with him from another restaurant where he had worked before buying the Wilmot Cafe in 1976. He slices apples into melted butter in a frying pan, then covers them with a cinnamon sugar glaze and egg batter and cooks the whole until set. The pancake is then transferred to the oven, where it bakes until done. The result is an eggy, gooey, appley pancake you'll drive out of your way for—even to Illinois and back. And like me, you'll eat the whole thing despite your best intentions.

In 1995 Russell passed the restaurant on to his sons, Mark and Tom, but stayed on to tend the kitchen. It is his hands that produce the home-made pies and pastries that fill the plastic case in the corner of the dining area. He is the master baker, and he will remain as long as he is able.

Mark says the family has operated the cafe as long as it has because it and they have become a big part of the Wilmot community. "It's just Mom's and Dad's personalities. People come here to talk to them, or each other. We're like the chamber of commerce of Wilmot."

Just how much the Badtkes and their cafe have meant to the people of Wilmot was evident at Edith's funeral in July 2001. "We were all at the funeral home for the visitation, and we stood greeting people for over three hours," Mark remembers. "I think everybody in Wilmot was there. The funeral was very big, very impressive. It meant so much to us to learn that Mom was so important to so many people."

Clearly, success is more than food. Despite what the sign over the kitchen window says—DANGER Men Cooking—you are safe at the Wilmot Cafe. You are among friends.

· ·

NEXT BEST BETS

BRISTOL
Red School Cafe
12320 Bristol Road
Where else in Wisconsin can you enjoy a chicken salad sandwich and Wisconsin cheese soup—and more—in a one-room schoolhouse?

Darien
RC's Country Cafe
39 North Wisconsin Street
Favorites at this cafe owned by a young brother-sister team include the hand-made potato chips, cheesy hash browns, and the Friday beer-battered fish fry served with homemade coleslaw and potato pancakes, plus pies, cakes, cookies, and other desserts.

Delavan
Elizabeth's Cafe
322 East Walworth Avenue
A fine representation of many small-town cafes in the southeast part of the state recently taken over by Macedonian and Albanian immigrants. Mostly homemade food in plentiful servings.

Delavan
Patti and Larry's Traveler Restaurant
319 East Walworth Avenue
Among the Traveler's best sellers are the all-day breakfasts—especially om-elettes—the ten daily soups, about half of which are homemade, the large and plentiful salad bar, and the daily sandwich specials. Steaks, ribs, and the Friday night seafood buffet are pleasers for those with a hunger for heftier fare.

Elkhorn
Elk Restaurant
13 West Walworth Street
Since 1971 the Wales family has carried on a tradition of "mostly home cooking." At the round table in the front window, the thrice daily men's klatches generally bypass food for coffee. About the ritual sip and chat, I'm told, "The six o'clock group creates all the problems of the world. The seven thirty group solves the problems created by the six o'clock group, and the two o'clock group rehashes the solutions. The next morning it starts all over again."

Fontana
Lucy's Coffee Shop
Main Street
Get there early for the homemade doughnuts, probably the most popular item on the menu.

Horicon
LeRoy Meats
85 Washington Street
Truth be told, this is a butcher shop not a cafe, but it serves fresh meats in a variety of daily specials between ten thirty and two o'clock Monday through Friday—the best unsung lunch in Horicon.

Iron Ridge
Cindy's Cafe
138 South Main Street

The promise of everything homemade lures Harley riders, bicyclists, drivers, and many others looking for a real burger, potato salad to die for, and pretty pies.

Jackson
Jimmy's Family Restaurant
N168 W21212 Main Street

A native of Greece, Jimmy Koutsios is a master of Wisconsin good home cooking. "I fix what they want," he says, "and what they want is what they'd make at home if they cooked." This includes ten pounds of meatloaf per day, fresh roasted meats, and plenty of potatoes with gravy. Those with a more adventurous palate opt for the huge Greek salads, gyros, and main dishes such as Greek style pork chops.

Lake Geneva
Fran's Cafe
522 Broad Street

Breakfast comprises almost 80 percent of the daily business. The locals also like the fresh muffins dripping with real butter, homemade soups, and a variety of sandwiches and plate specials.

Mayville
Backstreet Cafe
11 North School Road

A sign on the wall reads "Never Trust a Skinny Cook." A popular place for breakfast and Thursday's Mexican selections.

Palmyra
Nature's Trail
Highway 59 West

After two years behind the grill, Pat Marrari has come to realize that she is not going to upend the eating preferences of the locals. "People here are set in their ways. They like what they know the names of," she says. The sign out near the road promises "homemade soups and specials." Pat delivers. "Everything's homemade because it tastes better."

Trevor
Cowmark Cafe
28414 Wilmot Road

Feeling famished? Try the Mark Omelette made with ham, sausage, bacon, hash browns, and American, Swiss, and cheddar cheese. Feeling voracious? Prepare yourself for the Monster Omelette, made with six eggs, filled with fifteen different items, and topped with biscuits and gravy.

WATERFORD
Granny's Grand Cafe and Bakery
213 East Main Street
Plain old good food plus refreshing selections from the owners' native Greek repertoire, including baklava and a Greek salad, burger, omelette, and stuffed pita.

WAUPUN
Helen's Kitchen
1116 West Main Street.
More a restaurant than a cafe, but great real food and the gathering place for Waupunites of all ages.

Fox Valley, Lakefront, and Door County

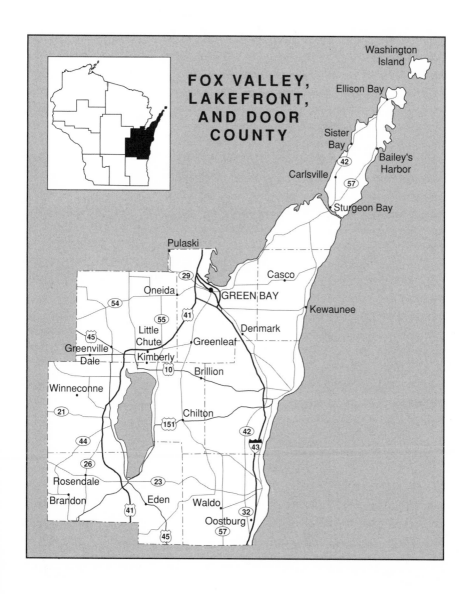

FOX VALLEY,
LAKEFRONT,
AND DOOR
COUNTY

Washington Island

Ellison Bay

Sister Bay

Carlsville

Bailey's Harbor

Sturgeon Bay

Pulaski

Casco

Oneida

GREEN BAY

Kewaunee

Little Chute

Denmark

Greenville

Greenleaf

Dale

Kimberly

Brillion

Winneconne

Chilton

Rosendale

Eden

Waldo

Brandon

Oostburg

BRILLION
Rudy's Diner 🍴 ⛲
117 West Ryan Street
(920) 756-2755
M 6 A.M.–2 P.M.; Tu–F 6 A.M.–7 P.M.; Sa 6 A.M.–2 P.M.; Su 7 A.M.–1 P.M.
Rosemary and Kevin Clarke

My West Bend friend and fellow pie rider, Kine Torinus, grew up in Green Bay and remembers visiting Rudy's Cafe—now Rudy's Diner—as a child, when she'd sit with her parents in a wall booth and sneak peeks at the local farmers and truckers seated at the counter. It's been years since she's been back to Rudy's, but she's never forgotten the homemade bread and pies and magical small town atmosphere that captivated her as a child.

Rudy's is a place people just don't forget. Not children grown up, not big city travelers or pie riders, not the fleets of truckers across the country who know it as the home of not merely good but exceptional home cooking. Trucker Robert Hansen, whom I met at a Juneau cafe, testifies, "I've met truckers in New Jersey and Texas who know about Rudy's. They ask, 'Is that little place still there along the highway?' They all know Rudy's. It's the supper club of luncheonettes."

In 1939 Rudy Seljan opened the doors of the little cafe to his very first customers. Fifty years later, after earning a remarkable reputation that made Rudy's a Wisconsin institution, he sold the business to Rosemary and Kevin Clarke, the current owners. A former teacher and caterer, Rosemary longed to have her own restaurant. When she and Kevin decided they wanted to get their kids out of Green Bay and raise them in a small town, they began to look for a business to buy. In Brillion, they discovered Rudy's Cafe and immediately fell in love with the squeeze-in size of the tiny roadside restaurant. But it was Rudy Seljan's reputation for honest home cooking—especially homemade bread—that clinched the sale.

"Rudy's was a place to be proud of," Rosemary explains. "When I first came here, I was really concerned that I wouldn't be able to live up to Rudy's reputation. Rudy's is such an institution. But I was lucky to get some of his same cooks to stay on for a few months and teach me how to make the famous white bread and pies. I wanted to follow in his traditions. I've added things of my own here and there, but I've been careful not to change too much. If it's not broken, don't fix it."

After passing on Rudy's secrets, the last of his employees finally retired, leaving Rosemary and Kevin to continue the little restaurant's homemade magic on their own. Rosemary expanded the bread line to include whole wheat—she developed her own recipe—buns and cinnamon rolls. In addition to the daily thirty-odd loaves of bread, she makes six or seven cream and fruit pies from scratch, slow-cooked daily specials with real pota-toes and gravy, a variety of soups, even her own jams from fresh Door County cherries and other fruit. (The most popular jam is cherry-pineapple.) In Rosemary's and Kevin's loving hands, the food at Rudy's Cafe tastes as good as it always has, if not better.

Even the best things can't go on the same forever, however. In Janu-ary 1993 the Clarkes completed an extensive remodeling project, expand-ing the cafe to almost twice its original size. In the process, they reconfigured the interior and enlarged and updated the kitchen. They wanted to capture the feeling of an old-time diner and have succeeded by stringing a band of windows over the front sidewalk and decorating in an almond and green color scheme. They restored the old counter stools and kept one of the original blond Formica-covered booths. It's against the far side wall, wait-ing for two people who are nostalgic about the Rudy's of the past. While digging in and tearing out, they found many receipts for building materials dating to the building's original construction, as well as food supplies Rudy bought for the restaurant. These they framed and hung on the wall.

People who have been coming to Rudy's for years heartily approve of the changes. They are confident in the consistently "good old food" and make the long trek from home—sometimes forty or fifty miles one way—for their favorite dishes. Rosemary relates, "A few weeks ago, I had one old guy, seventy or eighty years old, who sat down at the counter and said, 'I drove all the way from Appleton for a piece of cherry pie.' When he was done, I asked him how it was, and he said, 'Now I'll have dessert.' And he ordered a piece of apple pie with ice cream."

Some first-time visitors to Rudy's Diner have a hard time believing that everything is really homemade. Women, especially, are fond of quizzing the staff about the bread, which they suspect started as frozen dough. "We raise our own yeast," Rosemary tells them in response. She remembers one woman who then naively asked, "Oh, do you raise it in your backyard?"

"We make everything homemade here, but we do have to draw the line on some things," Rosemary smiles.

CASCO
Village Kitchen 𝕐
101 Old Orchard Avenue (Highway 54)
(920) 837-7333
M–F 5 A.M.–7 P.M.; Sa 5 A.M.–1 P.M.; Su 5 A.M.–12 P.M.
Chris and Gary Jacobs
A fellow adventure eater who promised unbelievably good home cook-ing—and plenty of it—at equally unbelievable prices had tipped me off to

the Friday fish fry at the Village Kitchen. Boy, was she right! I talked with my sister on the phone after gorging myself on beer-battered redfish, boiled red potatoes swimming in fresh melted butter, coleslaw, potato salad, and poppy seed torte and told her the food was divine.

"Did I say divine?" I asked with a laugh. "That's certainly appropriate. When I got there, two nuns were sitting at the counter. Then the local priest walked in wearing his blacks, with his clerical collar tucked into his shirt pocket." Leave it to Catholics to flock to the best fish fry in the area.

It may not be that everyone in the Village Kitchen that Friday night was Catholic, but they certainly were converts to the real food brought out from the back kitchen. The weekly pilgrimage of diners kept the restaurant full at all times, with people sliding into booths as soon as they were vacated. I was hardly out of mine before an elderly couple replaced me, ignoring the dirty dishes and crumpled napkins I left behind. As I stacked my three containers of leftovers into a take-out tower and carefully balanced them in one hand, the wife whispered, "You'll have enough for lunch tomorrow." My plan exactly.

The Friday night dining ritual at the Village Kitchen features five choices of fish and a variety of potato sides. I had a hard time selecting from perch, pike, baked cod, beer-battered cod, and beer-battered redfish, but finally chose the redfish because I had never had it before. It was lovely, lightly clothed in crispy, golden brown batter. Following the example of my neighbor in the next booth, I picked up the pieces with my fingers and dipped them into the homemade tartar sauce, served in a sizable paper cup. I did find myself wondering if there was any protocol at all to eating fried fish on a rainy Friday night in Casco. The finger method worked but did have one major drawback. When I reached for my Pepsi, the can slipped out of my oily fingers and clattered noisily onto the seat opposite me in the booth. As my fellow finger-eater neighbor turned to stare at me, I noticed he had moved on to eating a piece of cherry pie with a fist-wrapped fork.

That made me think of dessert, and when my waitress flashed by and stopped, I ordered a piece of poppy seed torte, adhering to the reliable adage, "Anything different is bound to be good." It consisted of poppy seeds folded into vanilla custard, with a graham cracker base and a non-dairy whipped topping. It, too, was divine—although the priest at the counter passed it over in favor of a chocolate malt, announcing to everyone in the restaurant, "I go back on the diet on Monday, so I've got to make today count."

After years of restaurant work, owner Chris Jacobs had the new restaurant built on the site of the former Hall's apple orchard—thus the road name—five years ago. Since that time, she has been amazed at how successful the business has become. It didn't take long for her excellent home cooking to be discovered by area eaters, including those who regularly make the trek from the cities of Manitowoc and Green Bay. The busiest days are Thursdays, when Chris makes roast pork, sauerkraut, and dumplings ("We're Belgian people around here," she says); Fridays, when fish takes center stage; and weekends, when breakfast is the big draw.

DALE
Old Store Cafe and Deli
W9718 Highway 10
(920) 779-6984
M 6:30 A.M.–7:30 P.M.; Tu 6:30 A.M.–2:30 P.M.; W–Th 6:30 A.M.–7:30 P.M.; F–Sa 6:30 A.M.–2:30 P.M.; Su 8:30 A.M.–2 P.M.
Deb and Bob Chonos

Deb and Bob Chonos, owners of the Old Store Cafe and Deli, sometimes stand in the back kitchen rolling their eyes in amazement at the wacky requests their customers make. "We ask each other, 'How in the world did they come up with that?'" Bob tells me. The two have not been on the job long enough to have heard everything, but Bob really isn't one to talk, since he is the inventor and namesake of the Bob Burger—without a doubt the quirkiest burger in Wisconsin. He has a sense of humor and knows how to laugh, which is important because I poked a lot of fun at his expense. But I also ate a Bob Burger, so I'm allowed.

What is a Bob Burger, you ask? It is a monster of a burger and "a slippery little devil," according to Bob. It's hard to eat because it refuses to stay neatly stacked and ordered. I had to finish mine with a fork. Bob starts with a good-sized burger and layers it from plate up in this order: bun bottom, peanut butter, sliced banana, hamburger patty, American cheese, bacon, fried egg, lettuce, tomato, mayonnaise—all crowned by the bun top. And he wonders about some of the things his customers concoct!

The Bob Burger is so weird, I just had to try it. Bob whipped it up in the kitchen and brought it out to me stacked a good five inches high on a white china plate. I had a hard time wrapping my hands around it, but I succeeded in gingerly taking a bite. The first one consisted of mostly bun bottom, peanut butter, and banana, since I approached it from an upward angle. With both Bob and Deb watching me closely, I reported, "Nothing strange here." I've always liked peanut butter and banana sandwiches. With the next bite, I got the full sensation . . . and it was amazingly good. A third bite and a fourth convinced me that as strange as it seemed, Bob had a winner with the Bob Burger. The flavors of all the incongruous ingredients blended into a pleasant surprise. I was savoring a Bob Burger, not tasting the individual items.

The obvious question is, how did Bob create the Bob Burger? "I just built it up over the years," he says matter-of-factly (as if there could be any other way). "Years ago a friend introduced me to peanut butter and bacon. When I was in the air force, we had a sack burger, which was a burger with a fried egg. Then when I was in Spokane at an A & W, I threw all of that out there, and they made it for me. When the girl brought it out, she stood there watching. I said, 'What, I didn't pay you enough?' 'You paid me enough,' she said, 'I just have to watch you eat it!'"

With Deb initially in charge of the menu and the kitchen, the Old Store Cafe and Deli didn't boast the Bob Burger. But one day, Bob made one up for himself and another guy saw it and said, "Make me one of those." Thus, the ball started rolling, picking up speed when a friend, a local radio broadcaster, encouraged everyone over the air to stop in for the "famous" Bob Burger. He said it as joke, but the Bob Burger soon became the talk of the town—and the talk in neighboring towns as well. It even found its way into this book.

While I recommend the Bob Burger to all true adventure eaters, those who prefer a little more mainline menu selections will be relieved to learn that Deb (the more sensible one of the two) and her sister, Maxine, offer a hefty variety of traditional cafe fare. Real mashed potatoes, clever soups (try the stuffed green pepper or macaroni and cheese soup), fresh roasted meats, and a variety of delectable pies and other baked goods—cakes, muffins, cinnamon rolls, bars—will please the tame palate. Deb's Beauty Pancakes are indeed beauties—and big, too. "It's fun to see people's eyes when they see them," Deb says. Pie artist Mary Morse pages through cookbooks and magazines in search of fresh alternatives to apple and cherry, whipping up nice little surprises like mystery pecan—made with a layer of cream cheese—which I ate right from the oven. She even takes the time to artistically decorate the tops with cutout pastry shapes, like stars and hearts.

With all this free-flowing goodness, the Old Store Cafe and Deli is bound to become one of the favorite destination cafes of Wisconsin eaters.

And what of the Bob Burger? That remains to be seen.

DENMARK
Lorrie's Home Town Cafe and Catering 🍽 ⚑
623 De Pere Road
(920) 863-8148
M–Sa 6 A.M.–4 P.M.; Su closed
Lorrie and Jim Steffek

When Lorrie and Jim Steffek bought Denmark's downtown cafe in 1990 to fulfill Lorrie's dream of owning her own restaurant, Jim paused in the doorway and thought of the previous owners, who had been in business for three years. "He thought three years was a long time then, and here we are into our fifteenth," Lorrie says. "They've gone really fast." Lorrie recently relocated to a new building on the other side of town complete with a deli and bakery counter and a gift shop specializing in Scandinavian items such as Royal Copenhagen plates and *nisse* (trolls). This is Denmark, after all.

In her position as cafe owner, Lorrie celebrates and promotes the town's Danish heritage in a variety of ways, something that was important to her from the very beginning of her tenure. Danes settled the town in the 1840s, and many of their Old World traditions have passed away. But at Lorrie's, you can find favorite specialties on the menu, particularly *æbleskiver*, served with maple syrup, homemade applesauce, and lingonberry jam. The æbleskiver is similar to a popover, made with buttermilk and egg whites and lightly flavored with cardamom. They're made in special, four-pound cast iron pans that Lorrie has found in local rummage sales. "The new ones aren't nearly as good as the old ones," she explains.

The menu is extensive and includes many items in Danish translation, provided by local residents who have retained a knowledge of the language. The Danish breakfast selections include Holger's *biksemad* (corned beef hash); *pandekager* (thin pancakes with lingonberries); *medisterpølse* (sausage links); æbleskiver with lingonberries; and *Nørske vaffler* (whole grain waffles). But what I really like are the witty Danish proverbs, including these choice ones: *"Alting har en Ende—uden pølsen, den har to"* (Everything has an end, except sausage, which has two); *"Smuler ere og brød"* (Even the crumbs are bread); *"Der er mange daggi aretm ig end flere maaltider"* (There are many days in the year, and still more meals); *"Det er strengt at trælle med tom tarm"* (It is hard to labor with an empty belly).

There is no danger of this last one after a stop at Lorrie's. Her "still home-cooked" daily specials are "the kinds of things your grandmother used to make for Sunday dinners." She has discovered that her mostly middle-aged customers prefer things they're familiar with, so she makes a lot of casseroles and meat and potato plate specials, like today's turkey and dumplings. Soups are also popular, and she offers different broth and cream soups every day; some, like Grandma's bean ("Anything with Grandma in it sells") and ham, cabbage, and caraway, are her own inventions. She lets loose pent-up creative energy on desserts, and her pies, such as apple-raisin-cinnamon, sour cream raisin, and lemon, sell out so fast she "can barely keep up with making them."

Lorrie's specialty isn't pie, however, but tortes filled with "everything ooey and gooey and sweet that you can dream of." Only people with super-human resolve can pass up her whipped cream, chocolate, nut, cream cheese, fruit, and candy concoctions. She also likes to experiment with a variety of cakes and puddings.

Lorrie has put her interest in reclaiming Denmark's ethnic traditions to use outside the restaurant as well. She was one of several people who planned and got the town's first Danish Festival off the ground ten years ago. Each year the festival has grown to include more activities, more Danish food, more representation by guests from the country of Denmark. The one-day festival is family-oriented fun, complete with an antique tractor pull, dance presentations, and an auction of homemade pies.

In addition to her community service, Lorrie is an active participant in her regional chapter of the Wisconsin Restaurant Association, winning the title of Restaurateur of the Year in 1998. "You have to give back be-cause no one gets far on their own," she says of her involvement.

ELLISON BAY
Viking Restaurant 🍽
12029 Highway 42
(920) 854-2998
February and March: Closed
April–May: M–Th 6 A.M.–2 P.M.; F 6 A.M.–7 P.M.; Sa–Su 6 A.M.–2 P.M.
June–October: M–Su 6 A.M.–8 P.M.
November–January: M–Th 6 A.M.–2 P.M.; F 6 A.M.–7 P.M.; Sa–Su 6 A.M.–2 P.M.

Dan Peterson
After only a day in Door County, I was ready for some long, rambling talk with the locals, so I drove up to Ellison Bay and parked the car in front of the Viking Restaurant. Inside, I spotted men in work clothes strung out along the green counter sipping coffee and discussing the tourist season that had just come to an end. Two tables of breakfasters kept up a lively conversation over the morning newspaper as newcomers stopped by with a hi and a few words. Although the sign on the roof says it is a "restaurant and lounge," don't be fooled into driving by. The Viking is really a small

town cafe in disguise and, until recently, one of the few restaurants open year-round for the locals.

The full-menu Viking Restaurant first opened in 1939 as the Viking Grill, serving mostly local residents and the few tourists who straggled this far north on the Door County Peninsula. ("Some of the real old-timers still write out checks to the Viking Grill," Dan laughs.) As the tourist population grew, so did the Viking Grill. A large, knotty pine-paneled dining room was added, followed by a basement indoor picnic area and a lounge, which replaced the longtime gift shop.

In 1961 then-owners Lawrence and Annette Wickman began the first commercial fish boil in Door County, offering tourists and locals heaping plates of steaming whitefish, new potatoes and tiny onions, pumpernickel rye bread, dill pickles, and cherry pie. "He was the founder of the Door County fish boils," Dan explains. "He even had 'Founder of the Viking Fish Boil' carved on his tombstone." (You can see it by driving one-quarter mile up Mink River Road to the second cemetery on the right. It's right in front and easy to find.)

In 1984 Dan became the owner of the Viking, and the title of master fish boiler fell to him. Dan grew up in Baileys Harbor, where his parents owned the former Cotton Club Hotel and conducted fish boils for guests. "I've been boiling fish for years, since about '48 or '49," Dan says. "The fish boil has been a Door County tradition for years, long before Lawrence started the Viking's. It was done in fishing boats, at church picnics. People think it originated in Door County, but when I ask people who have studied foods, they say it's not only Door County. All kinds of people—Swedes, Bohemians, Finns, Icelandics—they all have boiled dinners. But people, when they come to Door County, that's what they think of: the Door County fish boil."

I had my doubts that plain whitefish, red potatoes, and onions boiled together in a huge pot over an open wood fire could live up to such iconic reputation, so I decided to stay for the Viking fish boil. Unlike most other Door County restaurants, the Viking does not require a reservation. There was only a small crowd gathered around the outdoor kettle. A few people held cameras and video cameras to capture the "boilover," when a can of kerosene is tossed onto the fire, ridding the kettle of its fish oil and scum. (The cooks ring a bell ahead of time so you won't miss it.) After the boilover, the kettle is whisked off the fire and the fish, potatoes, and onions are removed to waiting bowls.

As I moved through the serving line, I admonished the girls against giving me a standard huge helping; I still doubted that plain fish, potatoes, and onions could be tasty enough to warrant it. Was I ever wrong!

Smothered in melted butter, the whitefish was so sweet, tender, and delicious that I could easily have eaten the pieces I turned down, and then some. The salt-encrusted potatoes and onions were also a wonderful surprise. The meal came with coleslaw, rye bread and butter, lemonade, and a piece of frozen "home-baked cherry pie." ("There's too many people to make pie," Dan explains.) For people who really don't like fish, broasted chicken is available as a substitute—but don't assume you don't like fish until you've tried the Viking fish boil.

For the past five years, Dan and his crew have taken the famous fish boil and other menu selections to the annual Norsk Høstfest, the country's largest Norwegian festival, held every October in Minot, North Dakota. They have returned three times with awards, including the Excellence in Food Taste award in 2000 and 2001. Moving the Door County fish boil to a large indoor festival building in Minot requires some adaptation, such as substituting gas for the wood that would otherwise be used for creating the fire. The end result is good boiled whitefish, but the presentation isn't nearly as dramatic as it is back home.

While the Viking Restaurant is synonymous with the Door County fish boil, you'll also find a delicious variety of homemade soups and chowders (don't miss Dan's award-winning whitefish chowder), sandwiches, burgers, specialty plates, salads, and dinners featuring homemade gravy and real mashed potatoes. For breakfast, Dan recommends the from-scratch buttermilk pancakes or the Swedish pancakes (also winners at the Norsk Høstfest) with lingonberries, an "Old World berry—kind of a cross between a cranberry and a currant." In addition, the Viking Restaurant has broasted chicken and other items suitable for picnics and ferry excursions.

GREENLEAF
D & G Restaurant
6794 Highway 57
(920) 864-7850
M–F 6 A.M.–7:30 P.M.; Sa 6 A.M.–2 P.M.; Su 7 A.M.–2 P.M.
Gloria Berg
Even the most intrepid adventure eater has a bad day once in a while and requires a mom. I drooped into the D & G Restaurant hot and exhausted, nearly starving, and also a great deal lonely. I had had a long stretch of days on the road and was missing my husband and son and just didn't want to go into another restaurant and ask questions of people I didn't know. I slumped in the booth and put my head in my hands. Gloria Berg came by to take my order and instead ordered me to drink a Pepsi for the caffeine and sugar.

She could tell I needed some home cooking with a mother's touch, and when I requested a grilled cheese sandwich, she asked me, "Can I make that on our homemade bread for you?" Can you? Is there any doubt? The sandwich came hot from the grill, with warm real butter soaked into both slices of the thick bread. If a cafe can make an excellent grilled cheese sandwich, you know you've stumbled onto a winner. Feeling a bit restored, I moved on to pie, opting for the French silk—which, as it turns out, is one of the three kinds of pie Gloria doesn't make from scratch.

Being the good mother that she is, Gloria took time out from the afternoon's business to offer me words of encouragement and support. By the time I left an hour and a half later, with two gift pieces of Gloria's Dutch apple and pecan pie nestled in a care package, I was ready to face the remainder of the day. Thanks, Gloria.

The D & G has been around for many years under the same name, which, coincidently, has been the initials of each member of the last two couples who have owned it. More than twenty years ago, Gloria's late husband Dave satisfied his wish of owning his own restaurant, and with Gloria's promise to "help out," the eatery thrived. Gloria eventually became first the chief operator and then, with Dave's death several years ago, its sole owner. "I couldn't ask for a better community," she says about the friends that have helped her through these difficult past years.

At first, Gloria remembers, she was very shy and hid in the back kitchen so she wouldn't have to face the customers in the dining room. But that didn't work because they'd often come looking for her, wondering about the person behind the excellent food they were enjoying. Gradually, Gloria came out of the kitchen and out of her shell. She is now the mother not only to sad, lonely adventure eaters but also to many of the members of the Greenleaf community. She watches over elderly people who live alone, even delivering meals to those who are housebound, and helps the recreation department with a Christmas party for seniors who would otherwise spend the holiday without companionship.

"Very few things are not made from scratch" at the restaurant, Gloria claims. "I just don't bother with things that are not real and homemade." She serves real mashed potatoes, homemade bread ("It was just something different to pull in customers"), and a tempting variety of fruit and cream pies. The favorite pie is without a doubt the cranberry-walnut made from a recipe brought in by a regular customer. Every day she offers nine or ten different varieties of soup and two or three different daily specials, such as meat loaf, beef stew, chicken, and pork chops. She celebrates the end of the workweek with a day-long fish fry consisting of seven varieties of fish plus salmon loaf. Father Bob, the local Catholic priest, is in attendance every Friday night without fail.

KIMBERLY
Larry's Parkside Restaurant
760 West Kimberly Avenue
(920) 739-6611
M–Su 6 A.M.–8 P.M.
Larry Williams, owner
Kelly Kolosso and Jeanette Rastall, co-managers

Jeanette Rastall has been away from Larry's Parkside Restaurant all day at a family reunion up in Marinette County. But before she goes home, she stops at the restaurant she co-manages with Kelly Kolosso to say hello to the girls working there and to grab a bite to eat. She'd rather spend the last hours of the day here among friends than go home to a dark house. "I never get tired of this place," she says as she eats a grilled ham and cheese sandwich.

Many of the regulars share her sentiment. So much good food and laughter are served here that it's a common saying that "if you're depressed, go to Larry's. You won't be for long." So rarely is there a dull moment that Kelly often adds an "entertainment charge" to the bill. "Coming here isn't much different than going out for dinner and a show," she laughs.

Kelly and Jeanette nearly trip over each other rushing to tell me stories about the Thursday morning crowd, especially "gullible Dan," who contributes to the football pool every week, but never seems to win. Jeanette often responds to his complaints with the phrase, "Can I get you some cheese with that whine?" When he finally did win the pool, Jeanette put on a bunny hat and served his twenty-five-dollar prize on a plate surrounded with shredded cheese and accompanied by a glass of cranberry juice.

Unlike many small town restaurants, Larry's enjoys a customer base of all ages, from young kids to senior citizens. The waitstaff consists of a few high school girls who bring in their friends, or who stop in to say hi or eat. Many of the girls are active in high school sports, which, Kelly and Jeanette have noticed, are the topic for many conversations around the restaurant. "The older people get so involved and interested in their lives that it's really hard when they graduate and go off to college," Kelly says.

Between the two of them, Kelly and Jeanette are at the restaurant from the time it opens until the time it closes. From their vantage point, they see some people several times a day and are usually the first to learn that someone has had a stroke, heart attack, or other disabling accident. The role of caretaker is often difficult to accept—and certainly not one they anticipated when they signed on at Larry's. Taped to the wall by the phone is a list of emergency contacts and phone numbers for several of the regular customers, a list that has been used more than once or twice.

Larry's Parkside is just like home to many of the regulars—in many cases, far better than home. There is always friendship and laughter, caring and camaraderie, and plenty of reliably good food. Both Jeanette and Kelly love to cook and keep it exciting by constantly paging through new cookbooks and food magazines, always keeping an eye out for something different and delicious. In this way, new menu items are introduced, such as the favorite crusty, onion-topped roll called bialy. Kelly found a recipe for the Jewish bread in a cookbook while shopping in Door County and couldn't wait to make it at the restaurant. The bialy has become such a hit that it is now difficult to keep enough on hand. Since Kelly is the bialy maker, she has to be sure the kitchen is well stocked before she goes on vacation.

Larry's Parkside is known for workingman's portions at a workingman's price. Try the omelettes and potato pancakes for breakfast—or spread the potato pancakes throughout the day by ordering them for lunch or supper. The kitchen has a hard time keeping up with the orders; for this reason, they're not available on Sunday, when the steady after-church crowd makes it the busiest day of the week. Other favorites are the meat loaf—which was my first choice, but I was told it was just out of the oven and still too hot to slice—roast beef, and spaghetti. (With the meat loaf out of the picture, I had the spaghetti, which was perfect the night I stopped in.) On weekends, homemade bread is available for toast, French toast, and sandwiches. The only beat Larry's misses is using instant potato pearls instead of homemade—but the rainbow selection of pie compensates for this sidestep.

I sampled the key lime pie because I had never before seen it served at a small town cafe and doubted it would be made with key lime juice. My teenage waitress wasn't familiar with this kind of pie and asked, "Do you want ice cream with that?" She gracefully rebounded from my comment that key lime pie wasn't served with ice cream by saying, "You can have it if you want it." I also refused the whipped cream. When she brought my slice of pie from the kitchen, Jeanette shook her head and held up her hand. "No, no, no, not that one," she cried. The poor girl was confused, as was I.

"I made a mistake with that one," Jeanette explained, as if the reason was obvious. "I got too busy and didn't pay attention to what I was doing and put it in the wrong crust. Key lime is supposed to have a graham cracker crust, not a pastry crust."

My waitress brought out a second piece, this time in a graham cracker crust. It was indeed made with real key lime juice, and it was very, very good. Despite this, I had the will power to push away half the piece. One taste, and I knew. Larry's is a place to come back to.

LITTLE CHUTE
Tucker's Inn
118 West Main Street
(920) 788-3778
M 6:30 A.M.–1 P.M.; Tu–F 5:30 A.M.–7 P.M.; Sa–Su 6:30 A.M.–1 P.M.
Larry and Carol Van Lankvelt

My friend Joanne advised that I check out Tucker's Inn in Little Chute and even drove me by it so I'd know just where it was located. "Their cinnamon rolls are fantastic," Joanne told me, so, of course, the next morning I ordered one. When I spied it being carried from the kitchen, I remembered Joanne had also told me they were huge, and so they are. Mine could have been mistaken for a small layer cake, with more than enough icing to cover one. My waitress laughed when I suggested she should have brought it in a bowl.

Owner Larry Van Lankvelt was away at a waterworks conference, so I ate my breakfast in silence and determined to stop again in a few days. That way I'd have a chance to sample more of the tempting selection of breakfast items, including French toast made with homemade bread, hot wheels (deep-fried doughnuts dipped in sugar), and potato pancakes.

Although breakfast is served all day, I arrived in early afternoon and opted for a bowl of cheesy bacon soup and a thick square of Carol Van Lankvelt's turtle cake for lunch. Larry Van Lankvelt tidied up after the last customers and waited for me to finish, then joined me at my table.

He and Carol have been owners of Tucker's Inn—named for the previous owner—for enough years to look forward to retirement. After observing the layoff of many of his fellow workers at the paper mill where he worked in maintenance, Larry decided the best way to keep a job was to work for himself. He'd played softball with Tucker, who wanted out of the restaurant. One night he went home and talked to Carol about buying the place. "She really had to be talked into it," he remembers, and she was thrilled when the deal Larry was working on with Tucker fell through. "But then it worked out," Larry remembers, and Carol got the job she had been dead set against.

Larry had always enjoyed cooking, but his chances were limited to the occasions the family went camping or to cottages. He'd developed a taste for restaurant work as a high school student working at Norb's Lunch, coincidentally located in the same building as Tucker's Inn. Norb's was a teen hangout serving burgers, chips, and sodas to students who walked up from the high school down the street for lunch and after-school rendezvous. "Every so often, Norb would tell me, 'Watch the store,' and go off to run errands," remembers Larry. Never in his wildest dreams did he imagine he'd be watching the store—and running it too—at this stage in his life.

Because Tucker's Inn was a successful business, Larry and Carol changed neither the name nor the menu. They did gradually add their own trademark items, such as the baked goods and hand-breaded fish, and extend the hours. "We made it a point to be open on Saturday and Sunday for the mill workers," Larry explains. The workload increased as Tucker's Inn became noteworthy for its home cooking and the regular counter crowd was joined by people who drove in from far out of town. "We have an influence as far away as Appleton," Larry says. "We have people who stop in whenever they pass by. We had three fishermen stop just this morning. And another couple drives in every morning from out near Mackville for oatmeal and coffee."

Breakfast is the mainstay at Tucker's Inn, but later in the day Larry and Carol have a hard time keeping in stock the popular meat loaf and roast pork—both served with mashed potatoes and gravy—and ham and scalloped potatoes. Another favorite is the "it's your call burger"— a quarter-pound patty with your choice of three toppings. You design it. You order it. You eat it. (And if that's your thing, don't miss the Bob Burger at the Old Store Cafe and Deli in nearby Dale.)

In Little Chute, which celebrates its Dutch heritage with the Kermis Festival every September, Tucker's Inn recognizes its links to the Old World with Dutch-inspired decor. Larry and Carol's daughter, Amy, a graphic artist, painted a windmill and tulips scene on the wall behind the counter and decorated the other walls with flowered garlands and Dutch phrases. (Larry is slightly embarrassed to confess that some of the words are misspelled because they don't know Dutch.) Other tokens of heritage are the tulip wallpaper border, a pair of wooden shoes, and pieces of blue and white Delftware. In previous years, Tucker's Inn prepared special Dutch dishes during the Kermis Festival, such as cabbage, sausage, and potato soup and pork cracklings called brye, which inspired a lot of comments of surprise. "Many people said, 'I haven't had that for a long time,'" Larry says. "And other people said, 'I've never had that before, and I'm not going to start now!'"

OOSTBURG
Knotty Pine Restaurant
941 Center Avenue
(920) 564-2600
M–Sa 6:30 A.M.–8:30 P.M.; Su closed
Deborah and Jeff Saueressig

For sixty years, the Knotty Pine Restaurant has been the halfway point on the run from Chicago to Door County, and now many of the kids who traveled in the back of their parents' Fords and Chevys are bringing their own kids—and even grandkids—for pancakes and burgers. Most are disappointed that the rustic, knotty pine paneling is gone; thirty years ago it was removed because it was scarred with hundreds of initials and hearts. Take a trip to the rear banquet room where the Kiwanis Club meets once a month and gaze on all the golden knotty pine that remains. Then imagine rolling a bowling ball down the length of the room, toward waiting pins. Can't quite see it? You'd never guess that the back room was indeed a bowling alley and that the wood lanes lie under the current floor.

Decorated now with white plastered walls, an ivy border, and lace curtains at the windows, the Knotty Pine manages to retain some of its long-ago charm. Owner Deborah Saueressig proudly points out the menu board resurrected from the 1960s hanging on the back wall. You can no longer get "aged t-bone or tenderloin steak for $1.79" or a stack of "wheat cakes w/ syrup for .35" but you can get the same wonderful homemade food for which tourists have been stopping for over sixty years. And served, I think, on the same old white Buffalo china with a rosy-colored rim.

Deborah grew up in Port Washington and moved to Oostburg ten years ago. She began working at the Knotty Pine for the previous owner and then stepped into the ownership role. The transition between owners was nearly seamless, and the loyal regulars didn't miss a beat in their daily rituals. They continue to line up before the official daily opening time of six thirty. The men still gather at the corner table every day between three and three thirty for coffee (which Deborah has waiting for them in full pots). Local artist Edwin Wynveen doesn't miss any of his six to eight visits a day. He comes in for talk and coffee, talk and cherry Coke, talk and pie, including his pie of choice, possum pie.

"Possum pie?" I ask.

Edwin launches into a long discussion about possums, how they're hunted and cooked and eaten in the southern United States. Deborah stands by smiling. Her possum pie includes no primordial marsupials, but is instead a sweet concoction of cream cheese, pecans, and vanilla and chocolate pudding in a graham cracker crust. To be on the safe side (my southern friends have told me about eating greasy old possums), I chose banana cream, with a sweet custardy filling made in the microwave and poured into a parchmentlike crust. It was delicious. But next time, I'll try the possum pie.

Edwin wears spotless black pants and a black vest over a crisp white shirt. At first I thought he was an undertaker, but he represents one of Wisconsin's largest nurseries. He speaks quickly and rather haltingly, and I miss about half of what he says. But there is no mistaking his praise for Deborah's cooking. "It's perfect. It's tops."

You'll no doubt agree. The top-choice favorites at the Knotty Pine include familiar old standbys: roast beef, meat loaf, mashed potatoes and gravy, scalloped potatoes and ham, thick and chunky soups. There are no surprises here (except for that possum pie)—just consistently good cooking that has characterized the Knotty Pine for sixty years. People know this and come back, no matter the distance. People like Ellis and Blanche Voskuil, who owned the place from 1946 to 1956, and who appear in the old black and white photos above the vintage menu board. "They stop in when they're visiting from Florida," Deborah says. "And just a few months ago, the man who has the Kirby Special named after him was here visiting. His old friends had a get-together in the back room, and fixed him a Kirby Special. That's a Coke float. They all had a good laugh about that."

The Kirby Special is found on the vintage menu board, but you can order one if you'd like. Deborah's four-year-old son, Jacob, who is too shy to talk, prefers root beer floats—perhaps the Jacob Special of the future.

PULASKI
Kroll's Family Diner
127 North St. Augustine Street
(920) 822-1888
M–Th 6 A.M.–8 P.M.; F 6 A.M.–9 P.M.; Sa 6 A.M.–6 P.M.; Su 8 A.M.–3 P.M.
Barbara Kroll

Like many other cafe owners, Barbara Kroll entered the job after making a major reassessment of her life and opting for a different course. For twelve years she'd been a stay-at-home mom to her four kids and then took an office job that helped to pay the bills but brought no satisfaction. She piled on the pounds, which made her depressed—which made her eat more. Grasping the seriousness of her unhappiness, she quit the office job and moved on to Festival Foods, where she worked as a "deli girl."

"It was then that it hit me: what I enjoyed doing. I liked to prepare food, and I liked to be around people," she says. With the support of her husband, Tony, and kids Amy, Rachael, Tony, and Jim, she began to contemplate the possibility of owning a little restaurant. She'd seen the for sale sign in the window of the small eatery across from Assumption of the Blessed Virgin Mary Catholic Church, and on March 4, 2002, she went in to take a look. "The place was really rough, but I saw the potential," she remembers. Armed with soap, water, buckets, and other cleaning supplies, she and her family—including sisters Shannon and Kathy who work alongside Barbara in the kitchen—took on the challenge of transforming the dark and dirty restaurant into Kroll's Family Diner.

It's amazing what some earnest elbow grease, some fresh paint, and a stubborn commitment to quality can produce. I remember the place before it was Kroll's Family Diner, and it was truly forgettable. And I had forgotten it until I walked into Barbara's version. I knew I had been there before but nothing looked or felt the same. Thank goodness. All the while the place was being transformed behind papered windows, the locals waited anxiously for the day when Barbara would open. The day she did, they perched at the counter before going to work as if their routines had never been interrupted. The rhythms of life in Pulaski beat as steady as a healthy heart after successful surgery.

Indeed, Barbara admits to having her customers' health constantly in mind. "I'm as health-conscious for them as I can be without going overboard," she says. Her concern for and interest in conscientious eating is due in large part to her own personal transformation during nineteen months in 1999–2000. Disgusted with her overeating, she joined Weight Watchers and lost eighty-six pounds through careful attention to what she was putting in her mouth. As a result of her weight loss, she gained confidence and self-esteem—so much so, in fact, that she found the courage to alter the course of her life. If it seems ironic that a weight watcher would wind up owning her own restaurant, consider this: by controlling her eating, she took control of her life and found herself. "I'm not just a mom," she says. "I'm not just a wife. I'm me, and this is where I can express myself."

Barbara brings special gifts to the restaurant. Not only is she an excellent cook who insists on homemade everything, she also focuses on healthful, inventive dishes. She is attentive to her customers who are diabetic and offers sugar-free alternatives, such as bottled Crystal Light and sugar-free pies. She's added a well-stocked salad bar for her friends in Weight Watchers (and for cafe hunters like myself who crave fresh, crisp vegetables). She also offers vegetarian and low-fat versions of popular items—garden lasagna, for example, and white chicken chili. She spruces up standard fare with clever additions: apples in the coleslaw and potato salad with chopped cucumber.

"One day a lady asked to see the owner, and I came out," remembers Barb. "'Are you the owner?' she asked. And I thought, oh-oh. She said, 'I just wanted to let you know that I have never had potato salad with cucumber in it before, and it is so good. Thank you.' That made me feel good and let me know I was doing things right.'"

Barbara also experiments with traditional Polish dishes because Pulaski is "a very Polish community." Her regulars appreciate her attempts to revive childhood memories and relish the opportunity to revisit Old World fare such as czarnina, or duck soup. Although the truly traditional version calls for a couple of tablespoons of duck blood, Barbara bows to state health regulations and omits it. Like Norwegians throughout the state who stick to their lutefisk, the Polish people of Pulaski stick to their czarnina. A more palatable and frequently requested Polish specialty is pierogi—small potato-filled pastry dumplings commonly served with pork and sauerkraut.

Whatever she cooks, the members of the "Old Farts Group," the Kiwanis, and the after-church crowds of Catholics have claimed Kroll's Family Diner as their home away from home. "My customers are just like family to me," Barbara says. "They make me so happy. I just love what I do so much, there's times I just cry."

ROSENDALE
Tabbert's Restaurant |●|
221 South Main Street (Highway 26)
(920) 872-2222
M–Th 5 A.M.–7 P.M.; F 5 A.M.–8:30 P.M.; Sa 5 A.M.–2 P.M.; Su closed
William and Kay Tabbert
Inside Tabbert's Restaurant, you'll find a wooden cutout of Rosendale depicting everything important in the little Fond du Lac County town: Tabbert's Restaurant, the United States Post Office, the Rosendale Shopping Center, and Tabbert's Insurance. Like a bookend, Tabbert's Restaurant supports the village, holding it upright and anchoring it. The sad thing, however, is that not much of what comprises the wooden Rosendale still exists. Rosie, the daytime waitress who grew up in Rosendale and has worked here for years, reports, "The post office moved, the grocery store closed, and Tabbert's Insurance closed. Bill's dad retired, and there's another agent there now."

For the time being, Tabbert's Restaurant is the sole survivor, holding its own since opening in 1954. Rosie explains that the past two years have been very hard on the little home-cooking cafe because the state highway was closed for reconstruction one year and the city streets the next. Bill and Kay Tabbert are hanging on, but Bill has had to take on another job to ensure a steady paycheck.

Fifty years ago, the restaurant was built as a small sit-down cafe with drive-up service in a cornfield on the south side of Rosendale. Rosie remembers coming here after high school basketball games for burgers, fries, and Cokes—"about the only thing they had!" At that time, the cafe consisted of a counter and a few booths, but later it added a dining room.

Bill Tabbert, owner since 1987 and a Rosendale native, was working in the restaurant business when he began eyeing the little cafe. "It was in a good location but needed rejuvenation, so I asked the owner to contact me if she ever wanted to sell." Bill was so certain the little restaurant would become his that two years before it did, he bought neighboring land for a parking lot. His optimism paid off. Today the parking lot regularly fills with cars and semitrucks, a reliable sign that Tabbert's is known near and far for its real, slow-cooked food.

Take the testimony of the trucker paying his bill at the counter who said of his noontime meal: "That was very, very good." He then climbed into the cab of a truck that had large pink cow snouts sticking out of the latticed sides.

Bill is proud of the homemade pies; fresh bakery bread, sweet rolls, buns, and hard rolls; real mashed potatoes; hand-pattied burgers; and homemade dinner specials that keep truckers and area residents from a twenty-five-mile radius well fed and satisfied. "We serve a lot of real food," he says, "because a lot of hard workers, a lot of truckers come in, and they don't want fancy croissants."

Spaghetti, roast beef and pork, meat loaf, and chow mein are among the favorite main meal specials at Tabbert's, but Bill also recommends breakfast features like "pancakes the size of manhole covers" and two-inch-thick slabs of French toast. "We serve generous portions," he points out.

STURGEON BAY
Perry's Cherry Diner ⏣
230 Michigan Street
(920) 743-4576
M–Sa 6:30 A.M.–9 P.M.; Su 8 A.M.–8 P.M.
Perry Andropolis
Taking a walk at dusk along the shores of Green Bay in Potawatomi State Park, I met a four-year-old boy who had just caught his first fish. With the fish dangling on the end of the line, he ran to me and cried, "See what I catched?" When his parents heard about my Wisconsin food foray they advised, "You'd better go to Andropolis Restaurant in Sturgeon Bay, just over the bridge."

The next day I dropped in for a visit with Perry Andropolis, who transformed the "home-style" Andropolis Restaurant into the pseudo-1950s-vintage Perry's Cherry Diner. It is decked out in black and white ceramic tiles, stainless steel and cherry red trim, pink and turquoise booths, chrome-edged black Formica tables and matching dinette chairs, and posters of Marilyn and Elvis. Perry refers to himself as the "current caretaker" of the restaurant, which began as Larsen's Lunch in the 1930s and became the Victory Grill after World War II and Andropolis Restaurant in the 1970s, when operated by his parents, Jack and Ann.

Despite its nostalgic, period theme, Perry's Cherry Diner doesn't completely disguise the old family-run eatery. Alongside blue plate specials and old-fashioned malts ("the elixir of the fifties"), inquisitive adventure eaters will be pleased to discover genuine Greek specialties, such as gyros—spicy lamb and beef, onions, tomatoes, and cucumber sauce in pita bread; spanakopita—spinach pie; and baklava—walnut and honey-layered pastry. You'll find plenty of other inspired best-sellers, too, including fajita chicken quesadillas, jerk chicken wrap, and the Andyjacks cherry wrap—chunks of tender chicken, Door County cherries, walnuts, and Perry's signature sauce. For timid eaters, the menu doesn't overlook traditional, mainstream Wisconsin favorites—"diner comfort food"—like meat loaf, hot beef, and hot hamburger, and to my surprise and delight, Kraft blue box macaroni and cheese served in a mound with a side dish. Spruce up the mac and cheese by adding grilled chicken.

Whatever you choose—and you won't go wrong with anything on Perry's menu—be sure to reserve room for Ann's excellent cherry pie, voted the "best cherry pie in Door County" by *Midwest Living* magazine. I ate plenty of cherry pie while I was on the peninsula, and I have to agree. Ann's crust is crisp and light—the top dusted with sugar—and the trademark Montmorency cherries are baked into a flavorful, rich filling. The recognition by *Midwest Living* is only one of several accolades bestowed on Perry's Cherry Diner by regional publications. In 1995, 1996, and 1997, Perry's was voted Best Hometown Diner/Cafe by readers of *Wisconsin Trails* magazine, and in 2000, the *Chicago Tribune* declared Perry's meat loaf to be "the best." Also in 2000, the diner was named Restaurant of the Year by the Wisconsin Red Cherry Growers, Inc.

Cherries appear in malts, pie, smoothies, crushes, the Andyjacks wrap, pancakes, and French toast—not to mention as garnishes speared on toothpicks.

The awards are deserved, but the most valued compliments come from Perry's customers, whose handwritten comments often find their way onto the "neato" pop-art menu designed by Perry himself. "Actual customer comments" include such gems as: "Either I'm really hungry or the steak and eggs are really good this morning." "You shouldn't ask the customers if they want pie. Just tell them they're having it." "You really do a disservice to customers who don't get to try your pie!" And (one customer to another about the strawberry pancakes), "Wow, that looks great. Maybe I don't want to share with you."

Perry Andropolis's goal is to make Perry's Cherry Diner "the best casual restaurant in Door County," and then take it into other areas in the Midwest through franchising. Perry's Cherry Diner would be the first small town restaurant in Wisconsin to franchise, but Jerry Bechard, owner of the Norske Nook in Osseo, who has established two other Norske Nooks in Hayward and Rice Lake, has successfully tried expansion. Says Perry, "I want to see where I can go with the business. We've done so well here that we're ready to move on and try more."

Popular with all ages—parents driving to Door County for family vacations report their kids' almost nonstop anticipation of Perry's Cherry Diner—the Sturgeon Bay eatery is home to visitors and locals alike. Over the past ten years, however, Perry has noted many changes. The retired men who met unfailingly every Monday, Wednesday, and Friday between seven and nine for companionship, conversation, and pipe smoking over games of sheepshead have mostly passed away. Their passing reflects a shift in Sturgeon Bay's demographics and a refocusing of community identity that is shaping current and future plans for civic development.

Perry notes that Sturgeon Bay is now a community of "mixed demographics, like a mini-Orlando" comprised of descendants of old-time settlers, professional and moneyed retired people, and aggressive young entrepreneurs and business people. Its future lies more and more in tourism and as a commercial hub for Door County. As its seasonal swell in population continues, more attention will be focused on infrastructure. Long anticipated is the replacement or restoration of the historic bridge linking southern and northern Door County, a bridge that feeds traffic directly into downtown Sturgeon Bay—and directly past Perry's Cherry Diner. Perry knows the year-long closure will be a strain on the downtown business, but with their eyes set on the future, both Perry and the city of Sturgeon Bay work toward seeing just how far they can go.

WASHINGTON ISLAND
KK Fiske
Main Road
(920) 847-2121
M–Su 7 A.M.–9 P.M.
Ken Koyen
When Ken Koyen says he serves the freshest fish in Door County—"They were swimming this morning"—you can believe him. He caught them.

He was out on his fish tug, *Sea Diver*, pulling in the gill nets when I was riding the ferry to Washington Island, a remote part of Door County where real people live, work, and raise families. Ken is a native islander who was raised on his multigenerational family's dairy farm, which is also the site of his restaurant, KK Fiske. It is a strange name for a restaurant, but it makes perfect sense to the informed. The KK stands for Ken Koyen. The Fiske is Danish for fish.

A Dane, a fisherman, a farmer, and restaurateur, Ken is a jack-of-all-trades—as anyone living year-round on the island must be. His right-hand man, Carl, says, "You've got to be able to do anything in order to live out here." Twenty years ago, Ken built a rectangular cedar building on the Main Road, at the edge of his parents' farm, as a fish market. He'd observed how the sport fishing industry had boomed with the interest of seasonal sportsmen and tourists and thought he'd get in on it. He added a few shops, only to witness the bottom fall out of the business. "We weren't really planning to run a restaurant," he explains, but slowly the fish market was transformed into the restaurant KK Fiske. And Ken fished, in part to keep the cost of running a restaurant at a profitable level. "If I need more fish, I don't go out and buy it like the next guy," he explains. "I just take the boat out."

This morning he caught 125 pounds of whitefish, which will be cleaned and cut into steaks for tonight's fish boil, and another 100 pounds of lawyers, or burbot. Lawyers can be served only fresh because the flesh turns to rubber when frozen. "The lawyers are not cooperating this summer," Ken complains, so in order to meet the constant customer demand for them, he must be on Lake Michigan five or six days a week. In other years, two or three days would have been enough.

Ken says the burbot, which is related to the cod, is nicknamed "lawyer" because "its heart is in its ass." It has a "humongous liver that cleans out the flesh," so it never tastes fishy. Ken dices the fresh catch into one-and-a-half-inch nuggets, then lightly batters and deep-fries them. Lawyers also find their way onto pizzas and into soup. Deep fried, they are "hands down" the most popular item on the menu, and people have been known to call from Chicago to make sure they're available before hopping into a plane. A hand-painted sign on the front window advertises Fresh Lawyers and attracts plenty of snickers and amateur photographers. "That's how we know it's spring—when the first tourist stops and takes a photo of the sign," jokes Ken and his son, Jesse, who has come from UW–Green Bay to help out with tonight's fish boil.

While the water is boiling in the large kettle at the edge of the parking lot, Ken brings out a red plastic basket of hot lawyers for me to eat.

They are delicious—and very hot. There is no hint of fishy flavor, and the meat is snow white inside the golden brown coating.

The night is cold, and this may well be the last fish boil of the season. It is late September and the tourists have gone home, leaving the islanders to themselves and the few friends that relish a quiet evening over sweet whitefish and red potatoes. A handful of people—friends of Ken—from Fairport and Escanaba have made the trip over for the fish boil. Because KK Fiske is about three miles from the ferry landing, they leave a van at the ferry dock when they come and go. Ken keeps an old limo on hand to pick up people there. If that's you, you'll want to call him ahead of time to arrange a rendezvous.

The Door County fish boil is a well-established tradition. The first commercial fish boil on the peninsula was begun in 1961 by Lawrence Wickman at the Viking Grill in Ellison Bay. Ken remembers observing him at both the restaurant and on the fish tug, where "the first fish off the roller went into the kettle." Food historians and folklorists have debated the origins of the fish boil, but Ken believes it is a tradition started by fishermen on tugs. Today, Ken's is the only commercial fish boil on Washington Island, but many civic organizations—the Lions, the American Legion—put them on as fundraisers each summer. Consequently, the local population is less likely to gather on Friday nights at KK Fiske than at these other fish boils.

But KK Fiske is definitely a local hangout, especially in the off season when the islanders idle a bit longer, drink a bit more coffee, and play another round or two of cribbage, sheepshead, dirty eight, or other favorite games. The cribbage board sits on a long rectangular table covered with a flannel-backed vinyl cloth, where every day between seven and eight in the morning the locals gather for coffee, recreation, and chat. They come to eat, too, of course, and are pleased with the all homemade offerings, including bread. They share the restaurant with tourists during the summer months but have it all to themselves in winter. All of the other restaurants are closed, and travel to and from the island is difficult, so by the time spring rolls around and the ice breaks up, "the locals are ready for something else. They're ready for a change of food, a change of scenery, and new people," Carl says.

With fifteen winter employees KK Fiske is the island's largest employer between November and May. During the summer months, twenty-one people are on the payroll. Ken credits the success of the restaurant to his help, saying, "They keep me going. I don't have to worry about how many hotdogs I'm going to eat. I feel I have an obligation to succeed because of them. I have the responsibility to earn enough to support them all."

Three hundred and sixty-four days of the year, the restaurant is open from six in the morning to nine at night. The addition of a bar a few years ago extended the working hours to past midnight. The bar is an old heavy timber granary that Ken discovered while haying near Zanders. He took it apart himself and moved it piece by piece to Washington Island, then reassembled it. He crafted the pine tables, benches, and stools and hung artifacts from pioneer days on the island. "I thought about how the pioneers made a living on the island farming and fishing," he explains. "The granary is on one end and on the other end is a dry-docked fishing boat strung with colored lights. We're still making a living farming and fishing. Not much changes on Washington Island."

WINNECONNE
Arrowhead Restaurant ⑩
104–108 West Main Street
(920) 582-4258
M–Su 5:30 A.M.–2:15 P.M.
Jim and Sue Brooks
Back in the 1960s, Jim Brooks had just gotten out of the service and gone back to work at the Midtown Dairy Lunch where he had earned spending money during high school. Sue was there too, working her way through college. They met, fell in love, got married, moved away, returned home, had one son, bought the place, had another son. In time, their two sons, Steve and Christopher, spent their after-school hours cooking, washing dishes, and waiting tables just as Jim did at their age, proving that life follows not a line but a circle.

The old Midtown Dairy Lunch has undergone many changes. Jim says things have been "streamlined a lot." Gone is the real-life soda fountain with carbonated water, the magazine and greeting card racks, the jukebox, the glass shelves stacked with tobacco and candy. In their place are paneled walls, a rack of color postcards for the tourists and summer residents, a bookcase filled with a rotating selection of paperbacks, blond Buckstaff chairs with orange vinyl seats, even a new name: Arrowhead Restaurant, the winner of a name contest sponsored by the previous owners. Amid the changes, one thing remains the same. The Arrowhead is still the central gathering place for the community, especially the men who come early, lining the counter for talk and coffee, and the women who crowd around the Round Table a little later, after the kids are off to school.

"A small town like this needs a place to congregate," Sue explains after Jim leaves to drive the high school soccer players to an away match. "They don't come for the coffee. It's a habit, a ritual, a routine that starts their day." The men arrive before the Arrowhead officially opens, sitting at the counter in the semidark. At five thirty they turn on the overhead light, signaling to Sue that she is now open for the day's business. "They come for the entertainment," Sue says. "Ninety percent of them just drink coffee. They come to find out the latest news and to goad each other. I enjoy it immensely. Some days it's a three-ring circus. Other times it's pretty stimulating."

At eight the women begin filling the Round Table next to the side wall, under the rack of personalized coffee mugs. The women (and the men, too) bring in their own mugs, each revealing a bit about its owner. Sue knows which mug belongs to which customer: this one is the school bus driver's, this one belongs to the summer resident who noticed all the regulars had their own mugs and brought one in for himself. There's even a mug for two of his friends who visit a few days out of the summer. They personalize the coffee corner in other ways as well, by taping to the wall comic strips, political cartoons, and postcards sent to the group by vacationing members. All of these bits and pieces are reflected in the metallic glass balls on the little artificial Christmas tree standing nearby, whose decorations are changed by the season. A second tree—the Packers tree— stands at the front of the restaurant every football season; it is decorated with green and gold ribbons, lights, and yellow ornaments, each inscribed with the name of a player.

Sue describes the Arrowhead regulars as an "extended family" and finds a place for both the regulars and her employees within her own family. Even family holiday celebrations, usually spent in the restaurant where dinners are prepared, are open to the regulars. "We're closed only Thanksgiving and Christmas," Sue explains, "although we're never really closed on Thanksgiving. People still walk in for free coffee and something off the grill."

And when they do, they often expect Sue to know exactly what it is they want. Some people are so consistent in what they eat day in and day out, and some are so dependent on Sue's knowledge of their habits, that they're thrown for a loop when she takes a rare day off. Sue laughs, "They'll tell the waitress, 'I don't know what I have. Sue knows, so you'll have to call her at home.'"

(On my first visit, Christopher Brooks joined in and told me: "Sometimes I'll go up to them and ask, 'Do you want to see a menu today, or do you want to recite it back to me today?'" Christopher is now a teacher. He and Steve grew up in the restaurant and moved into other careers, but they still can be counted on to fill in when hands are short. "It's still all in the family," says Sue.)

According to Christopher, menus are a mere formality, used by strangers and others still new to small town eating. The true sign, then, of an experienced adventure eater is the ability to order without using a menu. For the most part, Wisconsin cafe menus are predictable: pancakes and French toast, eggs and toast and all of the ordinary sides for breakfast; hot beef, burgers, soup, and daily specials for dinner—check the board on the wall for the meal of the day.

That pretty much sums up the food at the Arrowhead. Sue says, "It's a family restaurant. Nothing is unique, just meat, potatoes (the mashed are instant), and vegetables." Known especially for its Sunday roasted chicken and dressing dinner, the Arrowhead also has pancakes and hash browns the locals rave about. Breakfast is hands down the biggest meal of the day. On weekends, it is not unusual for Jim and Sue to serve between 200 and 250 people. "Everybody gets hungry at nine on Sunday morning," laughs Sue. "On the rare days it's slow, it's like waiting for the other shoe to drop."

Other menu favorites are the "consistently good" burgers and all variety of meats. Jim's daily special pie is homemade, and it goes quickly, much faster than its frozen, "home-baked" cousins. The streamlined Arrowhead no longer serves "real life" sodas, malts, or banana splits, but what it still has, Sue promises, is "good food, generous portions, and great prices."

. . . .

Next Best Bets

Bailey's Harbor
The Food Factory
8085 Highway 87
Winter and summer, the menu features sturdy stuff that fills the bellies of the cherry farmer, fisherman, and the lazy tourist. Hand-peeled and mashed potatoes, meat loaf, fried chicken, burgers, and a variety of other homemade favorites compete with the popular all-you-can-eat spaghetti and Friday fish fry specials. In summer, the tourist crush prohibits homemade desserts, but they return in winter in the form of pies, cakes, cobblers, and other sweets.

Brandon
Brandon Cafe
142 East Main Street
Thursdays are set aside for broasted chicken, a favorite of the locals but only fair-to-middlin' for me. A classy touch is the painted mural of Brandon's Main Street during the 1800s and 1900s.

CARLSVILLE
Laurie's Cafe
6224 Highway 42

On my first drive-by heading north, I didn't understand the sign: Laurie's Calf-A. On my way south, I stopped for lunch and had to groan at the other sign, Udderly Moolicious. As you might expect, the modest, do-it-yourself interior is decorated with a collection of Holsteins—a radical departure from the upscale restaurant decor characteristic of Door County. The food was like Mom's and worth going back for.

CHILTON
Julie's Uptown Cafe
32 West Main Street

Dive into the apple pie, made in the deepest pie pan in Wisconsin.

EDEN
Eden Cafe
303 West Main Street

Pump your gas and fill your tummy at this combination service station and cafe. Family-style food, but watch for the not-quite-homemade offerings in the potato and pie categories. Don't miss the collection of clever signs, including this one: "Cleaning the house while the children are growing is like shoveling snow while it's still snowing."

GREENVILLE
Mr. & Mrs. K's
N1671 Greenville Drive

Food like Mom made served with seasoning and sauce in the form of witty repartee. The menu cover promises "Something Superior for Your Interior." I had Wisconsin chili (with elbow macaroni), but I've been told the breakfasts are unbeatable.

KEWAUNEE
Larry and Mona's Restaurant
301 Ellis Street

Plenty of Kewaunee's citizens find the rustic barn board interior of this corner restaurant suitable for sitting, drinking coffee, and passing the time. Good food, too. A sign on the wall reads, "Using the winter as an alibi is just another snow job."

ONEIDA
Grama's Diner
N7284 County Highway U

Grama-style cooking in a little cafe attached to the Shell Hilltop station.

Sister Bay
Carroll House
645 South Bay Shore Drive
You won't find everything made from scratch at the Carroll House, a rather pricey Door County fixture since 1957, but you will find a great vintage look— take a seat at the counter—and breakfasts people drive up the shore for. Breakfast and lunch only.

Sturgeon Bay
My Sister's Cafe
325 North Third Street
Located in a former small box store—perhaps a grocery or hardware store?— this cafe at first confused me by all of the collectible kitchen pieces in the front window. I thought it was an antique store! It's full of relics of past days and plenty of huge portions of good home cooking, including pancakes touted as the best in the United States. While that may be a stretch, they are light, thin, tasty, and *huge*. Is there a competition among cafe owners to see who can make the biggest pancakes?

Sturgeon Bay
Pudgy Seagull Restaurant
113 North Third Street
A typical restaurant serving "basic, normal home food." The downtown hangout for seniors and families inside and, for some reason, teenage skate-boarder-types outside on the sidewalk.

Waldo
Tim's Waldo Cafe
235 Depot Street
Doubling as a gallery of the works of George Pollard, a hometown boy and renowned portrait artist, this cafe "Located in Bustling Downtown Waldo, Wisconsin," features a variety of fine cooking. Italian spaghetti, hot beef, omelettes, from-scratch buttermilk pancakes, cream and fruit pies, tortes and other desserts are favorites here, as are the burgers made with ultra-lean Black Angus beef—among the best I encountered in the state.

Epilogue

Looking Back

When I first conceived the idea for this book, I envisioned a directory to good home-cooking spots around Wisconsin. I planned to concentrate only on food, but soon after my cross-country trip was underway it became apparent that cafes are more than places to grab a quick sandwich or hot meal. They are the social hubs of small communities, where people gather to learn about election results, buy chances for the ladies' auxiliary quilt raffle, and share a game of sheepshead or dice over a cup of coffee. As if it had a life of its own, *Cafe Wisconsin* diverted from its original emphasis and developed into an examination of ways in which food is used to bring about social interaction.

Folklorists Charles Camp, Lin T. Humphrey, and others have long promoted the study of American food and food customs—foodways—in social context. Food should be studied not by itself but as part of the total event or festive gathering in which it plays a part, such as the family birthday party, community festival, or church supper. Humphrey suggests that the study of foodways include "places where people get together to eat, drink, and have a good time." Places like Mamie's Cafe in Stoddard, the Alma Hotel in Alma, Graff's Restaurant in Lena. Places like Cafe Wisconsin.[1]

The study of food leads to cookbooks and such restaurant guides as Duncan Hines's *Adventures in Good Eating* and Jane and Michael Stern's *Roadfood*. The addition of social context—food events and food places—leads to *Cafe Wisconsin*. During my search, I wanted to discover what roles cafes play in Wisconsin's small towns and in the lives of individuals both historically and today, so I treated cafes as texts that, like written materials, could be read for social information. Seemingly small details became important. In tulip-trimmed shutters I read cultural heritage; in retired men's coffee groups, the renegotiation of individual identities and social roles; in county guidebooks stacked in front windows, the promotion of the local area to outsiders. Certainly cafes play many roles, but in considering decor and architecture, oral and written words, social gatherings and performances, cafes function, most importantly, as heritage centers, senior centers, and chambers of commerce.

CAFES AS HERITAGE CENTERS
Local History: Photos and Artifacts, Oral Histories, and Food

As heritage centers, cafes allow communities to review and reshape their past and present it for public consumption as they wish it to be remembered. Walls are often decorated with black and white photographs depicting a town's history: street scenes with boardwalks and horse-drawn wagons, loggers on a river drive, families spending a Sunday afternoon at the lake. Photos are typically lent or donated from the private collections of regular customers and are especially popular with older members of the community, who enjoy studying the photos, hoping to find a relative or old friend they recall from their childhood. Natives who have moved away and return for visits are also pleased to find images of their past hanging on the walls, images that recall long-forgotten memories and inspire reminiscences and anecdotes. For newcomers to a community, these photographs establish the past as a knowable time and place.

Physical artifacts also tell the history of local areas. Among other things, you'll find cafes decorated with collections of logging equipment, antique household items, wooden cases from defunct local breweries, and railroad memorabilia. Raul Perez's Lumber Inn in Delafield, built on the site of the old Delafield Lumber and Fuel Company, is filled with bucksaws, carpenters' tools, and relics from the old lumberyard. Tracks Dining Car Cafe in Webster, owned by Joel Hakenson and Pam Durkee, is gradually taking on the appearance of a railroad museum. In Waldo, Tim Christensen's Waldo Cafe boasts a gallery offering the works of acclaimed portrait artist George Pollard, a native of the town. In Sauk City, hometown author August Derleth is honored with Augie's Room at Leystra's Venture Restaurant, owned by Jim and Janine Leystra.

Physical objects often stimulate oral histories in the forms of personal reminiscences, anecdotes about local characters and events, jokes and riddles, and retellings of practical jokes. Among the most common oral histories are those told by elderly and former cafe owners about their early days of business when farmers and townspeople would flood into towns for weekend shopping and dances and keep restaurants open until late at night. Back in those days, when you could buy a hamburger and malt for a quarter—and in winter you came into town for it on a horse-drawn sleigh—life was hard and vigorous, and the dedicated labor of men and women carved out family farms and industries from the Wisconsin land.

Familiar, comfortable, and conservative, Wisconsin cafe food—with a foundation of meat (mostly roast beef and pork), potatoes, and vegetables—is an artifact of this earlier way of life. Foods tend to reflect the local economic base, so that in the central cranberry bog region of Wood

County you'll find cranberry pies, breads, and muffins at Sherri Dessart's Country Cafe in Babcock. In the potato fields banding Highway 8 across the north, you won't find a cafe that dares to use instant potato flakes or buds. In Door County and on Washington Island, you'll find the fish boil— fresh whitefish, red potatoes, and small onions cooked over an open fire— a virtual icon begun commercially at the Viking Restaurant in Ellison Bay. And wherever you travel in Wisconsin, you'll find fish fries ritually held every Friday night, a remnant, some cafe owners believe, of the years when the state's heavy Catholic population was forbidden to eat meat on Fridays.[2]

Ethnicity: Foodways and Decor

Wisconsin cafe food is also influenced by the local ethnic heritage. You'll find Cornish pasties—hearty meat and potato pies—in the southwest (in the extreme north, they've been adopted by the Finns), lutefisk and lefse in the state's Norwegian areas, and kolache and shuleke in the Czechoslovakian settlements. Most ethnic selections tend to be cautious and familiar—shuleke, for example, is nothing more than chicken dumpling soup—and a safe and easy way of emphasizing ethnicity.[3] Others, however, like lutefisk—dried cod treated with lye and reconstituted before eating—require a daring palate and an iron stomach. (On the other hand, the potato flatbread known as lefse, lutefisk's partner on the plate, is not only easily tolerated but also easily substituted for flour tortillas, as at the Norske Nook in Osseo.) Safe and easy or daring and queasy, ethnic foods often become emblematic of ethnic groups, so that the pasty and figgyhobbin served at the Red Rooster Cafe in Mineral Point are the embodiment of Cornishness and lutefisk and lefse are viewed as edible capsules of Norwegian heritage (although the Swedes have their own version).[4]

Foods also reflect the heritage of people who settled in areas not of their own cultural background. When Appalachian families migrated to Forest, Langlade, and Vilas Counties at the turn of the century, they brought with them "foreign" foods such as biscuits and gravy and soup beans, which Larry and Susan Palubicki serve at their Log Cabin Cafe in Crandon. The Palubickis were among only a handful of owners offering this southern breakfast staple when I canvassed the state for the first *Cafe Wisconsin*, but since then it has become popular fare nearly everywhere. At Perry's Cherry Diner in Sturgeon Bay you'll find Perry Andropolis serving Greek moussakka, tyropita, and spanakopita, and in Greenwood, at the Greenwood Family Restaurant owned by Ernesto and Linda Rodriguez, burritos, chalupas, tostadas, fried ice cream, and other specialties from Mexico share menu space with hot beef and cheeseburgers. The peaceful coexistence of ethnic specialties and conservative Wisconsin meat-and-potatoes fare indicates that Wisconsin cafe food, like American food in general, is culturally diverse yet unified.[5]

Even more significant, ethnic foods recapture a lost or vanishing heritage for later generations whose parents and grandparents shed traditional foodways during their assimilation into mainstream American culture. In Denmark, Lorrie Steffek of Lorrie's Home Town Cafe and Catering serves hot, just-baked æbleskiver—a kind of apple popover—using her grandmother's recipe and cast iron æbleskiver pans she picks up at local yard sales. At Kroll's Family Diner in the Polish town of Pulaski, owner Barbara Kroll revives Old World fare such as czarnina (duck soup sans the blood) and pierogi.

Though foods are perhaps the most accessible of ethnic crafts, it is not necessary to prepare or eat foods to enforce one's ethnic identity. Jokes about food do this just as well. At the former Dallas Cafe in Barron County, featured in the first edition of *Cafe Wisconsin* but since closed, owners Tom and Jan Clarkin prepared neither lutefisk nor lefse (although Jan had a flat grill and roller for making lefse, something she always intended to do), yet a sign on the wall read, "Lutefisk—A Gift of Cod that passeth all understanding." Jan and I had a good laugh over the sign, and an even better one when I shared what I had mistakenly copied: "Lutefisk—A Gift of God that surpasseth all understanding." And in the Norske Nook in Osseo— the name alone reinforces the area's ethnic identity—where lutefisk and lefse are prepared during the winter months for the locals and again in May for the Norwegian independence celebration, Syttende Mai, another sign reads, "If lutefisk is outlawed, only outlaws will have lutefisk."[6]

Ethnic jokes also take the form of narratives and practical pranks. In coffee klatches from early morning to late afternoon, men tell jokes about their own ethnic group and those of outsiders. In Schubert's Old Fashioned Cafe and Bakery in the Norwegian town of Mt. Horeb, Roy Tvedt tells tales of foolish Swedes and even more foolish Norwegians, and quips about the Swiss from New Glarus who can't be trusted. Though they disparage and ridicule Norwegians, Norwegian jokes are largely told by people of Norwegian heritage who are free to tell them at any time. However, joke-telling and the playing of practical pranks by non-Norwegians is limited by cultural rules based on the degree of camaraderie between jokesters and their audience. For example, in the heavily Norwegian town of Hixton in Jackson County, the non-Norwegian and non-native Lohmar family, owners of the Hixton Cafe, gave their regular customers practical Norwegian joke Christmas gifts one year. The "Norwegian flashlight" consisting of a toilet paper tube with matches glued on the end was illuminating.

The success of the Lohmars' gag gifts affirm the mutual respect and love between them and their customers.[7]

Another way to express ethnicity is through cafe decor. In 1992, for example, the readers of *Wisconsin Trails* magazine voted Osseo's Norske Nook as their favorite "unusual or ethnic restaurant" in the state because of its "Norwegian flavor." The award puzzled owner Jerry Bechard, who questioned how the Nook's "most ordinary food" could be considered ethnic. The Nook's "Norwegian flavor" is derived not from the lutefisk and lefse made for the locals ("There's not many tourists who eat lutefisk," Jerry asserts), but rather from the pleasant Norwegian blue, cream, and earth tones, the beautiful rosemaled wall decorations, the large hand-painted wall mural of a Norwegian peasant girl and fjord village, and the Norwegian crafts and gift items for sale at the Gave Buttik across the street.

In similar ways, other cafes promote the ethnic heritage of their own communities. In the Vernon County village of Hillsboro, Julie Eder, founder and former owner of the Country Style Cookin' Restaurant, left the current owners her collection of Czechoslovakian dolls, folk art, Cesky Den buttons, flags, and ethnic jokes, such as the Bohunk 2-Holer, a miniature double-decker outhouse. In Westby, at Borgen's Norwegian Cafe and Bakery, you'll find trolls cavorting on the walls and full-size mannequins dressed in colorful bunad, or traditional regional costumes. In Blanchardville's Bit of Norway Restaurant, featured in the first edition of *Cafe Wisconsin* but since closed, a beautiful handmade Norwegian Viking ship hung from the ceiling. Until it closed in 2001, Bark's Dutch Oven Bakery and Cafe in Baldwin, the St. Croix County town that annually celebrates Let's Go Dutch Days, had a colorful mural of a windmill. The new owners chose to erase it with a coat of fresh white paint.

As with ethnic food, decor can define the heritage of whole towns or assert the personal heritage of individual owners whose ancestors were outsiders among other dominant ethnic groups. In the Welsh-settled town of Cambria, for example, Evelyn Leystra decorates Leystra's Venture, which she and her late husband, Sam, established, with Holland-blue siding and tulip-trimmed shutters. Inside, Evelyn displays her collection of blue and white Delftware, which she says is "real Delft" even if it was purchased in Cedar Grove, Wisconsin, not Delft, Holland. Evelyn believes she has inherited her affection for windmills and tulips from her Holland-born parents, and deliberately uses these Dutch motifs to assert her own family's ethnic heritage.

Collections have connective power, linking places and people through time and across space. Whereas Evelyn purchased her Delftware, many other collections often begin with the gifts of customers. In North Freedom at

Carol's Railroad Inn Cafe, former owner Carol Clendenning's impressive collection of vintage green kitchenware and railroad-related items began with a few pieces she brought in to fill out the cafe. Thanks to her customers, the cafe is filled with green sieves, sifters, colanders, salt and pepper shakers, match holders, and stoves, as well as ceramic train planters, toy trains, railroad signs, matchbooks, calendars, schedules, decorative plates, wind chimes, and much, much more. About two hundred miles away in Bruce, the locals christened Katie Verhagen's newly constructed Katie's Cafe with kitchen antiques and collectibles to replace items that were lost when fire destroyed the original cafe. Because collections accumulate over time as gifts from customers, they are a good indication of a cafe's stability and consistency, as well as a good measure of the esteem the community feels for a cafe and its owner.[8]

Some collections, such as the coffee mugs decorated with Norwegian folk dancers at Borgen's Norwegian Cafe and Bakery in Westby and the Finnish-American calendars at the Twin Gables in Brule, are offered for sale. Purchased primarily by out-of-town visitors, these items identify a community as special or unique and promote ethnicity by spreading emblematic forms of it outward to the larger public. Other items, such as the beautiful Cesky Den festival buttons sold at the Country Style Cookin' Restaurant, are purchased by local and area residents and pull the outer fringes of the community inward in a unifying ritual celebration of its shared heritage. Ethnic festivals find many cafe owners playing an integral role. In Hillsboro, Julie Eder helped prepare and serve traditional Czechoslovakian foods—roast pork, sauerkraut, potato dumplings, jaternice (liver sausage), applesauce, and kolaches—sold from the festival food booth. In Little Chute, Larry Van Lankvelt of Tucker's Inn prepared traditional Dutch foods including pork cracklings known as brye at the town's annual Kermis Festival. In ways such as this cafe owners act as "ritual specialists" expressing their own and their community's cultural identity through activities and edible symbols of heritage.[9]

Cafes Then and Now

In examining ethnicity, we look at the expression of cultural heritage as found in individual cafes. But if we step outside the individual frame and consider all cafes at once, the history of American restaurants comes into view. In Wisconsin, cafes represent a chronological development beginning with nineteenth-century boardinghouses, hotels, stagecoach inns, and taverns and moving on to 1920s-era combination cafe and confectioneries, tobacco shops, and bakeries; 1930s filling station eateries; midcentury drive-ins, soda fountain/grills, and full-menu restaurants; and culminating in the 2000s, with cafes being found in all variety of recycled buildings, some of which have been made over to resemble earlier restaurant types, such as the diner.[10]

Perhaps one of the oldest cafes in the state is the Dairyland Cafe in the northern Dunn County town of Ridgeland, which began about 120 years ago as a boardinghouse. Other featured cafes started life about the same time as hotel restaurants or sandwich shops. Among these are the cafe in the Alma Hotel, which still rents rooms; the Lakewood Cafe in the former Lakewood Hotel in Winter; and the Hotel Crandon Cafe in Crandon.

Jensen's in Galesville was one of the oldest cafes—and one of my favorites—until 1992 when it closed and its contents were auctioned off. Established in a two-story brick building erected in 1902, it was a working restaurant museum. Philip Jensen, son of founder Tollef Jensen, had saved many of the cafe's original furnishings and pieces of equipment, including leaded glassware, sundae trays, an early Hamilton Beach malt machine, and damask table linens used by his mother and aunts for special occasions. Philip entertained me by recalling from his early childhood the cafe's early customers—Norwegian immigrants and Indians. Featured in the original *Cafe Wisconsin*, Jensen's Cafe has been converted into a food co-op.

Other early cafes are notable for their sleek, angular lines and flowery art deco adornment, which characterized high style architecture and decorative arts in the 1920s and 1930s. Clyde and Debbie Hady's Cafe on the Park in Lake Mills, with its green, peach, and cream painted woodwork and exquisite marble counter, is one of the handsomest cafes in Wisconsin. But the title of Most Beautiful goes without a doubt to Steele's Restaurant in Berlin, owned since 1995 by Therese Lewallen. Steele's Restaurant is one of William Least Heat-Moon's "golden dreams from the past"—entirely unaltered since 1937, when it was fitted out with a black marble counter and red-topped stools on steel posts; high-backed oak booths now with yellow cracked ice Formica tops and individual amber glass wall lamps; and a stainless steel soda fountain in an oak back bar. Steele's is so remarkable, it takes your breath away.

Cafes were located primarily in town on the main business street until the 1930s, when drive-ins, grills, root beer stands, burger boxes, and motel and filling station eateries dependent on the automobile began appearing on the outer edges of towns. In Monticello, Jimmie's was built as a burger-only grill sometime in the late 1930s, replacing an earlier combination confectionery/tobacco/sandwich shop; in relatively unchanged form, it is now the M & M Cafe owned by Mike and Mary Davis. About the same time in Brillion, Rudy's Diner, formerly Rudy's Cafe, was built a few blocks out of town on Highway 10, where it attracted a loyal following of adventurous travelers and cross-country truckers who, over the next fifty years, would make Rudy's into a Wisconsin institution.

Small town economy and practicality led to the recycling of countless retail and private buildings, so that today it is possible to eat in a one-room schoolhouse (the Red School Cafe in Bristol), a former post office (the Corner Cafe in New Lisbon), a combination general mercantile and bank (the Unique Cafe in Boscobel), a pipe cutter's shop (the Brickhouse Cafe in Barronett), even a funeral home (the Hayseed Cafe in Wauzeka). As buildings were transformed, living quarters were typically added upstairs or off the back, so that owners were not only operators but also residents.

By the 1940s and 1950s, many small town restaurants were built or updated with neon signs, durable stainless steel, chrome, and Formica and featured soda fountains and jukeboxes. During this period the cafe became the local teen hang out, where high school kids consumed burgers and malts after school and after ball games. Many received or gave their first kiss in the privacy of a booth. Tabbert's Restaurant in Rosendale started life this way, as did Callen's Restaurant in Union Grove and the Dairy Bar Cafe in Thorp. Today's adventure eaters will be happy to discover that these cafes still look quite a lot like they did when they opened. As Earl Bruinsma, co-owner of Callen's Restaurant with his wife, Charlotte, says, wood and stainless steel just never wear out.

By midcentury Wisconsin cafes had also fallen under the influence of popular programmatic architecture that gave America roadside attractions like huge coffee pot-shaped eateries and filling stations resembling oversized gas pumps. In Williams Bay, the white dome known as Daddy Maxwell's Arctic Circle Cafe was an igloo-inspired, walk-up, burger-and-fries kind of place, looking as though it belongs on top of the nearby Yerkes Observatory. In fact, a black and white photo inside the entrance showing it superimposed on the Observatory demands a double, sometimes a triple take.[11]

Another popular midcentury restaurant type, evolved from turn-of-the-century horse-drawn food wagons, was the streamlined, stainless steel diner. The only authentic example in Wisconsin is the Delta Diner in Delta in Bayfield County. A fully restored 1940s Silk City Diner, the once urban Delta is quirkily (and enticingly) out of place in Wisconsin's northwoods. While the Delta's the real thing, three other cafes nostalgically revive the diner mystique in studied simulations: Perry's Cherry Diner in Sturgeon Bay, the Royal Cafe in Coloma, and the Wolf River Diner in Fremont. The first two are decked out in lipstick red, white and black, with chrome-edged tables and matching chrome-legged chairs. Perry's Cherry Diner, formerly Andropolis Restaurant, also sports pink and turquoise booths, Elvis and Marilyn posters, and stainless steel bands around the cement block exterior to give it an air of authenticity. The Wolf River Diner opts for green and cream, vintage toys, movie magazines, and posters in an interior interpretation so exact that I thought it was a rare survivor from the 1950s. Other cafes go for a similar rock and roll feel on a leaner budget, relying on old 45s glued to the walls (Cardo's Cafe in Hurley) and replicas of Coca Cola advertising signs and other pieces (Main Dish Family Restaurant in Luck).[12]

The history of American restaurants is told not only in Wisconsin cafe architecture but also in the obsolete restaurant items owners have recovered from basements, behind walls, under counters, and between floorboards, such as Philip Jensen's parents' electric malt machine, leaded glasses and candy dishes, and table linens. In Oostburg, at Deborah and Jeff Saueressig's Knotty Pine Restaurant, a menu board from the early 1960s advertises a stack of pancakes for 35¢ and aged T-bone or tenderloin for $1.79. At Steele's Restaurant in Berlin, a collection of vintage paper cup liners, dishes, advertisements, picture postcards, and old menus fills the glass case beneath the cash register.

Once the local teen hangout, small town cafes are foreign territories to many of today's teenagers. Ten years ago, many owners were optimistic that cafes would be instrumental in connecting today's youth with the past. At the now-defunct Country Cafe in Winter, Mary Canestorp proudly noted that grandchildren "still" sat with grandparents. In Merrill, Signa Lambrecht, former owner of Skipper's Restaurant with her husband, Bob, believed that today's generations, raised on impersonal, fast food of dubious nutritional value, would eventually return to the authentic, deliberately prepared food of their grandparents. And Rosie Fierek of Allan and Rosie's Kitchen in Shawano, now the Main Street Diner under a different owner, anticipated the day the younger generations would reject fast food and living and return to the home cooking of the slower paced, community-based small town cafe.

Has that happened? Today's cafe owners note that the largest percentage of their regular customers continues to be those of middle and advanced age. Although each year brings a certain number of deaths, the average age remains fairly stable. New people are added to the mix as they retire or undergo life-changes that make possible daily or at the least semiweekly visits to the cafe. The ten o'clock coffee group at Our Place Cafe in Cumberland, consisting of a stable core of about eight people ranging in age from thirty-five to sixty-five, is fairly representative. Craig, the youngest member, has participated in the coffee klatch since he was an eight- or ten-year-old boy accompanying his father. Dick, the jokester in residence the day I dropped in, schedules his work deliveries around the ten o'clock meeting. And the others—all retirees—roll out of bed and into the cafe almost every day without fail.

I saw few children in all of the cafes I visited, so few, in fact, that when I did see them, I noticed them. At Denise's Cafe in Randolph, three middle school boys wearing football jerseys ordered burgers, fries, and malts before their late-afternoon game, just as kids did in the 1950s and 1960s. A family of six with three children under the age of ten occupied a corner table at Lisa Jolin's Cookery in Sugar Camp on a Friday night in October. Mom, Dad, and Grandma enjoyed the fish fry, but the kids opted for burgers and fries. At yet another cafe, whose owner declined to be included in the book, students walked from the high school a few blocks away to eat lunch, which nine times out of ten consists of burgers and fries. Or rather, the boys eat burgers, fries, and Cokes. The girls eat only fries and Diet Coke. (One girl exclaimed how much cheaper lunch is at the cafe than at the school. It's no wonder, I thought, when you eat only fries.) Interestingly, though fries are the universal kids' food, at many cafes they are being snubbed for cheese curds, an increasingly popular choice. Only in Wisconsin.

Family Heritage

Like a community glue, cafes link the past and present, age and youth. Many are second-generation family businesses. Some children take to them eagerly, like Doyle and Nancy Lewis, who took over the five-star Unique Cafe in Boscobel from Doyle's mother. Other children leave home looking for new opportunities before returning to restaurant life, as did Heather (Oatsvall) Dahl, who as a teenager resented having to work in her parents' New Lisbon cafe but now embraces the opportunity. Whether they deliberately choose restaurant work or simply fall into it, these children are proud that their cafes are family businesses—an unbroken thread running from the past to the present. Some cafe owners hope their own children will continue the family tradition, and others urge theirs into an easier, more lucrative life.

Family heritage is emphasized by displaying family portraits, heirlooms, and other personal belongings in cafes and by using family recipes and cooking methods. Jill Poeschel, owner of Blondie's III in Mondovi, displays framed photographs of her children on the counter. At the Koffe Kup Restaurant in Stoughton, Trish Gulseth uses her husband's Norwegian grandmother's doughnut recipe. Ten years ago at Lauer's Restaurant in Brandon, now the Brandon Cafe under different ownership, Charlotte Marshall was making cream pies the way she remembered her grandmother making them—dumping ingredients together in a pot on top of her cook stove (she never used a recipe.) Though Charlotte substituted her microwave for the stove top, she noted that she used the same "dump" method. Family foodways, like portraits, heirlooms, and collections, link generations and bring the past into clearer focus.

CAFES AS SENIOR CENTERS
Coffee Klatches: Reviewing, Reshaping, and Renegotiating Lives

In cafes throughout Wisconsin, retired men gather at preset hours to pass the time over coffee, talk, and games. Naming themselves "The Liar's Club," "Old Farts Anonymous," "Social Security Group Coffee Drinkers," or "The Power Hour," these coffee klatches are a daily social ritual in which lives are reviewed and reshaped and identities renegotiated after retirement. The members are predominantly men, although from time to time a wife or another woman will sit in with the group. In cases such as this, however, women generally tend to be observers rather than active participants. Yet it is not uncommon for a woman to be a dominant member of a coffee group, as is Marie in the ten o'clock coffee group at Our Place Cafe in Cumberland. In other cases, women gather to make up their own groups—usually church groups, exercise groups, or widows sharing a meal.

Ironically, although women are traditionally associated with coffee parties and gossiping, in Wisconsin cafes men are by far the more notorious coffee klatchers. Says Dick at Our Place Cafe, "We do. We don't. We is what we is." Coffee klatches replace the daily social interaction men knew while they were employed. For example, Roy Saarbacker, a three-times-a-day coffee klatcher at Barb Paar's Lunch Bucket Cafe in Black Earth, saw just about everyone in town every day as the town postmaster. Now retired, he visits the cafe to remain in contact with friends and former customers.

Because he built a network of social contacts through his job as postmaster, Roy is perhaps more fortunate than other men who have retired from less public work. Through their participation in coffee klatches, men renegotiate identities that retirement has stripped away, using signs to declare who they have become—Old Farts and Social Security Group members—and personalized coffee mugs to emphasize the hobbies that now keep them busy. At the local cafe, men are remade. They become smooth lovers, under-par golfers, and fishermen à la Babe Winkleman. Some even become pig farmers. For example, ten years ago at the Corner Cafe in Lake Mills (now closed), a retired plumber reserved himself a spot at the end of the counter every morning between six forty-five and eight with a sign he crafted: "Milford the pig farmer." Yet, owner Donna Gnabsik pointed out with a laugh, "he doesn't have a pig on the place."

While they work out new, comfortable identities, the retired men review the past with reminiscences about the work they have done, the things they have experienced, the people they have known. "I remember when" stories are popular entertainments, and local raconteurs spin out tales about horses and buggies tied up along dirt main streets, their military service during World War II, and the cost of medical care a half-century ago. Through their eyes, the past is superior to the present, a time when life was happier and more secure and the young still had respect for the elderly.

Review of the past leads to commentary about the present, and coffee klatches "solve all the problems of the world." In 2002, the most common general topics of discussion were Wisconsin's gubernatorial race, Bush's presidency, and the weather. Less significant topics are also discussed and debated, such as the price of a cup of coffee, the preferred number of glasses of water drunk each day, Medicare payments, golfing, fishing, farming, and the best freeways and approaches to major cities. Talk about current conditions—on international, national, and personal levels—shapes and orders the present and provides the men with a sense of involvement in external events that are unpredictable and beyond their control.[13]

Coffee Klatches: Games and Jokes

The smaller, intimate world that coffee klatches enclose often requires daily doses of suspense and excitement. Fitting the bill are games of chance (dice, number guessing, and coin flipping) and games of skill (cribbage, sheepshead, euchre, gin). These games often bring together people who otherwise would have little or no social contact: retirees come together with bread delivery men, agnostics with Lutheran ministers, summer residents from Chicago with native farmers. The dice games appear complicated to the uninitiated, and though many are common around the state, such as Horse and 6-5-4 (or Ship, Captain, Crew), some coffee klatches play games invented by one of their members. Interestingly, it is the conversation that accompanies the games rather than the games themselves that unite the men. Submerged in their talk, the men pay little attention to the game's progress, so that when a turn comes, it is necessary to consult the previous shakers for an update on the game being played. Having taken their turn, players immediately return to the conversation. Card games replace dice games in many cafes, but the stakes are generally the same: a nickel, quarter, breakfast, or a round of coffee.[14]

Other forms of entertainment include sharing jokes, and members of coffee klatches bring in reams of photocopied material that accumulate as owners' under-the-counter collections. Ten years ago, the menu for the fictional Roadkill Cafe circulated throughout the state and included some of Wisconsin's Finest Entrees, like Center Line Bovine ("tastes real good straight from the hood"), Slab of Lab, and Guess That Mess. All the rage for a couple of years, the roadkill theme all but faded away—only to be revived in localized versions such as "Roadkills from the Great River Road" and "Treasures Found on the Mississippi," both printed on placemats at Mamie's Cafe in Stoddard.[15] Other common examples of photocopied "jokelore" include signs like this one, typically found posted behind the counter or on a wall: "LOST DOG 3 legs, blind in left eye, missing right ear, tail broke, recently castrated. Answers to the name of Lucky." PG-rated selections such as this make up less than 10 percent of the average collection, in which AIDS jokes, gay jokes, pictorial sex jokes, scatological jokes, and other X-rated material predominate.

If you think jokes such as these stray beyond the confines of good taste, consider what folklorist Roger Abrahams calls "Equal Opportunity Eating." He argues that only "in principle [do] we like to keep separate and discrete matters of talking, eating, engaging in sex." But in reality—especially in coffee klatches—talking, eating, and sex are frequently combined because they are, after all, forms of intercourse that bring meaning and value to relationships.[16]

Recreation and Employment Opportunities

Over plates of home cooking and bottomless cups of coffee, elderly men fill the social void brought by retirement with conversation and friendship. Mornings and afternoons are often spent playing cards, cribbage, dice, poker, and euchre at a wall table, out of the way of restaurant traffic. Their games are tolerated as long as the talk and laughter doesn't smother normal conversation of the other customers, and as long as their table isn't needed by people looking for a meal. Cafe owners often jokingly refer to themselves as "babysitters" and their businesses as "homes away from home." The local cafe is even better than home for many men, whose wives wait with endless "Honey, do" lists, and for single men, whose empty houses accentuate their isolation from family and friends.[17]

Homes require families. For senior citizens who are widowed or otherwise alone, some owners foster togetherness and kinship by opening up their own family celebrations—children's birthdays, graduations, weddings, and holidays—to include them.

For years, Ann Moerke prepared a huge Christmas feast at the Crystal Cafe in Iola for her own children and senior citizens from the community who might otherwise have been alone. Slowly the numbers of elderly dwindled as more of them moved to nursing homes, and Ann's Christmas dinners finally stopped. In Winneconne, Jim and Sue Brooks have held their family Christmas dinner at their Arrowhead Restaurant, but leave the door open to any customers who might wish to drop in. And for the past few years the Crystal Cafe in Phillips has prepared a free community Thanksgiving dinner for anyone who cares to attend.[18]

For senior citizens who live in nursing homes and planned communities, cafes offer an opportunity for occasional outings. Jerry Bechard, owner of the original Norske Nook in Osseo and two sibling Nooks in Rice Lake and Hayward, regularly receives busloads of day-trippers throughout the summer eager for a piece of the Nook's world-famous pie. A nursing home in Chippewa Falls plans excursions to area cafes at least once a summer, perhaps to remind the residents who sign up what real home-cooked food still tastes like.

Many people who have already retired from other work get part-time jobs at their local cafes to stay busy, keep in touch with other members of the community, or provide business opportunities to children and other family members. Examples from the first *Cafe Wisconsin* include Jerome Blaser, formerly a farmer and director of transportation for Oconto Falls area schools, who hired on at the Falls Restaurant and then bought himself the cafe in order to keep his job when the owner wanted to move on. Larry and Judy Butler retired from their California restaurant and peacefully settled in the quiet Clark County town of Owen. Not long after, they bought Kristie's Restaurant, named after their granddaughter, which they ran with the help of their daughter and her family. Similarly, Bob and Sharon Schlieger retired to Hawkins after running cafes in southeastern Wisconsin. Retirement was cast aside when they bought the Whispering Pines Cafe, operating it with the help of their family. All three cafes are now in different hands.

Community Health Watch

Coffee klatchers, as well as other elderly men and women customers, are so regular in their visits to local cafes that owners know it is nine o'clock when the Social Security Group Coffee Drinkers arrive, or two thirty when Loren drops in for an afternoon chat and a cup (or two or four) of coffee. Some customers' visits are so regular and their eating habits so predictable that owners or their employees can have orders ready when they arrive. And when such a customer fails to arrive without prior notice of the absence, cafe owners often worry that an accident or even death has occurred and call or visit to check up on the missing person. Because they are perhaps the only business in town that sees people on a regular, daily basis, cafes function as the "Community Health Watch," a name provided by Kathy Lohmar, whose parents own the Hixton Cafe in Hixton.

From their vantage point behind the counter, cafe owners, their families, and employees supervise the comings and goings of regular customers while keeping tabs on special health concerns and problems. They are often the first nonfamily members to know of heart attacks, strokes, accidents, or a doctor's order to restrict the diet. For customers who are supposed to be watching their cholesterol, owners supervise breakfast orders, ready to intercept the forbidden bacon or sausage. They scold diabetics who cannot stay away from the sweets, heart patients who cannot pass up the offer of a cigarette, and dieters who cannot refuse the daily assortment of baked goods. At Teri's in Baraboo, Teri Scott serves "down to earth foods" without heavy seasoning because a majority of her customers are "guys on low salt diets who can't stand spices." When a man who had survived a heart attack ordered his regular breakfast of eggs, sausage, and buttered toast, Teri brought him a bowl of oatmeal and dry wheat toast instead.

Regular customers who have met with an accident or other temporary disability often receive home deliveries from small town cafes. They may choose to phone in their orders or automatically receive whatever is the daily special. If they're able to get out, cafe owners or employees sometimes pick them up at home and bring them back to the cafe for a meal or an afternoon of coffee and conversation. A decade ago at the former Wagon Wheel Cafe in Arcadia (now Renee Brueggen's Kozy Kitchen) owner Sharon Waldera alternated turns with members of the afternoon dice-playing coffee klatch to pick up or deliver home a disabled man. She also "watched out for his diet." Other cafe owners, such as Sharon Kupietz at the Wildflower Cafe in Trempealeau, serve senior meals through their county's program on aging. Working with a professional nutritionist, they plan balanced meals suitable to the dietary needs of the elderly, especially single men, who no longer can or do cook for themselves.

Cafe owners repeatedly refer to themselves as "caretakers," both of the elderly and other marginal populations, such as the physically and mentally disabled, loners, and "the down and out." Some admit that if it weren't for such attention and care, quite a few individuals would simply slip through the cracks and disappear. One cafe owner gives a "loner" clothes to wear, especially coats in the winter, and takes him along on employee outings. "Without us, he'd have nobody," he says. Another employs a disabled war veteran, and another, a young man who is mentally handicapped. Until they closed Hanny's Restaurant in Lake Geneva, owners Kenneth and Joyce Bouhl took care of the "down and out" by trading a hot meal for a simple job, such as cleaning the weeds out of cracks in the sidewalk, or extending credit until a social security check came in at the end of the month. Even their waitresses sometimes chipped in to buy a meal for people who were broke and "needed a meal."[19]

CAFES AS CHAMBERS OF COMMERCE
Promoting Small Town Life and Tourism
In their role as chambers of commerce, cafes intercede with outsiders on behalf of the local and area community. On any given weekend during the summer—and especially during the fall color season—adventure eaters and other tourists seek out Wisconsin's small town cafes, where they hope to experience (for an hour or less) small town culture. Bicyclists all over the state make weekend pie rides to their favorite cafes. Motorcyclists from the Twin Cities and LaCrosse make regular weekend forays to Borgen's Norwegian Cafe and Bakery in Westby every Sunday morning. Fishermen on their way north drop in at the Roberts Kitchen in Roberts for the Friday night fish fry. Others fishing on Lake Chetek wouldn't dare begin the day without first feasting on breakfast at Bob's Grill in Chetek. And thousands of tourists a year visit the Norske Nook in search of the pie made famous by Jane and Michael Stern's *Roadfood*. To outsiders, the small town cafe is the most accessible public space, a microcosm of an alternative way of life that is appealing because it appears more vital and authentic: slower, intimate, and community-based.

In the cafe, many outsiders experience small town life through a process similar to osmosis: a kind of absorption through a semi-permeable screen of self-protection and privacy rather than direct involvement and participation. At Schubert's Old-Fashioned Cafe and Bakery in Mount Horeb, for example, the tourists tuck themselves into high-backed booths along the wall and occupy themselves with private conversations and extensive menu reading. They rarely join the locals at the counter, who, as Joe Revak, the owner of the former Audrey's Spot Cafe in Ladysmith, told me in 1991, tend to be people in a hurry who don't have the time or the interest to take part in the social activities going on around them. With their backs toward other diners, waitresses, and coffee groups gathered for laughter and gossip, counter sitters read newspapers, books, and business papers, spreading out the contents of brief cases along the counter next to them. The counter is where extra space can be appropriated for private use, unlike square tables set up with two or four chairs that invite company.

However, counter sitting is entirely different for strangers because they are so obvious, so exposed to the questioning stares of the regulars. Counter sitting puts strangers in the midst of the social activity and carries with it an obligation for conversation, especially about yourself: where you're from, what you do, why you're there. Perched on a counter stool, you can easily chat with owners and waitresses, swivel around to joke with the coffee crowd or share a game of dice, and covertly evaluate food carried from the kitchen and baked goods sitting behind the counter. For these reasons, I prefer sitting at counters.

In cafes, out-of-towners and local residents come together. Cafes, therefore, make excellent tourist information bureaus. They supply maps and brochures for local attractions, times for ferry crossings, locations of motels, and directions to destinations off the main routes. In Cassville, the Rivers Cafe regularly caters to tourists and provides copies of county guidebooks, brochures for an architectural tour of Cassville, and color pamphlets for the area's tourist attractions, such as Stonefield Village just up the road. In Holcombe, Jeff and Ronda Gulich's Lake Holcombe Cafe serves as the village center, where travelers seek directions, fishermen seek bait shops, hunters seek licensing stations, and snowmobilists seek maps of winter trails.

Cafes act as intercessors with visitors yet also provide refuge to the locals from seasonal swarms of sightseers. On a busy June day in Lake Geneva, tourists filled the trendy downtown restaurants, but Fran's Cafe on Broad Street, a few blocks off the lakefront, was quiet and cozy with a few locals at the counter shooting the breeze over coffee and fried eggs. In other cafes, such as Lucy's Coffee Shop in Fontana, the locals gather early in the morning and again after closing, their only respite from the summer residents and tourists who fill the tiny restaurant between breakfast and lunch and force them to either abandon or adjust their regular daily visits.

Integrating the Community

The community bonds in the small town cafe. During locals-only hours, in daily coffee klatches, cribbage games, and early morning breakfast groups, native, year-round residents and seasonal cabin dwellers come together for coffee and conversation, discovering commonalities upon which friendships develop and grow. At the Village Soda Grill in Manitowish Waters, for example, northwoods natives rub elbows with out-of-state "influential men," including a judge and the owner of a Chicago-based lumber chain. Not far away in Mercer at Tom's Country Cafe, retirees and other summer residents from Chicago and Milwaukee mix with local auto shop owners and motel keepers. As an owner of a northwoods cafe noted ten years ago, the locals quickly welcomed out-of-towners into their coffee group. "If you could come in every day for a week," she said, "you'd be sitting at the Round Table. One day a guy from Chicago came, and twenty minutes later he was at the Table talking and laughing with the locals."

Community members integrate in other ways as well. Natives who have moved away and return for visits often make the cafe one of their first stops. At the Alma Hotel in Alma ten years ago, I met a couple that had returned to the wife's hometown for a family funeral. Over apple pie and coffee, she caught up on news and gossip with the teenage waitress—the daughter of a former high school friend. So and so had moved away. This person had divorced. That person had died. Talk brought her temporarily back into the community, connecting her to people and places she had left long ago.

In the small town cafes, others who have never left establish and solidify relationships with members of the community whom they have known slightly or not at all. Retirees come together in coffee klatches and card games to reminisce about the years they spent farming, stringing telephone lines, or selling automobiles; though their past lives are different, retirement is something they have in common. Dice games bring together men who would otherwise have little to do with each other: retirees with working men, laborers with professionals, old men with young men.

Other people integrate into the community as well. From the Alma Hotel to the Woodville Cafe, widows network for friendship and support. At other cafes divorcees and stay-at-home mothers with kids grown and gone enter the social world of paid employment, and loners are pulled back into the community.

A recent phenomenon—I did not see it ten years ago—is the migration into small towns in primarily southeastern Wisconsin of relatively new immigrant groups, especially Albanians and Macedonians from former Yugoslavia and Mexicans, who are moving out of the Chicago, Rockford, and Milwaukee urban centers in search of affordable restaurants. The small town cafe perfectly suits these immigrants, and an amazing number are being bought and turned into family-style restaurants. The Albanian restaurants especially seem stamped out of nearly identical molds. The menu offerings and format (down to the misspellings) are the same, as are the restaurant names—easily distinguished by an individual's or town's name followed by "Family Restaurant," as in Milton Family Restaurant, Delavan Family Restaurant, and Andy's Family Restaurant (Jefferson).

I found the Albanian and Macedonian entrepreneurs generally to be earnest and hard working, as well as wary of all my questions. They have learned to prepare the traditional, meat-and-potatoes based fare that Wisconsinites love. Missing so far are homemade desserts and baked goods— pies and cakes, bread and donuts—and their own ethnic foods, with the exception of hybrid salads, omelettes, and pita sandwiches featuring feta cheese. It will be interesting to see how these immigrant-operated cafes and restaurants develop over the next few years and how they might both influence and be influenced by traditional Wisconsin food, small town residents, and Wisconsin culture in general.

Supporting the Community: "Living Newspapers," Fundraisers, Festivals and Civic Organizations
As the social hubs of small towns, cafes are "living newspapers," noted Donna French, former owner of Donna's Kitchen in Roberts, in the original *Cafe Wisconsin*. All the news that's worth knowing is channeled through the men perched at the counter or crowded around Round Tables and Medicare Tables, "Village Halls," and "Olde Town Halls." At the small town cafe, you'll hear the social column and learn about yesterday's funeral that brought in thirty cars. On the news page you'll learn who was elected county commissioner or school board member. On the editorial page you'll hear various opinions on topics ranging from politics to road construction. On the comics page you'll laugh about the regulars' Silly String assault on Deb Hantke, owner of the Squeeze Inn in Milton. On the sports page, you'll hear replays from last night's double header, a shot-by-shot analysis of the local men's golf outing, or a brief introduction to pistol and skeet shooting competitions.

In the classifieds—the bulletin board near the front door—you can find yourself a drywall contractor, a sidewalk layer, a chimney sweep. At many cafes, the bulletin board is also the entertainment section. There you'll find advertisements for next month's tractor pull in Tomah, the evangelistic crusade in Viroqua, the Twin O'Rama summer festival in Cassville. The minutes from the town board meeting are there, too. The ballpark is in need of regrading and reliming, the community center needs 150 new folding chairs, and so-and-so's dog is still running loose. All the news— and then some—that is fit to print.

Cafes also promote community fundraisers, events, and festivals. At the Pier Plaza in Bayfield, you can drop spare change into a can by the register and help send the French students to France or elect a Bay Days queen. At Joan's Country Cookin' in Hustisford, you can buy a chance on a Harley Davidson motorcycle being raffled by the local volunteer fire department. At Lorrie's Home Town Cafe in Denmark, owner Lorrie Steffek is an active promoter of the town's annual Danish Festival. Still other cafes support festivals by sponsoring floats in parades or candidates for queens and princesses.

Some cafe owners, like Bob Prevost of Prevost's in Solon Springs, sponsor league bowling and softball teams, as well as youth T-ball, baseball, soccer, and peewee football teams. Trophies, plaques, and other awards fill many shelves, walls, and glass display cases. Others support civic organizations like the Jaycees, Kiwanis, and Lions by providing meeting rooms and banquet facilities during or after the regular business day. Looking for yet another way to return the people of Osseo's commitment and loyalty to his business, Norske Nook owner Jerry Bechard implemented a continuing education scholarship for qualifying employees. "I believe in paying back," he explains.

Cafes as Business Associations

As chambers of commerce, cafes promote and support the local business economy. For example, every morning at about six thirty at the Home Plate Diner in Mishicot, until the business exchanged hands several years ago, construction workers, plumbers, electricians, and other contractors gathered at the "Town Hall" table over breakfast and coffee to discuss the day's work, lay out timetables, and schedule jobs. They were followed at eight thirty by the local merchants and businesspeople, the former village president, and other officials, who began the day with talk about local business, tourism, education, environment, and other community concerns. The informal morning breakfast network was an opportunity for members of the Mishicot business community to keep in daily contact, lend each other support, and promote local economic growth.

In Iola, the local businessmen leave notes on their doors telling clients they are at Judy Bolier's Crystal Cafe, and some people have taken to paying their bills and conducting other transactions over pie and coffee. This bit of small town flavor charms the tourists and adventure eaters who come to Iola for the Crystal Cafe's excellent home cooking, afterward browsing through the handful of gift shops that have sprung up as a result of the cafe's popularity. Similar economic regrowth has occurred in Osseo, home to the Norske Nook, which experienced a phenomenal rise to fame after being featured in Jane and Michael Stern's first edition (1977) of *Roadfood*. Since then, the Nook has attracted hundreds of thousands of adventure eaters so that today Osseo is a tempting tourist center filled with antique, gift, and craft shops—including the Nook's own Gave Buttik. Without the Nook, owner Jerry Bechard believes, Osseo might be just another obscure small town.

As chambers of commerce, cafes function as business associations, encouraging, supporting, and rejuvenating local economies. While the most successful cafes have the capacity to rejuvenate communities, many others boost their local and area economies in a more modest way by purchasing locally produced foods and supplies. At the Polonia Cafe in Polonia, owner Diane Dombrowski purchases fresh meats from Waller's meat locker in nearby Nelsonville. Renee Brueggen, owner of the Kozy Kitchen in Arcadia, places daily orders with Myer's Bakery, located right next door. When Pauc's Bakery in Amherst closed, leaving Amherst Cafe owner Diane Stroik without her favorite multigrain bread, she took Pauc's recipe to the local grocery store and convinced its bakery department to make the bread for her. "I like to spread the revenue around to local business," she explains. "After all, we're all in this together."

We are indeed—pie riders, adventure eaters, cafe owners, farmers, food suppliers, coffee klatchers, Wisconsin residents, and curious visitors. We're all in "it" together, and much of it can be found at Cafe Wisconsin. I'll be eating pie at the counter. Join me, won't you?

NOTES

1. See Charles Camp, *American Foodways: What, When, Why, and How We Eat in America* (Little Rock: August House, 1989); and Lin T. Humphrey, "Small Group Festive Gatherings," *Journal of the Folklore Institute* (1979): 190–201. For a concise social-oriented examination of the small town cafe as a "food place," where feminist politics are served along with scratch cooking, see the chapter entitled "On the Town: The Emma Chase" in William Least Heat-Moon's *PrairyErth* (Boston: Houghton Mifflin, 1991), 122–30.

2. The conservative nature of Wisconsin cafe food is perhaps a result of a compromise between conflicting ethnic and regional food habits, as Margaret Mead suggests of American food in general. Susan Kalčik explores Mead's observations on the "cultural standardization" of American food in "Ethnic Foodways in America: Symbol and the Performance of Identity," in *Ethnic and Regional Foodways in the United States: The Performance of Group Identity*, edited by Linda Keller Brown and Kay Mussell, (Knoxville: University of Tennessee Press, 1984), 52–53.

    Other popular explanations of Wisconsin's Friday night fish fry ritual credit tavern keepers who lured post-Prohibition customers back to the neighborhood beer hall by offering free fried fish. The poor Depression economy further fostered the tradition because people knew where to find a free meal at the end of the week. Often they brought their entire family, for Wisconsin taverns have historically been family-friendly businesses, unlike those in neighboring states with blue laws that prohibit patrons under the age of eighteen. It doesn't hurt that Wisconsin is blessed with ample lakes filled with all variety of freshwater fish, and that advances in the commercial fishing and frozen food products industries have made it possible to deliver cod, pollock, and other favorite ocean fish to the Badger state. For more reading, see Mary Bergin, "Fish Fry on Friday," *Capital Times* (5 January 2004); Jeff Hagen, *Codfather II* (Black Earth: Trails Media Group, Inc., 2001), "Friday Night in Dairyland," *Wisconsin Trails* (March/April 2002), and *Fry Me to the Moon* (Black Earth: Trails Media Group, Inc., 1999); and Susan Squires, "The Tradition of Friday Night Fish Fry," *Shawano Leader* (18 February 1996).

3. For more on this point, see Kalčik, "Ethnic Foodways," 55, and Anne R. Kaplan, Marjorie A. Hoover, and Willard B. Moore, *The Minnesota Ethnic Food Book* (St. Paul: Minnesota Historical Society, 2003).

4. In "We Are What We Eat: Omaha Food as Symbol" (*Keystone Folklore Quarterly* [1971] 16: 165–70) folklorist Roger Welsch notes that ritual foods "transcend historicity, economics, and taste" and act as an embodiment of cultural identity. An excellent exploration of Wisconsin's ethnic heritage is Fred L. Holmes, *Old World Wisconsin: Around Europe in the Badger State* (Eau Claire, Wis.: E. M. Hale and Co., 1944). You can learn more about Wisconsin's ethnic foodways in Harva Hachten, *The Flavor of Wisconsin: An Informal History of Food and Eating in the Badger State* (Madison: Wisconsin Historical Society Press, 1981); and Terese Allen, ed., *Home Cooked Culture: Wisconsin through Recipes* (Madison: Wisconsin Arts Board, 1998).

5. For more on this point, see Waverley Lewis Root and Richard de Rochemont, *Eating in America: A History* (New York: William Morrow, 1976), 276–312.

6. See also Kalčik, "Ethnic Foodways," 56.
7. Wisconsin folklorist James P. Leary lays out the cultural rules for telling ethnic jokes in "The 'Polack Joke' in a Polish-American Community" (*Midwestern Journal of Language and Folklore* 6 [Spring/Fall 1980]: 26–33). For more ethnic jokes collected in Wisconsin cafes and other places throughout the upper Midwest, see Leary, *So Ole Says to Lena: Folk Humor of the Upper Midwest* (Madison: University of Wisconsin Press, 2001) and selected chapters in *Wisconsin Folklore* (Madison: University of Wisconsin Press, 1998).
8. Folklorist Henry H. Glassie believes that collections are connective art derived from individual, useful objects. "What individual ornaments appear to be," he writes, "is the least significant thing about them. Their meaning lies less in their manifest content than in their magical capacity to bring events and human beings to life in the mind" (*Passing the Time in Ballymenone: Culture and History of an Ulster Community* [Philadelphia: University of Pennsylvania Press, 1982], 369–70). For his eloquent discussion of collections as connective art, see especially 361–65 and 370–72.
9. See also Kalčik, "Ethnic Foodways," 56–61.
10. For a nostalgic pictorial history of American restaurants, as well as quite a few Wisconsin road-side sites, see John Baeder, *Gas, Food, and Lodging: A Postcard Odyssey through the Great American Roadside* (New York: Abbeville Press, 1982). See also John Mariani, *America Eats Out: An Illustrated History of Restaurants, Taverns, Coffee Shops, Speakeasies, and Other Establishments that Have Fed Us for 350 Years* (New York: William Morrow and Co., 1991). A basic history is Richard Pillsbury, *From Boarding House to Bistro: The American Restaurant Then and Now* (Boston: Unwin Hyman, 1990). Don't miss the Norske Nook on 166 and 168–70.
11. For more about programmatic restaurants and other commercial ventures, see J. J. C. Andrews, *The Well-Built Elephant and Other Roadside Attractions: A Tribute to American Eccentricity* (New York: Congdon and Weed, 1984).
12. Diner devotees will enjoy John Baeder, *Diners* (New York: Harry N. Abrams, 1995); Richard J. S. Gutman, *American Diner Then and Now* (Baltimore: Johns Hopkins University Press, 2000); Gerd Kittel, *Diners: People and Places* (New York: Thames and Hudson, 1998); Alison Moss, ed., *Diners* (Naperville, Ill.: Sourcebooks, 2000); and Michael Karl Witzel, *The American Diner* (St. Paul: Motorbooks International, 1999).
13. For another traditional way older men deal with the problems of retirement, see Simon J. Bronner, *Chain Carvers: Old Men Crafting Meaning* (Lexington: University of Kentucky Press, 1985).
14. Leary does a creditable job of explaining dice games in "Wisconsin Tavern Amusements" in *Wisconsin Folklore*, 377–85. A related but brief look at dice shaking and card playing in a Green Bay tavern can be found in Kirk Lamond Gray, *Tavern-Based Leisure and Play in a Midwestern Working Class Community* (Santa Monica: Rand, 1978).
15. See also B. R. "Buck" Peterson, *The Original Road Kill Cookbook* (Berkeley: Ten Speed Press, 1987); and Richard Marcou, *How to Cook Roadkill* (Bradford, U.K.: M. C. B. Publications, 1993).
16. It is challenging reading, but you'll learn more about Roger Abrahams's views in "Equal Opportunity Eating: A Structural Excursus on Things of the Mouth," in *Ethnic and Regional Foodways in the United States: The Performance of Group Identity*, edited by Linda Keller Brown and Kay Mussell (Knoxville: University of Tennessee Press, 1984). For more examples of photocopier lore, don't miss Alan Dundes and Carl R. Pagter, comps., *Work Hard and You Shall Be Rewarded: Urban Folklore from the Paperwork Empire* (Detroit: Wayne State University Press, 1992) and *When You're Up to Your Ass in Alligators: More Urban Folklore from the Paperwork Empire* (Detroit: Wayne State University Press, 1987).
17. Other small town businesses often take on the role of "babysitter" for the elderly and disabled. In *Grand Opening* (New York: Ballantine Books, 1996), novelist Jon Hassler's portrait of small town Minnesota life in the 1940s, the Foster family owns a grocery and deposits a rather senile grandfather at the pool hall across the street, where he drinks coffee and passes the afternoons in idle talk.
18. See also Kalčik, "Ethnic Foodways," 48.
19. In Gloria Naylor's novel *Bailey's Cafe* (New York: Harcourt Brace Jovanovich, 1992), misfits and social outcasts come together at Bailey's Cafe for understanding, comfort, redemption, and the courage to go on.

Index

By Town

By Cafe